REFERENCE

DISCARDED

CLAYTN-RIV   REF
3101

☑ P9-DJL-180
Reagan.
The new encyclopedia of Southern
culture   10/13

The NEW ENCYCLOPEDIA *of* SOUTHERN CULTURE

VOLUME 19 : VIOLENCE

Volumes to appear in

The New Encyclopedia of Southern Culture

are:

The NEW

ENCYCLOPEDIA *of* SOUTHERN CULTURE

CHARLES REAGAN WILSON General Editor

JAMES G. THOMAS JR. Managing Editor

ANN J. ABADIE Associate Editor

VOLUME 19

Violence

AMY LOUISE WOOD   Volume Editor

Sponsored by

THE CENTER FOR THE STUDY OF SOUTHERN CULTURE

at the University of Mississippi

THE UNIVERSITY OF NORTH CAROLINA PRESS

Chapel Hill

This book was published with the
assistance of the Anniversary Endowment Fund
of the University of North Carolina Press.

© 2011 The University of North Carolina Press
All rights reserved
Designed by Richard Hendel
Set in Minion types by Tseng Information Systems, Inc.
Manufactured in the United States of America
The paper in this book meets the guidelines for permanence and
durability of the Committee on Production Guidelines for Book
Longevity of the Council on Library Resources.
The University of North Carolina Press has been a member
of the Green Press Initiative since 2003.
Library of Congress Cataloging-in-Publication Data
Violence / Amy Louise Wood, volume editor.
p. : ill. ; 24 cm. — (The new encyclopedia of Southern culture; v. 19)
"Published with the assistance of the Anniversary Endowment
Fund of the University of North Carolina Press."
"Sponsored by The Center for the Study of Southern Culture at the
University of Mississippi."
Includes bibliographical references and index.
ISBN 978-0-8078-3522-7 (alk. paper) —
ISBN 978-0-8078-7216-1 (pbk.: alk. paper)
1. Violence—Southern States—Encyclopedias. 2. Southern
States—Social conditions—Encyclopedias. 3. Southern States—
Race relations—Encyclopedias. I. Wood, Amy Louise, 1967-.
II. University of Mississippi. Center for the Study of
Southern Culture. III. Series.
F209 .N47 2006 vol. 19
[HN79.A13]
975.003 s—dc22
2011655030
The *Encyclopedia of Southern Culture*, sponsored by the Center for
the Study of Southern Culture at the University of Mississippi, was
published by the University of North Carolina Press in 1989.
cloth   15 14 13 12 11   5 4 3 2 1
paper   15 14 13 12 11   5 4 3 2 1

Tell about the South. What's it like there.

What do they do there. Why do they live there.

Why do they live at all.

WILLIAM FAULKNER

Absalom, Absalom!

CONTENTS

GENERAL INTRODUCTION

In 1989 years of planning and hard work came to fruition when the University of North Carolina Press joined the Center for the Study of Southern Culture at the University of Mississippi to publish the *Encyclopedia of Southern Culture*. While all those involved in writing, reviewing, editing, and producing the volume believed it would be received as a vital contribution to our understanding of the American South, no one could have anticipated fully the widespread acclaim it would receive from reviewers and other commentators. But the *Encyclopedia* was indeed celebrated, not only by scholars but also by popular audiences with a deep, abiding interest in the region. At a time when some people talked of the "vanishing South," the book helped remind a national audience that the region was alive and well, and it has continued to shape national perceptions of the South through the work of its many users—journalists, scholars, teachers, students, and general readers.

As the introduction to the *Encyclopedia* noted, its conceptualization and organization reflected a cultural approach to the South. It highlighted such issues as the core zones and margins of southern culture, the boundaries where "the South" overlapped with other cultures, the role of history in contemporary culture, and the centrality of regional consciousness, symbolism, and mythology. By 1989 scholars had moved beyond the idea of cultures as real, tangible entities, viewing them instead as abstractions. The *Encyclopedia*'s editors and contributors thus included a full range of social indicators, trait groupings, literary concepts, and historical evidence typically used in regional studies, carefully working to address the distinctive and characteristic traits that made the American South a particular place. The introduction to the *Encyclopedia* concluded that the fundamental uniqueness of southern culture was reflected in the volume's composite portrait of the South. We asked contributors to consider aspects that were unique to the region but also those that suggested its internal diversity. The volume was not a reference book of southern history, which explained something of the design of entries. There were fewer essays on colonial and antebellum history than on the postbellum and modern periods, befitting our conception of the volume as one trying not only to chart the cultural landscape of the South but also to illuminate the contemporary era.

When C. Vann Woodward reviewed the *Encyclopedia* in the *New York Review of Books*, he concluded his review by noting "the continued liveliness of interest in the South and its seeming inexhaustibility as a field of study." Research on the South, he wrote, furnishes "proof of the value of the *Encyclopedia* as a scholarly undertaking as well as suggesting future needs for revision or supplement to keep up with ongoing scholarship." The two decades since the publication of the *Encyclopedia of Southern Culture* have certainly suggested that Woodward was correct. The American South has undergone significant changes that make for a different context for the study of the region. The South has undergone social, economic, political, intellectual, and literary transformations, creating the need for a new edition of the *Encyclopedia* that will remain relevant to a changing region. Globalization has become a major issue, seen in the South through the appearance of Japanese automobile factories, Hispanic workers who have immigrated from Latin America or Cuba, and a new prominence for Asian and Middle Eastern religions that were hardly present in the 1980s South. The African American return migration to the South, which started in the 1970s, dramatically increased in the 1990s, as countless books simultaneously appeared asserting powerfully the claims of African Americans as formative influences on southern culture. Politically, southerners from both parties have played crucial leadership roles in national politics, and the Republican Party has dominated a near-solid South in national elections. Meanwhile, new forms of music, like hip-hop, have emerged with distinct southern expressions, and the term "dirty South" has taken on new musical meanings not thought of in 1989. New genres of writing by creative southerners, such as gay and lesbian literature and "white trash" writing, extend the southern literary tradition.

Meanwhile, as Woodward foresaw, scholars have continued their engagement with the history and culture of the South since the publication of the *Encyclopedia*, raising new scholarly issues and opening new areas of study. Historians have moved beyond their earlier preoccupation with social history to write new cultural history as well. They have used the categories of race, social class, and gender to illuminate the diversity of the South, rather than a unified "mind of the South." Previously underexplored areas within the field of southern historical studies, such as the colonial era, are now seen as formative periods of the region's character, with the South's positioning within a larger Atlantic world a productive new area of study. Cultural memory has become a major topic in the exploration of how the social construction of "the South" benefited some social groups and exploited others. Scholars in many disciplines have made the southern identity a major topic, and they have used a variety of methodologies to suggest what that identity has meant to different social groups. Literary critics have adapted cultural theories to the South and have raised the issue of postsouthern literature to a major category of concern as well as exploring the links between the literature of the American South and that of the Caribbean. Anthropologists have used different theoretical formulations from literary critics, providing models for their fieldwork in southern communities. In the past 30 years anthropologists have set increasing numbers of their ethnographic studies in the South, with many of them now exploring topics specifically linked to southern cultural issues. Scholars now place the Native American story, from prehistory to the contemporary era, as a central part of southern history. Comparative and interdisciplinary approaches to the South have encouraged scholars to look at such issues as the borders and boundaries of the South, specific places and spaces with distinct identities within the American South, and the global and transnational Souths, linking the American South with many formerly colonial societies around the world.

The first edition of the *Encyclopedia of Southern Culture* anticipated many of these approaches and indeed stimulated the growth of Southern Studies as a distinct interdisciplinary field. The Center for the Study of Southern Culture has worked for more than three decades to encourage research and teaching about the American South. Its academic programs have produced graduates who have gone on to write interdisciplinary studies of the South, while others have staffed the cultural institutions of the region and in turn encouraged those institutions to document and present the South's culture to broad public audiences. The center's conferences and publications have continued its long tradition of promoting understanding of the history, literature, and music of the South, with new initiatives focused on southern foodways, the future of the South, and the global Souths, expressing the center's mission to bring the best current scholarship to broad public audiences. Its documentary studies projects build oral and visual archives, and the New Directions in Southern Studies book series, published by the University of North Carolina Press, offers an important venue for innovative scholarship.

Since the *Encyclopedia of Southern Culture* appeared, the field of Southern Studies has dramatically developed, with an extensive network now of academic and research institutions whose projects focus specifically on the interdisciplinary study of the South. The Center for the Study of the American South at the University of North Carolina at Chapel Hill, led by Director Harry Watson and Associate Director and *Encyclopedia* coeditor William Ferris, publishes the lively journal *Southern Cultures* and is now at the organizational center of many other Southern Studies projects. The Institute for Southern Studies at the University of South Carolina, the Southern Intellectual History Circle, the Society for the Study of Southern Literature, the Southern Studies Forum of the European American Studies Association, Emory University's SouthernSpaces.org, and the South Atlantic Humanities Center (at the Virginia Foundation for the Humanities, the University of Virginia, and Virginia Polytechnic Institute and State University) express the recent expansion of interest in regional study.

Observers of the American South have had much to absorb, given the rapid pace of recent change. The institutional framework for studying the South is broader and deeper than ever, yet the relationship between the older verities of regional study and new realities remains unclear. Given the extent of changes in the American South and in Southern Studies since the publication of the *Encyclopedia of Southern Culture*, the need for a new edition of that work is clear. Therefore, the Center for the Study of Southern Culture has once again joined the University of North Carolina Press to produce *The New Encyclopedia of Southern Culture*. As readers of the original edition will quickly see, *The New Encyclopedia* follows many of the scholarly principles and editorial conventions established in the original, but with one key difference; rather than being published in a single hardback volume, *The New Encyclopedia* is presented in a series of shorter individual volumes that build on the 24 original subject categories used in the *Encyclopedia* and adapt them to new scholarly developments. Some earlier *Encyclopedia* categories have been reconceptualized in light of new academic interests. For example, the subject section originally titled "Women's Life" is reconceived as a new volume, *Gender*, and the original "Black Life" section is more broadly interpreted as a volume on race. These changes reflect new analytical concerns that place the study of women and blacks in broader cultural systems, reflecting the emergence of, among other topics, the study of male culture and of whiteness. Both volumes draw as well from the rich recent scholarship on women's life and black life. In addition, topics with some thematic coherence are combined in a volume, such as *Law and Politics* and *Agriculture and Industry*. One new topic, *Foodways*, is the basis of a separate volume, reflecting its new prominence in the interdisciplinary study of southern culture.

Numerous individual topical volumes together make up *The New Encyclopedia of Southern Culture* and extend the reach of the reference work to wider audiences. This approach should enhance the use of the *Encyclopedia* in academic courses and is intended to be convenient for readers with more focused interests within the larger context of southern culture. Readers will have handy access to one-volume, authoritative, and comprehensive scholarly treatments of the major areas of southern culture.

We have been fortunate that, in nearly all cases, subject consultants who offered crucial direction in shaping the topical sections for the original edition have agreed to join us in this new endeavor as volume editors. When new volume editors have been added, we have again looked for respected figures who can provide not only their own expertise but also strong networks of scholars to help develop relevant lists of topics and to serve as contributors in their areas. The reputations of all our volume editors as leading scholars in their areas encouraged the contributions of other scholars and added to *The New Encyclopedia*'s authority as a reference work.

The New Encyclopedia of Southern Culture builds on the strengths of articles in the original edition in several ways. For many existing articles, original authors agreed to update their contributions with new interpretations and theoretical perspectives, current statistics, new bibliographies, or simple factual developments that needed to be included. If the original contributor was unable to update an article, the editorial staff added new material or sent it to another scholar for assessment. In some cases, the general editor and volume editors selected a new contributor if an article seemed particularly dated and new work indicated the need for a fresh perspective. And importantly, where new developments have warranted treatment of topics not addressed in the original edition, volume editors have commissioned entirely new essays and articles that are published here for the first time.

The American South embodies a powerful historical and mythical presence, both a complex environmental and geographic landscape and a place of the imagination. Changes in the region's contemporary socioeconomic realities and new developments in scholarship have been incorporated in the conceptualization and approach of *The New Encyclopedia of Southern Culture*. Anthropologist Clifford Geertz has spoken of culture as context, and this encyclopedia looks at the American South as a complex place that has served as the context for cultural expression. This volume provides information and perspective on the diversity of cultures in a geographic and imaginative place with a long history and distinctive character.

The *Encyclopedia of Southern Culture* was produced through major grants from the Program for Research Tools and Reference Works of the National Endowment for the Humanities, the Ford Foundation, the Atlantic-Richfield Foundation, and the Mary Doyle Trust. We are grateful as well to the College of Liberal Arts at the University of Mississippi for support and to the individual donors to the Center for the Study of Southern Culture who have directly or indirectly supported work on *The New Encyclopedia of Southern Culture*. We thank the volume editors for their ideas in reimagining their subjects and the contributors of articles for their work in extending the usefulness of the book in new ways. We acknowledge the support and contributions of the faculty and staff at the Center for the Study of Southern Culture. Finally, we want especially to honor the work of William Ferris and Mary Hart on the *Encyclopedia of Southern Culture*. Bill, the founding director of the Center for the Study of Southern Culture, was coeditor, and his good work recruiting authors, editing text, selecting images, and publicizing the volume among a wide network of people was, of course, invaluable. Despite the many changes in the new encyclopedia, Bill's influence remains. Mary "Sue" Hart was also an invaluable member of the original encyclopedia team, bringing the careful and precise eye of the librarian, and an iconoclastic spirit, to our work.

Commentators on the American South often mention violence as a defining feature of the region, sometimes paired with a contrasting cultural trait, as in violence and religion, violence and manners, and violence and hospitality. The old saying was that a southerner would be polite to you up to the point of shooting you. Writer Willie Morris used to say you could not go wrong in talking about southern culture by using the word "juxtaposition," and violence and its seeming opposites in the South are good examples. From the colonial era, travelers to the region claimed that its people had a special propensity for fighting, and violent images of the South continue to reverberate in modern popular culture. Violence was surely connected to forces that shaped the South—from the Indian wars, to frontier rough justice, to Civil War fighting, to lynching and urban race riots, to civil rights murders. Poverty, long-standing rural isolation, reliance on close-knit kinship groups, a culture of honor, and racial tensions all figured somehow into the mix that resulted in expressions of violence through southern history, at both the public and private levels. The overview essay explores the factors contributing to the South's sometimes-violent climate and its relationship to violent national tendencies as well.

The contribution of the *Violence* volume of *The New Encyclopedia of Southern Culture* is a breadth of coverage of the topic, showing how violence has touched many areas of social, cultural, political, and economic life. Its 44 thematic articles and 58 topical entries expand the relatively modest coverage of violence in the *Encyclopedia of Southern Culture*, reflecting the productive research on violence since the earlier publication. As in the study of the South in general, issues of race relations figure prominently herein, from entries on slave patrols and slave revolts, to explorations of violence against Mexican Americans and American Indians, to examinations of lynching and black resistance. Authors open up specifically cultural aspects of violence in the South through analysis of honor and dueling, outlaw heroes, and representations of violence in song, literature, and film. Topical entries provide accessible information on symbolic sites of southern violence, including the Alamo, Angola Prison, the chain gang, the Trail of Tears, Rosewood, Fla., and Harlan County, Ky. Individuals who have been related to southern violence include such outlaw heroes as the James Gang and Bonnie and Clyde, lynching victim Leo Frank and lynching opponents Jessie Daniel Ames and Ida B. Wells-Barnett, Confederate warrior and Reconstruction terrorist Nathan Bedford Forrest, and civil rights martyr Emmett Till. Important events such as Bacon's Rebellion in the colonial era, the Wilmington, N.C., race riot in the 1890s, and the Birmingham church bombings in the 1960s are all detailed as iconic occasions of southern violence.

Consideration of violence in the South opens up connections between culture and the social relations that underlie it. Such major categories of analysis as social class, race relations, gender, and ethnicity all figure prominently. The topic provides a sharp lens on viewing broader attitudes and behaviors that have made the American South a particular place.

The NEW ENCYCLOPEDIA *of* SOUTHERN CULTURE

VOLUME 19 : VIOLENCE

VIOLENCE IN THE
AMERICAN SOUTH

Over the past 400 years, violence of all sorts has bloodied the southern landscape: from the whipping and torture of slaves to slave revolts, from gentlemen's duels to backwoods feuding, from the brutal backlash against Reconstruction in the 1860s to the massive resistance against civil rights protests in
the 1960s. Murder rates in southern states have long exceeded those in other
states, and southerners, both black and white, have historically been more dis-
posed than other Americans to step outside the law to settle personal grievances. Even today, southerners are more likely to own and use guns, to favor a
strong national defense, and to condone the corporal punishment of children,
all of which suggest a greater level of comfort with the use of violence to resolve
social problems.

All the same, it is difficult to think about violence as a particularly southern
phenomenon. Violence is endemic to most human societies. And the United
States as a whole, not just the South, has experienced gun ownership, homicidal
crime, police brutality, and mob violence on a scale unprecedented in modern,
Western democracies. Violence has been central to the formation of America
as a nation, from the first European battles with American Indians in the 17th
century, to the Revolution, to the Civil War, to the brutal expansion into the
West in the 19th century. As historian Richard Slotkin has shown, it has also
been central to American myths, the symbolic narratives that Americans have
told about themselves, through which national ideologies and identities have
been constructed and imparted. For Slotkin, the most significant myth has
been that of the frontier, that westward moving terrain where whites forged a
nation through the willful destruction of both the wilderness and the American
Indians who inhabited it. Our mythologies have represented that destruction in
redemptive terms, imagining the frontier as a place for both national progress
and personal renewal and opportunity.

This volume then is not making a case that the South has been exceptionally
violent. It was not only southerners who engaged in mob violence or who joined
the Ku Klux Klan, nor was it only southerners who imposed racial segregation
and resisted racial integration through force. Some forms of violence, such as
gang warfare, organized crime, or clashes between labor and capital, have been

more prevalent in other parts of the country. That is not to say, however, that southern violence has not had its own distinctiveness or its own particularities. The South has also been the site of national myths as lasting and as crucial as those born from the western frontier, through which Americans, north and south, have imagined the regenerative promise of tribulation and bloodshed—from the Civil War and Reconstruction to the civil rights movement.

This volume chronicles many of the varied ways in which violence erupted in the South and the impact it had, on individuals, on communities, and on the nation as a whole. It explores the texture and the trajectory of violent acts across various subregions and within different subcultures throughout the South. In many cases, entries address forms of violence more specific to the South, or at least more prevalent. Other thematic entries consider types of violence that were not particularly "southern" in nature or origin, but examine the particular forms they took in southern contexts, such as American Indian wars, or race riots, or suicide. Topical entries focus on certain violent episodes that were particularly remarkable or, conversely, particularly representative. Not every manner or dimension of human violence could be covered in one volume, of course. The entries included here are not meant to be comprehensive, nor could they be. Themes and topics, if not specific to the South, are significant in terms of understanding southern history and society. For this reason, for example, violence against animals in the form of hunting and blood sports are considered, while other acts against animals, such as vivisection, are not.

Although many entries address personal acts of violence and acts of intra-racial violence, the emphasis in this volume is on social or communal acts of violence, particularly those acts white southerners perpetrated on African Americans. To be sure, most violence committed in the South, as in the rest of the country, occurred within racial groups, and people were, and still are, more likely to commit violence against people they know, as entries on homicide, feuding, and dueling, to name a few, explore. Yet, it has been racial violence, in its various social and political forms, that has marked southern culture and that has shaped southern history in dramatic ways. If national identity was forged through bloodshed, so too was a Confederate identity. White supremacy was an ideology maintained through sheer force, whether through slave punishments, lynchings, or the terror exacted by the Ku Klux Klan. Moreover, its force has been so potent in southern culture—in particular, in the formation of masculinity in the South—that it has impinged upon the history of personal forms of violence. One cannot understand the history of, for instance, homicide or sexual violence in the South without taking stock of the ways in which white supremacy bore upon both white men's and black men's sense of masculinity or the values they placed on violence.

Importantly, white supremacy was forged not only along a black-white divide in the South, as entries on violence against Mexican Americans and against Native Americans reveal. These groups, as well as African Americans, also pushed back against white supremacy through legislative action, peaceful protest, or further acts of aggression. This volume pays attention to those acts of resistance and also to the role violence has played within minority cultures—for example, the use of war and torture within American Indian cultures, or outbreaks of violence within the slave quarters, or a kind of folk glorification of violence apparent in black music.

Although the entries center on physical acts of violence, violence is always, at the same time, psychological. For this reason, although the volume focuses on violations against persons, certain violations of property are included here—arson and church burnings, for instance—because those actions are meant to strike a psychological chord, serving as an act of protest or an act of terror. In that sense, what defines violence is not acts of destruction or violation as much as acts that cause suffering. It is uncomfortably easy when studying violence or reading account after account of violence to forget or immunize oneself to the human tragedy involved in the compendium of violence cataloged here. Behind these historical studies and sociological analyses are stories of real human loss and mourning, of unfathomable degrees of physical pain and psychological distress.

One hopes that to catalog southern violence as this volume does can help further our knowledge of southern culture and history as a whole. Violence was not a sensationalistic, subcultural phenomenon, exerting itself on the fringes of southern society. Violence was at the core of a southern social order based on stark class and especially racial hierarchies, the maintenance of which depended upon force and aggression. For this reason, violence intersected with and shaped the region's legal, political, religious, and economic institutions and had everything to do with southern attitudes about masculinity and femininity, crime and punishment, individualism and the state. Racial violence is certainly not particular to the South, but it did make its mark on southern society in ways that were historically distinctive.

For myriad reasons, southerners' violence has also been more conspicuous to outsiders and, in many cases, more widespread than elsewhere in the nation. From the 18th century on, memoirs, travel narratives, and diaries from the South revealed an attention to southerners' seeming penchant for violence, recording acts of feuding, dueling, fistfights, and vigilantism, not seen in comparable accounts from the North. Historian John Hope Franklin dubbed the region "the Militant South," because of white southerners' aggressiveness and enthusiasm for military ventures dating back to the 18th century. During the American Revolution, soldiers from Connecticut apparently refused to fight alongside soldiers from the Virginia colony because they saw their southern compatriots as too cruel and brutal as fighters. Not all southerners are violent or even bellicose, of course, but, according to Franklin and numerous other scholars, a climate of militancy and a quickness to settle disputes through violence dominated the region in a way that alternative codes or values did not. This fighting spirit can account, in part, for the historical overrepresentation of southerners in the military and in military schools.

The South's fighting spirit can also shed some light on why homicide rates have been higher in the region, a fact that has been true from the 19th century to the present. Some observers have been quick to attribute these rates to the larger numbers of African Americans residing in the South, yet, controlling for race, scholars have found that white southerners are more homicidal than whites in the rest of the country. Although felony crimes such as robbery and forcible rape are more common outside the South, southern murder rates are, in large part, the reason why southerners have a reputation for bellicosity and aggression. Homicide is crucial to understanding southern violence, because explaining why southerners have been disproportionately responsible for the murders committed in this country can help to account for related forms of violence most associated with the South, from slavery to the civil rights era. Journalist H. V. Redfield was the first to investigate southern homicide in any depth, cataloging acts of murder in southern news reports through the 1870s and comparing them to northern records. In his 1880 book, *Homicide, North and South*, he noted that murder rates in the former slave states were 10 times those in the North. These statistics held up some 40 years later when sociologist H. C. Brearley cheekily described the South as "that part of the United States lying below the Smith and Wesson line." According to Brearley, the top seven states with the highest homicide rates between 1920 and 1925 were former Confederate states, and southerners were two and half times more likely to kill than northerners.

Social scientists in the past 40 years have refined our understanding of these tendencies. Despite our image of blood-soaked northern cities, southern cities have higher homicide rates than northern cities, and rural southerners are more homicidal than their counterparts in other parts of the country. These trends are not unrelated to gun ownership. Southerners own guns at higher rates than other Americans and are more likely to use them in acts of rage or self-defense. These regional discrepancies hold only for white southerners, however; African American homicide rates do not differ by region. Certainly, poverty and structural racism can account for the fact that homicide rates for African Americans are as high in the North as they are in the South, but sociologists also theorize that because black migration to the North has been a relatively recent phenomenon, the values and customs from the South that black southerners carried with them to northern cities have persisted.

"Values and customs from the South" is significant. Although observers have offered a variety of explanations for this southern propensity toward murderous violence, most have attributed it to patterns of culture that led southerners to want to resolve disputes or avenge offenses through violence and to condone, even applaud, acts of aggression. Some have explained these cultural tendencies by looking to the South's frontier roots and the relative weakness of formal legal institutions to temper and restrain violent impulses. Journalist W. J. Cash, in his 1941 tome, *The Mind of the South*, posited that in the southern backcountry a particular brand of proud individualism asserted itself through violence. Indeed, in the backwoods of the South, traditions such as no-holds-barred fighting remained common long after they had disappeared in the North. As historian Elliott Gorn has shown, northern travelers to this country in the 19th century were astonished to find that southern men engaged in brutal, "rough and tumble" fights, where eyes were gouged and noses bitten. Southern propensities toward vigilantism and mob violence in the 19th and early 20th centuries can be traced to similar frontier values, which led to a certain distrust of legal institutions and reliance upon "rough justice" to avenge crime and settle scores. In the rural mountainous regions, feuds, such as that of the infamous Hatfields and McCoys, continued to be emblematic of southerners' lawlessness into the 20th century.

Yet, at the same time, other sparsely populated regions of the country have not witnessed the same levels of lethal violence as the South. In 2004 the former frontiers of the West and Midwest accounted for 23.7 percent and 19.3 percent of murders in the United States, in line with or below their percentage of the population. The South, meanwhile, accounts for 36 percent of the national population and 43 percent of its murders. Moreover, the South has hardly been a lawless region, nor have southern legal institutions been particularly weak or ineffective historically. Southerners, even in the most isolated parts, regularly settled disputes privately, but they also, at the same time, depended on the courts to adjudicate disputes, to enforce moral codes, and to maintain the social and racial order. Despite the South's tragic history of extralegal racial violence, it is important to recognize that most crimes allegedly committed by African Americans were judged and punished through the legal system (as biased and skewed against African Americans as that system has been). The South has had higher incarceration rates and higher execution rates than other sections of the country. Today, capital punishment is legal in every southern state, except for West Virginia. As Margaret Vandiver notes in this volume, about 90 percent of all executions since 1977, when the death penalty was reinstituted in the United States, have taken place in southern states. Southerners have relied upon the law to punish wrongdoing without mercy.

Certainly the fact that the South is the poorest region of the country might account for its higher murder rates. Sociologists and historians have argued that economic frustration in the 19th century and early 20th century led white southerners to lash out at African Americans, in lynchings, whitecappings, and other forms of mob violence. Outbreaks of violence correlated with falling cotton prices and economic depressions. Yet, while economic frustration may account for some acts of violence, for instance, when white farmers targeted successful black farmers, it does not explain why elite southerners engaged in dueling, or why white southerners of all classes joined the Klan or participated in and encouraged lynchings. Nor does it explain why poor southerners have been more violent than the poor in other parts of the country. Still today, white southerners living in poverty are more homicidal than their counterparts in the North, and white middle-class southerners are more homicidal than white middle-class northerners.

Rather than explanations of lawlessness or economic deprivation, scholars have reached a general consensus that a cultural mentality developed in the South, which expected and condoned violent responses to certain situations — to defend oneself against potential assaults, to avenge perceived insults, and to maintain social and racial control. In this view, it is not that the South lacks mechanisms for social control, such as strong legal institutions or moral codes, but that, in many cases, those mechanisms encouraged, even demanded, acts of violence. As sociologist John Shelton Reed has put it, violence in the South has often been considered "lawful," if not in the legal sense of the term, then in a sociological sense.

At the foundation of this mentality stands the concept of honor. Scholars have argued that a southern code of honor has persisted through time and across subregions. It not only explains the South's high homicide rates but can help make sense of a range of violent practices, from dueling, to rough-and-tumble fighting, to lynching. Honor, simply put, comprised a man's reputation or his external standing in his community, which in turn determined his internal sense of worth. In other words, a man's sense of self was predicated on his social power and status—his honor. Because honor formed the core of personal identity, southern men felt compelled to defend it at all costs. Violence was often the means through which a man could repair his honor and restore his public status, not just by knocking down his offender but also by demonstrating his own strength and valor. Acts of aggression, in this respect, were not committed against or outside the social system; rather, that system, at times, insisted upon them.

In his classic work, *Southern Honor*, historian Bertram Wyatt-Brown argued that, through the 19th century, honor was the driving force behind southern history, shaping family relationships, community hierarchies, the institution of slavery, and attitudes toward the law. Honor as a dominant ethic in the South can certainly clarify the kinds of violence that have been prevalent in the South, even into the 20th century and the present. It is not just that homicide rates are comparatively high in the South, but southerners are likely to murder people they already know, often as a consequence of fights or even personal affronts. In his study of southern violence, Brearley noted that juries were not likely to convict murder defendants who claimed they were retaliating against a personal insult. Journalist Hodding Carter found that to be true when he sat on the jury of a murder trial in Louisiana in the 1930s. The defendant lived next to a gas station, where a couple of men who gathered there began teasing him persistently. One day, he took out a shotgun and began to fire, injuring his persecutors and killing a bystander. Carter recounted that when he called for a guilty conviction, the other jurors objected, crying, "He ain't guilty. He wouldn't have been much of a man if he hadn't shot them fellows."

Even today, studies have shown that southern men are more likely to respond aggressively to perceived insults. In one well-known study done in the 1990s, social psychologists Richard Nisbett and Dov Cohen measured the levels of cortisol, the hormone associated with anxiety and stress, in the saliva of southern and northern white male college students after they had been insulted. The students, who thought their saliva was being tested for a different experiment, were approached in the hallway on their way to the lab by another man, who was in on the experiment. That man jostled each student and called him an "asshole." After this incident, cortisol levels had risen 79 percent in the southern students but only 33 percent in the northern students. In a related study, students were given a hypothetical scenario, involving one man flirting with another man's girlfriend at a party, to complete after they had been insulted in the hall; 75 percent of the insulted southern students imagined the scenario ending with an act of violence or threat of violence, while only 41 per-

Collecting bones of soldiers killed in a battle in Grant's Wilderness Campaign, May–June 1864. Cold Harbor, Va. Photograph taken April 1865. (John Reekie, photographer, Library of Congress [LC-B817-7926], Washington, D.C.)

cent of the northern students did so. Further experiments revealed that these southern students showed more hostility when they felt that their masculinity and their status had been threatened by the insult.

Indeed, this ethos of honor has been so powerful in the South because it defined one's gender identity—a man's sense of masculinity depended upon it. As Edward Ayers notes in this volume, women had, in place of honor, virtue, which was predicated on their personal decorum and restraint. That is not to say that women have played no role in the southern culture of violence. They helped to raise sons to be assertive and demanding and encouraged men to engage in violence, whether in acts of war or vigilantism. Southern women also themselves committed acts of violence. Even today, like their male counterparts, southern women commit more homicides than northern women do. In the past, a white woman's cry of rape could galvanize a lynching, and as the purported victim of black aggression, she at times played an exalted role in the ritual. In the 1920s, white women created their own auxiliary to the Ku Klux Klan, the WKKK, which, while it did not commit acts of violence, did embrace

the reactionary, angry outlook of the KKK. Southerners often justified the righteousness of the vigilantism by noting women's participation in it or their approval of it.

Although scholars have agreed that an ethic of honor has had overriding influence on southern men, explaining much about southern violence, it is not
clear where it derived from or why it has been so persistent across class and
racial boundaries, as well as subregions of the South. Wyatt-Brown and others
have maintained that white southerners inherited an ethic of honor from the
honor-bound culture of their Scots-Irish ancestors, who dominated European
migration into the southern colonies, and who had long been known for their
fiery tempers and ferocious pride. Scholars have attributed these qualities to
the Celtic herding economy, which led to a kind of hypervigilance and fierce
individualism, and to the fact that the Celts were relegated to the inhospit-
able fringes of British land and society, which led them to feel under siege. In
this view, Scots-Irish migrants to the South maintained this worldview even as
they transitioned into farmers in a market-driven society. This thesis, however,
does not explain why an honor-bound ethos, associated with premodern cultures, persisted into the modern era, amid other cultural influences or in the
face of widespread in-and-out migrations. It also does not explain why honor
held such sway for southerners of non-Celtic origins, such as elite slaveholders,
who tended to descend from English ancestry, or African Americans. If this
ethos was attractive enough or dominant enough to infect these other groups,
as some have argued, then how did this transmission of culture happen?

Honor is an ancient ethos, common throughout Europe through the 17th
century, but particular social and economic conditions offered it sure footing
in the South, which in turn gave rise to distinct forms of violence. As historian Edward Ayers has argued, the root cause of southern propensities for violence lies not in ethnicity or unchanging temperament but in the forces of history. We thus cannot consider southern violence without looking at slavery,
an institution based on the violent oppression of a people. Early observers
indeed blamed southerners' aggressiveness on slavery. Abigail Adams held
slavery responsible for the cruelty and arrogance she perceived in southerners,
and Thomas Jefferson lamented that slavery was having a deleterious effect on
southern morality. "The whole commerce between master and slave is a perpetual exercise of the most boisterous passions, the most unremitting despotism on the one part, and degrading submission on the other," he wrote in 1794
in *Notes on the State of Virginia*. "Our children see this, and learn to imitate it."
For Alexis de Tocqueville, writing some 40 years later in his classic study of
American institutions, *Democracy in America*, it was the idleness of the slave-

holder, his energies directed primarily to controlling his population, that could explain his militarism: "He delights in violent bodily exertion, he is familiar with the use of arms, and is accustomed from a very early age to expose his life in single combat."

For slaves, their masters' violence was brutal and arbitrary, with no functional purpose except to control every aspect of their lives. For slaveholders, violence was necessary to preserve plantation order and their own authority within that order. Even a slaveholder's misguided sense of his own paternalism, the view that he was a benevolent, fatherly figure to "his people," dictated that he use whippings to chastise and discipline them. This violence was thus full of contradiction: a slaveholder demonstrated and maintained his control by unleashing aggressive passions; his violence was a signal of his absolute power; yet it was, at the same, a signal of the inherent weakness of the institution that gave him that power—a slaveholder employed violence because he saw his plantation as fragile, unruliness and revolt ready to break out at any point.

Slavery can further help to explain why an archaic code of honor persisted in the South. Nonslaveholders, of course, also embraced this ethos; homicide rates have been at times highest in places where slavery was relatively weak. Nevertheless, nonslaveholders were still part of a larger social structure that prized hierarchy and public displays of status, and that social structure remained in place largely because of the institution of slavery. As Ayers has shown, urbanization and the rise of liberal capitalism in the antebellum North encouraged a culture of dignity, in which a man's sense of worth derived from his inward sense of character and restraint, rather than his outward reputation or status in his community; he was guided not by shame but by conscience. Although many southerners were as market-oriented as their northern counterparts, they perceived themselves as organized around feudal traditions of rank and patriarchy. Slavery allowed a premodern ethos of honor to persist because it ensured that southern communities remain rural, economically homogeneous, hierarchical, and, importantly, resistant to change.

Slavery also generated notions of power that shaped ideals of masculinity for slaveholding and nonslaveholding men alike. In a modern context, we think of mastery in terms of self-mastery, or our control over our emotions and passions. But in a slave society, the term "master" implied dominance over others, a control that depended on violence or the threat of violence. This understanding of mastery infiltrated all classes. As historian Stephanie McCurry has shown, yeoman and poor whites adopted conceptions of authority and power, if not over slaves, then over their wives and children—their households—that paralleled those of the elite classes.

Moreover, slavery can help to explain why conceptions of masculine honor have been so apparent in many African American communities. Slaves brought an ethos based in honor and shame with them from their African societies, which were also organized around notions of mastery and servility. As slaves, Africans were forced to adopt positions of dishonor, to subjugate themselves, at least in the presence of their masters. Among each other, black men jostled for respect, fostering an ideal of manhood based on bravado and swagger that matched that of white men. Sociologists have argued that black migrants brought this culture of honor with them to northern cities, where, amid the economic deprivations of urban ghettos, it morphed into what Elijah Anderson has called "a code of the streets." Those who live by this code demand respect and punish with force acts of disrespect; by this code, minor insults can become lethal. This adaptation of a southern code of honor was by no means absolute in African American communities. Many traditions of black resistance, most notably civil disobedience, have been rooted in Christian ideals of personal dignity, which dictate that one remains restrained, though resolute, in the face of insult.

Finally, slavery reminds us how much southern violence has been wrapped up in maintaining not only masculine authority but white domination. Just as the institution of slavery rested on violence, so too did the ideology of white supremacy. After the Civil War, southern whites continued to exert control and assert their power over African Americans through intimidation and bloodshed. Reconstruction was one of the bloodiest periods in U.S. history, as white southerners lashed out at ex-slaves demanding their freedom and civil rights, and various paramilitary groups attempted to overthrow the Republican rule that was guaranteeing that freedom. Beginning in the late 19th century, Jim Crow segregation and disenfranchisement operated not only through the force of law and custom but also through violence or the threat of violence. The specter of lynching and other acts of punishment, individual or collective, terrorized African Americans, threatening them with death for any transgression of the racial order.

Some elite, conservative whites, averse to the most brutal manifestations of reactionary racism, maintained that racial segregation was necessary to prevent violence, as, by maintaining a racial hierarchy, it would keep the races in peaceful harmony. It did just the opposite, of course. Although, to be sure, racial violence peaked in the 1890s, when southern states and municipalities first instituted Jim Crow laws, that bloodshed continued through the 20th century. Southern whites also reacted violently to attempts on the part of African Americans to resist white domination or federal forces to enforce racial equality.

White supremacy was also an ideology that refused to recognize its own violence. At its core stood the assumption that whites were inherently more civilized and restrained than African Americans, who were imagined as more aggressive and viciously criminal. White acts of violence were, in this view, simply a necessary mechanism to control and contain black savagery. The most gripping fear was that African American men, freed from the restraints of slavery and eager to claim the rights and privileges of white manhood, posed a threat to the virtue of white womanhood. The specter of the "black beast rapist" cut to the heart of whites' anxieties about their own power and the integrity of their social order. This stereotype became the primary trope through which white southerners defended lynching and other acts of white vigilantism, even though most of this violence was not actually committed to retaliate against rape. Rhetorically, however, the image of vulnerable white women in the clutches of lascivious black men effectively galvanized support not only for vigilante justice but also for more stringent legal penalties against black crime. Until 1977 rape was considered a capital crime in many southern states, and almost 90 percent of men executed for rape in southern states were African American. Even to this day, African American men are more likely than white men to receive a death sentence when convicted of crimes, especially when the victims of their crimes are white.

That white supremacy was bolstered on a perception that African Americans were innately more criminal can explain why images of black innocence and black nonviolent resistance that came out of the South in the civil rights era struck such an emotional chord nationwide. Images such as the photograph of the mutilated corpse of Emmett Till, the 14-year-old black boy murdered for wolf-whistling at a white woman in Mississippi in 1955, or news footage of black teenagers facing down fire hoses and police dogs in Birmingham in 1963, were, in part, so visually effective because they challenged an ugly assumption whites held about African Americans.

In these ways, violence was more than just a political act to maintain white power; it was also a cultural act that conveyed and even created meaning for its perpetrators and its witnesses. The effects of violence are, of course, traumatic and destructive, to victims, to their families and communities, and even to perpetrators. Still, violence is performative in the sense that it is action through which people construct identities and forge communities. As noted, southern men relied on violence to affirm their manliness—whether by avenging a personal affront or protecting, through force, their women. Even some of the rituals that marked a boy's entry into manhood were wrapped up in violence: his first fight, his first gun, or a first hunt. For African American men, in particular, violence could be the means to assert their manliness in a culture that denied them the privileges of their gender and, relatedly, a means to claim the rights of full citizenship. At the same time, freedom for African Americans entailed a freedom from violence, the right to live without terror.

Communities also used violence to establish and reinforce their boundaries, whether through the punishment of those within the group who break communal codes or through the retaliation against outsiders who threaten to disrupt the community. Southerners have been notorious for their fierce loyalty to local custom and their suspicion of outsiders, much of which was rooted in traditions of local sovereignty dating back to the colonial period. These traits were not exceptional to the South, but they have been particularly pronounced in certain subregions and at certain moments in southern history. For instance, historians have attributed southern vigilante practices, including lynching, to the value placed on localism. In this view, lynching was an expression of popular sovereignty, the notion that communities had a lawful right to punish crime when they viewed legal institutions as either ineffective or intruding upon their will. These traditions can also shed some light on the reasons why many white southerners blamed any attempts by African Americans to claim their rights on "outside agitators" and resisted with forceful passion any federal intervention to guarantee those rights under the clarion call of "states' rights." Indeed, in his work on southern homicide, historian Sheldon Hackney found that white southerners have had a tendency toward "extrapunitiveness," a mentality that led them to blame outsiders for their woes rather than themselves. According to Hackney, this mentality can explain why white southerners have higher homicide rates and are less likely to commit suicide than white northerners. It can also explain the tendency for many white southerners to feel that their way of life was under siege, that it is was constantly at risk of disintegration, and so needed to be defended at all costs.

And, at least since the beginnings of the abolition movement in the 18th century, the southern social order *had* been under assault. White southerners defended the principles of local control and states' rights so vociferously because their racial order depended on them. Although white supremacy was powerful and abiding, the sheer amount of blood that was shed to protect it signals just how tenuous and unstable it was as a social system. Violence was not only a mechanism through which whites tried to preserve that order, however; it was also performative in the way it helped construct a sense of racial identity and solidarity for whites. It was for this reason that many acts of white supremacist violence were ritualistic. Public lynchings, involving drawn-out tortures or Klan rallies, parades, or public acts of intimidation such as cross burnings were meant to terrorize African Americans, but they also served as public displays of white power, meant to foster a sense of superiority and collectivity among whites.

Liberal critics of the South, such as H. L. Mencken and Gunnar Myrdal, contended for many years that the region's propensity for certain kinds of violence was a sign of its backwardness and its refusal to enter the modern world. They believed that as the South modernized, that is, as it became urbanized and drew away from rural traditions, as its criminal justice system became more centralized, and as its people became more educated and less impoverished, violence across the region would inevitably decline. To an extent their predictions were right, in the sense that while its homicide rates remain higher than those in the rest of the country, the South is a far more peaceful place today than it was 100 or even 50 years ago.

Yet, the history of the South has not led to one long, inexorable decrease in violence. Moments of the most intense change in the South led to some of the bloodiest and most damaging outbreaks of violence. The Civil War, most notably, created a political and economic crisis in the South that exacerbated existing cultural tensions and created new ones. In the border states, for instance, the social instability after the war gave rise to outlaw gangs such as the James brothers, who themselves had been Confederate guerrilla fighters during the war. And arguably the war's most significant consequence—the emancipation of slaves—created a new group of citizens, which set off the horrifying racial and political conflicts of Reconstruction.

The process of modernization after the war, during what has been termed the New South era, also at times created conditions and circumstances that, rather than alleviating violence, intensified it. In the late 19th century, the rise of rural tenancy and the development of new industries in the South that placed whites and blacks in economic competition with each other aggravated existing tensions between the races. The growth of towns and cities and rising commercialism further upset traditional social hierarchies and generated fears of crime and moral decay, fears that were inseparable from whites' desire to maintain racial order. These tensions were unleashed in extraordinary waves of violence in southern cities, towns, and rural communities. Even feuding, which seems like a form of violence rooted in archaic traditions, escalated in the late 19th century as capitalist industries such as the railroad and coal mining entered into Appalachian communities, disrupting their self-sufficient stability.

In these ways, southern violence has been all too often reactionary, a lashing out against the forces of change that were disrupting traditional social arrangements and established class or racial hierarchies. This characteristic was true even as some forms of violence appeared utterly modern, as perpetrators made use of modern technologies and modern forms of communication. Lynch mobs hanged their victims from telephone poles on city streets, drawing crowds of spectators on trains and streetcars, and photographed the violence and sold them as postcards. The Ku Klux Klan in the 1920s transformed itself into a national organization with a sophisticated publicity machine. And white supremacists in the face of civil rights protestors in the 1960s used bombs and other incendiaries to impose their brand of terror.

Because violence is cultural—because it emerges from value systems and in turn shapes them—it has played a prominent role in southern popular, religious, musical, and literary cultural traditions. Sociologist John Shelton Reed has posited that southerners tend to be more at ease with stories about or images of violence in their everyday interactions to a greater degree than other Americans. In the South, he has written, "violence is not just something to be used when someone wants something, but something to be sung about, joked about, played with." Further social research has revealed that southerners are more likely than other Americans to consume and enjoy violence as entertainment. Part of this tendency might be due to a kind of casual acceptance of violence in everyday life, but it could also mean that southerners have used their strong cultural traditions to reflect upon violence, that they take it very seriously indeed. Culture is the medium through which southerners, black and white, have justified, conceptualized, and made sense of the violence they have committed and have suffered. This volume includes entries on the representation of violence in southern literature, music, religion, and public memory, for this reason.

Looking at southern history and culture through the focal point of violence inevitably shifts our perspective on them. What were in fact distinct events or historical moments, with their own causes and their own dynamics, begin to seem more similar. Historical particularity gives way to undercurrents of continuity. From the slave patrols of the antebellum period to lynchings at the turn of the 20th century, to the rise of massive resistance in the 1950s, violence has been a central means through which white southerners sought to maintain racial control and exert white authority. From the long tradition of dueling to the waves of whitecappings that terrorized the southern countryside in the late 19th century, to the success of the second Klan in the 1920s, to antiabortion extremists of the recent past, violence has been a means through which southerners have regulated moral conduct and sought to impose moral order. And from the Regulator movement that anticipated the American Revolution, to the guerrilla bands that formed during the Civil War, to the Klan terror of Reconstruction, it has been the means through which southerners have resisted what they considered corrupt and unlawful intrusions of state power.

The entries in this volume, however, are also meant to recover particularity—to uncover the meaning, the texture, and the tragedy of various forms of violence and specific episodes of violence from the colonial period to the present. This volume can document only a fraction of the violence that has been committed through southern history, though. In the past, many acts of violence simply went unrecorded and undocumented. But in chronicling some of the most significant acts of violence and examining the mentalities that surrounded violent crime and punishment in the South, we can enrich our understanding of not only the South but our national culture as a whole. At the same time, this volume can hopefully allow us to honor the suffering that lies beneath and that often goes unrecognized in the study of violence.

AMY LOUISE WOOD
Illinois State University

Elijah Anderson, *Code of the Street: Decency, Violence, and the Moral Life of the Inner City* (1999); Edward L. Ayers, *Vengeance and Justice: Crime and Punishment in the Nineteenth-Century American South* (1985); H. C. Brearley, in *Culture of the South*, ed. W. T. Conch (1934); Dickson D. Bruce, *Violence and Culture in the Antebellum South* (1979); W. Fitzhugh Brundage, *Lynching in the New South: Georgia and Virginia, 1880–1930*; William Carrigan, *The Making of a Lynching Culture: Violence and Vigilantism in Central Texas, 1836–1916* (2006); W. J. Cash, *The Mind of the South* (1941); Crystal Feimster, *Southern Horrors: Women and the Politics of Rape and Lynching* (2009); Richard B. Felson and Paul-Phillippe Pare, *Social Science Research* (March 2010); John Hope Franklin, *The Militant South, 1800–1861* (1956); Raymond Gastil, *American Sociological Review* (June 1971); Kenneth S. Greenberg, *Honor and Slavery: Lies, Duals, Noses, Masks, Dressing as a Woman, Gifts, Strangers, Humanitarianism, Death, Slave Rebellions, the Proslavery Argument, Baseball, Hunting, and Gambling in the Old South* (1996); Elliott Gorn, *American Historical Review* (February 1985); Sheldon Hackney, *American Historical Review* (February 1969); Saidiya Hartman, *Scenes of Subjugation: Terror, Slavery, and Self-Making in Nineteenth-Century America* (1997); Thomas Jefferson, *Notes on the State of Virginia* (1794); Matthew R. Lee et al., *Deviant Behavior* (January 2010); Nancy MacLean, *Behind the Mask of Chivalry: The Making of the Second Ku Klux Klan* (1994); Stephanie McCurry, *Masters of Small Worlds: Yeomen Households, Gender Relations, and the Political Culture of the Antebellum South Carolina Low Country* (1995); Richard E. Nisbett and Dov Cohen, *Culture of Honor: The Psychology of Violence in the South* (1996); Michael Pfeifer, *Rough Justice: Lynching and American Society, 1874–1947* (2004); George Rable, *But There Was No Peace: The Role of Violence in Politics of Reconstruction*

(1984); H. V. Redfield, *Homicide, North and South: Being a Comparative View of Crime against the Person in Several Parts of the United States* (1880); John Shelton Reed, *Political Science Quarterly* (September 1971), *One South: An Ethnic Approach to Regional Culture* (1982); Hannah Rosen, *Terror in the Heart of Freedom: Citizenship, Sexual Violence, and the Meaning of Race in the Post-Emancipation South* (2008); Richard Slotkin, *Regeneration through Violence: The Mythology of the American Frontier, 1600–1860* (1975); Alexis de Tocqueville, *Democracy in America* (1835); Christopher Waldrep, *Roots of Disorder: Race and Criminal Justice in the American South, 1817–1880* (1998); Altina Waller, *Feud: Hatfields, McCoys, and Social Change in Appalachia, 1860–1900* (1988); Joel Williamson, *Crucible of Race: Black-White Relations in the American South since Emancipation* (1984); Amy Louise Wood, *Lynching and Spectacle: Witnessing Racial Violence in America, 1890–1940* (2009); Bertram Wyatt-Brown, *Southern Honor: Ethics and Behavior in the Old South* (1982); Margaret Vandiver, *Lethal Punishment: Lynchings and Legal Executions in the South* (2005).

American Indians, Violence toward

Warfare was common among native chiefdoms in the pre-Columbian era, but Euro-American imperatives, especially the desire for slaves and land, ushered in an age of unprecedented violence. Although ominous, first encounters were fleeting. Spaniards captured and enslaved Indians along the South Carolina coast in the 1510s and 1520s, and in 1521 Juan Ponce de León attempted to colonize southern Florida as a base for mining and slaving. Much more devastating was the expedition of Hernando de Soto, whose four-year rampage throughout the region's interior exposed many Native American people to Europeans, horses, dogs of war, and firearms for the first time. Encounters with the De Soto expedition ranged from uneasy alliances to bloody battles, such as the one at Mabila in central Alabama. Tascaluza, a powerful chief, had rallied thousands of native warriors to the fortified town, where they attempted to trap and kill De Soto. The plan backfired when De Soto's army breached the palisade with steel axes and set fire to the houses inside, killing as many as 3,000 Indians. Throughout the expedition, De Soto took hundreds of native people captive, forcing them to serve as burden-bearers and sex slaves. When seeking information, he sometimes tortured these captives. By 1543, native people forced what remained of De Soto's starving army into the Gulf of Mexico, but Euro-American patterns of violence—warfare, slavery, rape, and occasional torture—would endure.

Major colonial conflicts in the South included the Powhatan Wars of 1622 and 1644, the Tuscarora War (1711–15), the Yamasee War (1715–18), the Natchez Revolt (1729–30), and the Cherokee War (1759–61). More than inevitable cultural clashes, these were conflicts over land, resources, and sovereignty, and native people often fought on both sides. Violence also punctuated everyday encounters as settlers and Indians quarreled at taverns and trading posts. During periods of strife, white southerners, like their Indian neighbors, took captives and subjected them to fates ranging from adoption to slavery. The most famous Indian captive was Pocahontas, daughter of Chief Powhatan, taken by the English of Jamestown in 1613. The English demanded a ransom, but Powhatan balked, and Pocahontas remained among her captors for the rest of her short life. Colonists, however, usually employed more indirect means to secure captives. From Native American middlemen and Euro-American traders, colonists bought Indian slaves, whom they put to work on their tobacco and rice plantations or sold to labor-starved colonies in the Caribbean or New England. Southern Indians traditionally had taken war captives, but the development of this external market encouraged them to enslave greater numbers, and the firearms they received from traders made warfare more deadly. The trade in

Indian slaves peaked from 1670 to 1715, when Carolina traders acquired between 24,000 and 51,000 souls. The devastation of the trade, however, is greater than these figures suggest, because for every captive taken, perhaps three died as a result of the violence that accompanied slave raiding. Such violence depleted native populations already reeling from European-introduced diseases. In the wake of the Yamasee War, a multitribal effort to reform British trade, the scale of captive exchange diminished significantly, but some southern whites continued to enslave Indians through the Removal era. In 1848, Creek headman Ward Co-cha-may reported that at least 100 recently captured Creeks toiled as slaves on Alabama plantations.

From the 1760s through the 1830s, native people endured increasing assaults on their land and sovereignty. As agriculturalists, southern Indians had long sought to mark their territorial holdings, but that need became increasingly urgent during this period of Anglo-American expansion. Driven by a Revolutionary-era ideology that united many eastern Indian groups against colonialism, native warriors attacked frontier settlements, and whites returned the volley with gusto. In 1776 Georgia, Virginia, and the Carolinas sent retaliatory forces to Cherokee country, where they destroyed 30 towns and thousands of acres of corn, bringing years of famine and misery to the Cherokees. War chief Dragging Canoe remarked, "It seemed to be the Intention of the White People to destroy them from being a people." Guerrilla warfare persisted for decades in the borderlands, where a new, cross-racial brand of southern masculinity emphasized individual courage, honor, and brutality. White warriors even collected war trophies, including scalps. In the aftermath of the Battle of Horseshoe Bend (1814), in which Andrew Jackson's forces killed about 800 Creek warriors, one white participant recalled, "Many of the Tennessee soldiers cut long strips of skin from the bodies of the dead Indians and with these made bridle reins."

Most of the Deep South remained Indian country until the 1810s when, in the aftermath of the Red Stick War (1813–14), the Treaty of Fort Jackson forced the Creeks to cede 23 million acres. In the 1820s Georgia and other southern states began to agitate for the expulsion of the Cherokee, Chickasaw, Choctaw, Creek, and Seminole nations. Under various degrees of coercion, most Native American southerners were forced to leave their homeland over the next 10 years, and violence marred every step of their expulsion. Each of these nations had exercised sovereignty over their lands and citizens, but now states extended their laws over Indian territories and crafted "Indian codes" that prevented native people from testifying against whites in court. Before they left Alabama, Creeks suffered beatings, theft, fraud, and even murder. The *Cherokee Phoenix* complained of a "pony club" of whites living on the Georgia frontier that stole livestock and harassed Cherokees, and when Cherokees tried to remove squatters on tribal land, the intruders attacked and sometimes killed them. Women were particularly vulnerable. According to the *Phoenix*, the Georgia militia had orders to "inflict corporeal punishment" on women who insulted them. Army lieutenant John G. Reynolds reported that many Creek women were raped by soldiers and civilians. Soldiers drove Cherokees from their homes and imprisoned them in stockades where, a missionary decried, "poor captive women" were "debauched, through terror and seduction." Oral tradition passed on by Seminole Betty Mae Jumper recounted how soldiers raped her great-great-grandmother and the woman's oldest daughter, prompting her to engineer the escape of her two other daughters. The Trail of Tears was fraught with violence that ranged from a soldier's stabbing of a pregnant woman in labor to the unsolved murder of two young Cherokee men who went into Golconda, Ill., for provisions.

After the removal of the five nations, southern states regarded many of the Indian people left behind as free people of color. For that reason, the Confederacy refused the army enlistment of Lumbee men in North Carolina but impressed them to build coastal fortifications. When Lumbees resisted, a war broke out that claimed lives on both sides. Indians benefited little from Reconstruction, and the Jim Crow system that followed relegated most Indians across the region to second-class status. Southerners enforced segregation with violence and intimidation, and Indians lived in fear. In Charenton, La., in 1901 a mob beat a Chitimacha man senseless and then descended on his father-in-law's house, murdering his wife, her brother, and her uncle. Authorities never arrested anyone for the murders. The man's offense had been trying to break up a fight between an Indian and an African American, a white prerogative, but his position as a Chitimacha whose tribe owned land on the edge of town was no doubt an underlying factor. Property ownership made Indians targets of violence. The Ashley Gang that terrorized south Florida began its crime spree in 1911 with the murder of a Seminole for his hides. After first a mistrial and then a guilty verdict, the Florida Supreme Court overturned the perpetrator's conviction. Fear of violence led some Seminole communities in the 1930s to give up their cattle to avoid confrontations with white cattlemen over grazing.

Interracial sex could precipitate violence. In late 19th-century North Carolina, whites forced a Coharie man who was living with a white woman to surrender his property. According to oral tradition, "The white folks told him that if he would sign the land over to the white folks, that they would let him live, but if he didn't they would take his life." The man took no chances and fled the community. In the mid-20th century, however, neighboring Lumbees routed the Ku Klux Klan, which had rallied to protest a relationship between Indian and white. Although whites considered most Indian-white sexual relationships taboo, white men did not hesitate to sexually exploit Indian women. In the 1930s missionaries among the Poarch Creeks in Alabama worried about white men preying on Indian schoolgirls, and government officials protested the sexual abuse of Seminole girls in the tourist camps of south Florida. Well-meaning whites discovered there was little they could do without the cooperation of local law enforcement, which often was not forthcoming. In the 1960s the rape of three Choctaw women by white Mississippians produced no indictments, although the sheriff had arrived on the scene during one rape. Officials in Washington responded by stating the obvious: "It appears that Indians may not be able to receive justice in local courts."

Officials were sometimes responsible for such violence. In the 1930s a white policeman severely beat a deaf Lumbee boy and then charged the boy with assault because he did not follow the officer's verbal order to clear the sidewalk. At the same time, law enforcement officials often denied Indians equal protection of the law by ignoring violence within their communities. This unwillingness to police native communities contributed to a stereotype of Indian savagery that, in turn, excused acts of violence against Indian people. Crimes perpetrated against whites by Indians seemed to confirm this stereotype and provoked demands for vigilante justice. Attempts to lynch three Lumbee men under indictment for robbery and murder in Georgia in the 1890s and a Cherokee man accused of rape and murder in North Carolina in 1911 suggest that Indians were appropriate targets, in the eyes of whites, for vigilante violence.

THEDA PERDUE
University of North Carolina at Chapel Hill

CHRISTINA SNYDER
Indiana University

Cherokee Phoenix (10 February 1830; 26 March and 16 July 1831); Grant Foreman, *Indian Removal: The Emigration of the Five Civilized Tribes of Indians* (1972); Alan Gallay, *The Indian Slave Trade: The Rise of English Empire in the American South, 1670–1717* (2002); H. S. Halbert and T. H. Ball, *The Creek War of 1813 and 1814*, ed. Frank L. Owsley (1969); Charles M. Hudson, *Knights of Spain, Warriors of the Sun: Hernando de Soto and the South's Ancient Chiefdoms* (1997); Betty Mae Jumper and Patsy West, *A Seminole Legend: The Life of Betty Mae Tiger Jumper* (2001); Theda Perdue, in *The Folly of Jim Crow: Rethinking the Segregated South*, ed. Stephanie Cole and Natalie J. Ring (2010); Theda Perdue and Michael D. Green, *The Cherokee Na-*

tion and the Trail of Tears (2007); Christina Snyder, *Slavery in Indian Country: The Changing Face of Captivity in Early America* (2010).

Arson

Arson can be defined as "deliberately setting fire to someone else's property for fraudulent or malicious purposes." Because the crime is typically committed anonymously, preventing arson is often hard, and bringing its perpetrators to justice is likewise difficult. Moreover, the motives behind illicit fire setting are often complex and diverse. Regional geographic patterns, however, may offer an intriguing glimpse into this anomalous behavior, for the southern United States manifests several unique forms of arson. The first type, an intentionally set wildland fire, is a legacy of the South's historical ecology, while a second, more current form of structural arson may have become unfairly associated with the region as a matter of popular misconception. Over the past several hundred years, rural incendiarism has indeed emerged as a characteristic southern culture trait that persists as a chronic problem affecting both private and public lands. Yet most recently, a notorious rash of church arsons has raised the specter of lingering racism across the region.

Overall, the crime of arson is no more prevalent in the South than it is in other parts of the country, yet certain practices have come to differentiate specific forms of arson in the South as distinct phenomena. A uniquely regional form of arson—southern woods burning—originally derived from its adaptive use within the human-environment system of hunting and gathering along with more intensive agricultural strategies undertaken by indigenous peoples. As frontier settlement proceeded during the 1700s and early 1800s, newly arrived European pioneers quickly learned the centuries-old technique of setting fire to wooded areas from the American Indian tribes who inhabited these landscapes and managed them for optimum productivity. For the Indians, burning the forest initially created and then maintained clearings that facilitated hunting, stimulated the proliferation of nut-bearing trees and berries, and later allowed for cultivation of crops. Following a brief period of genocide and removal of remaining Indian populations, Euro-American settlement systems that continued the use of established fire practices prevailed. The many stated reasons for recurrent burning included the renewal of forage, clearing vegetation for new fields, the removal of insect and reptile pests or unwanted weeds, and simply keeping the woods open and looking clean. Although burning vegetation on lawfully established homestead property was obviously not illegal behavior, a problem arose when participants in the free-range cattle economy set fire to extensive grazing areas that were widely regarded as a common resource.

The situation was exacerbated when absentee timber owners attempted to enforce a ban on burning and thereby infringed on what was perceived by local residents as their right to burn. In some cases, such fires have been set out of spiteful resentment or retaliation against either corporate ownership or federal control of these lands, and many fires were deliberately set as a protest over any attempt to prevent them. This is particularly true not only for large tracts of privately held land but for publicly owned forests as well. Following the termination of federal land alienation programs at the end of the 19th century, remaining public domain holdings were consolidated into national forests that initially maintained policies of fire suppression. Although reliance on controlled burns is now an accepted forest management strategy, arson is still the leading cause of wildfire in the national forests of the South. Thus, southern woods burning has persisted, viewed by some as criminal activity and by others as a vested traditional practice.

In the past, other fire-setting activity may also have developed as a form of social protest in certain areas. One researcher found that during the postbellum Reconstruction period in central Georgia "arson was a primarily interracial, black-on-white crime" that tended to flare up during cycles of economic turmoil and that "arson generally constituted a means by which the poor and the propertyless could strike out against those who dominated a racist and economically exploitive society." In any case, the idea that arson should be construed as an intrinsic element of the southern ethos has been made manifest in literary and popular culture alike. One of William Faulkner's greatest stories, "Barn Burning," published in 1939, portrays the inner conflicts of a young boy who ultimately rejects the lawless and aberrant pyromaniac behavior of his father, a shiftless and amoral sharecropper named Ab Snopes, who stealthily sets ablaze the barns of a succession of landowners over perceived slights or injustices. And even though the hit record by country music legend Hank Williams used the title "Settin' the Woods on Fire" merely as metaphor for having a good time in 1952, the illuminating lyrics of that popular song were clearly indicative of actions familiar to most rural southerners.

A more recent form of arson in the South has involved the widely publicized phenomenon of church burnings. During the early to mid-1990s a series of arson attacks on church buildings occurred across the region. Emotions ran high as national news media reported a pattern of rural African American places of worship being targeted, and a prominent court case in South Carolina established a punitive monetary settlement against a local Ku Klux Klan chapter for its complicity in an arson case there. The spate of church burnings in the region had become such a glaring political issue, even at the federal level, that it resulted in the passage of the Church Arson Prevention Act of 1996, which provided funds to rebuild damaged religious structures and established more severe penalties for those convicted of what would now be treated as a federal crime. The rhetoric behind its passage was racially contextualized and wrapped in hate crime terminology, with proponents of the bill pointing to the fact that a majority of those structures that were torched did indeed house African American congregations. But while it appears that many of these southern church arsons may have been motivated by racism, this is not so conclusive as an overall cogent explanation for the phenomenon. Recent critical analysis indicates that most of the churches set afire were not only situated within areas of predominantly black population but were in areas that already had higher rates of structural arson than other locations; moreover, counter to prevailing public perceptions nurtured by sensationalist press coverage, most fires were actually in urban rather than rural settings. Even so, incidences of arson across much of the South may be especially noticeable, however, because of the region's rural poverty, for a recent case study in Florida found that the more economically depressed counties suffered from higher rates of arson.

ROBERT KUHLKEN
Central Washington University

John P. Bartkowski, Frank M. Howell, and Shu-Chuan Lai, *Rural Sociology* (October 2002); M. L. Doolittle and M. L. Lightsey, *Southern Woods-Burners: A Descriptive Analysis* (1979); Ed Kerr, *Harper's* (July 1958); Jack Temple Kirby, *Mockingbird Song: Ecological Landscapes of the South* (2006); Robert Kuhlken, *Geographical Review* (July 1999); Jeffrey P. Prestemon and David T. Butry, *American Journal of Agricultural Economics* (August 2005); Stephen J. Pyne, *Fire in America: A Cultural History of Wildland and Rural Fire* (1982); Albert C. Smith, *Journal of Southern History* (November 1985); Sarah A. Soule and Nella VanDyke, *Ethnic and Racial Studies* (July 1999); Christopher B. Strain, *Burning Faith: Church Arson in the American South* (2008).

Black Armed Resistance

Throughout the history of the American South, African Americans resorted to armed resistance to defend themselves against racist violence. During slavery, successful armed revolts were small and relatively rare, but together with the numerous attempted rebellions that were discovered before they could be put into action, they were of significant symbolic value, demonstrating African Americans' longing for freedom. The two largest rebellions in the 18th century were the New York City insurrection of 1712 and the Stono Rebellion of 1739, which took place near Charleston, S.C. When slave conspiracies were revealed, white retaliation was swift and brutal. In the aftermath of revolts and conspiracies, white authorities put tight security measures into place to discourage further unrest.

Fewer slave revolts and conspiracies took place in the 19th century. In 1800 enslaved blacksmith Gabriel Prosser planned a massive revolt in Richmond, Va., but shortly before the rebellion was to begin, fellow slaves revealed the plan to white authorities. Gabriel, his followers, and other suspects were quickly rounded up and executed. In 1822 Denmark Vesey, a free black carpenter, was discovered to have planned a large slave revolt in Charleston, S.C. Vesey had intended to lead a slave army on Charleston, but as in the case of other conspiracies, a servant alerted his white master before the rebellion could take place. Local authorities quickly detained Gabriel, seized more than 100 suspects, and later executed the revolt's leader and 34 of his followers. The 1831 rebellion of Nat Turner in Southampton County, Va., was the most violent one in U.S. history, killing 59 people, including women and children. Once more, however, white militiamen quickly put down the revolt and captured its leader. In the end, white authorities executed Turner and almost 20 of his followers. Although rumors of slave conspiracies continued to swirl among southern planters in the following decades, the Turner revolt remained the last major slave rebellion in North America, but it inspired militant abolitionists, whose actions contributed to the outbreak of the Civil War and the subsequent end of slavery.

After the Civil War, blacks in the American South were faced with an upsurge of antiblack violence and frequently resorted to armed force to protect themselves and their communities. One of the most violent antiblack organizations was the Ku Klux Klan, a secret fraternal society that was founded by former Confederate soldiers in 1866 in Pulaski, Tenn. Yet many African Americans refused to remain passive in the face of white terror. Indeed, the end of the Civil War marked a watershed in the history of black militant resistance in the United States. Slaves had been prohibited from owning weapons, which made militant resistance extremely difficult. After the war, the Thirteenth and Fourteenth Amendments to the Constitution not only ended slavery and made African Americans citizens of the United States but also allowed them to carry weapons. As a result, African Americans across the South purchased rifles, shotguns, and pistols. For black men the right to bear arms became an important symbol of their new freedom.

Black Civil War veterans in particular were determined to fight back. In many parts of the South, former black Union soldiers formed paramilitary organizations to defend their communities against the Ku Klux Klan and other terrorist groups. Black militias were unable to stop entirely the reign of terror that whites launched in the aftermath of the war, and militant resistance frequently meant death for black defenders. But on several occasions, black militiamen successfully drove back white vigilantes with force. In 1876, for instance, African American men successfully repelled an attack by Klansmen near Laurens, S.C. Such forms of resistance were most effective in those areas of the South where blacks were in the majority. In the Lowcountry of South Carolina, for example, large black communities were well organized and could easily repel white attackers. Ultimately, however, black militant resistance during Reconstruction could not prevent the advent of segregation and disfranchisement. Racist violence also continued.

Black militant resistance played a significant role throughout the Jim Crow era. During the 1890s, lynching emerged as a new form of racial terror. Outspoken black intellectuals such as Ida B. Wells and W. E. B. Du Bois called for manly self-defense to confront white lynch mobs. When African Americans joined together, they were sometimes able to repel white murderers. In 1899, for example, during what came to be known as the Darrien Insurrection, a small army of armed black men in McIntosh County, Ga., thwarted the attempts of a white mob to seize a black prisoner accused of raping a white woman. Seven years later, blacks in Wiggins, Miss., traded hundreds of shots with white attackers who had vowed to lynch a member of the black community. More often, however, black militant resistance provoked rather than deterred racist aggression. Armed blacks who confronted exploitative employers, white lynch mobs, or abusive police officers frequently faced swift retaliation against themselves and their communities. Despite numerous appeals from African Americans to prosecute acts of racist violence, the federal government did nothing to stop the brutal reign of white supremacy.

In the first two decades of the 20th century, a number of blacks practiced and publicly advocated armed self-defense against racist terrorism. In the aftermath of World War I, when race riots broke out in Houston, Washington, D.C., and numerous other American cities, a number of combat-experienced black veterans organized the protection of black neighborhoods. Black nationalist leaders such as Marcus Garvey and Cecil Briggs applauded black veterans' militancy and urged their followers to confront white aggression in the same manner. During the 1920s, many African American intellectuals hailed the advent of a "New Negro," a black man who refused to be intimidated by white supremacist terrorism. But as in the case of African American resistance to lynching, self-defense could also trigger antiblack violence. In 1921 in Tulsa, Okla., for instance, blacks' attempt to protect a young African American from a lynch mob led to the invasion and complete destruction of the city's black neighborhood.

Despite such setbacks, black militant resistance continued in the 1930s and 1940s. During the Great Depression, black sharecroppers and tenants in Alabama relied on armed protection to safeguard the meetings of a nascent union movement. World War II further politicized and radicalized African Americans, many of whom refused to acquiesce to white violence. During the war years, black soldiers in the South frequently rose up against mistreatment, while African American civilians fought back when attacked by whites during hundreds of urban race riots that erupted between 1941 and 1943. After the war, numerous black veterans used their guns to defend themselves when confronted by racist attackers upon their return to the United States. In 1946 in Columbia, Tenn., several hundred black veterans guarded the city's black neighborhood against a rumored white attack but were later overwhelmed by white policemen, who destroyed black homes and businesses and arrested hundreds of African Americans.

During the southern civil rights struggle of the 1950s and 1960s, white supremacists again launched a reign of terror to stop blacks' quest for equality, but organized black self-defense frequently helped local civil rights campaigns survive in the face of white violence and sparked less brutal repercussions than in the past. Black activist Robert F. Williams emerged as an early proponent of what he called "armed self-reliance." In 1957 the military veteran founded a black self-defense organization in Monroe, N.C., to protect the local freedom movement against the revived Ku Klux Klan. That same year blacks in Birmingham, Ala., founded the "Civil Rights Guards" to prevent dynamite attacks against the church of local civil rights leader Rev. Fred Shuttlesworth. More sophisticated black self-defense groups emerged in the 1960s, when civil rights activists launched massive nonviolent demonstrations and voter registration drives in the Deep South. Confronted with the federal government's reluctance to provide protection against racist attacks, numerous African Americans resolved to rely on their own protection. In the summer of 1964, black military veterans in Tuscaloosa, Ala., organized a highly sophisticated defense squad, which guarded African American activists and their white allies. During the Freedom Summer project of 1964, a number of black Mississippians formed similar groups to repel segregationist attacks. That same year, blacks in Jonesboro, La., established the Deacons for Defense and Justice (DDJ), which patrolled black neighborhoods with guns and provided armed escorts for white and black activists. In 1965 African American activists formed another DDJ group in Bogalusa, La., achieving nationwide notoriety after shootouts with the Ku Klux Klan.

By the late 1960s, when federal authorities finally began to take seriously their responsibility to protect African American citizens, most southern self-defense groups had disbanded. For the emerging Black Power movement, however, armed resistance became a vital pillar of its multilayered program, even though it played a different role and underwent a process of radical reinterpretation. Black self-defense metamorphosed into a militant symbol of black defiance, which served primarily as a means to affirm and nurture black manhood. Militant groups such as the Black Panther Party for Self-Defense (BPP) or the Republic of New Africa also reinterpreted traditional concepts of self-defense. Inspired by the ideas of black nationalist Malcolm X, anticolonial theorist Frantz Fanon, and revolutionaries such as Che Guevara and Mao Tse Tung, they argued that race riots and revolutionary violence constituted a legitimate form of self-defense to resist white oppression.

Despite the largely symbolic nature of Black Power militancy, the Federal Bureau of Investigation (FBI) considered the new militants a threat to the nation's security. Beginning in 1967, it used the highly sophisticated counterintelligence program COINTELPRO to disrupt and destroy the BPP and other revolutionary groups that advocated self-defense. In the following years, Black Power militants either succumbed to the FBI's destructive tactics or toned down their provocative rhetoric. A few organizations, among them the Black Liberation Army, continued clandestine guerrilla warfare against the white police, but by 1972 most activists had abandoned their plans for armed revolution, focusing on political organizing instead. Nevertheless, the Black Power movement's reinterpretation of black self-defense as part of a protracted struggle for liberation remains one of the most visible forms of black militant resistance in the 20th century.

SIMON WENDT
University of Heidelberg

Herbert Aptheker, *American Negro Slave Revolts* (1943); Eugene D. Genovese, *From Rebellion to Revolution: Afro-American Slave Revolts in the Making of the Modern World* (1979); Lance E. Hill, *The Deacons for Defense: Armed Resistance and the Civil Rights Movement* (2004); Herbert Shapiro, *White Violence and Black Response: From Reconstruction to Montgomery* (1988); Tim Tyson, *Radio Free Dixie: Robert F. Williams and the Roots of Black Power* (1999); Simon Wendt, *The Spirit and the Shotgun: Armed Resistance and the Struggle for Civil Rights* (2007).

Blood Sports

The history of blood sports in the American South is as long as that of the region itself, and its definition just as amorphous. The term "blood sport" is used to refer to a range of geographically and historically disparate social practices that center on the baiting or killing of animals for the pleasure and entertainment of spectators. Remnants of 19th-century British and Irish blood sports, such as the baiting of bears and badgers, fighting of roosters and dogs, and hunting of foxes and hares, survived in the U.S. South and were transformed into folk traditions. In the 20th century the term has also come to refer to certain high-risk contact sports among humans, such as boxing, wrestling, and mixed martial arts competitions. This essay treats the following blood sports most strongly associated with the American South: bare-knuckle fighting, cockfighting, dogfighting, "hog-dogging," and fox hunting. While these are by no means the only blood sports enjoyed in the South, they are the most widespread, documented, and clear-cut examples.

It must be noted at the outset that blood sports are not distinctively southern. Southern studies scholars have soundly critiqued the notion of a "savage ideal" as being more characteristic of an imagined South than the complex and varied lives of individuals in the region. Moreover, as animal rights organizations have gained acceptance, blood sports have become increasingly controversial as activists dispute the classification of such practices as "sport" and decry them as exploitative of animals. Indeed, legislation prohibiting these practices and increasing penalties is proliferating across the United States; during the writing of this essay, cockfighting was criminalized in New Mexico and Louisiana, its last two strongholds. Sporting enthusiasts argue that in the context of a society highly dependent on animal exploitation for its products, such legislation may be motivated less by a concern for animals and more by a colonial impulse to police working-class pleasures. In any case, blood sports have been integral in the construction and expression of southern cultural identities.

The practice of southern backcountry brawling was traced by scholar Elliott J. Gorn through a review of oral histories and travelers' accounts. Bare-knuckle fighting in the English style (according to Broughton's Rules) was fashionable in the 18th-century South. According to these rules, a "fist battle" continued in timed rounds until one fighter was knocked out or thrown down. Yet, in the South, these rules were ignored in favor of a "no-holds-barred" style of fighting, which came to be known as "rough-and-tumble," or simply "gouging." This style of fighting was not limited to the peasant classes and in fact was popular as early as 1735 among Virginia gentlemen in Chesapeake Bay. As the names suggest, scratching, choking, tripping, and throwing were common elements of these fights, and gouging, with the intent of removing an eye, was considered the sine qua non of a tumble. The goal of each fight was the maximum disfigurement of one's opponent, which might include the severing of body parts, but a code of honor dictated that no external weapons be used (although long fingernails, often filed to a point, were fair game). Fights continued until one fighter gave up or was unable to continue.

In the late 18th century, ceremonial dueling gradually replaced hand-to-hand combat among the upper classes, but rough-and-tumble remained alive and well in rural and backwoods areas of the South. A rich oral history of rough-and-tumble speaks of a culture guided by notions of honor and kinship, where small slights might well provoke outrage and violence. Southern backcountry gouging became associated with moral turpitude and degeneracy, but it has been persuasively argued that, by embracing violence through actions and legends, southern men were better able to cope with the grief and alienation that surrounded them. By the mid-1800s, as weapons became more widely available, other contests gradually came to replace rough-and-tumble style of fighting.

Perhaps the most iconic of southern blood sports is cockfighting. Yet, as with the remaining blood sports treated in this essay, this term refers not merely to animals fighting in a wild or domestic setting but to a practice orchestrated by humans. Gamefowl are descended from the jungle fowl of India and Southeast Asia but were selectively cultivated for pit fighting in 19th-century England. Unlike many other breeds of farm and ornamental chickens, gamecocks (roosters of gamefowl bloodlines) are typically aggressive toward other roosters and will fight to the death or incapacity of one bird. Cockers, as their human handlers are known, come from a wide range of ethnic and socioeconomic backgrounds.

A cockfight typically involves the matching of two gamecocks, each with a handler and a referee who enforces the Modern Tournament or Derby Rules that govern the fight. The most common venue for a cockfight is a Derby, or series of fights that take place on a given day or weekend in an arena or "cockpit" that measures 16 feet across and is surrounded by bleacher seating conducive to spectatorship and betting. Birds are conditioned much like athletes, with special diets and exercise regimes for at least two weeks (a period known as a "keep"), in anticipation of Derby day.

On the morning of a Derby, birds are weighed and paired so that each bird will have an opponent within two or three ounces of his own weight. They are also paired according to fighting style; knives or gaffs are attached to the roosters' legs near their natural spurs. Knives resemble razor blades and can be long or short, whereas gaffs are long spikes. Gaff fighting is a more traditional style and requires more stamina from the chicken, whereas knives, which inflict damage more quickly, have become increasingly popular in the South. Animal welfare advocates condemn the use of these weapons, but cockers insist that the weapons, which facilitate a quick end to a match, actually make the practice more humane.

The cockfight commences when the referee orders the handlers, spaced nine feet apart, to "pit your birds." The birds are released and often "break," or fly up and meet in the air. They peck and strike each other with beaks and feet until a handle is called, when each handler must pick up his bird. A handle is called when one bird is "hung" or caught on a knife or gaff, and a count is called if one does not fight. If a bird is counted out in 30 seconds, or attempts to run away, the other bird is declared the winner. When a fight is prolonged, it is moved to a smaller "drag pit" to keep the action in the main arena moving. The cocker who has won the most matches at the end of the Derby is the victor.

As illegal, underground practices, many blood sports are difficult to measure through traditional data-gathering techniques, but a 1970 issue of the trade publication *Grit and Steel* estimated 500,000 cockers in the United States, a figure that has surely declined as legal penalties have increased. In 2006, at Sunset Gentlemen's Club at Lafayette, La., one of the few remaining historic cockpits in the United States, one of the final derbies before cockfighting was declared illegal attracted diehard cockers from around the South. Talk of states' rights abounded, along with peach brandy, Cajun French, and high-breaking, spectacular birds. Rather than appearing backward or cruel, the hosts were full of information and warm hospitality.

Although dogfighting has recently burst into public consciousness with the 2007 federal indictment of the Atlanta Falcons' quarterback Michael Vick, the practice was considered a "national institution" as far back as 1816. Fighting dogs (typically Staffordshire Bull Terriers) accompanied English and Irish immigrants to the United States and were later imported, primarily into New York and Boston, where dogfighting became popular among "sporting men," gentlemen and working class alike. The American Society for the Prevention of Cruelty to Animals mounted a campaign against dogfighting that resulted in its prohibition in the United States in 1860. However, it was still widely practiced, as demonstrated by the publication by the *Police Gazette* of its own version of rules for dogfighting in 1888.

In the early 20th century, the South became the locus of a particular culture of rural dogfighting built around the concept of the dog's gameness, or perceived desire to fight. The Cajun Rules were developed by G. A. Trahan to govern dog matches, and the American Pit Bull Terrier was bred specifically to excel under these rules. Contrary to popular belief, the Cajun Rules do not require a fight to the death or incapacity of one dog. "Dogmen," as dogfighters are known, argue these rules prevent a match from being inhumane, since they are designed to test a dog's gameness rather than mere fighting ability. According to these rules, a dog who crosses the pit to his opponent and takes hold (known as a "scratch") is seen as potentially game, whereas if a dog turns away from his opponent or shows other signs of hesitancy, time is called. A dog who turns is given another chance to scratch to his opponent, and if he is unwilling, he is branded a "cur," and the match is over. Thus, even if one dog is severely injured and barely able to fight, but keeps scratching, he can defeat a more capable but less willing opponent. The concept of gameness is valorized and frequently applied not only to the dogs in the context of fighting but to the men and their families in their daily lives and struggles.

In the late 20th century, dogfighting has shifted once again to more urban areas as certain inner-city African American and Latino men have taken up the sport. According to the Humane Society of the United States, these men are more likely to engage in street fights rather than organized fights, where dogs are matched "OTC" (off the chain), without formal rules or a referee. Old-time southern dogmen define themselves in opposition to mainstream American society but also to dogfighters who do not use the Cajun Rules. Although dogfighting has historical roots in the South, as well as a high concentration of dogmen in the region, dogfighting according to the Cajun Rules is not uniquely southern, as it is still practiced throughout the United States and abroad.

Hog hunting has taken place for much of recorded human history, but the capture of hogs with dogs has recently developed into a competitive spectator event known as "hog-dogging" or "hog dog rodeos." The hunting of feral hogs and wild boars, abundant throughout the South, has traditionally been accomplished through the use of specially trained "bay" dogs, which chase and corner the hog, and "catch" dogs that take hold of the hog and allow it to be captured. A demonstration called "Uncle Earl's Hog Dog Trials" was organized in 1995 in Winnfield, La., as part of former governor and hog hunter Earl K. Long's 100th birthday celebration. In a series of field trials, judges score the skill with which dogs are able to bay and catch a penned hog. As a spectator sport, this practice has since spread throughout the South and is particularly popular in Alabama. Although hog hunting still appears sacrosanct, hog dog rodeos are a new target of animal welfare legislation.

Fox hunting is distinct from other forms of blood sports in the South. It is a legal form of recreation, for example, and represents not only a folk tradition but one engaging considerable privilege and resources. It complicates the social-class basis of blood sports. Tracing its roots to British tradition, the running of the hounds took root in Maryland and Virginia in the mid-1600s, with hounds incorporated from Britain. Hunters imported the red fox from overseas to replace the gray fox found naturally in the southern woodlands. The red fox's great cunning was believed to offer hunters a greater challenge than the gray fox. The development of stronger bloodlines in the southern colonies also grew out of fox hunters' efforts.

Fox hunting developed its own distinctive culture, including black coats of the field and red coats of the staff, honoring of protocols, and appreciation of tradition. Hunters prize their hounds, often with pedigrees dating back to early southern history.

JERE ALEXANDER
Emory University

George C. Armitage, *Thirty Years with Fighting Dogs* (1935); Alan Dundes, ed., *The Cockfight: A Casebook* (1994); Charles W. Eagles, ed., *"The Mind of the South": Fifty Years Later* (1992); Richard K. Fox, *The Dog Pit* (1888); Adrian Franklin, *Animals and Modern Cultures: A Sociology of Human-Animal Relationships in Modernity* (1999); Elliott J. Gorn, *American Historical Review* (1985); Mike Homan, *A Complete History of Fighting Dogs* (1999); Ted Ownby, *Subduing Satan: Religion, Recreation, and Manhood in the Rural South, 1865–1920* (1990); Bob Stevens, *Dogs of Velvet and Steel: Pit Bulldogs; A Manual for Owners* (1983).

Capital Punishment

The law and practice of capital punishment in the United States have differed significantly by region. Slavery exerted a profound influence on capital punishment in the South, with southern states creating slave codes that specified numerous capital offenses applying to slaves and free blacks but not to whites. Historically, the South carried out more executions and was slower to institute reforms than other regions. Under current laws, many nonsouthern states continue to sentence people to death, but executions are overwhelmingly concentrated in southern and border states.

The total number of executions in the American colonies and the United States is not known, but some 20,000 have been documented. The earliest laws in most jurisdictions imposed mandatory death sentences, although the harshness of these laws was somewhat mitigated by frequent commutations. Most executions were for homicide or rape, but people were also executed for witchcraft, piracy, burglary, robbery, horse theft, slave revolt, and other crimes. Early

Lawrenceville, Ga., 8 May 1908. A crowd gathers to witness Henry Campbell's public hanging. He was tried and convicted of murdering Ella Hudson and her daughter. Campbell is seen wearing a dark suit and standing among the crowd in the center portion of the photograph. (Courtesy of Georgia Archives, Vanishing Georgia Collection)

executions were carried out under local authority, in public, most frequently by hanging.

Efforts to reform or abolish capital punishment began in northern states in the late 18th century. In 1847 Michigan became the first of several states to end executions. Legal reforms (including dividing the offense of murder into degrees, giving juries sentencing discretion, restricting capital punishment to fewer offenses) and reforms in practice (holding executions in a central location in state prisons before selected official witnesses and substituting other methods for hanging) occurred over a long period of time. With few exceptions, these reforms were adopted significantly later in the South than in the northern states.

In the 20th century nearly all executions were carried out for first-degree murder or for rape. Executions for rape occurred almost exclusively in southern or border states, and almost 90 percent of those executed for rape were African

American men. Electrocution was the most frequent method of execution. The decade of the 1930s had the most executions; the number fell throughout the 1940s and 1950s, and executions came to a halt in 1967 while federal courts considered appeals. Executions resumed under new statutes in 1977.

Capital punishment has always had a powerful fascination for Americans. Public executions were widely attended by crowds that ranged from reverent to raucous. Certain capital cases—the executions of the Italian anarchists Sacco and Vanzetti in Massachusetts in 1927, the death sentences and repeated trials of the Scottsboro defendants in Alabama in the 1930s, the long struggle of Caryl Chessman to save himself from death in California's gas chamber—almost seem to define their era. The 1977 execution of Gary Gilmore by firing squad in Utah was the first under current laws and received extensive media attention in the United States and abroad. Public interest in capital cases and executions continues unabated, with media reporting on the last statements and last meals of the condemned and crowds gathering outside prisons at the time of the execution of well-known inmates. Today, capital punishment is a contentious moral, political, and public policy issue, with strong opinions held by supporters and opponents.

Well into the 20th century, many prisoners were executed without appeals, some of them weeks or even days after trial; review by federal courts was rare. By the mid-1960s, the NAACP Legal Defense Fund was representing or assisting most condemned inmates and launched a coordinated effort to challenge the constitutionality of the death penalty. This strategy achieved its greatest success in 1972, when the U.S. Supreme Court ruled in *Furman v. Georgia* that the death penalty as applied violated the Eighth and Fourteenth Amendments. State legislatures reacted quickly, writing new laws in response to *Furman*. In general these laws bifurcated capital trials, mandating separate hearings to determine guilt and punishment, specifying aggravating and mitigating circumstances to guide sentencing decisions, and providing for direct appeals to state courts. In 1976 the U.S. Supreme Court ruled several variations of the new statutes to be constitutional and executions resumed in 1977.

Since upholding the constitutionality of capital punishment, the Court has restricted its use in a number of important ways, abolishing it for rape of an adult woman (*Coker v. Georgia*, 1977) and for rape of a child (*Kennedy v. Louisiana*, 2008). The Court also forbade the use of capital punishment for defendants who are insane (*Ford v. Wainwright*, 1986), who are mentally retarded (*Atkins v. Virginia*, 2002), and who were juveniles at the time of the crime (*Roper v. Simmons*, 2005).

The Court has refused relief based upon statistical evidence of racial disparities in sentencing (*McCleskey v. Kemp*, 1987), has upheld stringent procedural restrictions on condemned prisoners' appeals (*Felker v. Turpin*, 1996), and has ruled that claims of innocence unaccompanied by a constitutional violation are grounds for federal habeas relief only if "truly persuasive" (*Herrera v. Collins*, 1993). In 2008 the Court upheld the constitutionality of lethal injection, by far the most common current method of execution (*Baze v. Rees*, 2008).

Thirty-five states (including all southern and border states except West Virginia), the federal government, and the military currently provide for capital punishment, although two of those states and the military have not carried out executions post-*Furman*. Fifteen states and the District of Columbia are abolitionist. Under post-*Furman* statutes, more than 7,000 people have been sentenced to death; more than 3,000 remain on death row. Most of the removals from death row have been a result of state and federal courts overturning death sentences or convictions. The average time between sentence and execution was nearly 13 years for inmates executed in 2007. Longer stays are not uncommon, however; a few prisoners have spent nearly three and a half decades on death row.

Between 1977 and 2009, 1,188 people were executed. All but 11 were men. Fifty-six percent were white, 35 percent black, and the rest were Asian, Latino, American Indian, and other. Nearly 80 percent of the executions were carried out for the homicide of white victims. Eleven percent of post-*Furman* executions occurred after inmates dropped their appeals and requested execution. Commutations of death sentences are rare post-*Furman*, with only 245 granted. Post-*Furman* executions peaked in 1999, with 98 persons put to death that year. Since then, executions have declined steeply, as has the number of death sentences imposed annually.

Five states (Texas, Virginia, Oklahoma, Florida, and Missouri) have carried out two-thirds of post-*Furman* executions. More than one-third of the total have been in Texas, with Harris County (Houston) alone accounting for 112 executions. Public opinion polls indicate that support for the death penalty is no stronger in the South than in other regions, although approximately 90 percent of modern executions have taken place in states that permitted slavery up until the Civil War.

Why executions should be so concentrated in the South is not clear. The homicide rate in the South is higher than in other regions, but the difference is relatively small. The violence inherent in slavery and segregation, which were upheld by law, may have resulted in residual institutional and political inclination to use legal violence. Fundamentalist religious beliefs also may contribute to willingness to punish harshly. Long-standing problems with appellate representation may increase the likelihood that southern death sentences are carried out.

Post-*Furman* death penalty laws were intended to create a sentencing system that would reserve the death penalty for the worst homicides and that would eliminate capricious and discriminatory sentencing. Extensive research has documented continuing problems in the imposition and administration of capital punishment.

A large body of research documents significant racial disparities in the post-*Furman* death penalty, leading some to conclude that modern capital punishment is a form of "legal lynching," although research indicates the relationship between these two forms of lethal punishment is complex. The location of a homicide can also play a role in determining sentence; prosecutors in some counties are much more likely than others to seek and obtain death sentences. Both anecdotal evidence and systematic studies indicate that the quality of defense representation in capital cases is often very poor, adding a further element of capriciousness in sentencing. Of all the problems in the administration of capital punishment, the conviction of the innocent has caused the most concern among the public. One hundred thirty-nine condemned prisoners have been exonerated in 26 states since 1973 (there have been many exonerations of prisoners serving sentences other than death as well).

The effects of capital punishment continue to be studied and debated. There is a high level of agreement among criminologists that executions have no significant general deterrent effect beyond that provided by long prison sentences. Although the execution of an individual obviously incapacitates him or her from any further criminal behavior, a substantial body of research indicates that the condemned are unlikely to reoffend and do not present more severe disciplinary problems while incarcerated than do other inmates.

Some supporters of the death penalty argue that executions provide solace for families bereaved by homicide that other sentences cannot provide. Victims' families have a wide variety of opinions on capital punishment, however, ranging from strongly supporting executions to absolutely opposing them. Whatever the wishes of the victims' families, only about 1 percent of homicides result in a death sentence and even fewer in execution.

Legal and public policy challenges to capital punishment are certain to continue as long as the penalty is used. Several recent developments indicate that the death penalty's popularity is eroding and that its use will probably continue to decrease. Executions are increasingly concentrated in a few southern states, particularly in Texas, which accounted for more than half of the executions carried out 2007–9. Public support for capital punishment has fallen from a high of about 80 percent in the mid-1990s, leveling off with roughly two-thirds in favor. Many polls asking respondents to indicate their preferred punishment for capital homicide have found that Americans prefer life without parole to the death penalty. Several states have imposed moratoria on executions and/or have instituted study commissions on capital punishment. In 2007 New Jersey became the first state to legislatively abolish the death penalty post-*Furman*. New Mexico followed in 2009. Methods of execution other than lethal injection have nearly been abandoned, but botched lethal injections have led to concern over the humaneness of this method. The extraordinarily high financial, resource, and opportunity costs of capital punishment are likely to influence some policy makers toward rejecting it in favor of a sentence of life without parole, which is available as punishment for first-degree murder in every state except Alaska.

These developments in the United States take place against a background of increasing international rejection of capital punishment. The International Criminal Court prohibits capital punishment. The European Union and leading human rights groups have launched vigorous campaigns against the death penalty and have sharply criticized the United States for its continued use of capital punishment. Ninety-five countries have abolished the death penalty outright. Nine more have abolished it for all but exceptional crimes such as treason. Another 35 retain it in law but have executed no one in at least 10 years. Only 58 countries retain the death penalty, and many of those rarely use it. China executes by far the most prisoners, but the United States is consistently among the half dozen other countries with the highest annual number of executions.

MARGARET VANDIVER
University of Memphis

James R. Acker, Robert M. Bohm, and Charles S. Lanier, eds., *America's Experiment with Capital Punishment* (2003); Amnesty International, www.amnesty.org; Stuart Banner, *The Death Penalty: An American History* (2002); Hugo Adam Bedau, ed., *The Death Penalty in America: Current Controversies* (1997); Bureau of Justice Statistics, *Capital Punishment, 2007* (2008); Death Penalty Information Center, www .deathpenaltyinfo.org; Rolando del Carmen et al., *The Death Penalty: Constitutional Issues, Commentaries and Case Briefs* (2005); Roger Hood and Carolyn Hoyle, *The Death Penalty: A Worldwide Perspective* (2008).

Church Burnings

On 15 September 1963 a bomb exploded in the basement of the 16th Street Baptist Church in Birmingham, Ala. The ensuing fire and death of four little girls placed the violence of white supremacy on the front pages of the nation's newspapers. It also entered the 16th Street Church into a long history of attacks against houses of worship in the American South. Though churches burn for any number of reasons, including accident and insurance fraud, church arson in southern culture has frequently been associated with a symbolic assault on a community's core institution.

Because of the South's particular history of racial conflict, burning a predominately black or multiracial church has held even greater significance. In 1822 an African Methodist Episcopal church in Charleston, S.C., was burned as retribution for allegedly hosting a planning meeting for a slave insurrection. The attack presaged a key method of intimidating and controlling black southerners after emancipation. Barred from participation in most civic institutions in the South for a century after Reconstruction, black southerners turned churches into spiritual homes, community centers, and organizational clearinghouses.

Black church burnings have seemed to increase in moments of black assertion, such as the Reconstruction years, the hopeful days following World War I, and especially the civil rights activism of the 1960s. Reconstruction saw political assertiveness by African Americans trying to exercise their citizenship rights and develop cultural institutions, with black churches separate from whites emerging as a key focus for a variety of activities. Black churches became political organizing sites, often allied with the Union League. Whites burned black churches to intimidate black aspirations. In the 20th century, some southern whites expelled all blacks in their communities, burning churches to prevent their use as sanctuaries. According to the Southern Poverty Law Center, 92 black churches were attacked between 1963 and 1966. In the first two years of the period, more than 50 black churches were burned in Mississippi alone. These tragedies fit into a general pattern of white violence against black liberation.

In the mid-1990s, a spike in church burnings ignited a debate among Americans about the persistence of racism in American society. Though arson is the leading cause of church fires around the country, from the 1980s through 1994 the statistical trend had been downward. Suddenly, in 1995 it seemed that churches were being lit up everywhere. And black churches were frequent targets. Though more white churches burned, the share of black churches being burned was significantly out of proportion with the black population in the United States, especially in the South. In the worst year, 1996, 117 black churches were attacked, 88 of which were in the South.

Though civil rights leaders like Jesse Jackson, Joseph Lowery, and Myrlie

Evers-Williams insisted that a pattern was developing that strongly suggested conspiracy, Assistant Attorney General Deval Patrick asserted that no evidence existed for an organized effort by a specific hate group. Patrick added, however, that the absence of a conspiracy did not mean that the attacks were not racially motivated. The successful prosecution of a Ku Klux Klan organization for an arson attack on a black church in 1995 in Bloomville, S.C., seemed to confirm Patrick's point. Some conservative politicians and commentators declared that civil rights activists had falsely created the media hype around black church burnings. Nonetheless, between 1995 and 1997, African American churches were four times as likely to be burned as white churches.

In June 1996 Congress unanimously passed the Church Arson Prevention Act. The new law made it easier to prosecute arson attacks against houses of worship, increased the maximum sentence to 20 years, and created a $10 million federal loan program for rebuilding. Private efforts, such as those coordinated by the multiracial National Council of Churches, yielded millions more dollars as well as thousands of volunteers who traveled to burn sites to help with reconstruction. By 2000 the rate of arsons had decreased. Yet, the deliberate burning of 10 Alabama churches—five predominately black, five white—in a single week in 2006 suggested that church burning has not lost its terrible appeal in southern life.

ERIC S. YELLIN
University of Richmond

Michael Newton and Judy Ann Newton, *Racial and Religious Violence in America: A Chronology* (1991); Christopher B. Strain, *Burning Faith: Church Arson in the American South* (2008); Timothy J. Minchin, *Australasian Journal of American Studies* (December 2008); Sarah A. Soule and Nella Van Dyke, *Ethnic and Racial Studies* (July 1999).

Civil Rights, Federal Enforcement

Before 1957, federal intervention to protect the legal rights of black southerners was infrequent at best. Beginning with the Little Rock crisis, the passage of the Civil Rights Act of 1957, and the creation of the U.S. Commission on Civil Rights, however, a new era of federal legal action in the South was born. From 1957 through the late 1960s federal authorities faced three major and often intertwined legal questions concerning the South: how to ensure southern blacks' right to register and vote, how to secure the desegregation of southern schools and colleges, and how to protect civil rights activists from illegal and often violent harassment of their efforts. On all three fronts federal officials—

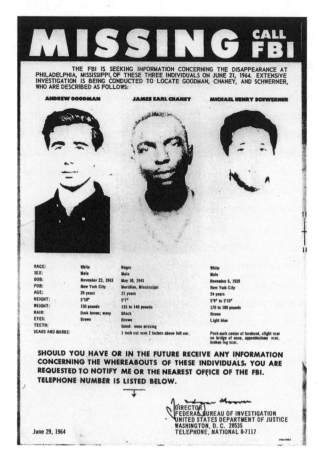

FBI poster seeking information on missing civil rights workers, Mississippi, 1964 (Mississippi Department of Archives and History, Jackson)

in the White House, at the Department of Justice, and in the Federal Bureau of Investigation—acted cautiously and conservatively in all but a few instances. That caution of three successive presidential administrations—Eisenhower, Kennedy, and Johnson—was strongly condemned by civil rights movement participants and supporters. At the same time, most white southerners failed to appreciate that the degree of federal action and intervention was much lower than could well have been the case, given the formal powers available to the federal authorities.

Critics of these administrations consistently pointed out that federal authorities were making only the most limited use of certain powers at their disposal: the voting rights provisions of the 1957 and 1960 civil rights acts, the Reconstruction-era criminal statutes codified as 18 U.S.C. 241 and 242, the statute giving the president very expansive federal police powers in any circumstance where state authorities are unable or unwilling to protect constitutional rights (10 U.S.C. 333), and the provisions authorizing all FBI agents and U.S. marshals to make warrantless arrests for any violation of a federal statute that they witnessed (18 U.S.C. 3052, 3053).

The degree of federal restraint was not a matter of happenstance or, as some have surmised, simply a result of presidential inability to mobilize the resources and energies of the FBI, whose longtime director, J. Edgar Hoover, was accurately regarded as extremely reluctant to involve the federal government in matters of race. Instead, in all three areas—schools, voting, and violence—limited federal intervention was based on a straightforward policy supported by all the presidents and attorneys general who were involved: that the racial transformation of southern society would proceed furthest, fastest, and with the fewest scars if federal authorities encouraged maximum voluntary compliance by southern officials and resorted to the coercive use of federal remedies and manpower as little as possible.

Throughout the 1957–64 period Justice Department officials seeking to eliminate racial discrimination from southern voter registration offices made persuasion their first and foremost tool. Only in counties or parishes where registrars rebuffed such approaches and continued to discriminate were federal civil suits brought. Similarly, even in such widely heralded federal-state confrontations as the integration of the University of Mississippi in 1962 and the University of Alabama in 1963, federal officials relied upon private conversations and negotiation and employed actual force only when all other means of obtaining obedience to the law had failed. Furthermore, even in instances where the very lives of civil rights activists were in danger, Justice Department officials moved with caution rather than alacrity. Many movement workers became deeply embittered at the lack of federal response to the shootings, burnings, and beatings that occurred throughout the Deep South between 1961 and 1965.

The summer of 1964 witnessed both a new assertion of federal power in the most violent of the southern states, Mississippi, and passage of the comprehensive Civil Rights Act. Prodded by the murder of three civil rights workers in June 1964, the Johnson administration established a substantial FBI presence in the state. At the same time, passage of the new law gave the government a powerful new tool for combating racial discrimination, particularly in public accommodations. Even in relative "hot spots" such as St. Augustine, Fla., and Selma, Ala., federal officials favored persuasion and conciliation before adopting stronger actions.

Passage of the 1965 Voting Rights Act, which provided for the appointment of federal registration officials in unregenerate southern counties, led many movement activists to expect the kind of extensive federal intervention throughout the South that the movement had sought but previously failed to obtain. To their great disappointment, however, federal officials at the Justice Department again applied the principle they had followed in previous years: direct federal authority should be exerted only where state and local officials failed to show good-faith compliance. Thus, far fewer federal registrars were sent into the South than civil rights proponents requested. A movement initiative to win passage of new federal statutes to eliminate jury discrimination and to specifically forbid any physical harassment of civil rights workers also failed to succeed in 1965–66.

Many movement participants and sympathizers, looking back at the so-called Second Reconstruction years, argue that a more aggressive and forceful federal stance would have meant more racial progress and at a lesser cost in dead, wounded, and emotionally scarred. Former federal officials, however— those men who served in the Justice Department hierarchy in the 1960s— believe that what many view as the South's tremendous racial progress since the late 1960s would not have occurred and that much of the previous bitterness would not have subsided had not the federal executive branch followed the moderate and restrained path that it did. Had federal authorities employed more heavily the coercive and punitive powers at their disposal, deep racial divisions might well have been further deepened and also prolonged. One's view of how sufficient the changes in southern race relations over the past 15 years have been will in large part determine whether one judges the federal law enforcement stance of the 1960s to have been intelligent or inadequate.

DAVID J. GARROW
City College of New York
CUNY *Graduate Center*

Carl M. Brauer, *John F. Kennedy and the Second Reconstruction* (1977); Richard Maxwell Brown, in *Perspectives on the American South*, vol. 1, ed. Merle Black and John Shelton Reed (1981); Haywood Burns, in *Southern Justice*, ed. Leon Friedman (1965); Robert K. Carr, *Federal Protection of Civil Rights: Quest for a Sword* (1947); John Doar and Dorothy Landsberg, U.S. Congress, Senate, Select Committee to Study Governmental Operations with Respect to Intelligence Activities, Hearings—Federal Bureau of Investigation, vol. 6, 94th Cong., 1st sess. (1976); John T. Elliff, *Perspectives in American History*, vol. 5 (1971); Allan Lichtman, *Journal of Negro History* (October 1969); Neil R. McMillen, *Journal of Southern History* (August 1977); Burke Marshall, *Federalism and Civil Rights* (1964).

Civil Rights–Era Violence

Although polls indicated that only about one-third of white southerners vociferously opposed the 1954 *Brown* decision that integrated public schools, massive resistance manifested among all levels of society in the second half of the decade. Among these efforts, physical violence and the threat of it were prominent. In 1956 alone, angry white protestors prevented the entry of one or a few black students at the University of Alabama, Texarkana Junior College, and Mansfield High School in Texas, schools in Clay and Sturgis, Ky., and Clinton, Tenn. The situations in Kentucky and Tennessee grew so alarming that the governors called out the National Guard. These episodes were followed in 1957 by mob frenzy in Little Rock, Ark., that grew so intense that President Dwight Eisenhower, who was by no means an ardent civil rights supporter, was forced to mobilize 1,000 soldiers from the 101st Airborne. In all, between 1955 and 1959, 225 incidents of anti–civil rights violence occurred across the South, most of it directed at the integration of educational institutions.

Ironically, while white violence accelerated in the early 1960s, African Americans used it to gain the attention and empathy of much of the media and the nation outside the South and thereby to achieve, in conjunction with the Johnson administration, significant civil rights legislation in the mid-1960s. They did so through a combination of courage and resilience in direct action campaigns in areas where white violent responses were anticipated.

Horrified as youngsters in 1955 by photographs of the bloated body of 14-year-old lynching victim Emmett Till, and inspired and emboldened by a sit-in at a Woolworth's lunch counter on 1 February 1960 in Greensboro, N.C., by four students from Agricultural and Technical College of North Carolina, thousands of college students began sit-ins across the South. Images of young people dressed in their Sunday best, sitting quietly at lunch counters studying, while surrounded by young white "toughs" jeering and pelting them with eggs, ketchup, and other food products, streamed into American living rooms via the three major television networks—ABC, NBC, and CBS—a first for an American social movement.

These revolting spectacles were followed the next year by scenes of black and white passengers being beaten by crowds of angry whites as they arrived from Washington, D.C., on interstate buses first in Anniston, then Birmingham, and finally Montgomery, Ala. Testing the 1960 *Boynton v. Virginia* ruling that facilities serving passengers on public transportation that crossed state lines should be integrated and determined to persist, despite Attorney General Robert Kennedy's efforts to dissuade them, a Freedom Ride Coordinating Committee pro-

Police dog attacking civil rights demonstrators, Birmingham, Ala., 1963
(Charles Moore, photographer, Birmingham News)

cured volunteers from around the country to continue into Mississippi where 328 riders were arrested by the police in a bus terminal in the state capital of Jackson and confined to Parchman Farm, one of the nation's most notorious prisons. The shocking images continued as riots roiled the town of Oxford, Miss., when Air Force veteran James Meredith, escorted by U.S. marshals, arrived on the Ole Miss (University of Mississippi) campus in October 1962; eventually military police, the Mississippi National guard, and the U.S. Border Patrol were summoned.

In Birmingham, in particular, the concordance between white supremacists and many law officers to control African Americans — a collaboration that had existed from the time black people set foot on southern soil — was demonstrated before national and international audiences as the city's public safety commissioner Eugene "Bull" Connor allowed members of the National States' Rights Party and Klansmen to beat Freedom Riders with lead pipes, baseball bats, and chains for 20 minutes before any police arrived. In the mid-1970s the revelation surfaced during committee hearings chaired by Sen. Frank Church that the 20-minute delay resulted from prior arrangements between a police sergeant and a Klansman-FBI informer, an agreement that Connor initiated as a way to successfully gain reelection in a tight race against another candidate that the Klan allegedly favored.

Two years later, in May 1963, Connor engineered a highly dramatic attack by Birmingham officers using police dogs and fire hoses against civil rights marchers, many of whom were children. This assault, coupled with the assassination of President John Kennedy in December in Dallas, Tex., enabled the highly experienced, politically astute president Lyndon Johnson to push through Congress a far stronger civil rights bill than the one on the table when Kennedy died. A tribute to the slain president, the Civil Rights Act of 1964 ended legal segregation in public places and mandated equal treatment in hiring and employment. The following year, two bloody attacks by state highway patrolmen and the Dallas County sheriff and his posse on marchers near Selma, Ala., facilitated passage of the Voting Rights Act.

Thus, white violence, coupled with media coverage, played a key role in the passage of important civil rights laws, but violence did not always occur—as when the Southern Christian Leadership Conference (SCLC) began civil rights demonstrations in Albany, Ga., in November 1961—and, without violence, the media largely ignored the protest. Additionally, not all violence made the news. Student Non-Violent Coordinating Committee (SNCC) activists, who headed for rural Mississippi to engage in voter registration efforts shortly after their organization was founded in 1960, experienced beatings and the horror of a man shot and killed when he tried to register to vote in McComb. The lack of media coverage of the violence inflicted on SNCC and the Congress of Racial Equality (CORE) activists and on local citizens with whom they stayed and worked contributed both to the development of informal and formal networks of armed, African American defenders and to the decision by Robert "Bob" Moses to bring hundreds of nonsouthern white students to the South to conduct voter registration campaigns in the summer of 1964. The subsequent disappearance and later discovery of the bodies of three civil rights workers—James Chaney, Michael Schwerner, and Andrew Goodman—did get extensive media coverage and helped facilitate passage of the 1965 voting rights legislation.

The horrific experiences of SNCC and CORE activists in the Deep South also contributed to growing frustration with a nonviolent approach among many. As CORE activist Dave Dennis explained as he reflected on his speech at James Chaney's funeral, "this country operates, operated then and still operates, on violence." This growing disillusionment occurred within an American culture saturated with the notion that violence is *manly*. These factors, coupled with an urban culture where black militancy was gaining momentum, contributed to expansion in local Black Power organizations.

Even more significantly in the long term, white violence in the American South, and the media's selected focus on it in the late 1950s and early 1960s, resulted in virtually no coverage of civil rights activities under way in the rest of the nation, a development begun in the 1940s and continuing in the 1950s and 1960s as African Americans moved in large numbers to cities outside the South and encountered prejudice and discrimination in housing, employment, education, and public services, including policing. Thus, most white Americans, including Lyndon Johnson, were confounded and incensed as the cameras zoomed in on the property riots in black communities that commenced in Harlem in 1964 and the Watts neighborhood in Los Angeles in 1965—both touched off, as was usually the case, by confrontations with the police—and the continuation of the "long hot summers," climaxing in the wake of the assassination of Dr. Martin Luther King Jr. in 1968. Similar dismayed, angry reactions on the part of whites greeted the highly publicized police wars with Black Panthers and other radicals in the late 1960s and early 1970s.

In sum, southern white violence and the media's selected coverage of it in the late 1950s and early 1960s left the impression that racism only existed in the "backward" South and that once "de jure" segregation was eliminated, the problem was solved. This "master narrative" overlooked ongoing prejudice among many whites and institutional racism deeply embedded in American society over centuries. Riots in the mid-sixties and subsequent black radical activity, along with continuing problems in urban ghettos, reinforced the view, enthusiastically articulated by conservative politicians, that African Americans themselves were the source of their dilemmas and that the Johnson administration had coddled them far too much.

GAIL WILLIAMS O'BRIEN
North Carolina State University

Mary Frances Berry, *Black Resistance, White Law: A History of Constitutional Racism in America* (1994); David Brown and Clive Webb, *Race in the American South: From Slavery to Civil Rights* (2007); Henry Hampton and Steve Fayer, eds., *Voices of Freedom: An Oral History of the Civil Rights Movement from the 1950s through the 1980s* (1995); George Lewis, *Massive Resistance: The White Response to the Civil Rights Movement* (2006); Jeanne Theoharis and Komozi Woodard, eds., *Freedom North: Black Freedom Struggles Outside the South, 1940–1980* (2003).

Civil War

The American Civil War is arguably the most violent event southerners have ever faced. Between 1861 and 1865, approximately 620,000 Americans died as

Embalming surgeon at work on soldier's body (Photographer unknown,
Library of Congress [LC-B811-2531], Washington, D.C.)

a direct result of the war. In a country that totaled more than 31 million in
1860, this meant that one out of every 50 Americans perished during the conflict. Following the war, the U.S. War Department totaled Union Army deaths
at 360,222, and scholarly estimates of the Confederate military deaths total
258,000. Combat deaths alone include 140,414 U.S. Army soldiers and 74,524
Confederates. For southerners in the seceding states, roughly 1 in every 19
whites out of a prewar white population of approximately 5 million died as a
result of military service. It was America's costliest conflict in the number of
total war-related deaths. The losses more than equal the death toll of all of the
other American wars combined through the end of the Vietnam War.

Yet, violence extended deeper than even these devastating figures suggest.
Historians have variously attributed the high costs of Civil War combat to the
new rifle technology available, inappropriate or overzealous use of Napoleonic

tactics, and aggressive or inept strategic thinking on the part of Civil War commanders. The July 1863 Battle of Gettysburg especially exhibits the toll that repeated clashes took with 53,000 total causalities in just three days of battle and more than 3,000 dead horses. The violence of the American Civil War took many forms, however, and combat on the conventional battlefields of Gettysburg or Shiloh, Antietam, and Vicksburg does not capture the entire story.

Civil War scholars continue to debate the role of each government's military policy and the harshness of violence directed by the opposing armies against the respective civilian populations. Some historians have argued that the Civil War was a "destructive war," a "savage conflict," and a modern "total war" as evidenced by the extensive mobilization of the Confederate population for war (roughly 80 percent of the military-age white male population of the Confederacy served in the army at some point during the conflict) and the U.S. Army's escalating use of violence to destroy southern property and the Confederate economy. These historians have also isolated acts of violence toward civilians by each army to prove that the war became as devastating as many 20th-century conflicts in this regard. Other historians have posited a limited-war argument. They have asserted that the death toll of the civilian population during the war caused by the armies does not merit the title "total war" when compared to earlier or later conflicts in world history but should instead be called "limited war" or "hard war." "Hard war" involves devastating economic warfare but restraint in the use of violence toward civilians. Regardless of whether the war earns the title "total war" or "hard war," the conflict remains the most devastating one in terms of loss of life for Americans and especially southern civilians in sheer numbers. Conservative estimates would place this figure at 50,000 war-related civilian deaths, with the majority of these occurring in the South.

Violence during the war also took the form of maiming and wounding, frequently scarring veterans for life. The rudimentary state of medical care in the 1860s meant that amputation was a common procedure in response to wounding, and frequently men did not survive the trauma of the experience. During the war, 281,881 U.S. Army troops were wounded, and while reliable statistics for Confederate soldiers are unavailable, some estimates place the number at over 200,000. While battle deaths did not cause the number of fatalities that disease wrought on Civil War armies (224,586 Union and more than 70,000 Confederate), soldiers spent an enormous amount of energy worried about maiming and death during combat. Fear of what cannon, rifle, bullet, shell, and powder could do to a man's body kept many men terrified or in a heighted state of awareness in combat. The loss of a limb could incapacitate a man and ruin his family's economic future in addition to damaging him psychologically for life. Edged weapons, however, caused only a small percentage of wounds, and many of these edged-weapon wounds were a result of fights and brawls in camp, rarely from bayonet and saber charges in battle. Violence took other forms during the war, including punishment, legal execution, and even frivolity. More than 500 soldiers from both northern and southern armies were executed by firing squad or hanging during the war; the crimes of desertion, murder, and rape were the most common reasons for the death penalty. Punishment for minor offenses in both armies frequently led to vicious punishments, such as riding a rail in camp, violent hazing, and even whippings. Occasionally violence could be more lighthearted as in the case of the large-scale snowball fights that broke out in the Army of Northern Virginia in January 1863.

Property destruction was another byproduct of the conflict; the total violence done to property during the war is difficult to estimate. Some of America's and the South's most important cities were left exhausted and in ruins by the war. Fire and explosions at the hands of U.S. and Confederate troops leveled sections of Atlanta, Ga., Columbia, S.C., and Chambersburg, Pa., and dozens of other southern cities including Fredericksburg, Va., Nashville, Tenn., and New Orleans, La., endured bombardment and military occupation. Gen. William Tecumseh Sherman's 1864 march through Georgia and Gen. Philip Sheridan's campaign in Virginia's Shenandoah Valley in 1864, which many historians have isolated as extreme examples of U.S. Army force toward the southern population, struck crippling blows at the southern economy and agricultural production in key breadbaskets of the Confederacy. In 1863 and 1864, riots over conscription, property impressments, and food shortages occurred throughout the South, notably in Richmond, Va., and Salisbury, N.C., and a massive draft riot in New York City in July 1863 required the Union Army's assistance to subdue. The violence of slavery was undone by the destruction of $4 billion in slave property when the Emancipation Proclamation issued on 1 January 1863, and the war ended the institution and freed 4 million slaves.

Atrocities, which included extralegal hangings, revenge shootings, mass killing, torture, and sexual assault, also occurred in numerous communities during the war. One recent study investigates no fewer than 12 mass killings, and racial animosity toward black soldiers and their white Union officers was the primary motivation for the Confederate soldiers who committed these atrocities. Famous battlefield racial atrocities at Fort Pillow, Tenn. (1864), Olustee, Fla. (1864), and the Battle of the Crater at Petersburg, Va. (1864), are evidence of racial hatred and racism motivating Confederate soldiers. But other atrocities were motivated by animosity toward political dissidents including southern unionists. One famous incident in January 1863 at Shelton Laurel, N.C., saw the murder of 13 Unionist men and boys at the hands of Confederate home guards. The Madden Branch massacre that occurred in northern Georgia in 1864 where six men were killed is also indicative of this type of Confederate violence against southern unionists. The state of Missouri experienced perhaps the worst guerrilla violence of any slaveholding state during the conflict, with women assaulted and raped in their homes. Many of these women experienced the horror of having their homes violated before seeing their male relatives taken from the home and killed in front of them. This community-level violence was frequently motivated by prewar hatreds, divided loyalties, and robbery.

The line between criminal violence and acts of war frequently became impossible to distinguish in the American Civil War's many local guerrilla conflicts. These conflicts often included some of the American Civil War's most colorful, dashing, and memorable characters, such as Gen. Nathan Bedford Forrest, Col. John Singleton Mosby, and Gen. Turner Ashby. The guerrilla conflict was savage and brutal, and men with murderous intent like Champion Ferguson, William Clarke Quantrill, and William "Bloody Bill" Anderson were also at work. The mass killing that occurred during William Quantrill's raid on Lawrence, Kan., on 21 August 1863 and which led to the deaths of nearly 200 civilians is one example of this guerrilla violence. Champion Ferguson, the Tennessee mountain guerrilla, admitted to killing more than 100 men personally during the war and was responsible for the Saltville, Va., massacre in October 1864, which killed at least 46 wounded and defenseless black U.S. soldiers. Ferguson was an example of violence motivated by politics and loyalty but also frequently by race hatred and prewar grudges held against local community members.

Given the short length of the American Civil War, the losses to the nation were staggering and difficult for many individuals to cope with emotionally and psychologically. A generation of southerners suffered trauma that would shape America for decades to come and the violence of the war is a key to understanding the southern response to defeat. Some of the postwar violence of the Ku Klux Klan, the White League, and Knights of the White Camelia can be directly attributed to settling accounts left open during the wartime violence. Many white southerners went into the war believing the South was invincible, and the violence of the war wrought losses that necessitated a strong explanation and justification. The Lost Cause mythology, which emerged in the South after the war to explain the causes, consequences of, and reasons for defeat, was a response to this trauma to the psyche of an entire population. The numerous works of writers Ambrose Bierce, William Faulkner, Robert Penn Warren, and Walt Whitman are also examples of the war's psychological toll on many Americans, North and South. Memory of the war's violence would continue to haunt Americans well into the 20th century.

BARTON A. MYERS
Texas Tech University

John Whiteclay Chambers, ed., *The Oxford Companion to American Military History* (1999); Drew Gilpin Faust, *This Republic of Suffering: Death and the American Civil War* (2008); Michael Fellman, *Inside War: The Guerrilla Conflict in Missouri during the American Civil War* (1989); Mark Grimsely, *The Hard Hand of War: Union Military Policy toward Southern Civilians* (1995); Philip Haythornthwaite, *Uniforms of the Civil War* (1990); Earl Hess, *The Rifle Musket in Civil War Combat: Reality and Myth* (2008); James M. McPherson, *Battle Cry of Freedom: The Civil War Era* (1988); Mark E. Neely, *The Civil War and the Limits of Destruction* (2007); Stephen J. Ramold, *Baring the Iron Hand: Discipline in the Union Army* (2009); Charles Royster, *The Destructive War: William Tecumseh Sherman, Stonewall Jackson, and the Americans* (1991); Daniel E. Sutherland, *A Savage Conflict: The Decisive Role of Guerrillas during the American Civil War* (2009); Gregory Urwin, *Black Flag over Dixie: Racial Atrocities and Reprisals in the Civil War* (2004).

Corporal Punishment in Schools

Corporal punishment is punishment inflicted on the body. It is a traditional form of discipline in American homes and schools commonly known as spanking, whipping, or paddling. American attitudes toward corporal punishment changed over the 20th century, but parents and educators in the southeastern United States were slow to embrace these trends in public opinion and policy. Paternalism, patriarchal religion, local control of schools, and a culture of honor explain why most 21st-century southern educators and parents continue to practice corporal punishment in addition to other disciplinary methods. Southern parents are more likely than those in other parts of the nation to discipline their children with force and to expect that teachers uphold corporal punishment.

Teachers had recourse to corporal punishment from colonial times to the 20th century. It was originally justified in the common-law doctrine of in loco parentis that delegated teachers the power to discipline children in the place of their parents. Parents and community members expected teachers, especially men, to efficiently discipline schoolchildren, which often meant physically dominating them. Schoolhouse discipline was a familiar topic for regional humorists in the 19th century; its practice, and the threat of it, was central to the imagery of the schoolhouse in *The Adventures of Tom Sawyer* by Mark Twain, for example. The practice also received attention from William Faulkner in book two of *The Hamlet*. Its schoolmaster, Labove, exemplified itinerant southern teachers who held school only in the absence of farm work, governed their pupils with brutality, and were always on the lookout for higher-paid employment.

Notable educators in the early republic, such as Horace Mann and Lyman Hall, were the first to contest schoolhouse discipline. Social scientists and educators further challenged corporal punishment in the 20th century. The debate over spanking, whether in homes or schools, continued among psychologists and educators until the late 1970s and early 1980s when state and federal courts began addressing litigation that questioned the prerogatives of teachers to administer corporal punishment in loco parentis.

In *Ingraham v. Wright* (1976), the United States Supreme Court affirmed the power of educators to use corporal punishment. In a split decision (5 to 4), reached after a vigorous dissent written by Justice Byron White, the Court dismissed the claims of two Dade County, Fla., youths who contended that corporal punishment by public school educators had violated their Eighth Amendment protections against cruel and unusual punishment and their Fourteenth Amendment rights to the due process of law. Although many southern cities have abolished corporal punishment in education, it persists in many rural southern schools.

DAVID HARGROVE
University of Mississippi

American Civil Liberties Union, *A Violent Education: Corporal Punishment of Children in U.S. Public Schools* (2008); Irwin A. Hyman and James H. Wise, eds., *Corporal Punishment in American Education: Readings in History, Practice, and Alternatives* (1979).

Criminal Justice through the Civil Rights Era

For much of their history, white southerners controlled crime with a prejudiced criminal justice system and extralegal violence. To black southerners, white southerners themselves acted criminally with their slavery and biased law enforcement. On the frontier between these two conceptions of crime and justice lay the true central theme in southern history: skepticism about whether due process—law in its regular course of administration through courts of justice—could effectively control crime. Both black and white southerners questioned whether the other side's darker impulses could be effectively controlled by abstract due process rules enforced bureaucratically. Doubt about the effectiveness of due process standards in the face of crime characterized the South, but that misgiving became the hallmark for all of American culture.

Race influenced white southerners' attitudes toward crime not immediately, when the first Africans landed in North America in 1619, but later, after slavery became the primary system for controlling labor. This happened around 1660, changing criminal justice, permanently setting the South on its course toward extralegal violent crime control. In 1669 the Virginia legislature wrote its toleration for extralegal crime control into law with a statute entitled "An Act about the Casuall Killing of Slaves." This law exempted slave owners from prosecution should they "chance" to kill a slave during the "extremity" of "correction." Since most crime control happened outside the formal institutions of government, such a law was necessary to safeguard from prosecution ordinary citizens using violence to control their black property.

White southerners understood their responsibility to control the South's black population as collective and best expressed through the slave patrol. Local governments organized and operated patrols. But the system had its roots in the more informal and private efforts organized by colonists in the Caribbean and Latin America. In 1661 the first comprehensive slave code in Barbados expected all whites to order and govern Negroes. This slave code also articulated whites' conviction that African descent implied a criminal character. The authors of the Barbados statutes feared blacks as heathens and brutes, people inherently dangerous. This detailed slave code might suggest a rigorous police state, but historians have found the opposite. In Barbados slaves evaded the law, trading in goods stolen or otherwise. In large measure, policing slaves meant controlling—with only limited success—this illicit trade.

South Carolina copied the Barbados slave code, and white patrollers watched for signs of trouble: secretive slave gatherings, slaves without passes, violations of the curfew. What had been a voluntary effort in Barbados became mandatory in South Carolina and the other American states. In 1696 South Carolina's legislature passed a more coercive law, organizing white men into squads to better whip and jail slaves from the countryside found in town on Sundays. Slaves wandering around on Sundays profaned Sabbath, but they also exchanged information outside white supervision, creating opportunities for insurrection.

The growth of towns in the South helped define and shape the nature of policing. Southern towns and cities organized the first uniformed police in America. Charleston introduced a police force, the city guards, in the 1780s.

Savannah, New Orleans, and Mobile followed later. These cities responded to complaints about slaves congregating in towns, engaged in criminal activities, and buying liquor and guns. White people complained that urban areas furnished slaves a refuge, places to hide from pursuing masters. The city guards patrolling those places wore uniforms and carried weapons. They received salaries rather than fees. They patrolled at night with a reserve force available during the daytime. They formed autonomous organizations because cities pleaded with legislatures for freedom from county interference. New Orleans had its own autonomous force after 1805. In 1832 Virginia cities won the right to organize their own patrols. One place to trace the origins of professional policing in America is in these urban slave patrols.

Professionalizing law enforcement increased through the late antebellum period when southern states subjected criminal trial court procedures to greater scrutiny. In the 1840s and 1850s southern state supreme courts increasingly tried to impose due process standards on trial courts. In Mississippi, the High Court of Errors and Appeals insisted that local magistrates inform slave suspects of their common-law right to remain silent. In Mississippi, trials carried out with biased jurors had to be done over; even slaves had a right to an unbiased jury. There were limits to these innovations. As late as 1849, Virginia still tried slaves charged with felonies before special courts of oyer and terminer, sitting without a jury and proceeding without a grand jury indictment. Slave defendants had lawyers, paid for by their owners, but the lawyers received no more than $25. Most scholars agree that due process protections really guarded the rights of the owner, not the slave defendant. Slaves received due process protections only when they stood accused of murder, rape, or arson, all capital crimes. Slave trials involving these serious crimes should be seen as condemnation proceedings, some scholars say. Due process protected the property owner rather than the defendant.

Such efforts to impose due process standards on slave trials actually changed the overall criminal justice system very little. At the end of slavery, southern courthouses still saw very few slave defendants, even in jurisdictions where slaves vastly outnumbered white people. For a criminal justice system dependent on slavery to control crime, emancipation was a catastrophic blow. White southerners brought their fears of African Americans into the postemancipation era. There are no regionwide statistics, but violent crime must have increased with the end of the Civil War. Normal mechanisms of policing, which included slavery, the patrol system, and the states' court systems, broke down. Confederate guerrillas and criminal gangs took advantage; when the federal government reimposed martial law in 1867, military patrols found they had to arrest white horse thieves more often than black criminals. Despite this, white southerners acted on their racial fears with a system of discriminatory laws northerners condemned as black codes. Mississippi passed the first of these laws in November 1865, and the rest of the South soon followed. These laws continued the pass system, requiring that African Americans carry proof of employment, punished slow working as "vagrancy," and authorized every white person to question blacks they encountered on the public highways. Blacks could not leave contracted employment prematurely, nor could they testify in court against white persons. Mississippi's law created county courts meeting continually to process the expected wave of black criminality. County courts could administer a quick beating; imprisonment would have deprived landlords of needed labor.

Such brutal laws produced demands by northerners for federal supervision of southern criminal justice procedures. When Congress assembled in December 1865, members debated how to bring order to the South as well as whether and how to intervene on behalf of the freed people. Congress passed the Civil Rights Act of 1866, defining citizenship and outlining the rights of citizens. Citizens could enter into contracts, buy and sell property, and, most important of all, testify in court, regardless of race. Federal authorities could prosecute crimes committed by state officers acting "under color of law." The Civil Rights Act also authorized federal judges to transfer into U.S. district courtrooms state ordinary criminal cases involving black people, if state courts discriminated. Congress, then, threatened the states' criminal justice systems. If the southern states persisted in their overt discrimination, they risked losing control of their criminal justice system to federal judges. Every southern state but one quickly backed down, repealing its black codes. Kentucky persisted, denying blacks the right to testify against whites until federal prosecutors took over a murder case against John Blyew and George Kennard, charged with murdering a black family on 29 August 1868. Two witnesses survived the attack, but they were both African American, and Kentucky law forbade their testimony in state court. Their testimony in federal court led to the convictions of Blyew and Kennard. The two convicted men appealed to the U.S. Supreme Court.

Between 1871, when the Supreme Court heard oral arguments in *Blyew v. United States*, and 1883, when the Court decided the *Civil Rights Cases*, the justices decided a series of cases designed to protect states' rights and prevent the imposition of due process standards on the southern states by federal judges. In *Blyew v. United States*, the Supreme Court ruled in favor of Blyew and Kennard, overturning their convictions, deciding that federal authorities should not have taken Blyew and Kennard's case out of state court. The justices wrote a strikingly narrow decision to justify this outcome. Witnesses to a murder, the justices said, could not be victims of discrimination because they had no interest in the case. Nor could the victims be subject to discrimination since they were dead. These decisions guaranteed that criminal justice in the South would get little federal supervision. After the Supreme Court's decision in this and other criminal cases, southern states excluded African Americans from their juries, did not seriously investigate, prosecute, or try persons accused of lynching, and often refused to extend criminal justice services to African American citizens.

Throughout the 19th century, and into the 20th, white southerners saw vigilantism as integral to their criminal justice system, a vital supplement to the slower and less effective processes administered by courts. When black defendants did go to trial, charged with crimes against white persons, mobs sometimes crowded the courtroom, intimidating jurors and court officers. This happened to white defendants as well. In 1915 the Supreme Court considered mob intimidation in the sensational Leo Frank case. The manager of an Atlanta pencil factory, Frank had been convicted in state court for murdering Mary Phagan. Frank claimed his trial had been dominated by a mob and asked for a federal writ of habeas corpus. The U.S. Supreme Court rebuffed Frank, seeing in his petition an attempt to unlawfully expand federal power. The Court charged that Frank's lawyers sought to deny Georgia the opportunity to supervise its own trials. Such a doctrine, the Court warned, would prevent the states from effectively repressing and punishing crime.

In 1923 the Supreme Court reversed itself and decided that, in trials where the mob so dominated the proceedings as to sweep aside the judge and jury, federal courts could step in and try the case. Oliver Wendell Holmes, dissenter in the Leo Frank case, wrote the opinion of the Court. It would, however, be hard to call *Moore et al. v. Dempsey* a turning point. After 1923 southern courts continued to hold their trials much as they always had, with all-white juries and amid persisting reports that mobs continued to crowd courtrooms, intimidating juries and court personnel.

In 1940, when the Federal Bureau of Investigation began researching reports of lynching, the agents reported that white southerners believed that they had a right to lynch black men accused of rape so long as they acted before an arrest. Once the accused person went into jail, many white persons thought the mob should step back, but not before. In fact, even that caveat did little to limit mob violence. Some sheriffs and deputies turned prisoners over to mobs, holding them only long enough for the mob to organize itself.

During the 1960s and afterward, southern courts asserted themselves more aggressively. Progressive political leaders insisted on more professional justice. The South became less tolerant of vigilante groups, including the infamous Ku Klux Klan. In part this development can be attributed to the political success of African American political candidates after the 1965 Voting Rights Law. Thereafter, black southerners became mayors and sheriffs across the South. At the same time, the U.S. Supreme Court increasingly demanded greater due process in criminal trials. Southerners, black and white, had reached a new social agreement that professional law enforcement and not private vengeance should control crime. In the popular culture, though, the image of the heroic vigilante acting to control crime outside the rule of law persisted, having become a national phenomenon, no longer only the central theme for the South.

CHRISTOPHER WALDREP
San Francisco State University

Edward L. Ayers, *Vengeance and Justice: Crime and Punishment in the Nineteenth-Century American South* (1984); Peter Bardaglio, *Reconstructing the Household: Families, Sex, and the Law in the Nineteenth-Century South* (1995); Michal R. Belknap, *Federal Law and Southern Honor: Racial Violence and Constitutional Conflict in the Post-Brown South* (1987); Charles C. Bolton and Scott P. Culclasure, eds., *The Confessions of Edward Isham: A Poor White Life of the Old South* (1998); Robert D. Goldstein, *Stanford Law Review* (February 1989); Sally E. Hadden, *Slave Patrols: Law and Violence in Virginia and the Carolinas* (2001); Michael J. Klarman, *From Jim Crow to Civil Rights: The Supreme Court and the Struggle for Racial Equality* (2004); Thomas D. Morris, *Southern Slavery and the Law, 1619–1860* (1999); Dennis Rousey, *Policing the Southern City: New Orleans, 1805–1889* (1996); Judith Kelleher Schafer, *Slavery, the Civil Law, and the Supreme Court of Louisiana* (1994); Richard Slotkin, *Gunfighter Nation: The Myth of the Frontier in Twentieth-Century America* (1992); Mark V. Tushnet, *Slave Law in the American South: "State v. Mann" in History and Literature* (2003); Gilles Vandal, *Rethinking Southern Violence: Homicides in Post-Civil War Louisiana, 1866–1884* (2000); Christopher Waldrep, *Roots of Disorder: Race and Criminal Justice in the American South, 1817–80* (1998).

Dueling

Dueling was introduced in America by French and British officers during the American Revolution. The practice was outlawed throughout the North after the Alexander Hamilton-Aaron Burr duel in 1804. The death of Hamilton shocked the North, which had already all but abolished the practice. In the South dueling became a criminal offense, with stiff penalties if the duel resulted in a death. Opposition to the practice was one of the few respectable social causes in the antebellum South. Despite statutes, antidueling societies, and public disapproval of the practice, dueling remained an important part of southern culture until the Civil War.

Many southern politicians and editors either engaged in duels or received or issued challenges. A list of such men reads like a "who's who" of the antebellum South and includes Andrew Jackson, William Clingman, William Yancey, Henry Clay, Cassius M. Clay, Henry Wise, Thomas Hart Benton, Sam Houston, William Crawford, Jefferson Davis, Judah P. Benjamin, John Randolph, George McCuffie, William Graves, Louis T. Wigfall, and Albert Sidney Johnston. Duels were not, however, limited to political and social leaders. Parvenus often used the duel as a vehicle for social advancement. Although it was not considered proper for a true gentleman to accept a challenge from a social inferior, such lines were often unclear, particularly in the Southwest.

Most duels were fought with pistols, although occasionally rifles were used. In New Orleans, swords remained the weapon of choice among some duelists. Duelists were supposed to follow elaborate rules, which were described in John Lyde Wilson's *The Code of Honor* (1838), but duels did not always proceed according to those rules. Indeed, before the publication of Wilson's book, most duelists, especially those not living in Charleston or New Orleans, likely knew little of the prescribed rules. The rules of dueling required that a challenge be sent, with an opportunity for the offending party to make amends and avoid a conflict. Nevertheless, spontaneous fights between gentlemen, with knives or canes as weapons, were considered by many a form of dueling. When Congressman Preston Brooks beat Charles Sumner with a cane until the Massachusetts senator was insensible, it was considered the equivalent of a duel by Brooks's Charleston constituents. Northerners, on the other hand, considered this act particularly barbaric because Sumner was seated, with his back to Brooks, when the attack began. Similarly, when Alexander H. Stephens, while unarmed, was attacked and knifed by a political rival, southerners considered the event within the bounds of political behavior.

The duel was one aspect of antebellum southern fascination with chivalry. Most duels were fought over alleged or perceived insults. The cause of a duel could be personal, social, professional, or political. Duels were often fought over the honor of one's family and, particularly, of women in the family. Social pressure, a desire to prove one's masculinity, or hotheadedness alone drove innumerable southern men to the field of honor.

PAUL FINKELMAN
University of Albany Law School

John Hope Franklin, *The Militant South, 1800–1861* (1956); Kenneth S. Greenberg, *Honor and Slavery: Lies, Duals, Noses, Masks, Dressing as a Woman, Gifts, Strangers, Humanitarianism, Death, Slave Rebellions, the Proslavery Argument, Baseball, Hunting, and Gambling in the Old South* (1996); Bertram Wyatt-Brown, *Southern Honor: Ethics and Behavior in the Old South* (1982).

Feuds and Feuding

Southern feuding shares many characteristics with feuding found elsewhere in the world. Feuding can be defined as blood revenge following an aggravated assault or homicide. The killings or attempted killings occur as revenge for perceived injustice. Terms such as duty, honor, righteous, and legitimate often appear in discussions of the motivation for the attacks.

A feud takes place within a political entity, which can be as large as a nation-state; it involves kin of the wounded or deceased victim; and the retaliatory attack usually leads to counterattacks. The attacks can alternate back and forth for decades, perhaps even centuries. This definition is meant to include feuds in which an unsuccessful attempt at a counterkilling leads to the killing of one or more of the revenge seekers, as occurred on several occasions in 19th-century eastern Kentucky in the Turner-Howard feud. Mortality in this feud was one-sided, as 13 Turners died while no Howards were killed.

Southern feuding lies on a continuum between violence and dueling. It is found from southern West Virginia, across western Virginia, Kentucky, Tennessee, Arkansas, and into eastern Texas. Feuds also occurred in Arizona and Colorado. In extremely isolated areas in the 19th century, where courts and kinship groups were absent, violence—from drunken brawling to banditry to cattle rustling—occurred with extremely high frequencies. The development of revolvers and repeating rifles in the last half of the century facilitated an escalation in homicides. At the other end of the continuum lies dueling, a highly structured and rule-based activity. Duels, which were fought by gentlemen to preserve their honor, were found in the Lowland South from Virginia through the Carolinas, to New Orleans. Feuding and dueling are usually not found in the same region. If a duel were to occur in an area where feuding kinship groups existed, the resulting injury or possible death would start a feud.

Several different approaches or theories have been used to explain feuding in general and southern feuding in particular. Because kinship groups are involved in feuds, anthropologists have often focused on the nature of these groups. Anthropologist Keith Otterbein has argued that the presence of fraternal interest groups—localized groups of related males—produces feuds when the interests of group members and the groups themselves are threatened. Another anthropologist, Christopher Boehm, has argued that feuding prevents all-out warfare—but it has to be feuding that can be stopped by payment of compensation. Since southern feuding rarely involves compensation, some feuds from this region led to such wholesale killing that they were called "wars" (e.g., the so-called wars of Clay County, Ky.).

Historians have come to prefer the world systems theory, an approach that argues that social change brought on by commercial expansion in the 19th century created the feuds. The Hatfield-McCoy feud is explained in this manner by Altina Waller, but not by Otis Rice or by Joe Ed Pearce. Historians with a folklore bent, such as David Hackett Fischer, look to the border region of Scotland and England for the origin of southern feuding. A culture of violence was brought from the border region to Appalachia by early settlers in the 18th century. Conditions were the same in both regions, and hence feuds persisted into the 20th century. Anthropologists and folklorists have also viewed feuding as "self-help," "folk justice," or "quasi law." In regions where courts are weak, folk justice may arise from an individual exercising what he believes is his right to get even. If fraternal interest groups are present, feuds occur. If fraternal interest groups are absent, retaliatory killings occur but the scattered kinsmen of the disputants do not become involved, as described by William Montell for an area along the Tennessee-Kentucky state line.

A comparative study of Kentucky feuds by Keith Otterbein is based on Joe Ed Pearce's detailed study of five Kentucky feuds. Similarities among the feuds include the structure of the feuding groups. The groups were large in membership, with descent traced through both sons and daughters (such a kinship group is termed an ambilineage by anthropologists). They were economically well off, they had members who held local political and judicial offices, and they had access to state governors' offices. The kinship groups were under the leadership of "clan" heads, typically vicious individuals who sought wealth and power through illegal activities such as distilling whiskey. Groups often violated the honor of members of rival kinship groups. Homicidal retaliation would occur. Homicidal encounters included ambushes (the most common type of armed combat employed), gun fights (next in frequency), house attacks, and encounter and arranged battles. Although there was no set sequence of homicidal encounters, ambushes and gunfights were likely to occur early in the feud sequence, while battles and house attacks were likely to occur late in the sequence. Otterbein concludes that since Kentucky feuds took place in a market economy, the pursuit of economic and political power was often more important than honor. "Market-based" feuding seems less concerned with righting a wrong than with eliminating a rival kinship group. Otterbein views feuding as a form of violent crime.

KEITH F. OTTERBEIN
University at Buffalo

Dwight B. Billings, Kathleen M. Blee, Pam Goldman, Sharon Hardesty, and Lee Hardesty, in *The Road to Poverty: The Making of Hardship in Appalachia*, ed. Dwight B. Billings and Kathleen M. Blee (2000); Christopher Boehm, *Blood Revenge: The Anthropology of Feuding in Montegegro and Other Tribal Societies* (1984); David Hackett Fischer, *Albion's Seed: Four British Folkways in America* (1989); William L. Montell, *Killings: Folk Justice in the Upper South* (1986); Keith F. Otterbein, ed., *Feuding and Warfare: Selected Works of Keith F. Otterbein* (1994), *American Anthropologist* (June 2000), in *The Encyclopedia of the Martial Arts*, ed. Thomas A. Green (2001); John Ed Pearce, *Days of Darkness: The Feuds of Eastern Kentucky* (1994, 2010); Charles Leland Sonnichsen, *I'll Die before I'll Run: The Story of the Great Feuds of Texas* (1962); Altina Waller, *Feud: Hatfields, McCoys, and Social Change in Appalachia, 1860–1900* (1988).

Films about Lynching

Since their beginnings in the mid-1890s, commercial motion pictures have registered the presence of lynching (or extralegal execution) in American society. By that decade lynching had become concentrated mostly in the South and had become overwhelmingly racial in nature, targeting African American men for crimes real and imagined. In the changing vocabularies of many eras since the early silent period, and particularly before lynching's diminution around the mid-20th century, film has been sensitive to the violence and trauma of the phenomenon in many ways. Among the many films to address the subject, explicitly or implicitly, have been one-shot "curiosity" films of lynchings and early narrative films with comic or dramatic chase sequences culminating in lynching or its symbolic equivalent. From the mid-1910s forward, full-length feature films across a number of genres integrated lynching into a broad range of presentational and narrative elements and into newsreels, documentaries, and other nonfiction films about extrajudicial execution.

As several films produced at Thomas Edison's West Orange, N.J., laboratory in 1895 suggest, early filmmakers perceived both the cinematic potential and the generic translatability of lynching. *A Frontier Scene/Lynching Scene* portrays a band of cowboys killing a horse thief. *Indian Scalping Scene/Scalping Scene* shows the same act performed by Indians on a prairie settler. Around the same time, another pair of films was produced with similar imagery.

Perhaps the earliest nonfiction lynching film was *The Hanging of William Carr*, produced on location in Liberty, Mo., on 17 December 1897. Though the farmer Carr was executed legally for the murder of his three-year-old daughter, a howling mob of outraged citizens attempted to break into the stockade where he was being held, hoping to kill him themselves.

As filmmakers began to produce narrative films, experimenting with increasingly complex editing and continuity styles, as well as with longer running times, lynching's violence found its way to the screen in new ways. *Tracked by Bloodhounds; or, A Lynching at Cripple Creek* (1904) features a wandering tramp who strangles a woman in view of her little daughter after a robbery attempt in the western mining town, followed by a series of chase scenes and his lynching at the hands of a mob of miners and cowboys. *Avenging a Crime; or, Burned at the Stake* has a nearly identical plot, complete with the attempted robbery and successful strangulation of a white woman (witnessed not by a daughter but by a little girl hiding in the bushes), and an elaborate chase sequence that culminates in a lynching. But *Avenging a Crime* is set in "a typical southern scene" rather than a western mining town, and its villain is a "very sulky" black man who commits his crimes after losing his money in a game of craps.

A small number of films with antilynching sentiments also appeared during this period. *The Parson of Hungry Gulch; or, The Right Man in the Right Place May Work Wonders* (1907) combines antilynching and temperance messages, portraying a young minister from New England, newly arrived in the far West, who not only prevents a gambling saloonkeeper from being lynched by a mob of townspeople but subsequently converts the gambler into a prayerful family man and brings the entire community together in harmony. *Banty Tim* (1913), based on a poem by John C. Hay, former secretary to Abraham Lincoln and U.S. ambassador to the United Kingdom, told the story of a Union soldier, back home in Illinois after the Civil War, who prevents the lynching of a hunchbacked black man who saved his life during the battle of Vicksburg. Even rarer than these films were films portraying black lynch mobs, like the one in *At the Cross Roads* (1914), an adaptation of a 1902 stage melodrama. The mob in this film pursues a white man who had raped the possibly mixed-race protagonist years ago, and a lynching is averted only by the woman's killing of the man in self-defense.

The 1915 lynching of Leo Frank of Atlanta made world headlines, and multiple fiction and nonfiction films connected to his trial and lynching were produced. Several films sympathetic to Frank emerged, including *Leo M. Frank (Showing Life in Jail) and Governor Slaton* (1915), which featured both the governor's wife and Frank's mother, and the five-reel *The Frank Case* (1915), which reenacted the entire case and predicted Frank's acquittal. Pathé News managed to get several shots of Frank's hanging corpse, and these were distributed nationally as part of its weekly newsreel. Gaumont News, another newsreel production company, filmed crowds gathered at the lynching site, a local judge pleading for them to let Frank's family remove his corpse peacefully, and Frank's mother collecting flowers in a separate location. In response to such films, the City of Atlanta quickly passed an ordinance outlawing public exhibition of any films of Leo Frank's lynching. The prolific African American filmmaker Oscar Micheaux twice produced films based on the Frank case: *The Gunsaulus Mystery* (1921) and *Lem Hawkins' Confession* (1935) (reedited and released as *Murder in Harlem*). The earlier film suggested that Frank (portrayed here as a sexual pervert named Anthony Brisbane) was in fact guilty of killing Mary Phagan (Myrtle Gunsaulus) and attempting to pin the crime on a black janitor. Like many in the black press, who had encountered countless cases of the scapegoating of blacks for crimes they did not commit, Micheaux seems to have believed that Frank was guilty and that his claims of innocence merely sought to shift culpability to the nearest black man.

More cinematically significant in 1915 than the Frank case was the unprecedented success of D. W. Griffith's epic *The Birth of a Nation*. With its lengthy sequence detailing the Ku Klux Klan's secret trial and murder of a black man, it guaranteed that more Americans would see lynching at the movies than ever before. Other filmmakers took notice, and lynching sequences indebted to Griffith's became common during subsequent years.

The interwar period was not without a tradition of antilynching filmmaking. Oscar Micheaux's early films *Symbol of the Unconquered* (1920), a Western featuring a heroic black homesteader, and especially *Within Our Gates* (1920), set largely in Mississippi, sought to expose the sheer trauma and injustice endured by African Americans under lynch law. As the Ku Klux Klan enjoyed resurgence during these years, blacks were not the only ones concerned about the organization. *Knight of the Eucharist* (1922) and *The Mask of the Ku Klux Klan* (1923) portrayed members of the Catholic fraternal organization Knights of Columbus denouncing the Ku Klux Klan and included scenes in which Klan members whipped and beat a young Catholic boy to death after the boy attempted to prevent them from desecrating the altar of his church.

A more comprehensive cycle of antilynching films was produced during the depths of the Depression. Many of these films were set outside the South and, like most of the "lynching" Westerns made during the same period, featured nonblack lynching victims. Fritz Lang's *Fury* (1936) condemned the overly congenial lynching culture that had prevailed in American society for so long.

Mervyn LeRoy revisited the Frank case to attack opportunistic politicians and journalists in *They Won't Forget* (1937). The 1935 murder of WPA worker Charles Poole by members of the Detroit Black Legion formed the basis of two anti-lynching films: *Legion of Terror* (1936) and *Black Legion* (1937). John Ford satirically revealed the narrowness and hypocrisy of communities where lynching occurs in *Judge Priest* (1934) and *Steamboat Round the Bend* (1935), a pair of Will Rogers vehicles. In Ford's *Young Mr. Lincoln* (1939), the country lawyer Lincoln faces down an entire lynch mob outside the jail where his clients, two white brothers accused of murder, are imprisoned, and deploys a rhetorical arsenal of humor, logic, pathos, and religion—along with physical strength—to persuade his peers to forgo their vengeance and allow the law to take its course.

Several years later, *The Ox-Bow Incident* (1943) and *Intruder in the Dust* (1949) challenged the authenticity of both the classic Western and Griffith's solid South. These powerful message films represented a culmination of the antilynching film tradition of the previous several decades. Ford's *The Sun Shines Bright* (1953) took a more nostalgic, less polemical tack, but served as perhaps the most humane antilynching film of the period, even as lynching in the South, and certainly in the rest of the United States, had become far rarer than it had been only several decades earlier.

World War II, economic recovery, and growing demands for civil rights contributed to lynching's decline. It has never entirely disappeared, though, and the possibility of its reappearance continues to animate American film. Spike Lee's *Summer of Sam* (1999) and Ang Lee's *Brokeback Mountain* (2005) made devastating indictments of lynching as a historical phenomenon. Perhaps more pressingly, though, they have also pointed to its enduring presence in mainstream American culture and its centrality to the ways Americans, southern and otherwise, have seen and understood themselves.

ROBERT JACKSON
University of Virginia

James Allen, Hilton Als, John Lewis, and Leon F. Litwack, *Without Sanctuary: Lynching Photography in America* (2000); W. Fitzhugh Brundage, ed., *Under Sentence of Death: Lynching in the South* (1997); Philip Dray, *At the Hands of Persons Unknown: The Lynching of Black America* (2002); Robert Jackson, *Southern Literary Journal* (Spring 2008); Charles Musser, *The Emergence of Cinema: The American Screen to 1907* (1990); Michael J. Pfeifer, *Rough Justice: Lynching and American Society, 1874–1947* (2004); Christopher Waldrep, ed., *Lynching in America: A History in Documents* (2006); Michele Faith Wallace, *Cinema Journal* (Autumn 2003); Amy Louise Wood, *Lynching and Spectacle: Witnessing Racial Violence in America, 1890–1940* (2009).

Films about Prison

Prison movies, set either wholly or partly in correctional institutions that focus on inmates and their keepers, date back to the silent era, but the genre really took off with a series of social- and political-conscience films that included Mervyn LeRoy's *I Am a Fugitive from a Chain Gang* (1932) and P. J. Wolfson's *Boy Slaves* (1938), the latter the story of reform school inmates enslaved on a turpentine farm. *I Am a Fugitive* was based on Robert E. Burns's exposé of Georgia's penal conditions. Paul Muni starred as James Allen, an unemployed war veteran wrongly accused of theft and sentenced to hard labor in a chain gang who made two daring escapes but was ultimately condemned to life as a permanent fugitive. The film's attack on social injustice and the state's complicity in the oppression of its citizens was summed up in the final scene when Allen's sweetheart asks "How do you live, Jim?" From the nighttime shadows, Allen whispers, "I steal."

The film's central motifs are imprisonment and entrapment, oppression, and degradation. It depicts beaten-down men in stripes and chains. Laboring for violent and sadistic guards became staples of the southern prison movie during the 20th century. Images of the southern landscape—long grass and cotton fields through which fugitives run, murky swamps in which they nearly drown, rivers always navigable with a handy boat, isolated shacks and cracker towns, and long, empty roads and highways—are used to kindle views of backwardness, strangeness, and otherness. Many of the later prison films' claims to depict an authentic prison experience were strengthened by the use of infamous southern prisons as filming locations. These included the Louisiana State Prison at Angola, itself the subject of a sobering documentary film, *The Farm: Angola, USA* (1998).

From the 1860s to the present, southern prisons contained disproportionate numbers of African American inmates, but prison movies have focused overwhelmingly on white males. Sympathetic black figures do appear, for example, in *I Am a Fugitive*, but they rarely say anything other than "Yes, Boss." Not until the late 1950s was there a major African American inmate character. In *The Defiant Ones* (1958), Sidney Poitier plays Noah Cullen (a role reprised by Lawrence Fishburne in the 1996 remake *Fled*) handcuffed to white racist John "Joker" Jackson (Tony Curtis). Literally chained together, their chain-gang escape is followed by adventure, heroism, and self-sacrifice, as a bond of brotherly love develops between the two and (as in many prison movies) a homosexual subtext is evident. Poitier received an Oscar nomination for best actor for his gritty performance.

More recent portraits of black inmates, such as Morgan Freeman's role as

Walter in *Brubaker* (1980) and the towering figure of John Coffey in *The Green Mile* (1999), still fail to capture the African American historical prison experience. Wrongly accused of the murder-rape of two white girls, Coffey (Michael Clarke Duncan) is held on Louisiana's death row in 1935, but his gentle character and supernatural powers of healing win over the guards and warden. Racial tensions are, of course, a stock theme in many southern prison movies. In the desegregated prison yard of Citrus State Prison, racial antagonisms abound, but black and white inmates find common cause when they take on the prison guards at football and win in *The Longest Yard* (1973).

The quintessential white prison hero and the celluloid chain gang returned in 1967 with Paul Newman's mesmerizing portrayal of Lucas "Luke" Jackson, war hero turned parking meter bandit doing time on Florida's hard road in *Cool Hand Luke*. Despite impossible odds of success, Luke's attempts to regain his freedom and selfhood by defying the control of the state and prison officials and the processes of dehumanization, by repeatedly baiting the guards and enduring many hours in the "sweatbox," enabled his fellow inmates to regain their own sense of manliness and self-respect. The southern chain gang returned in the later 20th century, both in reality and in film, but whereas it had been the vehicle for exposing social and racial injustice, particularly in the 1930s, in *O Brother, Where Art Thou?* (2000) it provided the backdrop for a series of escapades and comic encounters in a tale based loosely on Homer's *Odyssey*, but which also paid homage to earlier prison movies.

Prison film stories are usually told from the prisoners' perspective. There are instantly recognizable characters: the snitches or rats, the bad or murderous convict(s), the wise and worldly lifer, and the youthful hero—usually a good man who has made mistakes or bad choices, been framed or set up, or is guilty of a minor offense. Audiences applaud their efforts to defy the system or get one over on their brutal oppressors. Some prisoners win audiences over with song, such as Vince Everett (Elvis Presley) in *Jailhouse Rock* (1957) or the Soggy Bottom Boys in *O Brother, Where Art Thou?*; others with their athletic prowess and guile as with washed-up pro-football player Paul Cullen (Burt Lancaster) in *The Longest Yard* (and Adam Sandler in the 2005 remake); still others by boxing, poker, and egg-eating skills (Luke Jackson in *Cool Hand Luke*). Other prisoners are celebrated for their dogged and understated determination to take on the system and win as with Clarence Gideon's (Henry Fonda) hours of study in the prison library and subsequent pauper's petition to the U.S. Supreme Court that secures legal representation for all indigent inmates in *Gideon's Trumpet* (1980). By contrast, the central characters in Jim Jarmush's "neo-beat-noir comedy" *Down By Law* (1986), Ted Demme's 1999 film *Life* (starring Eddie Murphy and

Martin Lawrence), and the Coen brothers' *O Brother, Where Art Thou?* are likable rogues or misfits.

In *Cool Hand Luke*, the voyeuristic Boss Godfrey ("The Man with No Eyes" because of his penchant for reflector sunglasses) is the embodiment of evil. Like his later counterpart, the psychotic sheriff in *O Brother*, he can be read as representative of the legion of cruel guards and wardens in nearly every southern prison movie. All criminal justice personnel in the South seemed to be involved in nefarious and corrupt schemes. In *White Lightning* (1973), convicted moonshiner "Gator" McKlusky (Burt Reynolds) engineers his release from prison in a deal with "the feds" to rat out his former partners, but instead he determines to hunt down the crooked sheriff who killed his brother. The heroic warden figure, Henry Brubaker (Robert Redford) in his 1980 performance, is a rare exception, but Brubaker's task is to clean up a small prison farm in Arkansas where the previous corrupt warden has encouraged guard scams and inmate violence.

A more sympathetic portrayal of southern death-row guards as decent men doing a hateful job to the best of their ability is evident in *The Green Mile*. Their racist attitudes are less overt than in *Monster's Ball* (2001), for example, where reformation for one racist ex-prison guard, Hank Grotowski (Billy Bob Thornton), is through a sexual relationship with an African American waitress, Leticia Musgrove (Halle Berry), who is grieving for her son killed in a road accident and the husband Grotowski helped execute. Halle Berry won an Oscar for her performance, but her role underscores the fact that prison stories generally exclude female characters (1995's *Dead Man Walking*, starring Sean Penn and Susan Sarandon, notwithstanding). In recent years, however, focus has begun to shift to include female prisoners who have committed particularly lurid or heinous crimes, most notably highway-prostitute-turned-serial-killer Aileen Wuornos. The story of her life and crimes was at the center of two movies, *Overkill* (1992) and *Monster* (2003), as well as several documentary films, including *Aileen Wuornos: The Selling of a Serial Killer* (1992).

As the South developed a monopoly over state-sanctioned executions in the second half of the 20th century, death rows and executions replaced the chain gang as the vehicles for raising social and political consciousness about injustice. Tim Robbins's *Dead Man Walking*, centering on a convicted murderer on death row in Texas and the caring nun who befriends him in the days before his execution, suggests southern penal systems could be just as discriminatory, brutal, and oppressive as their 1930s counterparts. Similar themes permeate death row and execution documentaries, including Errol Morris's *The Thin Blue Line* (1988), also set in Texas, which reenacts the crime for which Randall Dale

Adams was wrongly convicted in 1977. The recent shift to mass incarceration in the United States and the continued use of capital punishment will undoubtedly ensure the longevity of the southern prison movie genre well into the 21st century.

VIVIEN MILLER
University of Nottingham

Frankie Y. Bailey and Donna Hale, eds., *Popular Culture, Crime, and Justice* (1998); Andrew Bergman, *We're in the Money: Depression America and Its Films* (1971); Donald Bogle, *Toms, Coons, Mulattoes, Mammies, and Bucks: An Interpretive History of Blacks in American Films* (2002); James Robert Parish, *Prison Pictures from Hollywood* (2000); Nicole Rafter, *Shots in the Mirror: Crime Films and Society*, (2000); Mark Wheeler, *Hollywood, Politics, and Society* (2006).

Guns

Since the early 1800s the image of southerners with firearms has served as a cliché for the nation and, indeed, the world. The firearm is certainly a secure cultural feature of the South, but that is true of rural groups in other geographical locations. Firearms, generalized violence, and "southernness" have, however, been historically linked in the popular and literary imagination and have served as negative features distorting overall perceptions of the southern reality. Since the 1960s the gun itself has taken on a larger meaning in the context of the American nation, and the traditional identification of southerners with guns has both reinforced stereotypes of regional violence and reaffirmed many southerners' interest in weapons.

The South has traditionally been portrayed as a gun-toting culture. In the 19th century, northern and European travelers frequently remarked on the prevalence of guns and knives in the region. Today many nonsoutherners, especially urbanites, express surprise at gun racks in pickup trucks, pro-gun-ownership bumper-sticker slogans, and the assertive attitudes of some southerners about the right to carry firearms.

Gun ownership and levels of gun usage are indeed relatively high in the South. According to a 2005 Gallup Poll, the South is the American region with the highest rate of personal gun ownership, at 36 percent, followed closely by the Midwest at 34 percent. The rates of total household gun ownership for the South and Midwest tied at 47 percent, well above the 31 percent rate in the eastern states (personal gun ownership in those states averaged 22 percent). Whether the existence of such statistics constitutes sufficient rationale for the

Mississippi Delta, 1968 (William R. Ferris Collection, Southern Folklife Collection,
Wilson Library, University of North Carolina at Chapel Hill)

widely held belief that a "southern subculture of violence" exists is difficult to
prove.

The belief in such a subculture flourished for many years. Persuasive arguments emanated from politicized campuses and newsrooms of the 1960s, and
authors of popular and academic articles asserted that violence was an inherent
quality of southerners' worldview. The "southern culture of honor" thesis had
been prevalent since the early 20th century, and it has been posited that retaliatory violence is normal behavior for southerners, many of whom are descendants of Scottish and Irish herding cultures, which valued defensive forms of
violence in protecting herds. In 2010 Richard Felson and Paul-Philippe Pare
studied regional and racial differences in weapon carrying in an article in the
sociological journal *Social Forces* and concluded that southern identity and behavior may not be so much distinguished by an "honor culture" as by a "gun
culture." Though regional rates of homicide and aggravated assault (10 percent of which involve guns) are highest in the South, those numbers are far
outweighed by higher rates of simple assault in other regions. Therefore, the
belief in the existence of a hyperviolent southern "honor culture" wavers, according to Felson and Pare, because overall rates of violence are actually lowest
in the South. The existence of a southern "gun culture" may more effectively
explain regional weapons-carrying and crime differences. The high rates of

firearm ownership in the South seem primarily related to the prevalence of shoulder weapons (i.e., shotguns and rifles) found there among sportsmen. Although handgun ownership in the South in 2001, according to a 2001 Harris Poll, hovered at 31 percent, shotgun and rifle ownership came in at 35 percent and 36 percent, respectively.

Handguns have been anecdotally linked to the South from antebellum times to the present, and statistics support the association. In 2001, 31 percent of southerners owned handguns, most often used in firearm-related violence, while only 14 percent of northeasterners claimed handgun ownership. Many handgun owners routinely carry revolvers or automatics in their glove compartments, briefcases, or, in the case of ladies, their handbags. Although some gun enthusiasts claim to use handguns for hunting, their primary function is cited as a weapon carried for protection. According to Felson and Pare's 2010 article, southern white men are twice as likely as their northern counterparts to carry guns for protection, and southern white women are more than six times more likely to carry guns for protection than are northern white women. (The article did not detect such drastic regional differences in populations of other races.) Many states have laws that allow for the carrying of concealed weapons, but in recent news in 2009 and 2010, several southern states joined Tennessee in its controversial ruling to remove the distinction between restaurants and bars in permit legislation, thus allowing handgun permit holders to carry guns into restaurants that serve alcohol. Similar laws are in place in Arkansas, Florida, Georgia, Kentucky, Mississippi, and Texas, and eight other (midwestern and western) states.

Such legislation is perhaps reflective of growing southern attitudes that support protecting gun ownership rights. A 2010 Pew Research Center report tracked different regions' attitudes toward protecting gun rights in 2008, 2009, and 2010. The South had the highest rate of support for protecting gun rights all three years. The 2010 survey indicated that 51 percent of southerners believed protecting gun rights to be more important than controlling gun ownership, which only 42 percent supported. Since 2008, southern support for gun control measures steadily declined from 57 percent to 42 percent, and support for protecting gun ownership rights rose from 40 percent to 51 percent. Some may attribute this to a suspected racially charged southern fear of President Barack Obama's passage of measures to ban gun ownership, despite his legislative silence on the subject.

Aside from its protective function, gun ownership in the South also seems to have a symbolic, ritual meaning. The presentation of a series of guns to young southerners often serves as a rite of passage, and the intricate progression in firearm socialization, many times in communal hunting settings, teaches basic safety and gun-use skills and perpetuates the existence of the southern gun culture. This progression often begins with the gift of a BB gun, which is used to develop essential safety skills and to impart basic principles of ballistics. The next stage of firearm socialization involves the receipt of the first "real gun"— the .22 rifle, a small-bore bolt- or pump-action weapon purchased or perhaps handed down from an older relative. Young hunters may also learn basic skills at fall dove hunts, for which they receive or borrow a shotgun, usually a 20-gauge (and later, a 12-gauge, when their upper-body strength allows them to master that weapon's recoil). The last stage of firearm presentation is often a graduation to a deer rifle.

The series of guns given to young hunters is but one reflection of the connection between guns and culture in the South. Communal hunting rituals are joined by recreational target shooting and marksmanship competitions, which reinforce the traditions of firearm socialization. Though not exclusively southern, 4-H and intercollegiate rifle, air rifle, shotgun, and pistol teams are embraced by many southerners and are included in the introduction of many young southerners to the southern gun culture. Firearms socialization is also often imbued with ideas of heritage and bound up in family traditions of gun collecting and inheritance. The gun culture embraced by much of the South is perpetuated by cultural productions like *Garden & Gun* magazine, a southern lifestyle magazine published in Charleston, S.C., since 2007 that calls itself "The Soul of the South" and acknowledges (as of 2010) its own membership in the National Rifle Association. The title of an article in the May–June 2008 issue reflects the perceived importance of southern gun collecting for recreational sport and perhaps even for class identification: "Game Changers: Eight Sporting Clays Guns That Will Help You Shoot Straight and Look Good Doing It (Even When You Miss)." A September 2010 posting on the magazine's Web site announced the upcoming auction of a double-barrel shotgun that once belonged to Teddy Roosevelt.

Many southern gun collectors possess and prominently display ancestral weaponry from "the war" and subsequent conflicts, as well as hunting rifles and shotguns passed down for generations and kept in working order. The preservation and maintenance of these old .44s and .36s suggest that weapons have a totemic significance that transcends the merely decorative and functional. For many rural families in the past, the gun was probably one of the most expensive items they owned and therefore one of the most valuable (next to land) that could be passed on to heirs. The weapons serve as a vital link to ancestors—one of the remaining physical evidences of who they were and of who contemporary southerners are. Old guns somehow connect the southerner to a mythic golden age or, alternately, to a hardscrabble but meaningful existence in the piney woods.

The pronounced cultural interest in weaponry evident in the South may stem from a perceived need for protection from animals and other humans, the enjoyment of hunting and the social constellation surrounding it, and a desire for a link with the past. This significant cultural symbolism has become entangled in a broader national debate over crime and gun control, but the South has not relaxed its grip on its multifaceted gun culture. That culture is not always the violent or "redneck" type of popular perception or of pickup truck decals, but it does reflect an identifying feature of the "southern reality."

FRED HAWLEY
Louisiana State University at Shreveport

MARY AMELIA TAYLOR
University of Mississippi

Pauline G. Brennan et al., *Journal of Quantitative Criminology* (1993); Dickson D. Bruce Jr., *Violence and Culture in the Antebellum South* (1979); Joseph Carroll, "Gun Ownership and Use in America," *Gallup Poll* (November 2005); Richard B. Felson and Paul-Philippe Pare, *Social Forces* (March 2010); Raymond D. Gastil, *Cultural Regions of the United States* (1975); Malcolm Gay, *New York Times* (3 October 2010); Sheldon Hackney, *American Historical Review* (February 1969); F. Frederick Hawley and Steve F. Messner, *Justice Quarterly* (December 1989); Lucas L. Johnson II, *Huffington Post* (21 September 2010); Lee Kennett and James L. Anderson, *The Gun in America: The Origins of a National Dilemma* (1975); Frank Newport, "Polling Matters" (June 2010); Pew Research Center for the People and the Press, "Gun Control Splits America" (March 2010); John Shelton Reed, *One South: An Ethnic Approach to Regional Culture* (1982); Phil West, *Memphis Commercial Appeal* (11 February 2010); Nancy Wong, *Harris Poll* (May 2001), www.harrisinteractive.com; James D. Wright, Peter Rossi, and Kathleen Daly, *Under the Gun: Weapons, Crime, and Violence in America* (1983).

Homicide

Compared to other American regions, the South has experienced relatively high rates of homicide throughout much of its history, and southern propensities to murder have been shaped by a number of historical factors. Early on, white southerners killed to defend racial slavery and then killed to reimpose racial hierarchy after its abolition. At the same time, powerful cultural systems of honor generated pressure to demonstrate masculine prowess within both the white and black communities. Further, heated contests for social respectability among whites in the 19th century caused southerners to kill as they sought to gain status in a hierarchical social order that revolved around the control of black labor in an unstable political climate. After Reconstruction, murder by African American men who were competing for social worth was a response to deprivation of political rights, white violence, Jim Crow racial segregation, and urban poverty.

From its origins as a colony of English planters and indentured servants, Virginia witnessed homicidal conflict between settlers and Indians and substantial social and political divisions related to the status of landless whites and Indian policy on the southern and western frontiers. Colonial Virginia saw a significantly higher murder rate than did colonial New England. In the last decades of the 17th century, murder rates in Virginia declined from 37 per 100,000 adults to 10 per 100,000, while the same period saw a decline from 6 per 100,000 to 1 per 100,000 in New England. By the early 18th century, however, a comprehensive system of racial slavery had arisen across the expanding southern colonies, promoting white solidarity and reducing homicide among whites but deploying chronic lethal violence to discourage and punish African American resistance and rebellion. In the initial years of racial slavery, Africans were murdered at a higher rate than European colonists (approximately 10 to 15 per 100,000 versus 9 per 100,000) as whites used brutal force to impose the prerogatives of racial slavery, but the rate at which southern whites killed blacks declined (to around 4 per 100,000) by the mid-1700s as slavery became more firmly ensconced. Failing to transfer western and central Africa's elevated murder rate to the American colonies, 18th-century slaves forged an African American community that saw low numbers of intraracial homicide. The colonial South experienced a relatively low black-on-black murder rate, as blacks were killed by other blacks only half as often as they were killed by whites. However, murders of whites by slaves rebelling against racial oppression surged in the mid 18th-century, inspiring white fears and more elaborate mechanisms of racial oppression, such as the organization of the white community into the slave patrol. Deepening the focus of southern folkways around the physical defense of personal and familial reputation, immigrants from north Britain carried a warrior culture and fierce fighting techniques to the southern frontier in the 18th century, but Scots-Irish murder rates declined to resemble those of other white Virginians by the end of the century.

The American Revolution destabilized southern society, unleashing social and cultural conflicts that fueled high rates of homicide. The revolutionary southern backcountry experienced a vicious civil war between Patriots and

Tories and extensive murderous depredations between settlers and Indians. Murder rates in the backcountry may have exceeded 200 per 100,000 between the mid-1760s and the end of the War of 1812. After the return of political stability in the 1810s, homicide rates declined precipitously in the Mountain South but remained relatively high in the Plantation South. In the antebellum era, whites increasingly murdered whites in honor-based disputes over status as a hierarchical social order revolving around the ownership of land and slaves squared uneasily with the egalitarian ethos inspired by the Revolution and Jacksonian Democracy. Slaveholding whites sometimes reacted with homicidal violence, including campaigns of vigilante killings, to perceived threats to the peculiar institution from rebellious slaves and the rise of abolitionism in the North. In the early to mid-19th century, the murder rate among whites grew to 6 per 100,000 in Virginia, 13 per 100,000 in Edgefield County, S.C., and 27 per 100,000 in Horry County, S.C.

Secession, the Civil War, and Reconstruction exacerbated political and social tensions across the plantation and mountain regions of the South. Prolonged contention over legal and political legitimacy and the preservation of white supremacy spiraled into elevated rates of intra- and interracial homicide that would plague the South for decades, even with the return of political stability and the implementation of Jim Crow racial segregation in the early 20th century. Mountain counties, which had seen a low incidence of homicide in the antebellum years, saw entrenched guerrilla warfare between Confederate and Union sympathizers during the war and patterns of extensive revenge and property-dispute murders in the years that followed. In the Reconstruction years, Gilmer and Rabun counties in northern Georgia experienced murder rates exceeding 55 per 100,000 adults, while Fentress and Wayne counties in the upper Cumberland Plateau in Kentucky and Tennessee witnessed rates of more than 250 per 100,000. Homicide also surged across the Plantation South, as ex-Confederates murdered thousands of African Americans, white Republicans, and other southern whites, sometimes collectively in paramilitary organizations such as the Ku Klux Klan and sometimes in individual confrontations. In Piedmont Georgia, the murder rate in Reconstruction rose from 10 per 100,000 to 25 per 100,000; in Louisiana, the rural murder rate in the 1870s may have exceeded 90 per 100,000.

The aftermath of Reconstruction established the contours for southern homicide well into the 20th century. Murder rates fell across the South after conservative Democratic "Redeemer" governments consolidated power by the early 1880s, but rose precipitously again in the 1890s as the price of cotton fell, farmers organized, and the Populists competed with the Democrats for white and black votes. As African Americans experienced the disappointing failure of Reconstruction to secure their rights and the subsequent rise of Jim Crow and disfranchisement, black-on-black homicide rates spiraled upward. In the latter decades of the 19th century, blacks migrated to southern cities where they encountered impoverished living conditions, murderous white police forces, and increasing white efforts to segregate public accommodations. Rage at the limited social space available for African American self-definition in the Jim Crow South channeled into elevated rates of black-on-black murder that would persist for decades. Intraracial homicide rates among blacks rose to 20 per 100,000 in rural Louisiana and to 30 per 100,000 in New Orleans by the 1880s.

Vividly remembering Reconstruction as an era in which they had lost control of criminal courts and political offices, many white southerners turned once again to collective murder outside the law amid racial and political conflict shaped by the depressed cotton economy of the 1890s. In a contagion of collective murder that was less overtly political and less systematically organized but even more racial than the collective violence of Reconstruction, southern whites lynched several thousand African Americans between the 1890s and the 1930s. Lynching became a primary means of punishing black resistance and criminality for white southerners skeptical of the efficacy of law and legal processes in the perpetuation of racial order in the New South. Southern urbanization and industrialization at the turn of the 20th century catalyzed anxieties over racial mixing and in some cases evoked large-scale spectacle lynchings, but eventually a southern middle class coalesced against mob violence. Embarrassed by the increasing spotlight African American activists and a nationalizing culture shone upon lynching and fearing the loss of investment that might promote economic growth and prosperity in the region, middle-class white southerners in the early 20th century pressed instead for "legal lynchings," expedited trials, and executions that merged legal forms with the popular clamor for rough justice. As the frequency of lynchings in the South plummeted in the middle decades of the 20th century, the practice went underground as lynchers no longer acted in large public mobs but instead in small, secretive groups that murdered in an expression of racial intimidation that by the late 20th century was more often called a "hate crime" than a "lynching."

Lynching was an aspect of a pattern of homicide that made the South the most violent region in the country (exceeding the Southwest, which had long contended for the label) by the 1920s and 1930s, when homicide rates ranged from 15 to 25 per 100,000 in most border states and from 25 to 40 per 100,000 in the Lower South. Subsequent transformations of the South, including urbanization and the civil rights movement, have reconfigured southern social circumstances but have not altered the South's status as the nation's most homicidal region. In 2007, Louisiana, Maryland, and Alabama led all states with murder rates of 14.2, 9.8, and 8.9 per 100,000, respectively.

MICHAEL J. PFEIFER
John Jay College of Criminal Justice
City University of New York

Edward L. Ayers, *Vengeance and Justice: Crime and Punishment in the Nineteenth-Century American South* (1984); Sheldon Hackney, *American Historical Review* (February 1969); Michael J. Pfeifer, *Rough Justice: Lynching and American Society, 1874–1947* (2004), *The Roots of Rough Justice: Origins of American Lynching* (2011); Randolph Roth, *American Homicide* (2009); Gilles Vandal, *Rethinking Southern Violence: Homicides in Post–Civil War Louisiana, 1866–1884* (2000); Bertram Wyatt-Brown, *Southern Honor: Ethics and Behavior in the Old South* (1982).

Honor

Southerners of the antebellum era made it clear that they subscribed to an ethic of honor, but they never specified exactly what honor meant. In large part, this was because the meaning of honor depended on its immediate context, on who claimed and who acknowledged it. In fact, honor might be defined as a system of beliefs in which a person has exactly as much worth as others confer upon him. Antebellum northerners and most 21st-century Americans have some difficulty understanding the idea of honor, for it runs contrary to what has come to be a national article of faith: each person, regardless of race, class, sex, or religion, possesses equal intrinsic worth—regardless of what others think of him. Insult has little meaning to people who share such a faith, but if one takes honor seriously, insult from a respected person can cut to the quick. Accordingly, much of the violence in the South from the 18th century to the present appears to have been sparked by insult, by challenges to honor. Southerners believed a man had to guard his reputation and his honor, by good manners and, if necessary, by violence. Insult literally could not be tolerated.

Women, although traditionally venerated in the South, could have no honor—only virtue. The ultimate protection of honor lay in physical courage, an attribute not considered to be within a woman's sphere. White men also refused to concede that black men could possess honor, although black southerners recognized honor among one another. Further, the honor of wealthy white men could not be damaged by men of lesser rank. Honor came into play only among equals. Contrary to stereotype, though, honor was not restricted to the southern aristocracy. Men of every class felt themselves to be honorable and could not tolerate affront and still enjoy the respect of their peers. The elite alone dueled, of course, but the duel was only the most refined manifestation of honorable conflict, the tip of the iceberg. Fighting, shooting, stabbing, feuding, and shotgun weddings were considered legitimate and inevitable results of honor confronting honor.

An emphasis on honor, concurrently with high homicide rates, prevailed in the 19th-century South, although the cult of honor became less formalized (and probably more dangerous in the process) after the Civil War. Duels faded away; shooting scrapes became more common. The concept of honor also spanned the subregions of the South, lowland and upland, slaveholding and nonslaveholding. It even persisted in southern cities, where volatile rural folkways combined with urban poverty and crowding to make southern cities peculiarly dangerous places to live.

The South was not alone in this culture of honor. In different variations, it has flourished for centuries in Mediterranean cultures such as those of Sicily and Greece. Cultures of honor also flourished among the aristocracy of 17th-century England and among the Scots-Irish, both of whom exerted decisive influences on southern culture in its formative states. The idea of honor did not prosper among the Puritans, Quakers, or Congregationalists and seems to be at odds with the impersonal relations of a predominantly commercial society. Honor never sank deep roots in the North.

The South, on the other hand, from its very beginnings seemed designed to nurture honor. Slavery and the society it spawned provided the conditions in which the notion of honor could flourish. Honor thrives in a rural society of face-to-face contact, of a limited number of relationships, of one system of values. Honor depends upon a hierarchical society, where one is defined by who is above or below him. Honor grows well in a society where the rationalizing power of the state is weak; an adherence to honor makes the state, at best, irrelevant in settling personal disputes.

Honor found itself increasingly on the defensive in the 19th century, not only from the North and England, but also from within the South. Honor, necessarily a secular system of values, clashed with the ideals of Christian virtue. Evangelical southerners deplored and denounced the violence and pride honor condoned. In their eyes, people who let their actions be dictated by honor allowed themselves to become mere slaves of public opinion. The vast majority of southerners, of course, whatever their religious inclination, killed or assaulted no one, and even those who did resort to violence did so only once or twice in a lifetime—still enough to send many more southerners than northerners to jail and penitentiary for violent crimes, although southerners were notorious for not prosecuting crimes of violence.

Black southerners, once liberated from slavery, also adapted to southern codes of honor. White observers, particularly those from the North, were appalled that blacks fought and killed each other over the same apparently trivial provocations as white southerners. Southerners of both races, consciously or not, held to their notions of honor far into the 20th century, even in northern cities. Those who find that high homicide rates today correlate with southern culture seem to be measuring the fallout of a culture of honor. Those who find a correlation with low literacy rates or poverty are describing the characteristics of a place in which honor can best survive in the present.

EDWARD L. AYERS
University of Richmond

Edward L. Ayers, *Vengeance and Justice: Crime and Punishment in the Nineteenth-Century American South* (1983); Peter Berger, Brigitte Berger, and Hansfried Kellner, *The Homeless Mind: Modernization and Consciousness* (1973); Pierre Bourdieu, in *Honor and Shame: The Values of Mediterranean Society*, ed. J. G. Peristiany (1965); Kenneth S. Greenberg, *Honor and Slavery: Lies, Duals, Noses, Masks, Dressing as a Woman, Gifts, Strangers, Humanitarianism, Death, Slave Rebellions, the Proslavery Argument, Baseball, Hunting, and Gambling in the Old South* (1996); Bertram Wyatt-Brown, *Southern Honor: Ethics and Behavior in the Old South* (1982), *The Shaping of Southern Culture: Honor, Grace, and War, 1760s–1880s* (2000).

Hunting

During the South's colonial and antebellum periods, the pursuit of wildlife provided settlers with both a diversion from their ordinary work routines and a supplement to their sometimes meager stocks of food. Settlers also hunted to control the numbers of larger mammals in their vicinity, for their crops were vulnerable to grazing by deer and by flocks of birds, while their free-roaming livestock fell prey to wolves.

During this period, some wealthy planters sought to emulate the privileges and refinements of European aristocrats. In some areas, hunting certain wild game became identified with the prerogatives of power and status; as such, it emerged as an important social activity for influential, wealthy individuals. The elite hunting narratives of the antebellum years offer detailed descriptions of the hunt, the chase, and the shoot. Although claiming to be factual, these narratives are actually standardized accounts whose recurrent themes provide in-

Hunter at Sea Island Hunting Lodge with his day's kill. Sea Island, Glynn County, Ga.,
1933 or 1934. (Courtesy of Georgia Archives, Vanishing Georgia Collection)

sights into the ideology of affluent planters and the ways in which they sought
to distinguish themselves from other social classes.

Many planters believed that hunting enabled them to understand nature and
man's place in the world. Southern hunters loved nature for its supposed order
and stability, which their own organized social life (based in a hierarchical arrangement of people and contingent upon the judicial application of force)
could only approximate. For these planters, hunting was a socially sanctioned
expression of power; they saw its violence as a requirement for participating

in the natural world and appreciating its indestructible order. This perspective allowed planters to differentiate their modes of hunting from others on the basis of presumed motive and purpose. If most whites and blacks in the South hunted out of necessity, planters did so for sport and for amusement. While other classes pursued wild animals for meat and tangible trophies, planters saw the process itself as the most important part of the chase. For them, the end was both unimportant and inconsequential. Hunting conventions (sportsmanship) became prerequisites for membership in polite society, and they provided its participants the opportunity to learn the important lessons of self-discipline and control. Plantation-style hunting, of course, was not for everyone. Outside the restricted circles of gentility, most men hunted wildlife for food and for profit. The majority of these hunters subsisted on the land and sold skins and game meat whenever they found buyers.

After the Civil War, the processes of urbanization and industrialization gradually concentrated many southerners in towns and cities. Leisure and wealth for growing numbers of these urban dwellers made a return to nature and the land increasingly attractive. This "escape" to nature became possible for those who owned or leased large tracts of land; outside of these tracts, however, city hunters came into increasing conflict with rural landowners, market hunters, and game dealers over the declining stocks of wild game. State trespass laws and federal game regulations became a solution to these conflicts; to legislators, they seemed the most democratic way to handle access to wildlife for those aspiring to hunt. By 1910 most southern states had joined the rest of the nation in enacting trespass and game laws and providing cadres of officers to enforce them. With these legal structures in place, market hunting and the sale of wild animals became illegal. State legislatures, in turn, gave wildlife agencies the power to monitor the populations of species now defined by law as "game" and to determine the ways and means by which these species became legal to hunt. Hence, as a direct result of legal processes initiated by city dwellers, states across the South restricted the variety of hunted species and formalized many hunting norms. These statutes and regulations still provide the ground rules and boundaries determining what, where, when, and how species are hunted. Although many southern hunters continue to hunt for food, most hunting in the South is now for sport and recreation.

Most of the current initiatives affecting field sports have come not from the South's rural populations but from organized groups in the cities; these groups include antihunting leagues and such hunting and conservation organizations as Ducks Unlimited, the National Turkey Federation, and the National Wildlife Federation. Each of these organizations, as well as their many counterparts, publishes its own journal, solicits contributions, and maintains lobbies that seek to influence legislation favorable to their causes. From these journals, contemporary hunters glean the latest tips, techniques, and technologies for tracking their game; find out about what to wear while pursuing it; learn about the big ones that escaped; and read about current fads in men's games.

Modernizing developments have influenced some types of hunting more than others. Particular varieties of dogs/hounds are bred, trained, and certified for specific types of hunters. A number of national organizations focus on these particular breeds, keep breeding records, and sponsor annual series of field trials and bench shows to authenticate their products. The trading, purchase, and breeding of hounds and dogs is a big business in many rural areas of the South, particularly in those that host the various field trials.

The influences of technology and the changing patterns of landownership are also apparent in the organization of hunt clubs. Hunt clubs began in colonial days when neighbors joined together for game drives. At that time, their organization was informal, often spontaneous, and involved no fees or formal membership. Later, when the large estates were divided or sold, individuals joined together to lease land for game and to alleviate the costs of maintaining hunting dogs throughout the year. Formal hunt clubs began about 1900. These clubs had a paid and limited membership and set specific times for hunting. In the latter decades of the 20th century, agribusiness—with its mechanized operations on large tracts of land—dramatically reduced game habitat on the better lands; most of the marginal lands, which had previously been occupied and tilled by tenants, reverted to pine plantations and scrub. With this secondary growth, deer returned to these marginal lands; so too did hunt clubs, now frequently headquartered in refurbished tenant shacks.

Today, precision firearms have largely replaced the muskets of former times (although many purists still prefer to stalk their deer with muzzle loaders or bows and arrows). Four-wheel-drive vehicles have superseded horses and wagons, dirt roads the foot trails, and CB radios and loudspeakers the hunter's horn. Yet the informal, intimate rituals between hunting buddies and the traditions of time and place continue to make the hunt club a seasonal feature of southern life.

The distinctiveness of southern hunting stems from a peculiar combination of traits found in the region. The myth of the plantation lifestyle continues to inform the traditions of those who can afford to live the image of this lifestyle and to influence others. Its reality persists in the hunting plantations for quail and deer (many of which were purchased and maintained by northern wealth in the late 19th and early 20th centuries) and in the colorful pageantries of the exclusive hunt clubs located throughout the South. Extensive landownership, wealth, power, and leisure sustain these plantations and clubs, luring some to join and many others to observe their seasonal rituals. Still others read about them or participate in regional or national field trials for fox, quail, and coon — species associated with earlier plantation life.

Most hunting in the rural South lacks the pretentiousness of the plantation tradition; nonetheless, it continues to reflect regional traditions of gender, racial, and socioeconomic stratification. More than two-thirds of southern hunters come from small towns or live in rural areas. Most are whites and Indians. Among these groups, youngsters typically learn to hunt from their fathers or close relatives. Guns are often heirlooms passed between generations. African Americans are proportionately underrepresented in the ranks of southern hunters; in contrast to the other cultural groups, they learn to hunt later in life and tend to learn from peers rather than from their fathers. Most southern hunters come from the working classes and are generally under 40 years of age. Although the expressed motivation for hunting varies, most hunters say that they hunt for sport rather than for food; nonetheless, they eat most of the game they take.

Hunting is still very much a masculine domain. Historically, most women who hunt have come from the far ends of the economic spectrum; this pattern seems to be shifting, however, as more southern women in the middle economic class take up the sport. Yet, hunting remains an activity dominated by men, and it is to them that the cleaning, cooking, and serving of game meat usually falls.

Socialization as a hunter begins at an early age, guided by fathers or an intimate circle of friends. In these close groups, young boys learn lessons about masculinity and their identity within a given community, together with skills useful in their transitions to manhood. A variety of coming of age rituals (aptly described by William Faulkner in *Go Down, Moses*) celebrate their maturation and accomplishments. Most boys' initial kills are small game such as squirrels and rabbits, which make relatively easy targets. Youngsters generally pursue a variety of mammals and birds as their time allows, but as they mature, they tend to specialize in one or a few species, depending upon their associations with other men, their jobs, and the costs of maintaining trained dogs.

Men who hunt together are also influential in other areas of community social and political life. Increasingly, however, family and work commitments disrupt these male hunting fraternities. Although jobs outside of the local community may temporarily dislodge these networks, many men return home religiously for the fall hunting season.

The types of game that southern hunters pursue reflect stratification along socioeconomic and racial lines. Ownership of trained dogs and the availability of extensive tracts of land are prerequisites for game that many count as the most "prestigious," including quail, deer, fox, and turkey. Access to these species remains difficult for many, although they may be hunted on public lands. Dove shoots, which usually open the fall hunting season, are generally open to most people because the shoot requires guns positioned in as many places as possible around a recently harvested field to keep the birds flying. (In many northern states, doves and quail are classified as songbirds and thus not hunted.) Many African Americans and working-class whites hunt squirrels, rabbits, raccoons, and possums, species normally avoided by other, more specialized sportsmen.

As a region, the South still retains an edge over other areas in the number of households that include a hunter. In 1959 Gallup Polls revealed that slightly over half of southern white households contained a hunter, compared to one-third for the rest of the nation. Fifty years later, these percentages have dropped dramatically. A cumulative tabulation of survey data from 1972 to 2006, compiled by the University of Chicago's National Opinion Research Survey, showed that the number of southern households with hunters now barely edges above 25 percent. This still suggests that one of every four households in the South includes a hunter—a figure that continues to lead most other regions of the country.

Every five years, the U.S. Fish and Wildlife Service publishes a national survey of wildlife-associated outdoor recreation. Its 2005 surveys in North Carolina estimated that 277,000 hunters spent 4.6 million days afield. That year, these hunters reportedly spent $512 million on their pursuits within the state, a sum that contributed to 8,800 jobs. The majority of these sportsmen (8 out of 10) say that a political candidate's position on hunting-related environmental issues is an important factor in determining for whom they cast their votes. Sportsmen and women have powerful voices in legislation through the Congressional Sportsmen's Foundation and the National Assembly of Sportsmen's Caucuses.

STUART A. MARKS
Durham, North Carolina

Dickson D. Bruce Jr., *Violence and Culture in the Antebellum South* (1979); Hennig Cohen and William B. Dillingham, eds., *Humor of the Old Southwest* (2nd ed., 1975); William Elliot, *Carolina Sports by Land and Water* (1859); William Faulkner, *Go Down, Moses* (1942); H. Gibson, "Deer Hunting Clubs in Concordia Parish: The Role of Male Sodalities in the Maintenance of Social Values" (M.A. thesis, Louisiana State University, 1976); C. Gondes, ed., *Hunting in the Old South* (1967); Clifton Paisley,

From Cotton to Quail: An Agricultural Chronicle of Leon County, Florida, 1860–1967 (1968); Robert Ruark, *The Old Man and the Boy* (1957); Louis D. Rubin Jr., *William Elliot Shoots a Bear: Essays on the Southern Literary Imagination* (1976); Francis Utley, Lynn Bloom, and Arthur F. Kinney, eds., *Bear, Man, and God: Seven Approaches to William Faulkner's "The Bear"* (1964).

Labor Violence

The United States' emergence as a major industrial power in the late 19th century, and as a political and economic superpower after World War II, has been marked by a striking paradox. America is usually regarded as a stable democracy not usually prone to social upheaval and conflict, yet arguably it has experienced more intense and bloody labor-related violence than any other industrial society in the world. No section of the country has been immune from such conflict, and many of the most protracted and violent confrontations occurred outside the South. Nevertheless, the region's antebellum history left an enduring legacy: planters and aspiring industrialists accustomed to the authoritarian cast of labor relations under slavery were reluctant to concede authority to workers' representatives, and the region showed an abiding hostility to organized labor.

The South's defeat in the Civil War meant the collapse of the region's labor system, but in the early years of Reconstruction former masters seemed determined to retain as much of their authority as possible. Emancipation detonated a series of far-flung struggles over land and labor, leading eventually to a surge in violence that would not abate until propertied whites had been restored to power across the South. A substantial proportion of the paramilitary violence that we associate with this period—led by organizations like the White Leagues or the Ku Klux Klan—was aimed at restoring discipline and submission among former slaves, whose expectations about the meaning of freedom in the new order clashed with employers' aims to control free labor.

The contest between planters and freed people was intensified by grass-roots mobilization of ex-slaves through the Union Leagues, local clubs set up by the Republican Party to rally the black vote. By 1867 the leagues and other secret societies had evolved beyond their vote-gathering role, often serving the same functions as trade unions. Through them, black workers launched strikes for better wages and conditions and engaged in reprisals against planters who continued to resort to physical abuse against laborers. Although it is difficult to generalize about the composition and motives of white paramilitaries, in many places the Klan was directed by substantial planters and engaged primarily in terrorizing the agrarian workforce into submission.

This mostly localized violence had evolved by the early 1870s into broad state-to-state campaigns aimed at restoring white supremacy and placing the state machinery back in the hands of propertied white southerners. By 1877 these had succeeded across the South, and planters noted with satisfaction a marked change in the disposition of plantation laborers. The political reversal sharply curtailed militancy among former slaves, and the conservative governments that now assumed power made no attempt to conceal their support for landed elites against the claims of a mostly black agricultural workforce.

While on the whole, the period immediately following this restoration was marked by quiescence and submission, the South was buffeted by new social and economic pressures, and by the mid-1880s a new round of confrontations was developing. A steep decline in cotton prices aggravated a more general crisis in southern agriculture, and many who made their living off the land— especially black and white sharecroppers and farm laborers—were being driven to desperate measures.

Small-scale violence everywhere attended the rise of the Populist movement, as white conservatives responded with deep concern over the challenge to the Democratic Party's monopoly on political power. Where the Populists' ascent was marked by vigorous grass-roots activism, authorities mobilized vigorously to suppress it. The itinerant agitator Hiram Hover had some early success in attempts to organize agricultural workers in the Carolinas and Georgia in the mid-1880s, but officials responded by raising the specter of "negro insurrection," rounding up and interrogating his supporters and, eventually, shooting and seriously wounding Hover himself. An unsuccessful regional strike by cotton pickers in 1891 met its most lethal opposition in the Arkansas Delta, where planter-led vigilantes rounded up 15 African American strikers, lynching nine of them. The closing decades of the 19th century saw a dramatic rise in lynching across the South, much of it directed against black laborers and often arising out of labor disputes.

Simultaneously with growing unrest on the land, the industrial transformation of rural communities intensified labor conflict, moving it into new urban settings. The new industry, funded by northern capital, aimed at exploiting the region's vast natural resources, and alongside textile mill villages springing up in the cotton-supplied Piedmont there appeared coal and iron mines, timber camps, and—in the new century—oil derricks. Much of the new industrial workforce was confined in company-run camps and towns, where it were subject to close surveillance and the authority of employer-run police forces.

In these harsh conditions, labor organizers sometimes found an eager constituency. Across the South, workers mobilized in third-party movements and in the Knights of Labor, which began to win a substantial following in the pockets throughout the region. Although the Knights formally eschewed strikes, local assemblies became the vehicles for militant industrial action and met with organized opposition from employers and state and local authorities. Sugar workers in southern Louisiana affiliated with the Knights in 1886 and a year later presented a list of demands to the Louisiana Sugar Planters Association. When planters rejected these, a strike was scheduled to commence at the peak of the grinding season in November, and in response the governor dispatched militiamen to the district, evicting strikers from the plantations and setting the scene for armed confrontation. Enraged by rumors that black strikers were set to burn the town of Thibodaux, white militiamen went on the offensive in July, murdering between dozens and perhaps hundreds of strikers in an incident that became known as the Thibodaux Massacre.

The pattern of confrontation was repeated elsewhere. The Knights were centrally involved in the Great Southwest Railroad Strike of 1886, with violence flaring at Fort Worth, Tex., and at points along the Louisville-Nashville line. Federal troops were dispatched to Tennessee in 1891 and 1892, where a rolling series of strikes against the convict lease system culminated in a confrontation involving upward of a thousand armed miners and, in one case, a successful attempt to spring convicts from the camp at Briceville. The coal and iron industries in northern Alabama proved a fertile ground for third-party agitation and would become the site of chronic labor conflict. In 1894 Gov. Thomas Jones dispatched state guards to the Birmingham district to suppress an interracial miners' strike in which four people—including three black strikebreakers—were killed. Like Tennessee, Alabama would also see dramatic action around the employers' use of convict labor, including several rebellions led by convicts themselves. At least one of these ended tragically, with 36 convicts being burned to death when they attempted to escape by setting fire to a company stockade.

Early in the new century a racially mixed workforce grew up around the lumber and sawmill towns in the forests of Mississippi, Louisiana, and east Texas, and by 1910 the tightly controlled timber camps were seething with dissatisfaction. The International Workers of the World–affiliated Brotherhood of Timber Workers launched a series of strikes in 1911 and 1912, and a low-level "timber war" culminated in July 1912 in a lethal confrontation at Grabow, La., where four men were killed and upward of 50 wounded in a shootout between strikers and company guards. Pitched battles took place that summer in the Appalachian coalfields, where members of the United Mine Workers (UMW) came out on top in a series of early confrontations with armed Baldwin-Felts guards, only to find themselves faced with a heavy militia presence and the imposition of military courts.

Southern labor relations were transformed by the First World War, as the federal government intervened to maintain labor peace and local employers were compelled to improve conditions to stem outmigration. But the end of the war saw a wave of strikes as workers attempted to make up for the austerity of the war years. In the South, the highly charged industrial situation was compounded by hysteria over radicalization and renewed black militancy. Attempts at interracial collaboration in Bogalusa, La., were suppressed with violence. In Birmingham, employers organized vigilantes to stifle organization of district steel mills, contributing to the revival of the Ku Klux Klan. Unrest in the coal mines was barely contained until it exploded in a six-month strike in 1920–21. More than 500 men were discharged for union sympathies, and tensions erupted in a series of large-scale skirmishes pitching "striking miners with pump guns, shotguns, pistols, and dynamite" against heavily armed company guards and state militiamen. Union meetings were outlawed under martial law, and the military seemed to single out black strikers for especially harsh treatment. In January members of the Alabama guard were indicted for lynching a mine union leader in Walker County. Such violence helped deliver a crippling blow to the UMW.

Suppression of the postwar strike wave and the economic recovery of the early 1920s ushered in an extended period of labor peace, which began to unravel dramatically in the aftermath of the 1929 Wall Street crash. In May 1931 a protracted battle between company guard and armed miners at Evarts, Ky., inaugurated a "coal war" that would roil Harlan and Bell counties for several years. Over a thousand shots were fired in the early skirmish, leaving at least four dead, and a dozen more would lose their lives by the end of 1935, leading state investigators to conclude that mine operators in collusion with state officials had imposed a "reign of terror" on "Bloody Harlan."

Elsewhere in the South, workers were not slow to take advantage of new openings for union organization made possible under Section 7(a) of the National Recovery Act. An early indication of what southern textile workers were up against was apparent in a 1929 strike at the Loray Mill, in Gastonia, N.C. There a series of skirmishes between the local sheriff and the communist-led strikers escalated into serious violence, culminating in an ambush on strikers in which union activist and mother-of-five Ella Mae Wiggins was killed. Gastonia went down to defeat, but in the summer of 1934 southern cotton mill operatives launched a general strike. By July some 20,000 workers had walked off the job in Alabama, and the strike spread across the region. In Decatur, union supporters were beaten and at least one organizer was shot. Two thousand strikers were interred and at least four people died in strike-related violence in Georgia. But the most serious violence took place in September at Honea Path, S.C., where deputies shot into a picket line, killing seven and wounding 20 more. The strike's defeat marked the last large-scale effort to organize the mills.

The South shared in the economic expansion brought on by World War II, and increased demand for labor granted women and African Americans access to industrial work from which they had long been excluded. White workers registered their opposition to these changes, sometimes through strike action: in the Mobile shipyards, which employed more than 40,000 workers at the height of war production, white workers staged a bloody race riot in May 1943 after their employer agreed to comply with federal regulations and promote 12 black workers into skilled positions. In Memphis and elsewhere, similar tensions marked the entry of black workers into industrial employment.

The postwar period saw another wave of strikes across the United States, but in the South the weak hold of industrial unionism and the combative disposition of the region's employers made organization difficult. Anticommunism was critical to containing postwar militancy, and in the South, where hostility to left-wing ideas merged with mounting racial hysteria, conservative Democrats and local employers joined forces to demonize the Congress of Industrial Organizations and thwart attempts to bring industrial unionism to the region. The association of labor radicalism with demands for racial equality became especially potent after the rise of the modern civil rights movement and, in a region where organized labor was already weakened by disadvantages, growing racial all-white regional unions. An upturn in black worker's militancy, evident at Memphis in 1968 and in the Charleston hospital workers' strike a year later, found almost no resonance among white workers in the region. The combination of enduring racial division and intermittent violence left southern labor in a weakened state as the American economy was opened up to intense global competition at the end of the 20th century.

BRIAN KELLY
Queen's University Belfast

Bruce E. Baker, *Labor History* (August 1999); James E. Fickle, *Louisiana History* (Autumn 1999); Michael W. Fitzgerald, *The Union League Movement in the Deep South: Politics and Agricultural Change during Reconstruction* (1989); Covington Hall, in *Labor Struggles in the Deep South and Other Writings*, ed. David R. Roediger (1999); Michael Honey, *Southern Labor and Black Civil Rights: Organizing Memphis Workers* (1993); Brian Kelly, *Race, Class, and Power in the Alabama Coalfields, 1908–*

1921 (2001); Melton McLaurin, *The Knights of Labor in the South* (1978); Daniel L. Letwin, *The Challenge of Interracial Unionism: Alabama Coal Miners, 1878–1921* (1998); Stephen H. Norwood, *Journal of Southern History* (August 1997); John C. Rodrigue, *Reconstruction in the Cane Fields: From Slavery to Free Labor in Louisiana's Sugar Parishes, 1862–1880* (2001); Karin A. Shapiro, *A New South Rebellion: The Battle against Convict Labor in the Tennessee Coalfields, 1871–1896* (1998); Phillip Taft and Philip Ross, in *The History of Violence in America: A Report to the National Commission on the Causes and Prevention of Violence*, ed. Hugh Davis Graham and Ted Robert Gurr (1969).

Literature, Violence in

Figurative and physical violence has shaped the form and content of literature emerging out of the American South since 16th-century chroniclers Garcilaso de la Vega and Alvar Nuñez Cabeza de Vaca recorded the bloody progress and wreckage of Spanish expeditions led by Hernando de Soto and Pánfilo de Narváez through Florida and the Southeast. Central to those earliest European accounts were the pitched battles between Spanish conquistadors and the indigenous corn cultivators and mound builders whose resistance to invasion and repudiation of conquistador declarations of superiority were recorded at length by chroniclers themselves hesitant at times about their own allegiances and the emerging racial categorizations of European selves and Indian others. Remote in time and place from literary efforts of later British seaboard colonies, those early chronicles nonetheless foreshadowed the centrality of racialization and racial categorization in southern literature, the violence required in drawing racial lines under slavery and segregation, and above all the heated dialogue/debate forged in the crucible of race that defined both white and black literary productions for three centuries to come.

Captivity narratives and travel accounts in British America made similar equations between violent early encounters and emerging identities of "white" settler and "red" Indian. John Smith's *A Generall Historie of Virginia, New England, and the Summer Isles* (1624), the most famous of Smith's eight books, featured the tale that helped to shape Virginia's mythology of origins — Smith's "rescue" by Matoaka, or Pocahontas, from execution by her father, the Powhatan Indian chief Wahunsunacock. Narratives to follow, like Robert Beverley's *The History and Present State of Virginia* (1704) and Thomas Jefferson's *Notes on the State of Virginia*, completed in 1784 and published in 1785 for a French audience, also linked the violence of encounter and war to emerging identities of "Indians" and "Virginians," defined, respectively, by categorizations of "red" decline and "white" progress. Both of these texts contributed to a growing discourse of racial categorizations in the region designating whiteness as the norm and darkness as alterity, but Jefferson's *Notes on the State of Virginia* would prove to be particularly important for anticipating both antislavery denunciations of the peculiar institution's inherent violence and proslavery rejoinders of silence, denial, and nonrecognition. In one of the book's most famous passages, Jefferson agonized over the corrupting power of slavery and its potential for violence: "The whole commerce between master and slave is a perpetual exercise of the most boisterous passions, the most unremitting despotism on the one part, and degrading submission on the other." At the same time, though, Jefferson resisted assertions of black equality, mused on the possibilities of white superiority, and resolutely refused to recognize the literary productions of Phillis Wheatley or Ignatius Sancho, among the earliest African American writers, as worthy of acknowledgment or affirmation.

That denial in turn anticipated the literary strategies of slavery's defenders, who answered early abolitionist charges of abuse, violence, and oppression with idyllic, pastoral portraits of plantation life unifying white and black families under the benevolent paternalism of slavery. John Pendleton Kennedy's *Swallow Barn* (1832) and Caroline Howard Gilman's *Recollections of a Southern Matron* (1837) set the pattern for a century of white plantation novels to come by portraying their slave owners as benevolent caretakers of black charges, who in turn professed their devotion to white masters. If any violence could be detected at all in these early plantation novels, it was in narrative corners and shadows, in marginal characters, like a single, malcontent slave in *Swallow Barn*, represented as an anomaly rather than as a symptom of potential rebellion. By the 1850s, such characters would more often than not be portrayed as frauds, abolitionist agitators masquerading as runaway slaves and seeking to foment rebellion on peaceful plantations, as in Caroline Lee Hentz's *The Planter's Northern Bride* (1854), one of a long line of "anti-Tom" novels responding to Harriet Beecher Stowe's stunning condemnation of slavery and its brutalities in *Uncle Tom's Cabin* (1852). Continuing in the 20th century with Thomas Nelson Page's *Red Rock* and Thomas Dixon's rabidly racist novels *The Leopard's Spots* (1902) and *The Clansman* (1905) and culminating with the 1936 publication of Margaret Mitchell's *Gone with the Wind*, plantation novels and stories stubbornly adhered to the proslavery argument and ultimately signaled the refusal to recognize and affirm charges of atrocities by slave narrative writers or even their very subjectivity, refusals that were paralleled and reinforced in the political and legal sphere by the tightening of slave code restrictions on assembly and education, self-censorship in newspapers, and confiscation of abolitionist publications.

Plantation pastorals, in short, constructed a façade of denial and silence regarding the violence required in the making and perpetuation of slavery, largely in response to abolitionist publications and slave narratives rolling off northern presses in mounting numbers, the latter eventually totaling 6,000 in extant form. Slave narratives recounting the brutalities of slavery were among the best sellers of the antebellum period and made celebrities of many of their authors, chief among them William Grimes, Charles Ball, Moses Roper, James Williams, William Wells Brown, and Josiah Henson. The most famous of these writers was Frederick Douglass, whose 1845 narrative highlighted incidents of brutal beatings and his own achievement of self-definition after defeating a slave breaker in single combat. Pitting his own will against the physical and institutional violence of slavery in that incident, he made the famous declaration: "You have seen how a man was made a slave; now you will see how a slave was made a man." It was a declaration — and a call to resist the violence of slavery with violence — that was anticipated by David Walker's 1829 call for armed resistance to slavery in *Appeal to the Coloured Citizens of the World*. Douglass's own call for resistance underscored the primary imperative of exposing violence at the heart of slavery and in the making of oppositional black identity. The narrative strategies to which Douglass and other slave narrators resorted — antipastoral and gothic scenes of confrontation, subjugation, and revelation — would be utilized as well by slave narratives to come, such as Harriet Jacobs's 1861 *Incidents in the Life of a Slave Girl*, and by African American fiction responding to the slave controversy: William Wells Brown's 1853 novel *Clotel*, Martin Delany's *Blake; or, The Huts of America* (1859), Frances Ellen Watkins Harper's *Iola Leroy* (1892), Booker T. Washington's *Up from Slavery* (1900), and Pauline Hopkins's *Contending Forces* (1900).

Locked in combat over the issue of slavery, plantation novels and slave narratives served as "dark twins" of one another, refracted reflections dependent on and contesting each other's representations of slavery, the violence it required, and its accompanying racial categorizations. On the smallest scale that struggle was captured in the confrontation between Frederick Douglass and the slave breaker Covey and the sexually charged contest between Harriet Jacobs's besieged slave girl and her slave owner, and on the largest it suggested something of the master-bondsman struggle for self-affirmation and recognition envisioned as the engine of history in Hegel's *Phenomenology of Spirit* (1807), itself partly a product of Hegel's close engagement with the 12-year slave rebellion that ended with the establishment of the republic of Haiti in 1804.

In the slavery controversy, the struggle over representation took the form of pastorals of denial and nonrecognition and of antipastorals of exposure and challenge. After Emancipation and Reconstruction, in response to the rise of lynchings, race riots, and white terrorism, the struggle took on a new set of competing narratives pondering and constructing changing representations of race and racial categorizations in the absence of slavery. To chart those changes and their accompanying violence, free-born African American writers, such as Charles W. Chesnutt and Sutton E. Griggs, and a few white writers, including Mark Twain and George W. Cable, resorted to narratives of estrangement, alienation, and denunciation, among them Chesnutt's *The Conjure Woman* (1899) and *The Marrow of Tradition* (1901); Griggs's *Imperium in Imperio* (1899) and *The Hindered Hand; or, The Reign of the Repressionist* (1905); Twain's *Adventures of Huckleberry Finn* (1885) and *Pudd'nhead Wilson* (1894); and Cable's *The Grandissimes* (1880). For these writers the night-ridings, burnings, and lynchings that seemed to define the postwar South imbued the very landscape with hostility and danger, and the novels and short stories they published featured scenarios of dehumanization, humiliation, and sudden death.

Not a few of them, like Chesnutt, Suggs, and James Weldon Johnson, would conclude that to remain in the region constituted a death sentence for anyone black, and hence those initial narratives of estrangement gave rise to the genre that critic Farah Jasmine Griffin has defined as the migration narrative, reflecting and constructing strategies of flight and survival in the huge 20th-century demographic shift of African Americans from the rural South to the urban North that became known as the Great Migration. Providing impetus for those stories of flights north, recounted in genres ranging from blues songs to James Weldon Johnson's anonymously published *Autobiography of an Ex-Coloured Man* (1912) and Jean Toomer's *Cane* (1923), was the sharp rise in racial terrorism, economic vandalism, and above all lynching that had become synonymous with the region by the first two decades of the 20th century. In blues songs and in widely hailed narratives and poems by Harlem Renaissance writers like Toomer and Langston Hughes, lynching was treated as an ever-looming danger and as a synecdoche for southern white hegemony and its supporting institutions of slavery, segregation, and officially designated categories of race. In the hands of Richard Wright, who made the migration narrative his own with the publications of *Uncle Tom's Children* (1938), *Native Son* (1940), *Twelve Million Black Voices* (1941), and *Black Boy* (1945), fears of lynching and whiteness merged with suffocating force in the dreams and imaginations of his young protagonists and drove them headlong into flight, reciprocal violence, and complete isolation. For him and for his protagonists, the violence of whiteness ultimately meant a repudiation of all things southern and an existential claiming of black identity apart from all ties and entanglements.

Poems, fiction, and plays of the Harlem Renaissance, in short, produced representations of region, history, and memory at sharp odds with plantation fictions evoking the slave past as harmonious and the era of Emancipation and Reconstruction as disruptive, misguided, and conflict-ridden. In those critiques of the region and its past, early 20th-century black writers found curious allies in white women writers in particular, including Ellen Glasgow, Elizabeth Madox Roberts, Evelyn Scott, and Frances Newman, who took issue with the nostalgia of plantation fiction for lost certainties of racial, gender, and class hierarchies. A good many white male writers, though, from the Fugitive poets in Nashville, Tenn., to a young Mississippi writer named William Faulkner, responded to the literature of the Harlem Renaissance and to the social and economic transformations of the new century with something very like a melancholy grieving for the losses of a postslavery world—for the "Old Negroes" who seemed to have fled the region and its traditions for the life of "New Negroes" in the urban North and for white women who no longer seemed to serve as custodians of memory, tradition, and white patriarchy. The poetry and essays produced by the men known first as the Fugitives and then as the Southern Agrarians reverberated with nostalgia for an ordered, hierarchical society and for lost configurations of white mastery. A similar nostalgia suffused the pages of the white writers of the Charleston Renaissance, including DuBose Heyward and Hervey Allen, and Faulkner's early novels, culminating in *The Sound and the Fury* (1929), which charted the disintegration of a white family amid the transformative forces symbolized by the rise of the New Woman and the New Negro.

These were representations that replicated to a striking degree the denials, silences, and repudiations marking the plantation pastorals that had earlier defended slavery against the representations and charges of violence so central to antebellum and postbellum literary texts by African American writers. Those denials would be largely echoed in popular plantation novels of the 1930s— Caroline Gordon's *Penhally* (1931), Margaret Mitchell's *Gone with the Wind* (1936), and Allen Tate's *The Fathers* (1938)—but the very popularity of those novels would prompt ripostes in novels and short stories by both black and white writers, who turned their attention to the repressions and silences required in nostalgic representations of slavery, its hierarchies, and its legacies. In increasingly self-reflexive works anticipating the postmodern turn, writers including Faulkner himself, Columbia-trained Zora Neale Hurston, Katherine Anne Porter, Carson McCullers, Eudora Welty, and later Robert Penn Warren, Ralph Ellison, and Walker Percy would highlight the violence required in the making of nostalgic stories, whether of the regional past in general or of the legacies of slavery and segregation. Faulkner's great novels of the 1930s and early 1940s—*Light in August* (1932), *Absalom, Absalom!* (1936), and *Go Down, Moses* (1942)—turned a glaring light onto the strategies of exclusion and abjection required in the making of community and racial hierarchies as well as the defining impact of narrative violence upon both white and black psyches. Hurston, McCullers, Welty, Porter, and Warren, for their part, scrutinized the psychic disruption wrought by narrative legacies of denial and nonrecognition and probed the dynamic of remembering and forgetting that had come to define the erasure of slavery in the white regional imagination.

Those literary interrogations of the psychic damage wrought by the figurative violence of southern narratives deepened with the publication of Ralph Ellison's pivotal 1953 novel *Invisible Man*, which presented its narrator as an uncanny voice of disruption bursting forth from the nation's racial unconscious of denied histories of oppression and abjection. Walker Percy's self-consciously antipastoral novels in turn, from *The Moviegoer* (1960) to *Lancelot* (1977) and *The Second Coming* (1980), evoked both the postslavery melancholia for lost certainties defining earlier white novels and newer searches for narrative foundations in the wake of the civil rights movement's "Second Reconstruction." Heeding Ellison's own declaration in 1968 that the movement required new histories and fictions of the national and regional past, two generations of black and white writers to follow, among them William Styron, Ernest Gaines, Alice Walker, Gayl Jones, Cormac McCarthy, Toni Morrison, Ellen Douglas, Madison Smartt Bell, Randall Kenan, Edward P. Jones, and Natasha Trethewey, allied themselves with the project of recovering what Morrison herself called "discredited knowledge," subjugated and invisible histories of slavery, segregation, and racialization from the silences imposed by official histories of national reunion, progress, and white hegemony. Accordingly, their poems, fiction, and nonfiction resorted to self-conscious rewritings of *Gone with the Wind* in particular and plantation novels and southern pastorals in general and thereby produced new genres of neo–slave narratives and neo–gothic texts of plural voices, identities, and possibilities for mutual recognition, exchange, and reconfigurations of race and community.

SUSAN V. DONALDSON
College of William and Mary

Walter Benjamin, in *Selected Writings*, vol. 1, *1913–1926*, ed. Marcellus Bullock and Michael W. Jennings (1996); David W. Blight, *Race and Reunion: The Civil War in American Memory* (2002); Susan Buck-Morss, *Hegel, Haiti, and Universal History* (2009); Jerry H. Bryant, *Born in a Mighty Bad Land: The Violent Man in African*

American Folklore and Fiction (2003); Gary M. Ciuba, *Desire, Violence, and Divinity in Modern Southern Fiction: Katherine Anne Porter, Flannery O'Connor, Cormac McCarthy, Walker Percy* (2007); Ron Eyerman, *Cultural Trauma: Slavery and the Formation of African American Identity* (2001); Louise Y. Gossett, *Violence in Recent Southern Fiction* (1965); Farah Jasmine Griffin, *"Who Set You Flowin'?" The African-American Migrant Narrative* (1995); Sandra Gunning, *Race, Rape, and Lynching: The Red Record of American Literature, 1890–1919* (1996); Adam Gussow, *Seems Like Murder Here: Southern Violence and the Blues Tradition* (2002); Grace Elizabeth Hale, *Making Whiteness: The Culture of Segregation in the South, 1890–1940* (1998); Jacqueline Dowd Hall, in *Powers of Desire: The Politics of Sexuality*, ed. Ann Snitow, Christine Stansell, and Sharon Thompson (1983); Trudier Harris, *Exorcising Blackness: Historical and Literary Lynching and Burning Rituals* (1984); Saidiya V. Hartman, *Scenes of Subjection: Terror, Slavery, and Self-Making in Nineteenth-Century America* (1997); Dominick LaCapra, *Writing History, Writing Trauma* (2001); Toni Morrison, *Playing in the Dark: Whiteness and the Literary Imagination* (1992); Tim A. Ryan, *Calls and Responses: The American Novel of Slavery since "Gone with the Wind"* (2008); Lillian Smith, *Killers of the Dream* (1949); Eric J. Sundquist, *To Wake the Nations: Race in the Making of American Literature* (1993); Amy Louise Wood, *Lynching and Spectacle: Witnessing Racial Violence in America, 1890–1940* (2009); Patricia Yaeger, *Dirt and Desire: Reconstructing Southern Women's Writing, 1930–1990* (2000).

Lynching

Lynching was arguably the most conspicuous form of a long-standing American tradition of vigilantism. In popular usage, it referred to a killing perpetrated by a group of persons working outside the law to avenge an alleged crime or to impose social order. By the 20th century, however, lynching also came to stand for racial oppression at its most horrifying, a result of the vast numbers of lynchings committed against African Americans during the Jim Crow era as a means to instill racial terror and enforce white supremacy. Even today, the term "lynching" denotes an act of violence perpetrated out of racial animosity, fueled by a mob mentality that is quick to ascribe guilt outside the bounds of due process. Lynching, however, has had a long and complex history in the United States; the meaning of the term lynching has changed considerably over time, and acts of lynching are not easily categorized.

The origin of the term has most commonly been attributed to Col. Charles Lynch of Virginia, whose extralegal "court" sentenced Tories to floggings during the American Revolution. "Lynch law" at first referred to any form of extralegal corporal punishment. By the mid-19th century, however, it came to refer primarily to lethal punishments. Hanging was the most common form of lynching, although mobs also shot their victims, dragged, beat, and tortured them, or burned them at the stake. Despite the gruesomeness of the practice, it was considered, through most of the 19th century, to be a legitimate, community-sanctioned form of violence. It was rooted in traditions of popular justice and local sovereignty, in which a community punished crime and established social order outside official legal institutions. In the antebellum period, lynching was not a predominantly southern practice; it was most commonly practiced in frontier regions, particularly in western states and territories. At this time, whites, Mexicans, and Native Americans were more likely to be the victims of a lynching than African Americans, although historians are uncovering more and more the extent to which slaves were subject to lynching. Lynching began to increase in the South just before the Civil War, when southern vigilantes, particularly in Louisiana and Texas, routinely inflicted death upon outlaws and on individuals suspected of plotting slave insurrections.

The Civil War and Reconstruction intensified lynching activity in southern states. Vigilantism in Texas alone during the war probably accounted for more than 150 deaths. Lynching became even more widespread during Reconstruction and was directed mostly at ex-slaves as a form of political terror. The Ku Klux Klan and other vigilante groups killed hundreds of African Americans, as well as white Republicans, in what were often ritualized ceremonies that presaged the ritual and public nature of many Jim Crow lynchings. Significantly, however, these killings were not at the time called "lynchings," since that term still connoted community sanction, and the violence of Reconstruction did not garner widespread and undisputed white support.

After a brief decline in violence just after Reconstruction, lynching rose in both intensity and frequency in the mid-1880s, peaking in 1892 and 1893, and, though on the decline after the 1890s, the practice persisted well into the 20th century. Although lynchings still took place throughout most of the United States in this period, the vast majority occurred in the southern states and involved white mobs targeting African Americans. Indeed, by the turn of the 20th century, the term lynching came to be primarily associated with racial control and oppression, even as defenders of the practice still sought to justify it as a legitimate form of criminal vengeance. In fact, many African Americans supported the practice of lynching as a form of community vigilantism in the late 19th century, even engaging in acts of lynching themselves. Once lynching came to be seen as tool of white supremacists to exert racial control, however, their support for the practice withered.

Lynching increased at the start of the Jim Crow era for a number of reasons.

Postcard of lynching in Floyd County, Ga., ca. 1913–19
(Courtesy of Georgia Archives, Vanishing Georgia Collection)

Economic stress and uncertainty provoked struggling white farmers and petty merchants to lash out at African Americans seeking political and economic advancement and impelled white planters to exert control over their black labor force. Moreover, increased urbanization and industrialization threatened traditional racial hierarchies and created a sense of social instability. In southern towns and cities, fears of black advancement and diminished white power became coupled with intense fears of black criminality—in particular, the fear that black men would rape white women and thus violate white purity. In this context, lynching coincided with the institutionalization of white supremacy, in the form of segregation and disenfranchisement, and served as a means to enforce new racial codes and to protect white male authority.

Efforts made to gather data on lynching across the United States did not begin until 1882. For this reason, the number of lynchings before 1882 may be underestimated. And even these post-1882 data are not comprehensive, because many lynchings went unreported or uncounted. Nevertheless, scholars have ascertained that from 1882 through the early 1950s, by which time lynching had virtually ended, at least 4,739 persons reportedly died at the hands of lynch mobs in the United States. The likely total is probably nearer to 6,000. More than 80 percent of lynchings occurred in southern states, and almost 90 percent of those were committed by white mobs against African American men. These statistics do not include those who died in race riots; nor do they include interracial homicides. Among the southern states, Mississippi, Georgia, and Texas saw the most lynchings, although, in proportion to the African American population in each state, lynching rates were actually higher in Florida, Arkansas, and Kentucky.

Other ethnic minorities, especially Mexicans, as well as immigrant and native-born whites, were also the targets of lynch mobs in this period. The largest mass lynching in the country, which took place in 1891 in New Orleans, was committed against eleven Italian immigrants who had been indicted for the assassination of the local police chief. A mob of thousands stormed the jail where the men were detained and dragged them to the street, shooting to death ten of them and hanging the other.

Lynchings drew more attention in the Jim Crow period not only because of the sheer numbers of them, but because a good number of them were committed as public rituals, before crowds of hundreds and sometimes thousands of spectators. The spread of newswires in the late 19th century ensured that Americans across the country were more likely to learn of the most horrific lynchings, and, because, on the whole, the news media became more sensationalistic in this period, reports of lynchings lingered over the ghastly details of mob executions. Not infrequently, local photographers, and sometimes members of the mob, snapped pictures of the violence, often rendering them into postcards to send to family and friends.

The 1899 lynching of Sam Hose in Newnan, Georgia, was one such sensationalized and gruesome event, which garnered national attention after news of the lynching spread across the wires. Hose was a black farm laborer, accused of murdering his white employer and raping his wife. A mob tortured and mutilated Hose before burning him to death. Crowds swarmed the town to witness the lynching, and excursion trains brought spectators in from Atlanta. Hose's body parts were distributed and sold afterwards, and a photographer advertised the sale of photographs of lynching in the local newspaper. That lynching set off a series of lynchings throughout the countryside around Newnan, as local whites feared a black conspiracy to attack and kill white citizens.

The lynching of Sam Hose was atypical in its excess, but most lynchings received the same kind of widespread community sanction. Lynch mobs are not easily categorized since they were made up of men from all strata of society. Lynching is most associated with the poorest members of white society, those who might have been in direct economic competition with African Americans. But that stereotype is only true of a segment of lynchings. Many mobs comprised yeoman farmers, as well as solid working-class and lower-middle class townspeople. Mobs also operated with the tacit, and at times vocal, approval of wealthy planters, civic and business leaders, ministers, judges, lawyers, and newspaper editors. Very few participants in lynch mobs were prosecuted in any state, and before World War II almost none ever served time in prison.

Lynching especially garnered public support when the target of the mob was accused of sexually violating a white woman. Those lynchings that resulted from accusations of rape were also more likely to be public and sadistic. Ridding society of "black brutes" who violated white women was indeed the most common justification for lynching. South Carolina Governor Cole Blease echoed the sentiments of many white southerners when he declared in one infamous speech: "Whenever the Constitution comes between me and the virtue of the white women of South Carolina, then I say 'to hell with the Constitution.'" In fact, however, only about one-third of all lynching victims were suspected of rape or attempted rape. Murder or attempted murder was more often the alleged crime. Others who died at the hands of lynch mobs were accused of transgressions of descending importance, such as arson, burglary, slapping a white person, stealing chickens, chronic impudence, or simply being "vagrant and lewd." Whatever the supposed crime, most southern whites considered lynching to be a significant deterrent to black criminality. In cases in which they felt white authority or white purity to be threatened, many southern whites believed that the law was too slow and that it bestowed too many rights on criminals; some crimes, they believed, simply stood beyond the purview of man's law—they required a form of justice that was swifter and more severe.

Although white southerners largely defended the practice until the 1930s, lynching rates decreased with each decade in the 20th century, except for brief flare-ups just after World War I and at the start of the Great Depression. This decline was due to a number of factors. As southern blacks increasingly migrated to the North and West in the 1910s and 1920s, white elites were less likely to condone the violence. Local police departments, meanwhile, were professionalizing, and thus took greater pains to protect potential lynching victims. Moreover, antilynching activists, both inside and outside the South, were increasingly successful at publicizing the atrocity of lynching. And in light of the National Association for the Advancement of Colored People's campaign for federal antilynching legislation, local and state officials grew more willing to arrest and indict alleged mob members, if only to keep federal action at bay. Over time then, public attitudes toward lynching shifted, and by the start of World War II, white southerners for the most part had come to disdain the practice. Lynchings still occurred in the 1940s and into the civil rights era, but they were, significantly, not committed publicly.

The public presentation of lynching photographs and postcards in the past decade has focused renewed attention on lynching, and a spate of academic studies reflects the growing interest in lynching and its role in southern culture. This recent attention to lynching led to a Senate resolution in 2005 that officially apologized for the Senate's repeated failure to pass antilynching legislation in the 1920s and 1930s.

WILLIAM I. HAIR
Georgia College

AMY LOUISE WOOD
Illinois State University

Edwin T. Arnold, *What Virtue There Is in Fire: Cultural Memory and the Lynching of Sam Hose* (2009); Edward L. Ayers, *Vengeance and Justice: Crime and Punishment in the Nineteenth-Century American South* (1984); Ray Stannard Baker, *Following the Color Line* (1908; repr., 1969); Richard Maxwell Brown, *Strain of Violence: Historical Studies of American Violence and Vigilantism* (1975); Bruce E. Baker, *This Mob Will Surely Take My Life: Lynchings in the Carolinas, 1871–1947* (2008); W. Fitzhugh Brundage, *Lynching in the New South: Georgia and Virginia, 1880–1930* (1992); William Carrigan, *The Making of Lynching Culture: Violence and Vigilantism in Cen-*

tral Texas, 1836–1916 (2004); James H. Chadbourn, *Lynching and the Law* (1933); James E. Cutler, *Lynch-Law: An Investigation into the History of Lynching in the United States* (1905); Phillip Dray, *At the Hands of the Unknown: Lynching of Black America* (2002); Michael J. Pfeifer, *Rough Justice: Lynching and American Society, 1874–1947* (2004); Arthur F. Raper, *The Tragedy of Lynching* (1933); Stewart E. Tolnay and E. M. Beck, *Festival of Violence: An Analysis of Southern Lynchings, 1882–1930* (1995); Christopher Waldrep, *The Many Faces of Judge Lynch: Extralegal Violence and Punishment in America* (2002); Walter White, *Rope and Faggot* (1929); Amy Louise Wood, *Lynching and Spectacle: Witnessing Racial Violence in America, 1890–1940* (2009); George C. Wright, *Racial Violence in Kentucky, 1865–1940: Lynchings, Mob Rule, and "Legal Lynchings"* (1990).

Memory

If we accept that there is something distinctive about violence in the South and also take seriously the Confederate anthem's claim that in Dixie "old times there are not forgotten," then it is no wonder that the violence the South has seen looms large in the region's historical memory. In fact, Sheldon Hackney suggested in the late 1960s that "the development of a southern world view that defines the social, political, and physical environment as hostile and casts the white southerner in the role of the passive victim of malevolent forces" accounted for the South's propensity for violence. But beyond a general sense that the region has long been under attack (from revolting slaves, abolitionists, Yankee soldiers, carpetbaggers, boll weevils, fire ants, and Yankee retirees), the South has been shaped by the specific effects of remembering its history as the scene of violence.

Oral tradition in local communities has been the most important means for perpetuating the historical memory of violence. With high levels of persistence and relatively low levels of in-migration after the early 19th century, much of the South was ideal for the creation of very durable communities with a strong sense of their own history. Perpetrators and victims of violence were often deeply connected to a community and a place, and members of the community generations later might still have a keen sense of the violent events of the past and how they connect to people and places in the present.

The various wars fought on southern soil all remained alive in memory to one degree or another. Throughout much of the South, especially the backcountry, the Revolutionary War was truly a civil war, fought brutally between small partisan bands. Some of the more stunning acts of violence, such as the 1781 massacre of 16 men and boys at Hayes Station in South Carolina, were discussed locally until at least the 1930s. The War of 1812 was a more structured conflict, with backcountry settlers taking pride in their role in winning the Battle of New Orleans. Some fiddler in Kentucky or Tennessee commemorated the date of that battle in a fiddle tune called "The Eighth of January," and an Alabama fiddler named a tune for Horseshoe Bend, where Andrew Jackson defeated the Creeks.

The violence of the Civil War became deeply ingrained in southern life and memory. Most immediately, the maimed bodies of veterans, tens of thousands of whom lost limbs, were daily reminders. Other wounds were less visible but no less real. Historian Eric T. Dean Jr. argues that Confederate veterans suffered from post-traumatic stress disorder. The epic battles of the war were recounted in reunion speeches and magazine articles and, even long after the last veteran had passed away, reenacted on hundreds of southern battlefields. The darker side of the war, the guerrilla war that often threatened to spiral out of control and unravel the entire social fabric, created hostilities in communities that endured for decades. Families with roots in the border states, such as Missouri and Kentucky, still tell stories of wartime brutality.

Much of the violence of Reconstruction was caught up with the tangled politics of the time and seems to have been less likely to persist in memory. Partly this is because the losers in such confrontations often fled the place and, if they stayed, found themselves with little access to the means of shaping public memory. White perpetrators of violence during Reconstruction, on the other hand, liked to remember their overthrow of Republican governments and black voters as a foreordained, effortless, and natural thing, omitting the very real but messy and morally questionable violence they used to achieve these ends. The large exception to this was the Ku Klux Klan. The Reconstruction Klan itself drew on the ritualistic world of 19th-century fraternal societies and the conventions of popular entertainment, and some Klansmen claimed to be ghosts of Confederate soldiers. They, in turn, were remembered and invoked when a new version of the Ku Klux Klan formed in 1915, though there was little emphasis on the violence of the original Klan.

Other violent episodes became significant in historical memory, but usually only in their locales where the context that gave memory meaning was readily accessible. The general practice of lynching became a familiar part of the region's past, but specific lynchings were remembered most powerfully by family and near neighbors of the victims, and many were forgotten. Labor violence was likely to be remembered when it played a role in the oppositional culture of an active labor movement, but where organizing was decisively defeated, as in the 1934 General Textile Strike, the violent scenes associated with it, as the killings at Chiquola Mill in Honea Path, S.C., could be buried for decades. Some conflicts based around class and livelihood exploded into broader community conflicts. The Black Patch War in western Kentucky and Tennessee during the first decade of the 20th century pitted local elites trying to control the production of tobacco and protect prices against small farmers and black laborers who threatened to undersell them. The vigilante violence they used was still remembered 70 years later. Similarly, in Clarke County, Ala., in 1893, political disputes erupted into a small-scale war between poor farmers in Mitcham Beat estranged from the mainstream and middle-class Democrats from the county seat. Several of the Mitcham Beat residents were killed, and families were terrorized. When a historian was writing about the Mitcham War in the 1980s, he found that the descendants of those who carried out the violence had learned little about it, while the people of Mitcham Beat had detailed oral traditions about the killings. Feuds between families were essentially reliant on memory: each killing became the justification for the next. Local color writers in the 1880s latched onto feuds as something characteristic of and distinctive to the southern mountains, so over the years, newspaper articles and books planted the idea in the American mind as one of the South's defining characteristics. Innumerable local killings and fights became integral to the historical memory of the communities in which they occurred. When abused wife Frankie Silver chopped off her husband's head with an ax on a cold winter's evening in 1831, she did not necessarily know that residents of Kona in North Carolina's Toe River Valley would continue to talk (and sing) about it for nearly two centuries.

One of the greatest legacies of violence in the South was silence. There were many reasons for this. In the case of African Americans, or indeed the poor and dispossessed of whatever race, the victims of violence were without much social power for decades, if not longer. They had little access to public space and few opportunities to speak publicly of what they had suffered. And if speaking of it could not change the situation or bring justice but only remind everyone of their status as victims and discomfit the perpetrators and their descendants, what was the point of remembering? The renewed public discussion of lynching and prosecutions of those guilty of killing civil rights activists only came long after African Americans had gained the social power to declare the truth of their ordeals. The fate of labor violence has been similar, without such a redemptive ending. The General Textile Strike of 1934 was the largest strike in the nation's history, but it was crushed and several people were killed. Because the most ardent unionists had been the textile workers most rooted in their communities, many had to find a way to live peacefully in their hometowns afterward. The price of this peace, however, was an enduring silence about the strike and the union, to the extent that children of those killed in 1934 never knew that the strike had happened at all. Only when scholars began to interview old mill hands in the 1980s and 1990s did awareness of the violence of the strike begin to seep back into public life. This story could be repeated in dozens, if not hundreds, of cases across the South.

Recently efforts to officially or formally acknowledge violent episodes from the southern past have occurred. In 1994 the Florida legislature authorized financial payments to nine survivors of the 1923 Rosewood Massacre and university scholarships to descendants of African American victims who were terrorized by white mobs. In 2000 the North Carolina legislature established the 1898 Wilmington Race Riot Commission to document that event and assess its impact on blacks in the state and region, and in 2008 the city dedicated a monument to individuals affected by the expulsion of black citizens from the city. In 1997 the 75th anniversary of the Tulsa Race Riot led to the establishment of the Tulsa Race Riot Commission, which recommended in 2001 that the city pay reparations to descendants of the 31 May 1921 riot that destroyed 35 city blocks. Greensboro, N.C., was the site on 3 November 1979 of the killing by members of the Ku Klux Klan and the American Nazi Party of five communist activists during a Death to the Klan march. A biracial group of citizens—without support of the city government—launched a Truth and Reconciliation Commission, modeled on that in South Africa, and its report assessed responsibilities for the massacre as part of an effort to promote community reconciliation. In a distinctive commemoration, each year since 2005, members of a group of multiracial activists have reenacted a civil rights–era rural Georgia lynching in which four young African Americans were killed. The purpose is to urge prosecution of those responsible for it and to call attention to the long history of violence against people of color. Films documenting some of these events have been a key part of nurturing the memory of southern violence, including *Before They Die* (Reggie Turner, director, 2008), *Rosewood* (John Singleton, director, 1997), and *Greensboro: Closer to the Truth* (Adam Zucker, director, 2007).

BRUCE E. BAKER
Royal Holloway, University of London

Bruce E. Baker, in *Where These Memories Grow: History, Memory, and Southern Identity*, ed. W. Fitzhugh Brundage (2000); W. Fitzhugh Brundage, *The Southern Past: A Clash of Race and Memory* (2005); Lawrence Goodwyn, *American Historical Review* (December 1971); Sheldon Hackney, *American Historical Review* (February 1969); William Lynwood Montell, *Killings: Folk Justice in the Upper South* (1986); Phillip Shaw Paludan, *Victims: A True Story of the Civil War* (2004); Daniel W. Patterson, *A Tree Accurst: Bobby McMillon and Stories of Frankie Silver* (2000);

Altina L. Waller, *Feud: Hatfields, McCoys, and Social Change in Appalachia, 1860–1890* (1988).

Mexican Americans, Violence toward

During the 19th and early 20th centuries, Mexicans in the Southwest suffered systematic persecution and violence at the hands of white vigilantes. This violence was wide ranging and included vigilante-organized mock trials with executions, hastily arranged mob hangings, forced expulsion of Mexican immigrants from communities by mobs, the burning of Mexican homes and Catholic churches, as well as a variety of nonlethal punishments such as whipping, branding, and maiming. A conservative estimate for the number of Mexicans executed by mobs is in the thousands.

Until the late 20th century, the number of Mexicans resident in the southeastern United States was relatively small, but more Mexicans lived in Texas in 1930 than in the rest of the United States combined. Consequently, it is not surprising to learn that more Mexicans died at the hands of mobs in Texas than anywhere else in the United States. Precise numbers are impossible to obtain, but it seems doubtful that even states with a robust history of extralegal violence against Mexicans, such as California, can match Texas's dismal record.

Mob violence against Mexicans in Texas did not follow the timeline of mob violence against African Americans. Most African American mob victims died after the Civil War, with the 1860s and 1890s deemed by most scholars to have been the most deadly. By contrast, those two decades witnessed a relative absence of acts of mob violence against Mexicans. Mob violence against Mexicans occurred with greatest frequency during the decades of the 1850s, the 1870s, and the 1910s.

As with black and white victims of mobs in the United States, vigilantes most commonly alleged murder as the reason for their extralegal execution of Mexicans. However, mobs targeting Mexicans rarely alleged rape, as was so often the case with black victims. Instead, lynchers of Mexicans frequently described their victims as "bandits" and accused them of theft.

Although there can be genuine debate over the relative balance of the many factors underlying anti-Mexican mob violence, there is no doubt that economic competition played a substantial role in motivating lynch mobs and vigilantes. In case after case, the backdrop to so much violence between whites and Mexicans was tied to the seemingly constant conflict over land and livestock or to the battle over terms and conditions of labor.

Several infamous episodes in which economic tensions precipitated mob violence deserve particular mention. In 1856 vigilantes ordered Mexicans living in Colorado County to flee after allegations were made that Spanish speakers were "exercising a mischievous influence among the slaves." The alleged conspiracy of the slaves called for the rebels to "make their way to Mexico." In the wake of the plot's discovery, Mexicans in the county were driven out. Colorado County was not the only place in Texas where Mexicans were expelled during the 1850s as tensions over slavery mounted.

During the summer of 1857 white vigilantes composed at least in part of working-class men who transported goods in the Texas interior savagely attacked their Mexican competitors in what has become known as the "Cart War." These vigilantes not only destroyed the property and disrupted the business of these Mexicans but also hanged or shot an unknown number of their rivals. Most estimates place the number of murdered Mexicans above 75. The *Austin Southern Intelligencer* opposed the vigilantes, alleging that the purpose of the violence was "to get rid of competition which in dispatch and cheapness excels" that of the white cartmen. The paper concluded that this economic conflict was "the sole cause of the war" and warned that it "behooves the property holders of San Antonio to put down the warfare." Instead, the paper urged that the average white man find a way to live with Mexicans, making these cheap laborers "the means of his own prosperity."

While few years would rival 1857 in terms of the number of attacks on Mexicans, economic competition continued to be a catalyst for mob violence. As the 19th century progressed, more and more Mexicans moved north into central Texas to work in the cotton fields. White vigilantes, often small farmers, laborers, and sharecroppers calling themselves "white caps," used warnings and mob violence to intimidate Mexican workers who they believed depressed wages. In 1898 a group of vigilantes in Gonzalez posted the following warning: "Hell, Texas, Feb. 16. Notice to the Mexicans: You all have got ten days to leave in. Mr. May Renfro and brother get your Mexicans all off your place. If not, you will get the same that they do. Signed, Whitecaps."

If mob violence against Mexicans in central Texas was often connected to labor and competition between Mexicans and working-class whites, vigilantism in south Texas more often revolved around issues of property. In 1848 the Treaty of Guadalupe Hidalgo guaranteed the rights of Mexicans who resided within the new boundaries of the United States to vote and to own property. In the short term, this meant that the vast majority of property in south Texas remained in the hands of Tejanos and that Spanish speakers gained some local influence in the reshaped political order. In the long term, however, Anglos found ways to acquire Tejano property and to assert political control.

As the travel writer Frederick Law Olmsted recorded during his visit to Texas in 1854, the "Americans are very jealous" of the "few Mexican land-holders" and "frequently with injustice" accuse the Mexicans "of every crime which cannot be directly traced to its perpetrators." Olmsted noted that "valuable lands" in the region belonged to Mexican families 20 years ago but have "come into the possession of Americans" with the original proprietors "rarely, if ever, being paid anything." He further observed that it was in vain to point out the protections afforded to these people by the laws of the United States and Texas, for the citizens of Texas believed in a "higher law," namely "the great and glorious law of selfish, passionate power—Lynch Law."

Economics alone, however, cannot explain the lynching of persons of Mexican descent. If mobs had considered only economics, they would have been just as likely to murder or expel any ethnic group standing in their way. But, in fact, mobs specifically targeted Mexicans and other Spanish speakers in the southwestern United States. A virulent prejudice played a critical role in inciting, antagonizing, and vindicating anti-Mexican violence. Other factors— such as cultural distance, the predominance of single men on the frontier, and a culture of honor and vengeance—were also important, but racial prejudice was one of the foundational causes of mob violence against Mexicans.

Negative attitudes toward Mexicans were in place long before the United States acquired Texas, New Mexico, California, and other parts of the Mexican North. The American colonists viewed Spaniards through the lens of the "Black Legend." Beginning at least as early as the 16th century, English writers portrayed Spanish culture as rich in "cruelty, superstition, and oppression without measure." The War for Texas Independence and the U.S.-Mexican War greatly enflamed these preexisting prejudices. On 6 April 1850 the *Stockton Times* printed the following from a Mexican War veteran: "Mexicans have no business in this country. I don't believe in them. The men were made to be shot at, and the women were made for our purposes. I'm a white man—I am! A Mexican is pretty near black. I hate all Mexicans."

The Treaty of Guadalupe Hidalgo officially concluded hostilities but did not erase this kind of bitter enmity. The law classified Mexicans as "white," but in practice they were seldom afforded the same rights and privileges as English speakers of European descent. Mexicans were often considered to be a racial hybrid of European, Indian, and African blood that had inherited none of the good and all of the bad from their ancestors. Mexicans were weakened not only by their racial characteristics but also by an inferior religion and culture. Numerous whites looked disparagingly upon the religion of most Mexicans, Roman Catholicism. The most convincing proof of the power of anti-Mexican attitudes is not so much in the words and thoughts of whites but in their deeds. Over and over again, Anglos treated Mexicans as if they were second-class citizens. Anglos believed that only whites had the capacity for effective self-government. As a consequence, they created obstacles to Mexican political participation, often by denying them the right to vote. Many Anglos also refused to socialize with Mexicans. Western communities segregated Mexican children from white children in local schools.

One final point that must be raised is Mexican resistance to mob violence. Mexicans implemented numerous strategies of resistance that challenged the legitimacy of mob law in the southwestern states. The scope of Mexican resistance differed considerably from that of African Americans. Although some black leaders such as Ida B. Wells and W. E. B. Du Bois advocated armed resistance against lynch mobs, most believed that a militant stance would prove counterproductive since whites would employ the full power of their resources to crush political opposition.

Because of the presence of the U.S.-Mexican border, persons of Mexican descent were in a much stronger position to employ self-defense against white mobs. Mexican resistance was embodied in a group of men whom whites categorized as "bandits" but who were folk heroes to the mass of Mexicans resident in the United States. These Mexicans were able to execute daring raids upon Anglo persons and property before escaping across the border. Among these vigilante leaders were Tiburcio Vasquez, Joaquin Murietta, and Juan Cortina. Between 1859 and 1873 Juan Cortina conducted a relentless campaign against the legal and military authorities in Texas. Cortina claimed that he had been divinely ordained to avenge the oppression of his people. He therefore attempted to rally Mexican Americans to his cause: "Many of you have been robbed of your property, incarcerated, chased, murdered, and hunted like wild beasts, because your labor was fruitful, and because your industry excited the vile avarice which led them." To whites, Cortina was a murderer and a cattle thief. To mistreated Mexicans, he personified the spirit of rebellion.

Although Mexicans in Texas possessed more opportunities for violent reprisal than African Americans, their resistance to mob violence should not be overstated, as the balance of power still lay firmly with whites. Ultimately, a more important instrument of Mexican resistance was diplomatic protest. Throughout the late 19th and early 20th centuries the Mexican government vigorously disputed violence against its citizens resident in the United States. Washington initially insisted that it had no constitutional authority to intervene in state internal affairs. Nonetheless, the persistence of Mexican protest in time produced positive results. In the 1890s relatives of Mexican mob victims in Texas and other parts of the United States began to receive indemnities from the United States government. In the 1920s federal authorities began arresting those complicit in mob violence against Mexicans. Although extralegal violence against Mexicans continued, by the 1930s it had become shrouded in secrecy and was no longer done in public without fear of legal punishment.

WILLIAM D. CARRIGAN
Rowan University

CLIVE WEBB
University of Sussex

William D. Carrigan, *Making of a Lynching Culture: Violence and Vigilantism in Central Texas, 1836–1916* (2006); Arnoldo De León, *They Called Them Greasers: Anglo Attitudes toward Mexicans in Texas, 1821–1900* (1983); Neil Foley, *The White Scourge: Mexicans, Blacks, and Poor Whites in Texas Cotton Culture* (1997); Ken Gonzalez-Day, *Lynching in the West, 1850–1935* (2006); Manuel G. Gonzalez, *Mexicanos: A History of Mexicans in the United States* (1999); Benjamin Heber Johnson, *Revolution in Texas: How a Forgotten Rebellion and Its Bloody Suppression Turned Mexicans into Americans* (2003); Susan Lee Johnson, *Roaring Camp: The Social World of the California Gold Rush* (2000); Patricia Nelson Limerick, *Legacy of Conquest: The Unbroken Past of the American West* (1987); Clare McKanna, *Race and Justice in the American West, 1880–1920* (1997); Carey McWilliams, *North from Mexico: The Spanish-Speaking People of the United States* (1949); Douglas Monroy, *Thrown among Strangers: The Making of Mexican Culture in Frontier California* (1990); Philip Wayne Powell, *Tree of Hate: Propaganda and Prejudice Affecting United States Relations with the Hispanic World* (1971); F. Arturo Rosales, *Pobre Raza! Violence, Justice, and Mobilization among México Lindo Immigrants, 1900–1936* (1999); David J. Weber, *Myth and the History of the Hispanic Southwest* (1988).

Militarism

For at least 150 years many Americans have perceived the South as being a uniquely militaristic region, possessing a prominent and unique "military tradition." Some of the earliest expressions of this idea emerged from the late antebellum era; according to historian Michael C. C. Adams, many northerners came to see the southern man as a "superior martial figure." During the Civil War white southerners often boasted that one southern man "could whip ten yankees." As southern generals piled up battlefield victories and forced the North to spend four years and 360,000 lives subduing an economically and numerically weaker Confederate nation, northerners too were ready to explain their difficulty by ascribing to theories of a militaristic South. During and after the war some charged that southern states had deliberately prepared for war by establishing dozens of military schools in the antebellum period and building up a southern soldiery prior to secession. Thus, northerners in this period of lingering sectional bitterness were apt to associate southern militarism with treason rather than virtue. Meanwhile, in the South, the culture of the Lost Cause praised southern valor and deified Confederate heroes such as Robert E. Lee and Stonewall Jackson, and Confederate veterans commanded tremendous prestige and authority in the postwar era.

Southerners enthusiastically volunteered for the Spanish-American War, determined to prove their national patriotism even as they boasted of the valor of their rebellious Confederate fathers. The entire cadet corps at Virginia Polytechnic Institute, for example, while volunteering its services to President McKinley, asserted that just as the South's soldiers had shown their "Yankee brethren" how well they could fight against them, they would now "show how Southern soldiers can fight with them."

For those who define a southern military tradition as either eagerness for war or as the prominence of southerners in the United States military, there are data from the 20th century to support their argument. Southerners eventually came to be by far the strongest supporters of American entry into World War I, albeit only after President Woodrow Wilson defined support of overseas intervention as a test of patriotism. Similarly, a Gallup Poll in 1941 indicated that 88 percent of southerners favored war against Hitler's Germany, as opposed to 70 percent for the nation as a whole. The World War I exploits of Sergeant Alvin York, a born-again Christian from the mountains of east Tennessee, strengthened national perceptions of southern military prowess. The southern roots of Dwight D. Eisenhower, Audie Murphy, George S. Patton, and others had the same effect in the World War II era. For most of the 20th century, in fact, southerners were statistically overrepresented in the military officer corps.

By the mid-20th century, professional scholars expressed interest in the idea of a militaristic or "militant" South. Some pointed to the high number of West Point cadets in the antebellum period who were southerners, an apparent enthusiasm for war and military display in southern culture, and the frequency of military "filibustering" expeditions by southerners in Latin America. John Hope Franklin noted all these trends in his classic *The Militant South, 1800–1861*, while also conflating an allegedly "militaristic" culture with a "militant" one—that is, with a very high frequency of personal violence such as dueling and brawling, and a greater acceptance of violence in general. Frontier conditions, slavery, weak law enforcement, and a cultural tradition of venerating martial forebears, Franklin asserted, made respect for military service and for certain forms of violence key components of southern society. Other historians, however, countered that while personal, individual violence was more common in the rural South, mob violence was more prominent in the more urban North. And Don C. Higginbotham argued that, at least in the colonial period, it was the northern colonies that showed more enthusiasm and aptitude for war.

Southerners' alleged enthusiasm for military education has drawn particular attention, and the topic has served as a battleground in which historians have waged a war of statistics. Opponents of Franklin's "militant South" thesis point out that the statistical preponderance of southern West Point cadets to northern ones was slight or nonexistent; in any event, northern cadets were more likely to *graduate* from the national military academy. A recent book on southern military schools responds by pointing out that roughly 100 military colleges and academies were founded in the South between 1827 and 1860, in comparison to 15 in the North. Meanwhile, every slave state in the antebellum period either established at least one state-supported military school or provided state support to private ones, while the northern states, supposedly more committed to public education, established none. Perhaps more important than these statistics is why southerners established such schools and why parents enrolled their sons in them. The evidence indicates that, contrary to the suspicions of contemporary northerners, the most important motivation was not preparation for civil war. Rather, white southerners associated martial virtues such as duty, courage, discipline, and patriotism with the civic duties needed to make a republic function; by training young men as soldiers, they thought, they were preparing them for republican citizenship. Northern parents and educators sometimes recognized these same associations but, at times, could also view military institutions and values as potentially threatening and undemocratic and therefore unsuitable for higher education.

This trend continued after the war, as every southern white land-grant college founded under the Morrill Act before 1900 functioned on a daily basis as a military school. Even black southerners recognized the connection between training young men as soldiers and educating them as citizens. In the age of Jim Crow, several black colleges also required their male students to join a corps of cadets and to learn discipline and military drill, even as white state authorities denied them the opportunity to train with weapons.

Some observers suspect that if there was a distinct southern military tradition, it has waned recently as the South has modernized and seemingly moved closer to the American cultural mainstream. Again, the evidence is mixed and provides another example of how difficult it is either to debunk the notion of a militaristic South or to prove its existence with hard facts. During the Vietnam era, there was far less antiwar unrest on southern college campuses than elsewhere. More recently, opposition to the Iraq War, though present in the South, has been relatively muted. It does seem that the South's overrepresentation in the military officer corps may be coming to an end. On the other hand, military recruiters in the early 21st century still find their job much easier in the South, a trend that has continued since at least World War II. Young southerners continue to follow their forebears into military service at a higher rate than those from other regions.

Moving beyond statistical comparisons on recruiting, numbers of military schools, and popular support for the nation's wars, it is possible to make several larger generalizations about southern militarism. First, it is clear that the bitter experience of defeat in 1865 did not diminish white southerners' veneration of martial forebears and enthusiasm for military institutions. Another trend in southern culture has been the relative or nearly complete absence of pacifism and suspicion of the military since the late antebellum period. Thus, one way to express the difference between "North" and South is to recognize that nonsoutherners also frequently honor military service and martial valor. Respect for martial sacrifice has always been a key component of American patriotism. And yet the larger American military tradition outside the South also includes, or exists alongside, a countervailing pacifist or antimilitaristic attitude. Opposition to war is always stronger outside the South, military educational traditions are often seen as "undemocratic" or "un-American" ways to run a college, and military recruiting is often difficult or even officially banned on nonsouthern college campuses. Thus, what seems unique about the southern military tradition as opposed to the larger American military tradition is the almost complete lack of this antimilitarist, pacifist sentiment.

Another increasingly recognized historical trend is that respect for military service and military education crossed, and still crosses, racial lines in the South. After emancipation, black men staunchly upheld their state militia units and volunteer companies until southern state governments forcibly disbanded them in the 1900s. Even today strong military traditions continue on historically black campuses such as South Carolina State, Savannah State, Florida A&M, and Hampton University.

Finally, the southern military tradition has been very much in tune with American ideas about personal autonomy and self-government. The South's style of militarism has never resembled that of 19th-century Prussia or imperial Japan, inflexibly demanding blind obedience and submission to authority. Indeed, the southern military tradition is a curious one in that it honors rebellion, or resistance to tyranny, as much as it does obedience. Southern militarism and perceptions of it have evolved over time. But popular memory of the partisan frontiersmen of the American Revolution and the Confederate heroes who, according to Lost Cause mythology, nobly resisted tyranny and outside coercion, have always influenced how white southerners thought about military service. Likewise, black southerners have always viewed military service as an assertion of their own citizenship rather than as an act of submission. In many ways, then, the southern military tradition has always been uniquely American, and uniquely southern.

ROD ANDREW JR.
Clemson University

Michael C. C. Adams, *Our Masters the Rebels: A Speculation on Union Military Failure in the East, 1861–1865* (1978); Rod Andrew Jr., *Long Gray Lines: The Southern Military School Tradition, 1839–1915* (2001); F. N. Boney, *Southerners All* (1984); James C. Bonner, *Georgia Review* (Spring 1955); Marcus Cunliffe, *Soldiers and Civilians: Martial Spirit in America, 1775–1865* (1968); John Hope Franklin, *The Militant South, 1800–1861* (1956); Anthony Gaughan, *Journal of Southern History* (November 1999); John Temple Graves II, *The Fighting South* (1943) Don C. Higginbotham, *Journal of Southern History* (February 1992); John Hawkins Napier III, *Alabama Review* (October 1980).

Nonviolent Protest (Civil Disobedience)

Nonviolent protest goes far back in American history. The Boston Tea Party was civil disobedience that led to national independence. The First Amendment to the federal Constitution, with its protection of free speech and the right to assemble, established the legal context for nonviolent protest. Henry David Thoreau famously went to jail for refusing to pay a tax to support the Mexican War. Harriet Tubman's Underground Railroad helped escaped slaves to freedom, combating slavery without violence. The women's rights movement used nonviolent strategies, leading to the right to vote in 1920. The labor movement used strikes and boycotts in seeking better working conditions and higher pay. Such individuals and groups have long resisted injustice or worked to achieve social change without violence, but the combination of organized mass resistance and nonviolent strategies reached a new level of philosophical coherence and sociopolitical effectiveness in the 20th century. The U.S. South became the site for one of the most significant uses of nonviolent protest to effect social change through the civil rights movement of the 1950s and 1960s.

Nonviolent resistance is anchored in two separate traditions. One is the religious insistence that harming another person is always immoral and that loving one's enemies can transform individuals and societies. The second, a political tradition, organizes economic, social, and political power to force changes in laws and policies regarded as unjust. Dissenters to unjust policies organize sources of power outside of government to compel official authorities to recognize the need for change. Nonviolent direct action efforts in the South were linked to national organizations in the early 20th century, those supporting pacifist activities and those promoting labor union organization.

The Fellowship of Reconciliation (FOR) was an international pacifist organization that began its work in the United States in 1915. During World War II it broadened its efforts beyond international affairs to address the problem of racial segregation in the nation. As early as the 1940s FOR members wanted to establish chapters in the South to launch a nonviolent campaign against Jim Crow. A. J. Muste, the FOR national secretary, and Bayard Rustin and James Farmer, field organizers for Muste, began in that decade articulating a philosophy and practice of nonviolence aimed at challenging the South's segregated social system. They drew from such books as Richard B. Gregg's *The Power of Non-Violence* (1944) and Krishnalal Shridharani's *War without Violence* (1939), the latter of which came from a disciple of Mahatma Gandhi and detailed his procedures for organizing social change coming out of the struggle for Indian national independence from the British. FOR's approach was through appeals to social morality, based in civil dialogue and lived example, to win over those entrenched defenders of segregation. Muste and his pacifist colleagues expanded the definition of pacifism from a message to a means of action to achieve reconciliation after the end of injustice.

The Congress of Racial Equality (CORE) championed nonviolent direct action from its emergence as a separate organization out of FOR in 1942. FOR provided paid staff, nonviolence training, and information on social activism across the South through the 1950s for CORE and other civil rights groups. CORE remained an informal, decentralized organization in its early days, with James Farmer becoming the first national CORE chairman in 1943 and remaining with the group until 1966. It succeeded in integrating movie houses and roller skating rinks in northern and western cities in the 1940s and developed relationships with white and black students in the upper South to plant the seeds for later use of nonviolent resistance. CORE pioneered modern nonviolent direct action for civil rights with sit-ins in the 1940s and a freedom ride, called the Journey to Reconciliation, in 1947. Still, one observer of race relations in the region, Constance Rumbough, noted in 1948 that "most Southern leaders think that the nonviolent direct action technique is not advisable in this area."

CORE persevered in establishing a network of chapters across the South, with 24 by 1960. CORE provided guidance to the Greensboro, N.C., students who launched a sit-in at a lunch counter in that same year, and the group initiated the "jail-in" strategy of activists serving out jail terms when arrested, rather than paying bail. "Jail, no bail" attracted considerable national publicity and became a significant direct action technique in the civil rights movement. In May 1961 CORE launched the first Freedom Ride of the movement, sending seven white and six black activists on bus rides into the South. Harassment, intimidation, fire bombings, beatings, and prison sentences met the freedom riders, but they succeeded in bringing an end to segregated seating in interstate travel. CORE was one of the sponsors of the seminal March on Washington in 1963.

CORE represented the expansion of Christian pacifism to civil rights struggle, but another source for nonviolent protest in the South was the labor movement, with Highlander Folk School the most direct institutional connection between labor and civil rights. Labor organizers had worked in the South since the late 19th century to organize industrial workers in coal mines, textile mills, timber camps, and other work places but had met violent resistance from corporate owners and government authorities. Founded in 1932 by Myles Horton, Don West, and Rev. James A. Dombrowski, Highlander was an adult education facility that at first specialized in training leaders of the labor movement in Appalachia and in nurturing appreciation and preservation of mountain cultural values. It achieved modest success in contributing to organizing workers in areas surrounding the school's east Tennessee location in Grundy County in its first decade. During the 1940s the school's faculty concentrated on unionizing textile workers in Tennessee and the Carolinas, directing labor education programs throughout the South, and developing residential workshops that promoted a racially integrated and politically engaged labor movement.

In 1953 Highlander launched new initiatives to encourage racial integration in the South, holding its first workshop on school desegregation in the year before the landmark *Brown v. the Board of Education* Supreme Court decision. Hundreds of people attended these workshops, which quickly made Highlander the educational center of early civil rights efforts. Literacy programs addressed the needs of blacks prevented from voting by state literacy requirements. Highlander music director Zilphia Horton adapted an old gospel song, which had been sung by striking tobacco factory workers in 1946, into the civil rights anthem "We Shall Overcome." In July 1955 Rosa Parks, before her role in touching off the Montgomery Bus Boycott, went to Highlander for a workshop, later speaking of that experience as the first time she had lived in "an atmosphere of equality with members of the other race." Highlander trained key civil rights figures in nonviolent direct action techniques in the mid- and late 1950s, including Martin Luther King Jr., James Bevel, Bernard Lafayette, Ralph Abernathy, and John Lewis. In the early 1960s, when student sit-ins began, college students gathered at Highlander to consider the next stages of the black freedom struggle. Regarding the group as truly subversive—even if nonviolent in philosophy—the state of Tennessee revoked Highlander's charter in 1962 and confiscated its property.

The Montgomery Bus Boycott became the crucible that brought connections between nonviolent direct action protest and civil rights together. Representatives from national organizations long working in civil rights came to Montgomery in 1955 to offer advice, ideas, and resources to local leaders. A committed pacifist, Bayard Rustin had long been a key figure in the FOR/CORE alliance, holding positions in both organizations and participating in the Journey of Reconciliation in 1947, for which he was arrested in North Carolina and spent a month on a chain gang. Afterward, he went to India to meet with Gandhi's sons and came away blending Gandhian nonviolent protest into his pacifism, all of which he shared with Montgomery leaders. Rev. Glenn E. Smiley, a white official with FOR, also came to Montgomery to visit with the emerging leader of the bus boycott, Dr. Martin Luther King Jr. Smiley, a Texan who was a devout believer in Gandhi's methods, carried an array of books about nonviolence for King, who confessed to Smiley that, at that point, he could not claim to know much about Gandhi's principles. Some leaders of national organizations hoped to control the boycott, but seeing the energy and organization at the local level, they came to provide funding and ideas instead of control. Perhaps the most significant civil rights leader of the early 1950s, A. Philip Randolph, head of the Brotherhood of Sleeping Car Porters, observed that Montgomery leaders had "managed thus far more successfully than any of 'our so-called nonviolence experts' a mass resistance campaign and we should learn from them rather than assume that we knew it all."

The immediacy of leading the Montgomery boycott surely led Martin Luther King Jr. to new understandings of the sources of nonviolence resistance and their applicability to the movement. King had long been interested in how religion could be used to combat social problems, especially the segregation he had grown up with in Atlanta. The black church had given him focus on Christian love, which he now combined with his growing appreciation of how Gandhian nonviolence could provide strategies for protest. In 1957 King identified nonviolent techniques for racial justice as "creative forms," including mass boycotts, sit-down protests and strikes, sit-ins, refusals to pay bail for unjust arrests, mass marches, and prayer sessions. King embraced Gandhi's concept of satyagraha, which he defined as "truth-force," "love-force," or "soul-force." "I came to see for the first time that the Christian doctrine of love operating through the Gandhian method of nonviolence was one of the most potent weapons available to oppressed people in their struggle for freedom." As leader of the bus boycott, he found his thoughts driven back to the Sermon on the Mount and the Gandhian method of nonviolent resistance. As he observed, "Christ furnished the spirit and motivation while Gandhi furnished the method."

King put forward key principles of nonviolence. He stressed it was "not a method for cowards; it *does* resist." It sought not to humiliate its opponents but to win their friendship and respect. Its attack was directed against the forces of evil and not the individuals caught in those forces. Nonviolent protest should avoid a violence of spirit within protestors as well as avoiding external physical violence; in struggling for human dignity, protestors should not give into bitterness and hate. Finally, "the method of nonviolence is based on the conviction that the universe is on the side of justice." King based much of his thinking in this regard not only on Gandhi's writings but on the idea of Christian love, as embodied in the concept of *agape*. King defined this as a kind of love wherein individuals love people "because God loves them and here we love the person who does the evil deed while hating the deed that the person does. It is the type of love that stands at the center of the movement that we are trying to carry on in the Southland—*agape*."

King admitted the difficulties at first of convincing the Montgomery boycotters of the value of nonviolence. "There was always the problem of getting this method over because it didn't make sense to most of the people in the beginning." King and other leaders used their mass meetings "to explain nonviolence to a community of people who had never heard of the philosophy and in many instances were not sympathetic to it." In the early days of the movement, the phrase "Christian love" was used by boycotters, reflecting the specifically Christian outlook that informed African Americans in Montgomery. "It was Jesus of Nazareth that stirred the Negroes to protest with the creative weapons of love," King noted. As time passed, "the inspiration of Mahatma Gandhi began to exert its influence." King praised Montgomery's blacks for their willingness to grapple with a new approach to the crisis in race relations. His experience in Montgomery, he later wrote, "did more to clarify my thinking on the question of nonviolence than all of the books that I had read." For him, living through the protests, "nonviolence became more than a method to which I gave intellectual assent; it became a commitment to a way of life." More than a strategic expedient, nonviolence became for King and others in the movement a philosophy "that men live by because of the sheer morality of its claim." Through countless sermons, lectures, classes, interviews, and publications, at endless mass meetings, protest events, and public gatherings, King became the nation's foremost exponent of nonviolent resistance, a philosophy grounded in the specific experiences of protest on southern soil.

Out of Montgomery came two organizations embodying nonviolent resistance—the Southern Christian Leadership Conference (SCLC) and the Student Nonviolent Coordinating Committee (SNCC). King and others founded the SCLC in 1957 to coordinate civil rights direct-action protests across the South and to offer a reform voice to the nation, with nonviolence and civil disobedience central to its mission. The organization offered leadership training workshops and citizenship education programs. It held voter registration drives and undertook a major campaign to attack segregation in Birmingham, Ala., which came to a head in 1963. James Bevel, who had trained at Highlander before becoming a leader in the Nashville student sit-ins in 1961, became the central strategist and conductor of the "children's crusade," a march of black young people that crystallized the city's black community in support of the protests. James Lawson, who as a Methodist missionary in India observed Gandhi's nonviolent methods, and who became committed to nonviolence as a governing philosophy in the 1940s, first met King in 1957 and soon became chair of the SCLC's direct-action committee and later became director of its nonviolent education work. Lawson called in 1961 for a "nonviolent army" to challenge segregation, pushing the organization in ever more militant directions. The same was true for another key activist, Ella Baker, who became interim director of SCLC when it was founded and was important in combining nonviolent philosophy with calls for economic justice.

Baker was a bridge from the SCLC to the establishment of SNCC, which became another central civil rights organization built around nonviolence. Baker called a meeting at Shaw University in Raleigh, N.C., in 1960 to encourage student sit-ins, and out of that meeting came the student-led group whose members participated in Freedom Rides to end segregation in interstate travel and supported voter registration drives and citizenship education projects, including a crucial role in Mississippi Freedom Summer in 1964. SNCC members in the late 1960s came to question the effectiveness of the interracial coalition that had long been central to civil rights work, and they rejected the nonviolent philosophy and tactics with the rise of the Black Power movement. The organization disbanded in 1970.

Since then, many social movements, from environmental activists to anti-abortion advocates, have employed nonviolent civil disobedience in support of their goals in the South, but doing so without the breadth and depth of the civil rights movement's embrace of nonviolence in the decades of the 1950s and 1960s. The Martin Luther King federal holiday often is the occasion for continued public reflection on the principles of nonviolence.

CHARLES REAGAN WILSON
University of Mississippi

David Garrow, *Bearing the Cross: Martin Luther King Jr. and the Southern Christian Leadership Conference* (1986); John M. Glen, *Highlander: No Ordinary School* (1996); Wesley C. Hogan, *Many Minds, One Heart: SNCC's Dream for a New America* (2007); Joseph Kip Kosek, *Journal of American History* (March 2005); Rhonda Mawhood Lee, *Journal of Southern History* (May 2010); August Meier and Elliott Rudwick, *CORE: A Study in the Civil Rights Movement, 1942–1968* (1973); Aldon D. Morris, *The Origins of the Civil Right Movement: Black Communities Organizing for Change* (1984); Adam Roberts and Timothy Garton Ash, eds., *Civil Resistance and Power Politics: The Experience of Nonviolent Action from Gandhi to the Present* (2009); James M. Washington, ed., *A Testament of Hope: The Essential Writings and Speeches of Martin Luther King Jr.* (1991).

Organized Crime

In both historical and fictional literature, the South has often been portrayed as a region characterized by crime and violence. The vigilante, the lyncher, the duelist, the race rioter, and the frontier ruffian have played prominent roles in the region's history. Writers such as W. J. Cash and Sheldon Hackney have described the pervasiveness of violence in southern history, and many writers have concluded that crime and violence assume a distinctive pattern in the region's development. Despite the numerous accounts of a southern propensity for violence, one aspect of it that has received little attention is organized crime in the South.

The term organized crime lacks precise definition but is generally employed to describe the illegal enterprises and operations of those underworld organizations commonly called the Mafia, La Cosa Nostra, and the Mob. In the 20th century these organizations have dominated criminal activities such as gambling, prostitution, narcotics, bootlegging, and extortion. Centered in large metropolitan areas throughout the United States, these "families," as they are called, are headed by "bosses," or "godfathers." Each boss is a member of a national organized crime "commission," which dictates overall syndicate policy. Although most of these families are located in large cities in the Northeast, Midwest, and West, three have been assumed to operate from the southern cities of New Orleans, Miami, and Dallas.

According to the organized crime unit of the FBI, the first formal Mafia family in America was established in New Orleans during the Reconstruction era by Italian and Sicilian immigrants who used Mafia organizations in their native country as the basis for a Louisiana family. Recent scholarly studies have shown that this account is not supported by concrete evidence. The earliest publicity given to a Mafia organization in Louisiana came from widespread newspaper coverage of the 1890 assassination of New Orleans police chief David C. Hennessy. In 1891, 16 Italian and Sicilian residents of the city were tried and acquitted of the Hennessy murder. Inflamed by sensational newspaper accounts and stirred to action by anti-Italian remarks made by Mayor Joseph Shakespeare, a mob broke into the Orleans Parish prison and lynched 11 of the defendants. Many writers have described the Hennessy killing as the action of a Mafia vendetta, but an exhaustive study by Humbert Nelli uncovered no evidence to substantiate that version.

The first reliable evidence of organized crime in Louisiana came with the establishment of a slot machine empire in the state by New York mobster Frank Costello in 1935. Costello evidently made a deal with Sen. Huey P. Long, whereby the state government would allow the machines in return for a share of the profits for the Long political machine. The Costello operation soon branched into "lotto" (the numbers game), bookmaking, and pinball machines. Shortly after the end of World War II, Costello, Meyer Lansky, the notorious financial wizard of the national syndicate, and Carlos Marcello, a Louisiana entrepreneur, opened two gambling casinos in Jefferson Parish. During the 1948–52 administration of Gov. Earl K. Long, casino gambling, slot machines, pinball machines, handbook operations, and lotto flourished openly in the southern half of the state.

Since the early 1950s Carlos Marcello was reputed to control organized crime in Louisiana and in neighboring states. According to such sources as the Metropolitan Crime Commission of Greater New Orleans and Sen. Estes Kefauver's committee on organized crime, Marcello headed an organized criminal empire that took in almost $1 billion annually from vice, theft, blackmail, extortion, robbery, and political graft. After intensive investigation by the Justice Department of Attorney General Robert Kennedy, Marcello in 1962 was forcibly deported to Guatemala because he had never become a naturalized citizen. Within a few months, Marcello returned to Louisiana and for many years managed to evade the concerted efforts of law enforcement agencies to uncover concrete evidence of his criminal activities. He did serve a brief sentence in a federal penitentiary for assaulting an FBI agent in 1967, and in 1981 he was convicted of attempting to bribe a federal judge and of conspiracy to influence federal officials. He served a lengthy term in a federal penitentiary. Released early from prison because of advanced Alzheimer's disease, Marcello returned home to Louisiana, where he died in 1993. Despite the many allegations about Marcello's Mafia family in Louisiana, virtually nothing is known about the organization, and little evidence has been produced to support those allegations.

In Florida, Santo Trafficante Jr. reputedly took over leadership of a Mafia family after his father died in 1954. Originally headquartered in Tampa, the syndicate moved to Miami in the late 1960s. Trafficante reportedly served as the coordinator of Meyer Lansky's casino gambling and wide-open vice, which flourished in Havana during the 1952–59 regime of Cuban dictator Fulgencio Batista. When Fidel Castro came to power in 1959, he jailed Trafficante and closed down the mob's operations on the island. In retaliation, Trafficante, along with Chicago Mafia boss Sam Giancana, conspired with the CIA in several futile attempts to assassinate Castro. Trafficante died in Florida in 1987. Today, the Trafficante organization supposedly dominates the lucrative narcotics trade between Latin America and Florida and is currently engaged in a struggle with Latin American narcotics traffickers.

Little is known about the Dallas family of Joseph Civello. Some accounts depict it as an independent Mafia family; others describe it as the Texas arm of the Marcello empire. Civello allegedly controls illegal vice in Texas and serves as a conduit for communications among various Mafia families. Civello came most prominently into the news when he was identified as one of the 57 mobsters who attended the infamous Appalachian meeting at the upstate New York home of organized crime figure Joseph Barbera Sr. on 14 November 1957.

Probably the best-known individual in the history of organized crime in the South was Jacob Rubenstein, better known as Jack Ruby. Born in Chicago in 1911, Ruby began his career in the Al Capone organization. He moved to Dallas in 1947, where he joined the Civello organization. Ruby operated several nightclubs, or "strip-tease joints," handled bookmaking operations and prostitution, and had close contacts with the Dallas police. In 1959 Ruby visited the Havana prison where Santo Trafficante was incarcerated, and he assisted in smuggling arms and supplies to anti-Castro guerrilla fighters in Cuba. Ruby had frequent contacts with close associates of Teamsters union boss Jimmy Hoffa, and he communicated with members of the Civello, Marcello, and Trafficante organizations. During the month prior to the assassination of President John F. Kennedy, he made numerous long-distance telephone calls to known mobsters. When Kennedy was assassinated, Ruby was seen at Dallas police headquarters, where Kennedy's accused assassin, Lee Harvey Oswald, was held in custody. On the morning of 24 November 1963 Ruby shot and killed Oswald in the basement of police headquarters. Convicted of the Oswald killing, Ruby spent the next three years in a Dallas jail. He died in January 1967.

In 1979 the Select Committee on Assassinations of the U.S. House of Representatives issued its final report on the Kennedy assassination, and it concluded that either Marcello or Trafficante may have conspired to kill the president. Kennedy's war on organized crime, his failure to eliminate Castro, and his sexual intimacy with Judith Exner, the girlfriend of Sam Giancana, provided possible motives. The committee found evidence that both Marcello and Trafficante had expressed the desire to be rid of Kennedy and that Lee Harvey Oswald's uncle, as well as several of the people with whom he associated during his stay in New Orleans in 1963, had connections with the Marcello family. The committee, however, could not furnish reliable proof of its speculations.

The subject of organized crime in the South has received scant attention from historians and other scholars. Much of the available material on the subject contains a considerable amount of sensationalism, speculation, and unfounded accusations. Because of its highly controversial nature, organized crime has attracted the attention of journalists and popular writers whose works lack documentation. The reports and studies of congressional committees and government agencies likewise fail to employ the proper techniques of historical inquiry. Much more research into the topic is necessary before an accurate and responsible history of organized crime in the South is possible.

MICHAEL L. KURTZ
Southeastern Louisiana University

G. Robert Blakely and Richard N. Billings, *The Plot to Kill the President* (1981); Michael L. Kurtz, *Louisiana History* (Fall 1983); Humbert S. Nelli, *The Business of Crime: Italians and Syndicate Crime in the United States* (1976); U.S. Congress, House of Representatives, *Investigation of the Assassination of President John F. Kennedy: Hearings before the Select Committee on Assassinations of the U. S. House of Representatives* (1978–79); U.S. Congress, Senate, *Report on the Select Committee to Investigate Organized Crime in Interstate Commerce* (1951).

Outlaw-Heroes

Southern history and legend have been marked by a procession of outlaws whose illegal behavior in the service of some noble cause or ideal has elevated them to heroic status. Most southern outlaws, like the Harpe brothers who wantonly robbed and murdered across the frontier South, were notorious rather than heroic. But there have always been southern outlaws who fit E. J. Hobsbawm's definition of "social bandits": those who are forced to break the law to avenge a wrong or to defend their honor, family, or community from some oppressive power or circumstance. From the Regulators of colonial South Carolina (1767–69), the first organized vigilantes in America, to Luke and Bo Duke of *The Dukes of Hazzard*, "good old boy" lawbreakers in one of the most popular television programs of the 1980s, honorable outlaws have been celebrated in southern folklore, popular culture, and high arts. Other regions and nations have celebrated them as well.

Southerners have enshrined a wide range of outlaw-heroes in myth and legend. The outlaws' diversity reflects the complexity of a region that embraces the extremes of colonial Virginia and frontier Texas, black and white, planter and mountaineer, yeoman and slave. In 1676 Nathaniel Bacon achieved heroic status by leading an illegal armed rebellion against the legitimate but unresponsive government of Virginia. The South Carolina Regulators stepped outside the law with popular support to control the backcountry in the 1760s. A significant number of southern outlaw-heroes were spawned and found their justification in the events of the Civil War and Reconstruction. In the white southern mind and myth, and eventually in the mythology of other regions, southerners were driven into outlawry by rapacious Yankee armies, corrupt Radical Republican politicians, predatory carpetbaggers, and vindictive former slaves. Guerrilla fighter and bank robber Jesse James protected southern women and children in frontier Missouri from violent northern persecution during the war. For years afterward he protected them from usurious banks and railroads. Similarly, the Ku Klux Klan and other white vigilante/terrorist groups were active in the South during Reconstruction. Harriet Tubman and John Brown were outlaw heroes to black southerners and abolitionists for their attempts to free slaves.

In the late 19th century the Hatfields and McCoys were two of the well-known feuding mountain clans who ignored points of law and fought over issues of honor and family loyalty. Morris Slater ("Railroad Bill"), the legendary black Robin Hood of Alabama, fought the law and stole for his poverty-stricken people until he was cut down in 1896. During the Depression of the 1930s in the Southwest, Bonnie Parker and Clyde Barrow, "Pretty Boy" Floyd, and other rural outlaws stole from the rich and gave to the poor in the tradition of Jesse James. Junior Johnson was a champion stock car racer in the 1960s who learned his driving skills while running moonshine in the hills of North Carolina, evading the meddling federal agents who put his daddy in jail. Johnson was compared to "Robin Hood or Jesse James" and was called the "last American hero" by Virginia-born writer Thomas Wolfe. Since the early 1970s southern actor Burt Reynolds has appeared in a long series of popular movies with Dixie settings in which he has played lovable outlaws who fought corrupt sheriffs, transported illegal beer, and robbed the gas stations of a heartless oil corporation. In the early 1980s cousins Luke and Bo Duke broke the law each week in their stock car *General Lee* while untangling themselves and their down-home kin from the corrupt operations of the judiciary and police in their mythical southern county.

The outlaw-hero's marginal status has defined the limits of acceptable behavior within southern society. He has provided traditional southern culture with a safety valve: honorable models for rebellion. Moreover, southern outlaw-heroes have reflected and reconciled what W. J. Cash called the "social schizophrenia" of the southern character: intense individualism versus a deep sense of responsibility for others, "hedonism" versus "Puritanism," unrestrained violence versus a gentlemanly code of conduct, wanderlust versus a profound sense of place and tradition. Nowhere has this "split" psyche been more apparent than in the southern outlaw-hero and nowhere have these contradictions been so well reconciled. The outlaw-hero is the single figure who can engage with impunity in explosive, illegal behavior because it is justified by some noble purpose.

There has never been unanimity regarding individual outlaw-heroes, especially when race is involved. The knights of the Ku Klux Klan have always had both white and black detractors in the South. And the status of many outlaw-heroes has varied over time. Klansmen enjoyed less heroic status during the "Second Reconstruction" of the 1960s than they had in earlier eras. The outlaw-heroes of the southern black and Mexican American fit the standard southern pattern except that they were seen as mere badmen by the white culture they fought. The 1831 slave revolt led by Nat Turner and the violent struggles of Gregorio Cortez with Texas lawmen were justified in the eyes of their people on the familiar basis of resisting legal but oppressive forces: the cruelties of slavery in Virginia and the uneven hand of justice in the Rio Grande Valley. In some cases no justification was offered for black outlaw heroes such as the bullying badmen in black folksongs: Stackolee, John Hardy, the Bully of the Town. Their tough defiance and ability to survive in a hostile white world were the stuff of black heroism with no need for moral justification.

There has been a fine line in southern culture between a rebellious hero celebrated for his uninhibited vitality and the true outlaw-hero who is completely beyond the law. Southern frontier heroes like Davy Crockett and Jim Bowie were widely celebrated in folklore and popular southwestern humor for behavior that was often violent and illegal, but they were not generally considered outlaws. Although the southern gentleman who skirted the law to duel for his honor was sometimes seen as a heroic figure representing the best of his culture, this did not make him an outlaw. Heroic Confederate military figures such as Robert E. Lee and "Stonewall" Jackson were outlaws perhaps in the eyes of the North but not to southerners. Confederate Partisan Rangers John Hunt Morgan, John Singleton Mosby, and William Clarke Quantrill owed their heroic status to dashing guerrilla warfare behind enemy lines. However, only Jesse James and a few other southern guerrillas clearly crossed over the line to outlaw-hero status by robbing banks and railroads long after the war had ended.

Since the beginnings of commercial country music in the South in the 1920s, some of its most popular figures have celebrated rebellious, rambling behavior in their songs. Much of the popularity and heroic status of Jimmie Rodgers, Hank Williams, Johnny Cash, and Merle Haggard have derived from their legendary participation in this lifestyle. The same was true for southern rockabilly rebels Elvis Presley and Jerry Lee Lewis. In the 1970s Texans Willie Nelson and Waylon Jennings were marketed with great success as "outlaw" country musicians because of their spirited rebellion against strait-laced Nashville's musical and social norms. Yet none of these were traditional outlaw-heroes driven beyond the law. Rather they were rebel heroes celebrated for their ability to pursue an independent lifestyle while maintaining, just as the outlaw-hero did, some allegiance to church, home, and mother. Ironically, all these country musicians have used the image of the free-spirited western cowboy to suggest their rugged independence. Despite country music's southern lineage, its performers have often rejected the "hillbilly" image in favor of western motifs that provide more positive and widely accepted images of heroism and rebellion.

A related regional borrowing occurred in the century following the Civil War when the western hero with his personal "code" that transcended the law began to bear a striking resemblance to the southern outlaw hero with his code of honor. Western heroes of all kinds were fashioned out of real and fictional southerners with outlaw qualities: guerrilla-bandit Jesse James, cowboy-vigilante "The Virginian," farmhand-gunfighter Shane. When such western heroes took the law into their own hands they did it with the southern outlaw-hero's sense of honor and purpose—usually to aid a community besieged by savage forces.

There was a historical basis for this western adaptation of southern characters and traditions; Texas's cowboys and Missouri's outlaws were largely southern in origin and worldview. An equally important reason for this borrowing was the climate of the post–Civil War era. The relatively homogeneous South, with its romantic myths of a gracious, agricultural past and noble Anglo-Saxon heroes (outlaws and otherwise), exerted a strong pull on a nation fearful of urbanization, industrialization, and immigration. The nation turned readily to western heroes who embodied traditional qualities of the southern outlaw-hero in a frontier setting free of urbanization and immigration, yet also free of controversial factors associated with the South such as slavery, aristocracy, and defeat.

Regardless of an outlaw-hero's morality as judged by outsiders, or the historical accuracy of the legends surrounding him, glorified "social bandits" like England's Robin Hood have long served significant psychological, sociological, and mythological functions for those who feel frustrated, victimized, and powerless. Southern outlaw-heroes demonstrated the continuing utility of the "social bandit" in the 20th century by becoming heroes of national and international proportion, such as Jesse James, Bonnie and Clyde, Burt Reynolds's outlaw persona, and the fictitious Dukes of Hazzard. These southern outlaw-heroes have had a universal appeal in tumultuous times because they embody the comforting values of a traditional culture yet have the strength and courage to break the law and successfully rebel against the injustices of life.

GEORGE B. WARD
Texas State Historical Association

Roger D. Abrahams, *Deep Down in the Jungle: Negro Narrative Fiction from the Streets of Philadelphia* (1970); W. J. Cash, *The Mind of the South* (1941); David Brion Davis, *American Quarterly* (Summer 1954); Hugh Davis Graham and Ted Robert Gurr, eds., *Violence in America: Historical and Comparative Perspectives* (1969); E. J. Hobsbawm, *Primitive Rebels* (1965); John A. Lomax and Alan Lomax, *Folksong U.S.A.* (1947); William A. Settle Jr., *Jesse James Was His Name* (1966); T. J. Stiles, *Jesse James: Last Rebel of the Civil War* (2002); Tom Wolfe, *The Kandy-Kolored Tangerine-Flake Streamline Baby* (1965).

Peonage

Peonage, a Latin American labor system that entered the United States through Mexican land acquisitions, relies on debt to bind laborers to the land. In 1867

Congress passed a law (14 Stat. 546) that prohibited peonage both in territories recently acquired from Mexico and throughout the United States. The law lay dormant until 1901, when U.S. attorney Fred Cubberly uncovered it and brought a case against Samuel T. Clyatt for using laborers in his turpentine operation to work off debts. During the statute's dormancy, the intricate farm labor system that developed in the South blurred the distinctions between law and custom. State legislatures enacted enticement laws, emigrant agent restrictions, contract laws, vagrancy statutes, the criminal surety system, and convict labor laws, while planters used both laws and rural customs to keep laborers, in most cases black sharecroppers, from leaving their employ. Such labor laws, like discrimination and disfranchisement statutes, became more severe in the 1890s and the first decade of the 20th century.

As the *Clyatt* case (*Clyatt v. United States*, 197 U.S. 207) progressed through appeals that ultimately decided the constitutionality of the law, the extent of peonage in the South became more apparent. In Alabama, Judge Thomas G. Jones, experimenting with light sentences and publicity in 1903, dramatized how pervasive peonage had become. In 1906 Booker T. Washington joined with local whites in Alabama and brought another precedent-setting case that exposed, through the plight of Alonzo Bailey, the tight legal framework that trapped men who took cash advances under "false pretenses" and left their jobs before completing the contract. The case also showed the draconian nature of southern rural labor laws. The basic "false pretenses" law had been on the books since 1885, but laborers had won a series of Alabama cases, for employers had been unable to establish the intent of laborers who left their jobs. In 1903 Alabama tightened its law, as did Georgia; Florida followed in 1907. Under the amended law, a laborer's taking the money and failing to either pay it back or work it out was "prima facie evidence of the intent to injure or defraud his employer." A 1907 rule of evidence prohibited the laborer from taking the witness stand to explain his intent. After two appeals, in 1911 the Supreme Court struck down the law (*Bailey v. Alabama*, 211 U.S. 452; *Bailey v. Alabama*, 219 U.S. 219). Yet other states, particularly Florida and Georgia, persisted with similar laws until the 1940s. The Supreme Court also ruled against the widespread practice of allowing planters to pay off fines of laborers who were facing jail sentences and then working them as criminals (*United States v. Reynolds*, 235 U.S. 133). This series of cases successfully unraveled much of the legal net that caught vulnerable farm workers and sucked them into the vortex of peonage. Still, peonage continued outside the law.

Most peonage cases originated in the old cotton belt that ran from South Carolina through the Black Belt of Georgia and Alabama and into the Mississippi and Arkansas deltas. During the first decade of the century many immigrants who were transported to the South became the focus of a series of cases and glaring publicity lasting several years. While successful court cases made southerners aware of the law, peonage continued as evinced in numerous complaints and prosecutions. The vast complaint file in the National Archives suggests not only the extent of involuntary servitude but also the helplessness of barely literate workers who tried to escape. Local law enforcement officials either ignored such conditions or actively supported planters. Most rural laborers did not understand the workings of the law and were caught up in the customary relationship of landlord and tenant; relatively few questioned their conditions. In some cases planters did not understand the law either. Court cases and complaints revealed clearly the bottom rung of the southern rural labor system and showed the confusion in distinguishing freedom from bondage.

Complaints and cases declined during the 1930s, although a landmark Arkansas case in 1936 used an 1866 statute (14 Stat. 50) outlawing slave kidnapping to prosecute lawman Paul Peacher and thus extend federal jurisdiction over any kind of involuntary servitude—not just that which involved debt. In recent years most peonage complaints have come from migrant laborers, and a number of successful prosecutions since the 1980s have revealed the vulnerability of such agricultural workers. Thus, in a larger sense, peonage has represented continuity with the South's slave past. Since its founding in 1993, the Coalition for Immokalee Workers, based in Florida, has earned national recognition for its role in investigating and pursuing cases of modern slavery. Most recently, in 2008, the U.S. Department of Justice brought charges against the Navarette family for shackling and beating undocumented workers from Mexico and Guatemala and forcing them to work on farms in Florida, North Carolina, and South Carolina. Brothers Cesar and Geovanni Navarette pleaded guilty to all counts and were each sentenced to 12 years in federal prison.

PETE DANIEL
Smithsonian Institution

William Cohen, *Journal of Southern History* (February 1976); Pete Daniel, *The Shadow of Slavery: Peonage in the South, 1901–1969* (1990); Daniel A. Novak, *The Wheel of Servitude: Black Forced Labor after Slavery* (1978); Jerrold M. Packard, *American Nightmare: The History of Jim Crow* (2002).

Police Brutality

Police brutality in the American South has its historical roots in the violent suppression of African American resistance within the southern system of slavery.

During the colonial period and the antebellum era, southern slave patrollers used means of physical coercion and violence to deter slave rebellions and capture fugitive slaves. Southern police institutions emerged from the slave patrol system. Following the failure of Reconstruction, police brutality became a crucial tool for white southerners in their attempt to reinforce white supremacy and build up segregation. In addition to that, southern sheriffs, deputies, and urban police officers used excessive physical violence to protect the economic, social, and political status quo. Consequently, police brutality was predominantly directed against African Americans but also against other minority racial and ethnic groups.

In order to sanction and enforce Jim Crow laws and regulations, police officers used undue violence against those African American women and men whose behavior seemed to challenge segregation and white supremacy. Southern policemen commonly referred to physical violence as a necessary means to keep African Americans "in their place." Consequently, police brutality against African Americans was widely practiced during arrests, house searches, and criminal interrogations. It encompassed homicides, shootings, beatings, whippings, and sexual violence. As a contemporary observer noted, the use of physical force to gain confessions from African American suspects was a "routine device" in many southern police stations. By using unwarranted physical force against African Americans, police officers sought to reinforce the claim of white superiority and black inferiority on an everyday basis. To achieve this goal, police violence was used as a means of intimidation and informal punishment. Archival sources document both the endemic use of police brutality throughout the American South as well as the willingness of African Americans to fight against this form of oppression. Despite the protests of local citizens, black newspapers, and civil rights activists, however, southern district attorneys and courts usually refused to prosecute and punish acts of police brutality. Only after 1940 did federal agencies start to initiate civil rights prosecutions in some of the most severe cases of southern police brutality against African Americans. Police officers also used disproportionate force during race riots that spread in the American South during the 20th century. In several instances race riots resulted out of, or were fueled by, incidents of police brutality against African Americans that instigated protest and rebellion within the local black community. In addition to that, police officers also participated in numerous lynchings by willingly releasing African American prisoners to lynch mobs, standing by while lynch victims were killed, and refusing to arrest mob members.

After World War II, police brutality became a major focus of black protest and local civil rights activism. Following decades of political struggle, African Americans were reluctantly appointed to southern urban police forces during the end of the 1940s. While their presence reduced crime rates within the black community, it did not end police brutality against blacks. Instead, southern police departments remained bastions of white interests and continued to uphold racial segregation in the American South. During the civil rights movement, white police officers attacked black and white civil rights activists and used disproportionate violence to prevent and interrupt peaceful demonstrations and sit-ins. In many southern communities, incidents of police brutality led to the formation of African American self-defense organizations. When Black Power activists reacted with open protest and armed resistance to acts of police brutality, they became targets of violent police actions. While civil rights activism led to a variety of reforms in southern policing, the massive corruption in southern urban police departments and the "war on drugs" during the 1980s and 1990s led to the continuation of police violence against minority racial and ethnic groups. Into the first decades of the 21st century, police brutality in the American South remains a racially charged matter that continues to set off controversial debates on southern race relations.

SILVAN NIEDERMEIER
University of Erfurt

W. Marvin Dulaney, *Black Police in America* (1996); Robin D. G. Kelley, in *Police Brutality: An Anthology*, ed. Jill Nelson (2000); Leonard N. Moore, *Black Rage in New Orleans: Police Brutality and African American Activism from World War II to Hurricane Katrina* (2010); Gunnar Myrdal, *An American Dilemma: The Negro Problem and Modern Democracy* (1944); Arthur F. Raper, *The Tragedy of Lynching* (1933).

Political Violence

No major section of the country can match the South's record of violence, political and otherwise. Southern political violence, like organized violence nationally, has featured repression by social and political elites of those who threatened (or were perceived to threaten) their control. The rare colonial insurrections—Bacon's Rebellion in Virginia (1675–76) and Culpepper's Rebellion in North Carolina (1677–78)—were in the main middle-class or upper-class revolts against ruling factions in their respective colonies and involved very little bloodshed. The Regulator movements of North and South Carolina in the 1760s and 1770s arose out of frontier conditions in the backcountry. The North Carolina movement sought to force the colonial authorities in the east to provide more responsible government in the west. The rebels were defeated on

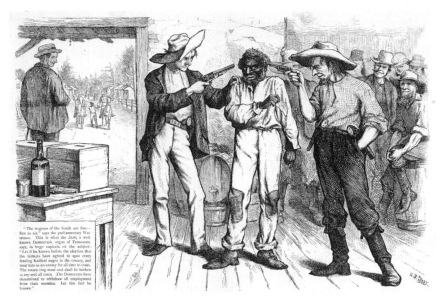

Cartoon that appeared in Harper's Weekly on 21 October 1876, illustrating intimidation of likely Republican voters. The cartoon's caption reads: "'Of course he wants to vote the Democrat ticket!' Democratic 'Reformer': 'You're as free as air, ain't you? Say you are, or I'll blow yer black head off!'" (Courtesy of the Tennessee State Library and Archives)

the battlefield of Alamance in 1771, after which six of their leaders were hanged. The South Carolina Regulators were vigilantes, organized to suppress anarchy and force the colonial authorities in Charleston to bring government to the frontier. Neither movement aimed seriously to modify the structure of colonial government, much less to overthrow it.

In fact, many backcountry settlers felt a greater kinship with England after 1775 than with the eastern planters who led the movement for independence. Organized North Carolina Loyalists were decisively defeated at the battle of Moore's Creek Bridge in 1776, but partisan warfare raged between Whigs and Tories for several years in some interior districts of the Carolinas and Georgia.

Antebellum vigilantism, aimed at actual or suspected slave insurrections and their white instigators, had not been political, strictly speaking. But the goal of keeping the slaves in subjection, by force if necessary, and the day-to-day requirements of slave discipline conditioned southerners to the use of force as a regular instrument of policy. Even greater discord followed in the wake of southern secession in 1861. Unionist sentiment existed in varying measure throughout the South, reflected in active or passive opposition to the Confederacy. It was strongest in the border states and in the mountain areas of Virginia,

North Carolina, Tennessee, Georgia, Alabama, and Arkansas. Opinion was not uniform in these regions, however, and warfare of family against family, even brother against brother, was not unknown. Such hostilities engendered bitterness that lasted for many years, sometimes in the form of blood feuds.

These wartime differences were translated after the war into political party divisions: former Unionists became Republicans, and ex-Confederates affiliated with the Conservative or Democratic Party. Federal Reconstruction policy introduced the Republican Party to the South in 1867 as the champion of Unionism, black freedom, and civil rights. Regional opposition to these goals drew heavily on prewar precedents.

It was but a short step from the militia musters and the slave patrols of the 1850s to Ku Klux Klans and the so-called home guards, white leagues, and redshirt clubs of the Reconstruction era. All were designed to enforce white supremacy. For more than a decade after 1865, therefore, white southerners of a certain age and disposition felt it their duty and privilege to continue the twin struggles against Unionism and for white supremacy, now joined as a crusade against the "Black Republican" Party. The crusade took several forms. All were more or less inspired, organized, and led by the middle and upper classes, appearances sometimes to the contrary notwithstanding.

The most spectacular form of resistance, but the least effective in the long run, was the midnight raiding of the Ku Klux Klan and its kindred organizations. Formed in Tennessee in 1866, the Klan spread throughout the South in the spring of 1868 as congressional Reconstruction policies went into effect. It killed, flogged, and intimidated hosts of black and white Republicans in the areas where it flourished, but by 1872 it was put down by a combination of state and federal judicial and military action. The Klan helped to impeach and remove Gov. William W. Holden of North Carolina, but it failed to end Reconstruction in any state.

Probably the most successful form of political violence was the urban riot. Seventy-eight have been counted for the years 1865 through 1876 in cities such as Memphis and New Orleans and villages including Camilla, Ga., and Clinton, Miss. Generally planned in advance, they often resulted in the death or banishment of Republican leaders of both races and the demoralization of their followers. Such riots occurred throughout the Reconstruction period and sporadically afterward, the last of them in Wilmington, N.C., in 1898 and Atlanta in 1906.

Closely related to the urban riots were the activities of the white league, redshirt club, and other paramilitary groups that dispensed with the bizarre disguises of the Ku Klux Klan and operated in broad daylight. They rode about before elections, breaking up Republican meetings and intimidating Republican candidates and voters. Georgians pioneered this tactic in 1870, and it was repeated with increasing sophistication throughout the Deep South from 1874 to 1876. With the urban riots, it was largely responsible for bringing southern Reconstruction to a close by 1877.

From the 1870s to the 1890s, southern Democrats controlled their respective states by means of honest electoral victories (where possible) and partial disfranchisement, fraud, and violence (where necessary). Republicans were permitted to vote and to elect candidates in the mountains and the black belts, but only as long as they did not threaten statewide Democratic control. In the 1890s, after a variety of agrarian insurgent movements, sometimes featuring coalitions with Republicans, Democrats began more systematically to disfranchise their opponents through constitutional or legislative action. Henceforth, the law would accomplish peacefully what riots and red shirt campaigns had done through threats and violence. The generation after 1890 saw the climax not only of black disfranchisement but of lynching and enforced racial segregation as well.

The violence of the second Ku Klux Klan in the 1920s was not primarily political, and, except for such isolated events as the assassinations of Gov. William Goebel of Kentucky in 1900 and Sen. Huey P. Long of Louisiana in 1935, substantial political violence did not return until the advent of the civil rights movement, or Second Reconstruction, of the 1950s and 1960s. The civil rights laws of 1957–64, and especially the Voting Rights Act of 1965, helped return millions of black voters to the polls after the lapse of three generations.

The civil rights movement used nonviolent protest as a means of winning public opinion throughout the country to peaceful change. Most of the violence that came was directed by whites against the desegregation of schools, businesses, and public facilities rather than the voting booth. It was not, therefore, specifically political until Martin Luther King Jr. and his colleagues shifted their emphasis in 1964 to black voter registration. The killing of Michael Schwerner, Andrew Goodman, and James Chaney in the registration drive in Mississippi and other acts of violence in 1964 hastened congressional passage of the Voting Rights Act the following year.

In 1979 members of the Ku Klux Klan and the American Nazi Party shot and killed five Communist Worker's Party demonstrators at Greensboro, N.C. Unlike most of the political violence since the Civil War, this event had little or no direct racial bearing; the perpetrators and the victims were all white. The incident dramatized the enmity that developed after World War II between political fringe groups of the far left and right. The enmity was most volatile in the South, where violence-prone Klansmen and Nazis were in evidence.

The reasons for the South's affinity for violence are not easy to pinpoint with assurance, but surely racial dissension has played a central role. So too, perhaps, has the region's rural, scattered population, which traditionally encouraged hunting, self-protection, private settlement of grievances, and attendant carrying of weapons. Politically, the South has experienced more bitter conflict, arising from deep racial and class divisions, than any other section of the country. Even when these conditions change and internal differences abate, old cultural patterns retain a life of their own.

ALLEN W. TRELEASE
University of North Carolina at Greensboro

Richard Maxwell Brown, *Strain of Violence: Historical Studies of American Violence and Vigilantism* (1975); Jane Dailey, Glenda Elizabeth Gilmore, and Bryant Simon, *Jumpin' Jim Crow: Southern Politics from Civil War to Civil Rights* (2000); Hugh Davis Graham and Ted Robert Gurr, eds., *Violence in America: Historical and Comparative Perspectives* (1969); Michael K. Honey, *Southern Labor and Black Civil Rights: Organizing Memphis Workers* (1993); Steven F. Lawson, *Black Ballots: Voting Rights in the South, 1944–1969* (1976); George C. Rable, *But There Was No Peace: The Role of Violence in the Politics of Reconstruction* (1984); Bryant Simon, *A Fabric of Defeat: The Politics of South Carolina Millhands, 1910–1948* (1998); Allen W. Trelease, *White Terror: The Ku Klux Klan Conspiracy and Southern Reconstruction* (1971); Christopher Waldrep, *Roots of Disorder: Race and Criminal Justice in the American South, 1817–70* (1998); Wilcomb E. Washburn, *The Governor and the Rebel: A History of Bacon's Rebellion in Virginia* (1957).

Prisons

American penitentiaries developed in two distinct phases, and southern states participated in both. Virginia, Kentucky, Maryland, and Georgia built prisons before 1820, and between 1829 and 1842 new or newly reorganized institutions were established in Maryland, Tennessee, Georgia, Louisiana, Missouri, Mississippi, and Alabama. Only the Carolinas and Florida resisted the penitentiary before the Civil War.

Southerners fiercely debated the justice and utility of the penitentiary throughout the antebellum era. Some citizens and legislators argued that the institution constituted an essential part of any enlightened government, whereas

Convict labor chain gang, North Carolina, 1910 (Jack Delano,
photographer, Library of Congress [LC-USF-33-20863-M3])

other southerners warned that the penitentiary posed a real and direct threat
to freedom and republican government. Advocates of the institution believed
that the law would be more effective if punishment were less physically brutal;
opponents of the institution believed that locking men up out of public sight to
"reform" them was a farce and a dangerous precedent. They preferred that their
states adhere to the older methods of punishment: fines, branding, imprisonment in local jails, or hanging. In the only two referenda on the penitentiary—
in Alabama in 1834 and in North Carolina in 1846—southern voters expressed
overwhelming opposition to the institution, but southern states nonetheless
created one penitentiary after another. Virtually no reformers championed the
cause of penal innovation; rather, obscure state legislators took it upon themselves to keep the South abreast of "progress" made in the rest of the Anglo-
American world. The new institutions they created closely resembled one another and their northern counterparts.

Most of the prisoners in these antebellum southern prisons were white
men, disproportionately from cities, and of immigrant background. Almost
no women received penitentiary terms. After 1818 only Louisiana consistently
sentenced slaves to prison. Most states of the Deep South incarcerated exceedingly few free blacks in their prisons, but Virginia and Maryland sent many

free blacks to their penitentiaries. Neither state was happy with this situation, however, and both experimented with ways to avoid imprisoning free blacks — including selling them into slavery or leasing them to outside contractors.

Southern governments were not enthusiastic about spending money for any prisoners and always sought ways to make prisons pay for themselves. Pressure mounted for the inmates to be leased to businessmen to make shoes, pails, wagons, and other articles, and leasing was instituted in Alabama, Texas, Kentucky, Missouri, and Louisiana. Often free workers demanded that convict labor be kept out of competition with "honest workmen."

Antebellum southern prisons were not substantially different from northern prisons. Most people in both regions had little faith in reformation, and prison officials North and South dealt out harsh physical punishment, supplied poor food, spent most of their energies on financial matters, became entangled in political patronage, and let contractors or lessees assume real control of the prisons.

The similarity between northern and southern prisons, however, abruptly disappeared with the Civil War and emancipation. Virtually all southern prisons were destroyed or badly damaged in the war, and southern governments had few resources with which to rebuild them. Southerners had become accustomed to the idea of centralized state penal institutions, but they now confronted a radically different situation: postwar prisons would no longer be reserved primarily for white men. Four million ex-slaves were now liable for incarceration, and the number of defendants who received penitentiary sentences soon outstripped even ambitious attempts by state officials to build penitentiaries. Many southern states, often with reluctance, turned to leasing convicts to work outside the prison walls. More than 9 of 10 prisoners were black men, most of them in their early twenties, most of them convicted of the lesser degrees of larceny. Many of them died in prison, and nearly all were mistreated.

No single political group in the postwar South bore sole responsibility for inaugurating the convict lease system — although the Democrats reaped most of its benefits. Black and white politicians, Republicans and Democrats, tolerated the system. Within 15 years after the Civil War all the ex-Confederate states allowed businessmen to submit bids for the labor of the state's felons.

In the late 1860s and early 1870s, a time of experimentation, leases ran for relatively short periods and convicts worked primarily as agricultural and railroad laborers. Railroad work on an expanded scale absorbed most of the penal labor of virtually every state in the 1870s. In the 1880s and 1890s convicts became increasingly concentrated in mining, especially in the states leasing the largest number of convicts: Alabama, Georgia, Florida, and Tennessee.

The lease system grew out of not only the inertia of the Old South but also the demands of the expanding capitalist system of Gilded Age America. On railroads and then in mines, the convict lease system served as the only labor force capitalists investing in the South knew they could count on to penetrate swamps and primitive mines. Indeed, as businessmen and officeholders haggled over convict leases, widespread corruption grew up around the system.

Because the New South had so few industries, because those industries were concentrated in relatively small areas, because the products of those industries (especially coal) were so crucial to the growth of the southern economy, and because southern labor was relatively unorganized, convict labor undermined the wage scale and working conditions of entire southern industries. In the early 1890s, after 20 years of suffering at the hands of the convict lease system, miners in Tennessee and Alabama launched large-scale revolts. Their opposition was joined with that from residents of communities where lessees established camps, cynical politicians of opposition parties, and people of conscience (such as Julia Tutwiler and George Washington Cable) who opposed the lease because it offended their sense of justice.

These protests helped bring the convict lease system to a very gradual end. Although some southern states—Virginia, Texas, Tennessee, Kentucky, and Missouri—had long used manufacturing prisons in addition to the lease system, as late as 1890 the majority of southern convicts passed their sentences in convict camps run by absentee businessmen. Only three southern states (Mississippi, Tennessee, and Louisiana) completely abolished the convict lease system before the turn of the century. Even those states that ended the lease system did not build new penitentiaries. Inmates were moved to state-run prison farms, which were considered more healthy and more secure than scattered convict camps. Different classes of prisoners were separated from one another, and death rates declined. Reformers continued to agitate for and gradually established juvenile reformatories, as well as prison schools, libraries, and commutation laws. Scandals continued to surface throughout the 20th century, highlighting the brutality and corruption of southern prisons.

In the 1980s a continued dramatic rise in prison populations and decline in state government revenues prompted the emergence of prison privatization efforts, or the contracting out of prison facilities, services, and management to private corporations. Private operation of prisons and systems became a convenient way to relieve overcrowding and high operating costs of federal and state-run facilities. In 1983 the first private correctional corporation, the Corrections Corporation of America (CCA), was founded in Nashville, Tenn., and soon began the operation of several facilities in Texas, Tennessee, Florida, and

New Mexico. Today the CCA, the country's largest private corrections corporation, operates only a few facilities outside the southern United States, and the southern states still lead the country's other regions in the use of private contractors. In 2005 private-institution inmates in the South made up 8 percent of the total inmates under state and federal jurisdiction in the United States, when the national private inmate population average was 6.7 percent.

The South today keeps a far higher percentage of its population in prison than any other part of the country. Though in 2008 crime rates in most southern states, with the exception of Mississippi, were higher than the national average crime rate (Mississippi's crime rate was 12 percent lower than the national average), incarceration rates (per 100,000 residents) for state and local prisons and jails were consistently higher in the southern states. Mississippi's incarceration rate was 38 percent higher than the national average incarceration rate, and Louisiana's rate was 48 percent higher than the national average. Most southern states, however, spend far less than the national average per convict; in 2009 taxpayer cost per inmate was 47 percent lower than the national average in Mississippi and 50 percent lower in Louisiana. The prisons in many of the southern states are usually crowded far beyond their designed capacity, and as has been the case since the first decade after the Civil War, blacks make up a disproportionately large percentage of the inmate population in the region and are sentenced for considerably longer terms than their white counterparts.

Cultural predispositions lie behind the South's bleak penal history. Southerners have generally held a less optimistic view of human nature than many other Americans and thus have placed less faith in the state in general and "reformatory" institutions in particular. Southerners have tended to adhere to the stern retributive justice of the Old Testament rather than the more compassionate ideals of the New Testament. Southerners in political power long operated in a one-party system that allowed penal corruption and neglect to go unchallenged by other parties. The history of prisons in the South suggests that southern culture is intimately linked with the often-tragic history of southern class and race relations.

EDWARD L. AYERS
University of Richmond

MARY AMELIA TAYLOR
University of Mississippi

Edward L. Ayers, *Vengeance and Justice: Crime and Punishment in the Nineteenth-Century South* (1984); National Institute of Corrections, State Corrections Statistics (2008–9), http://nicic.gov/Features/StateStats; P. J. Wood, *International Political Soci-*

ology (September 2007); Hilda Jane Zimmerman, "Penal Systems and Penal Reform in the South since the Civil War" (Ph.D. dissertation, University of North Carolina at Chapel Hill, 1947); *Southern Exposure* (Winter 1978) (special issue on prisons).

Race Riots

A race riot is a transient, racially motivated, communal act of civilian violence against multiple targets that results in injury, death, or the destruction of property. Historians generally avoid using the term race riot to describe southern acts of violence associated with slavery. Instead, scholars of American history prior to 1865 primarily employ the term in reference to approximately 44 separate white attacks on African Americans in northern and midwestern cities such as New York, Boston, Philadelphia, Detroit, and Cincinnati. Fears of black labor competition, jealousies toward black advancement, and a determination to maintain racial boundaries helped fuel many of those riots. In 1863 animus toward the enforcement of the federal government's first conscription laws sparked the New York City Draft Riots, which climaxed in an orgy of antiblack violence.

Reconstruction represented one of the bloodiest periods of racial conflict in the South. Historians have estimated that white terrorists killed approximately 3,000 African Americans during that period, and scholars have documented at least 78 race riots between 1865 and 1876. In the aftermath of the Civil War, African Americans resolutely pursued freedom, full civil rights, and economic self-reliance. White supremacists, Democrats, and large landowners were just as determined to check the political and economic empowerment of former slaves. In 1866 rising racial tensions and growing white hostility toward the presence of black soldiers and veterans boiled over into bloody raids against African Americans in Memphis and New Orleans. During the Memphis riot, white mobs invaded black settlements, murdered at least 46 African Americans, raped black women, and looted and razed dwellings and churches. In New Orleans, a mob, under the direction of Confederate veterans and local law enforcement officials, assailed activists seeking to secure voting rights for African Americans. At least 34 African Americans and three of their white supporters were killed.

Northern outrage toward the massacres in Memphis and New Orleans helped pave the way for Radical Reconstruction. In response, white Democrats and their allies waged a campaign of terror aimed at curbing black political activity and weakening the Republican Party. Following a contested 1872 state election marred by fraud and violence, white extremists in Louisiana attempted to force their candidates into office in a series of offensives. During the

A group of captured detainees are being marched in downtown Tulsa under armed guard,
1 June 1921. (Tulsa Race Riot of 1921 Archive, 1921–2000, Department of Special Collections
and University Archives, McFarin Library, University of Tulsa, Tulsa, Okla.)

Colfax Massacre of 1873, for example, members of the White League, seeking to replace the recently ensconced sheriff and judge of Grant Parish with their own candidates, brutally killed as many as 150 African Americans defending the courthouse. Between 1874 and 1876, southern whites orchestrated additional massacres against a range of targets that included Republican activists, teachers, ministers, officeholders, and militiamen. White mobs killed approximately 300 African Americans in greater Vicksburg in 1874, 30 in and around Clinton, Miss., in 1875, and six or seven in Hamburg, S.C., in 1876. During those and other incidents, rioters frequently looted and destroyed black property. The race riots of the Reconstruction era played a crucial role in rallying southern whites behind the banner of the Democratic Party and hastening the retreat of the national Republican Party from intervening in southern affairs.

Despite the success of the southern Democrats and their allies in seizing political power during Reconstruction, the forces of white supremacy continued to face repeated challenges to their hegemony in coming years. Race riots emerged as a vital component of a larger white supremacist campaign that reached its height in the South between the 1890s and early 1900s. When the Populists succeeded in mobilizing substantial numbers of whites and African Americans behind their platform during the 1890s, the Democrats fought off their new political challengers with a groundswell of bloodshed and voter fraud. State governments enacted a flurry of segregation and disfranchisement laws. Democrats and their allies openly embraced racial violence as a tool for checking black labor activism and political participation. In North Carolina's 1894 elections, a Fusionist coalition of Republicans and Populists secured majorities in both houses of the state assembly. Two years later, the interracial coalition augmented its power in the state legislature and won the governorship. In 1898 Democratic leaders deployed voter fraud, intimidation, and racist demagoguery to reestablish their control over state government. In the aftermath of the 1898 election a white mob under the leadership of prominent Democrats instigated an assault on African Americans and Fusionist public officials in the predominantly black city of Wilmington that culminated in an armed takeover of the local government. Estimates of the number killed during the riot range from seven African Americans to 300. Over 1,000 more fled the city during what became known as the Wilmington Race Riot.

Journalists and Democratic candidates in Georgia openly applauded the Wilmington massacre in the months leading up to a 1906 gubernatorial primary that centered on the issue of disfranchisement. Linking black voting rights with the crime of black-on-white rape, newspapers openly advocated extralegal violence. That September a white mob numbering in the thousands shot, stomped, bricked, and knifed to death African Americans trapped in downtown Atlanta. White rioters ransacked black businesses and beat black workers who competed with whites for jobs. Armed African Americans successfully turned back mobs on multiple occasions. At least 25 blacks and two whites died during the four-day Atlanta riot. The Springfield, Ill., race riot of 1908, which resulted in the deaths of at least two African Americans and the widespread demolition of black property, shared key similarities with the Atlanta riot. The massacre broke out after city officials succeeded in preventing an angry mob from capturing two black men—one charged with raping a white woman, the other accused of killing a white man after attempting to rape his daughter. The mob focused much of its fury on black business owners and upwardly mobile African Americans.

The outbreak of World War I accelerated the migration of African Americans into northern and midwestern cities and dramatically intensified racial animosities. Many whites perceived the new migrants as potential job competitors and were enraged by their presence in public spaces traditionally monopolized by whites. In 1917 angry whites in East St. Louis launched an invasion of black neighborhoods that resulted in at least 39 black deaths and the dislocation of thousands of African Americans. In the war's aftermath, many whites resented what they perceived to be a new sense of racial pride and militancy among African Americans, particularly veterans. During the "Red Summer" of 1919 a wave of 26 race riots surged across America, engulfing southern and northern cities and seeping into rural crossroads such as Elaine, Ark. A veritable race war broke out in Chicago in the aftermath of a confrontation arising along the border between segregated black and white beaches. In the chaos that followed, white mobs brutalized black trolley riders as well as many African Americans caught crossing into "white areas" by foot or by car. Whites drove into black neighborhoods and fired bullets into black residences. As was the case in other cities that summer, African Americans repeatedly defended themselves. Fifteen whites and 23 blacks died in Chicago. Hundreds more suffered serious injuries.

In Tulsa, Okla., in 1921, more than 2,000 white rioters, angered at false reports that a black man had sexually assaulted a white woman, overwhelmed the determined efforts of armed black defenders to protect their community. The mob decimated the prosperous black district of Greenwood, killed at least 26 African Americans, injured hundreds more, and displaced approximately 10,000 from their homes. (Many experts place the death toll of African Americans in Tulsa above 60). In Florida in 1923, a white woman's allegation that a black man had raped her set in motion a series of white-initiated attacks and shootouts that ended in the death of least six African Americans and two whites and the destruction of the predominantly black town of Rosewood.

World War II generated renewed racial tensions as growing numbers of blacks and whites sought new job opportunities in American cities. Housing and food shortages intensified frictions arising from job competition between whites and African Americans in rapidly growing industrial centers. In Detroit in 1943 a series of racial skirmishes and the spread of inflammatory rumors exploded into a large-scale riot. Police joined in the attacks on African Americans and their property. In the end, 25 African Americans and 9 whites lay dead.

Since the 1960s commentators and journalists have primarily used the term race riot to refer to African American urban unrest. Inner-city riots broke out in Harlem as early as 1935 and 1943. In 1964 similar outbursts erupted in cities throughout the North. A year later the Watts riot in Los Angeles resulted in 34 deaths and property damage estimated at $35 million. In both 1967 and 1968 more than 125 uprisings exploded in large and small cities throughout America. In coming decades, similar riots occasionally flared up, most notably in Miami in 1980 and in Los Angeles and other large cities in 1992.

Many scholars have linked the riots of the 1960s with the relative impoverishment of inner-city blacks and their limited access to employment opportunities, adequate housing, and basic social services. Many African Americans had come to regard white police officers, absentee landlords, and shopkeepers as outsiders and the principal agents of their marginalization and deprivation. Rumors or actual incidents of police brutality preceded almost all the urban revolts. The arson and violence of the rioters primarily targeted property. The looting focused on white-owned stores. African Americans suffered most of the riot-related casualties, which generally resulted from confrontations between law enforcement officials and local residents.

The past two decades have witnessed a growing interest among scholars and the general public in race riots. State legislatures in North Carolina, Oklahoma, and Florida have appointed commissions to prepare reports on individual riots in their states, and racial massacres are assuming a central role in reparations and racial reconciliation movements. Emerging from these developments is a greater awareness of the extensiveness of American racial violence and a fuller recognition of its legacies.

DAVID FORT GODSHALK
Shippensburg, Pennsylvania

Richard Maxwell Brown, *Strain of Violence: Historical Studies of American Violence and Vigilantism* (1975); David S. Cecelski and Timothy B. Tyson, eds., *Democracy Betrayed: The Wilmington Race Riot of 1898 and Its Legacy* (1998); Philip Dray, *At the Hands of Persons Unknown: The Lynching of Black America* (2002); Eric Foner, *Reconstruction: America's Unfinished Revolution, 1863–1877* (1988); David Fort Godshalk, *Veiled Visions: The 1906 Atlanta Race Riot and the Reshaping of American Race Relations* (2005); Donald L. Horowitz, *The Deadly Ethnic Riot* (2001); Nell Irvin Painter, *Creating Black Americans: African-American History and Its Meanings, 1619 to the Present* (2005); Michael Perman, *Pursuit of Unity: A Political History of the American South* (2009); Thomas J. Sugrue, *Sweet Land of Liberty: The Forgotten Struggle for Civil Rights in the North* (2008).

Rape

Any analysis of rape in the South must lead to a discussion about race and class. Sexual violence was part of the complex system of social control that maintained the racial, gender, and class hierarchies that structured the southern social order. Commonly held beliefs about rape mapped the contours of southern society and provide a shorthand description of power relations in the South. From the colonial period into the 1960s, African American women received little protection from the legal system, thus allowing rape to be an effective weapon used to colonize black women's bodies. The law did not recognize the rape of a slave woman as a crime, except insofar as it represented damage to her master's property, and slave owners could rape their female property with impunity. Black women fared little better in the 20th century.

In the same period, the rape of white women, theoretically at least, represented an assault on the honor of her husband or father, and thus represented a serious crime, unless, of course, she was a woman of little social standing or dubious reputation. Rape convictions were often difficult to obtain because of persistent doubts about women's veracity regarding sexual matters. While the contours of the law shifted over the course of southern history, and the ideological underpinnings of rape evolved as part of the development of racial segregation, these broad outlines of rape remained constant. Black women were vulnerable to sexual assault, especially at the hands of white men. White women were theoretically placed on a pedestal, on which their protection from sexual violation came to represent protection of white supremacy. For poor white women, protection was considerably less absolute.

From the outset of the development of race-based slavery in the American colonies, the sexual exploitation of slave women worked to entrench a labor system of perpetual and inherited servitude. Bolstered by European assumptions that African women were inherently more libidinous than white women, the rape of slave women served to demonstrate white power. Slave men had little ability to defend African women, and the children produced through rape increased the capital of owners once the law determined that children inherited their slave status through their mothers.

That the legal system offered slave women little in the way of protection from sexual assault, however, does not mean that African American women meekly submitted to violence. Despite the odds against them, black women resisted their attackers through ingenuity and violence. Some even killed white predators rather than submit. Other black women used their master's sexual interest as leverage, gaining privileges and resources for themselves and their children. In other cases, there is evidence that the sexual relationships between slave women and white men grew out of affection. The law did not always dictate individual actions, despite the coding of racial hierarchy in rape law. Criminal statutes regarding forcible rape in the antebellum period were race specific, singling out white women for protection from black men and implicitly assuming that white men could be charged with rape only for crimes against white women. Statutes determining punishment for convicted rapists were also race specific, calling for prison terms for white men and castration or the death penalty for slaves. Despite the racial elements of the law, not all slaves were convicted when accused of rape by white women. Slaves represented valuable property and often received competent legal counsel provided by their owners.

While some slave men were executed, others were pardoned or transported, and their owners compensated by the state. Unlike the postbellum period, white southerners in the antebellum period were not consumed by the fear of black men's assaults of white women.

Once the defeated states of the former Confederacy rewrote their state constitutions to comply with the Fourteenth Amendment during Reconstruction, explicit racial distinctions in the criminal code were no longer permissible. Black women now were able to bring charges of rape against white men, and formal discrepancies in punishments were removed. Maintaining rape as a tool of racial control nonetheless continued during segregation, however, as whites determined how to apply the law in individual cases. The legal system continued to ignore black women's charges of sexual violation and allowed judges or jury members to continue to inflict differential punishments on convicted defenders depending on race. For example, in Virginia, during Reconstruction, racial disparities in punishment were removed from the criminal code, allowing convicted rapists of either race to be imprisoned for anywhere from 5 to 20 years or sentenced to death. In practice, while 54 men were executed for rape or attempted rape between 1908 and 1954, not one of them was white. Well into the 20th century, rape remained a crime in which black men faced considerable legal jeopardy or even lynching for being accused of a sexual crime by a white woman. They faced almost certain conviction, they were punished more severely than white men, and they were far more likely to pay for their alleged crime with their lives, either through execution after trial or through extralegal violence.

White men, however, faced few consequences for their abuse of black women. For men accused of sexual assault by women of their own race, the results were more ambiguous. Few historians have systematically examined these cases at the county level. Anecdotal evidence suggests, however, that jurors routinely were suspicious of women's claims of rape. Charges that the victim was promiscuous, of poor character, or from a poor or marginalized family frequently implied that she was likely to consent to any sexual overtures, and the requirements that victims corroborate their allegations of nonconsent with evidence of violence usually confirmed those assumptions. As long as men were not accused of raping family members or particularly prominent women of unblemished reputation, punishments, in the unlikely event of convictions, were usually minor.

The adjudication of rape cases in southern courtrooms, however, did not always reflect the rhetoric about rape in the post-Reconstruction South. Discussions of rape in the South have usually meant invoking denunciations of "black beast rapists" and until recently have appeared in historical scholarship only as part of discussions of lynching. After Reconstruction, many white southerners believed that emancipation caused freed slaves to revert to their former state of savagery. Separated from the civilizing institution of slavery, African American men had developed an uncontrollable sexual desire for white women and a willingness to use violence to satisfy that desire. In response, white southerners felt themselves justified in inflicting immediate and severe punishment in an effort to deter future rapists, including the public torture and mutilation of accused black men without the benefit of trial. Analyzing the pervasive and heated rhetoric about "beasts in human form" who desecrated pure white womanhood, historians have concluded that white southerners conflated black men's desires for the political, economic, and civil rights of white men—indeed for manhood—with a desire for white women. Lynching, justified by the alleged propensity of black men to rape white women, thus became a critical tool of racial control during Jim Crow, and white women, assumed to be pure and virginal, came to represent the entire edifice of white supremacy. The convergence of racial and sexual violence became one important means by which historians analyzed racial terror in the South and African Americans' lack of basic rights. While the rhetoric of black men's propensity to rape white women appeared frequently in cases of lynching, most extralegal violence against blacks did not involve charges of rape. The insistence that white southerners had a right and a duty to protect white women from black men, however, proved difficult for nonsoutherners to counter. It also placed considerable power in the hands of white women, who could falsely accuse black men to serve their own or their family's interests. Some white women, though certainly not all who made allegations of rape, seized this opportunity.

Although the myth of the black beast rapist, or what W. J. Cash termed the "rape complex," served as a tool to enforce white supremacy, the fear of rape by black men on the part of white women also reified white men's patriarchal control over white women. White men's rhetorical promises of protection came only in return for white women's promise of obedience and adherence to the dictates of middle-class respectability. White men theoretically offered the cloak of chivalry to any woman with white skin, but protection, or, more accurately, retribution in response to charges of rape against a black man, in reality was not guaranteed. Women who failed to behave according to the mandates of ladyhood, or whose families did not abide by accepted standards of white behavior, might find their charges of rape treated with suspicion. Occasionally, juries acquitted the men such women accused. More often, while their accused assailant was convicted, he received a less severe punishment or was released early through a conditional pardon. Such actions placed qualifications on a white woman's claim to protection and served as a warning to other white women to uphold the values associated with pure white womanhood.

By the mid-20th century, many African Americans recognized that the prosecution of rape cases was part of the fight for civil rights. Notorious cases of allegations of rape, such as the Scottsboro case in 1931 and the Martinsville Seven case in 1951, became one vehicle through which civil rights organizations began to insist on legal protections for black men accused of rape. By the 1950s in Virginia, civil rights lawyers not only defended black men who were accused of rape by white women but also represented black women who brought charges of rape against white men. Although black women still faced an uphill struggle in holding white men to account for their sexual crimes, white men increasingly faced trial, and occasionally conviction, for their assaults of black women. At the same time, white women's charges against black men faced increasing scrutiny in the legal system. Despite the gains made by the civil rights movement in protecting the rights of black victims and accused assailants, and despite the gains made by the women's movement in demanding more reasonable standards of evidence at trial, race continues to matter in cases of rape. Many Americans continue to envision rapists as black men, and black women still face insinuations of promiscuity more than other groups of women. Nevertheless, lynchings for charges of rape have virtually ended, and all women, white or black, have the possibility of a fair hearing in court.

LISA LINDQUIST DORR
University of Alabama

Peter Bardaglio, *Reconstructing the Household: Families, Sex, and the Law in the Nineteenth-Century South* (1995); W. Fitzhugh Brundage, *Lynching in the New South: Georgia and Virginia, 1880–1930* (1993); Daniel Carter, *Scottsboro: A Tragedy of the American South* (1969); Lisa Lindquist Dorr, *White Women, Rape, and the Power of Race in Virginia, 1900–1960* (2004); Jacquelyn Dowd Hall, *Revolt against Chivalry: Jessie Daniel Ames and the Women's Campaign against Lynching* (1993); Eric W. Rise, *The Martinsville Seven: Race, Rape, and Capital Punishment* (1995); Diane Miller Sommerville, *Rape and Race in the Nineteenth-Century South* (2004).

Reconstruction-Era Violence

It is well known that Reconstruction in the former Confederacy precipitated considerable violence. Ravaged by four years of civil war, the South in 1865 suffered the death throes of military defeat and political revolution. Like the Confederacy itself, most local and state governments were defunct. Civil courts did not operate and law enforcement, such as it was, consisted mostly of bands of irregular soldiers or home guards who created as much terror and disorder as they claimed to protect citizens against. Larger towns and cities fared somewhat better in this state of affairs than backcountry areas that were far removed from the presence of federal troops and at the mercy of so-called regulators who preyed upon blacks and whites alike. Urban areas, however, experienced an influx of freed people from the countryside who, although looking for safety, too often found that conditions in southern cities could be as dangerous as they were on the plantations. Clashes between urban blacks and whites were frequent. In the spring and summer of 1866, as Radical Republicans in Congress attempted to wrest control of Reconstruction away from President Andrew Johnson, bloody riots in Memphis (1–2 May) and New Orleans (30 July) claimed scores of black lives and helped convince the nation that Johnson's policy of amnesty to former Confederates and quick restoration of the two sections was untenable. As a result, Congress embarked upon a plan of Radical Reconstruction, which included dividing the South into five military districts, expanding the Freedmen's Bureau, and passing both the Fourteenth and Fifteenth Amendments to the Constitution. Radicals hoped that by guaranteeing black southerners equal protection of the laws and the right to vote that they could secure the Republican Party's ascendancy and stabilize the region.

Stability, however, was hard to come by. Further reforms were needed to ensure the safety of southern blacks and their white allies. In addition to the new constitutional amendments establishing the rights of citizenship for African Americans and giving the federal government jurisdiction over violations of those rights by the individual states, southern Republicans also instituted a number of policies aimed at diffusing the hostility and violence that characterized the post–Civil War South. For instance, in 1867 Congress disbanded southern state militias, which had become havens for disgruntled ex-Confederate soldiers who terrorized former slaves. Next they lifted the federal ban on black participation in militias, which had been in place since colonial days, and allowed black southern men to become active members. In Arkansas, South Carolina, and Louisiana, where Republican governors enthusiastically employed them, these new "black militias" helped elect Republican officials and protect them from white vigilantes, such as the Ku Klux Klan. The dismantling of the Ku Klux Klan was, perhaps, the most noteworthy victory against white violence. In response to the Enforcement Acts (1871), which declared that conspiratorial actions to deprive citizens of their rights by violence and intimidation were subject to federal prosecution, the newly formed Department of Justice succeeded in bringing to trial hundreds of accused Klansmen for con-

A Prospective Scene in the "City of Oaks," 4th of March, 1869.

"Hang, curs, hang! * * * * * *Their* complexion is perfect gallows. Stand fast, good fate, to *their* hanging! * * * * * If they be not born to be hanged, our case is miserable."

"A Prospective Scene in the 'City of Oaks,' 4th of March, 1869," published in the Tuscaloosa Independent Monitor. The editorial cartoon depicts the lynching of carpetbaggers by the Ku Klux Klan, 1 September 1868. (Courtesy of the Alabama Department of Archives and History)

spiring to violate African Americans' right to vote and their right to bear arms and for murder. Although the number of convictions was less than what many southern Republicans had hoped, the prosecutions effectively broke the organization and made the act of "night riding" and disguised intimidation too risky for white southerners to continue.

Despite these unprecedented efforts to quell southern violence, it remained a defining feature of Reconstruction. After the Klan's defeat, white southerners continued their paramilitary campaigns against freed people and white Republicans, only this time without masks or disguises. After 1872 a self-consciously counterrevolutionary movement began in the Black Belt region designed to end Reconstruction once and for all. The "White Leagues" in Mississippi and Louisiana, and the "Red Shirts" in South Carolina used unmitigated violence to drive their opponents from political office and out of the South altogether. Following the Mississippi Plan, a strategy for breaking Republican political organization by targeting party leaders and keeping black voters from the polls first devised by hard-liners in the Magnolia State, paramilitary units across the Deep South set about an armed overthrow of Republican state governments. In September 1874 the Crescent City White League in New Orleans routed the

Metropolitan Police and drove the Republican governor, William Kellogg, from office. Although President Ulysses S. Grant sent federal troops to restore order and Kellogg a few days later, the White League continued to circumvent the Republican legislature. Rival governments claimed victory in that fall's elections, and when Grant hesitated to send troops a second time in January to install Republican officials, the White League effectively won. With federal military support waning along with public sentiment in the North, white paramilitaries effected similar outcomes in Mississippi and finally in South Carolina, the last holdout for Reconstruction. By the time Rutherford B. Hayes took the oath of office in 1877, the last federal troops had been removed from the South in return for southern Democrats' support for Hayes's election.

Although it is clear that violence became an effective tool used by whites to combat Reconstruction, violence was more than just an instrument of political or social control. In many instances violence, particularly sexual assault against freedwomen, constituted a performance of social inequality that emerged from the larger cultural discourse about race and black inferiority in the postwar South. In essence, southern whites reconstructed racial hierarchy, which had been upended owing to emancipation, through violence. Many of the ritualistic components that would become characteristics of lynching later in the century have their origins in Reconstruction-era violence. The intimate nature of the violence freed people experienced took place mainly outside the purview of state authorities and therefore was exceptionally difficult to police or control. The intimate violence between planters and their former bond people held deeply symbolic meaning and represented ideas of self, personhood, and freedom that transcended its instrumental function. The violence of the postwar period was part of a larger culture of violence that continued patterns and traditions of slave society and connected honor, power, and physical aggression. In other words, southerners—both black and white—did not turn to violence when other methods at social transformation failed. Rather they continued to use violence as an expression of personal as well as political identity, as a badge of freedom. It is important to note that freed people were not merely victims of this culture of violence but were also active participants in it. Freed people used violence to settle disputes, discipline children, and police the boundaries of households.

Reconstruction-era violence had a significant, long-term impact on both the South and the nation. Southern leaders, such as South Carolina governor and white supremacist Ben Tillman, experienced difficulties controlling the meaning of the violence they used during Reconstruction. Like other apostles of southern home rule, Tillman used the memory of Reconstruction-era violence to create an image of the South as inherently violent. With the proliferation of lynching and other forms of Jim Crow justice, it seemed to others in the nation impossible to challenge or change the southern way of life. Men like Tillman exploited poverty and disaffection to nurture reactionary politics that ensured the South would remain set apart, benighted, and backward in the eyes of the nation.

CAROLE EMBERTON
University at Buffalo

Thavolia Glymph, *Out of the House of Bondage: The Transformation of the Plantation Household* (2008); Steven Hahn, *A Nation under Our Feet: Black Political Struggles in the Rural South from Slavery to the Great Migration* (2003); Stephen Kantrowitz, *Ben Tillman and the Reconstruction of White Supremacy* (2000); Leon Litwack, *Been in the Storm So Long: The Aftermath of Slavery* (1979); Susan E. O'Donovan, *Becoming Free in the Cotton South* (2007); George Rable, *But There Was No Peace: The Role of Violence in the Politics of Reconstruction* (1984); Hannah Rosen, *Terror in the Heart of Freedom: Citizenship, Sexual Violence, and the Meaning of Race in the Postemancipation South* (2009); Otis Singletary, *Negro Militia and Reconstruction* (1959); Dorothy Sterling, ed., *The Trouble They Seen: Black People Tell the Story of Reconstruction* (1976); Allen Trelease, *White Terror: The Ku Klux Klan Conspiracy and Southern Reconstruction* (1971).

Religion and Violence

When journalist W. J. Cash described his southern "man at the center" in 1941, his composite white southerner was characterized by his violence as well as his fervent religiosity. Cash described "the boast, voiced or not, on the part of every Southerner, that he would knock the hell out of whoever dared cross him." Cash also noted his southerner's attraction to "a faith as simple and emotional as himself. A faith to draw men together in hordes, to terrify them with Apocalyptic rhetoric, to cast them into the pit, rescue them, and at last bring them shouting into the fold of Grace." Cash saw this combination as no coincidence but rather as a natural development arising out of the southerner's unique social environment and personality. The naked violence of slavery, along with the rural nature of southern society for much of its history, combined with the southerner's "simple, direct, and immensely personal character" to produce the figure of the hot-tempered, hallelujah-singing southerner that observers have remarked on ever since.

The prevalence of both violence and religion in southern life has not always been characteristic of the region, however. In the mid-18th century, while undoubtedly religious, the majority of southerners, both black and white, were unchurched. And, at least according to a recent study, homicide rates in the mid-18th-century South were no greater than elsewhere in the country. In the early 19th century, the South experienced a rise in homicide rates that would differentiate southern patterns of violence from northern and European patterns for the next two centuries. This rise largely coincided with the region's embrace of evangelical Christianity in this same period. By the mid-19th-century travelers remarked on both the religious fervor and ferocity of southerners with equal wonder. Traveling through the South in the 1850s, northerner Frederick Law Olmsted remarked on the ubiquity of religious conversation. "Men talk in public places, in the churches, and in bar-rooms, in the stage coach, and at the fireside, of their personal communions with the Deity, and of the mutations of their harmony with His Spirit, just as they do about their family and business matters," wrote an amazed Olmsted. In 1842 English traveler J. S. Buckingham recorded his belief that the proportion of violent crimes in the South was five times greater than that of the North and 10 times greater than that of any country in Europe.

But despite what seems at times a family resemblance, the relationship between religion and violence in the South has always been complicated. Throughout the 19th century, evangelical churches consistently opposed the eye-gouging, ear-biting, hair-pulling fights in which many of their male congregants, black and white, frequently participated. Clergy were also consistently critical of the most famous example of upper-class southern violence: the duel. In 1807 Rev. Nathaniel Bowen of Charleston, an Episcopalian, preached a sermon titled "Duelling, Under Any Circumstances, the Extreme of Folly," in which he lamented that the practice had "even intruded where the mild and peaceful religion of the Saviour should have totally excluded it."

Despite their opposition to most forms of interpersonal violence throughout the 19th century, the clergy of the South wholeheartedly proclaimed the righteousness of the South's cause and the bravery of its soldiers during and after the Civil War. The violence of the war seared into the white southern mind the abiding image of the noble, Christian soldier, and the prodigious loss of life sacralized the southern soldier, giving rise to the amalgam of memory and civil religion that historians call the Lost Cause. The southern clergy were among the main stewards of the war's memory. Before the war even ended, Presbyterian minister R. L. Dabney was hard at work on his biography of the fallen and famously pious Stonewall Jackson, whom Dabney called "God's sermon to us, his embodied admonition." Accounts of revivals in Robert E. Lee's Army of Northern Virginia were quickly published, as well. And though the majority of southern soldiers probably identified with one of the three major evangelical Protestant denominations, it was a Roman Catholic priest, Abram Joseph Ryan, who would become the poet laureate of the Lost Cause, most famously in his elegiac poem "The Conquered Banner."

It was not coincidence that W. J. Cash linked religion, violence, and slavery in his description of the archetypal southerner. Race has been an ever-present ingredient of both southern religion and southern violence, and some of the most incendiary moments in southern history have occurred at the intersection of these three forces. In 1831 in Virginia the sometime Baptist slave preacher Nat Turner led one of the most successful slave rebellions in American history, in which approximately 60 whites and many more blacks eventually died. Turner's actions were influenced, as he told his amanuensis Thomas Gray before his execution, by apocalyptic visions and his belief that he was God's instrument of justice. When asked by Gray, "Do you not find yourself mistaken now?" Gray reported that Turner answered, "Was not Christ crucified?" In response to Turner's Rebellion, black worship meetings across the South were scrutinized and suppressed as many white southerners questioned the link between Turner's religion and his rebellion.

Decades later black southerners would again turn to the image of the crucified Christ as white lynch mobs tortured and killed black men with increasing regularity beginning in the 1880s. Historians have only recently lent weight to W. J. Cash's evocation of "primitive frenzy" and "blood sacrifice" in southern religion by describing the religious significance of lynching for both the white crowd and black victim. One historian provocatively described lynching as "the southern rite of human sacrifice," arguing that for whites lynching operated at a subconscious and symbolic level to resolve communal conflicts and repair the sacred boundary that separated black and white in the South by offering a black victim as a sacrificial scapegoat. Although it was not a product of evangelical Christianity, lynching in the South seems at least to have been informed by the context of evangelical discourse and ritual. Mobs eagerly sought confessions and expressions of penitence from their victims and frequently allowed them to pray before dying. The crowds that gathered to watch a lynching also bore witness to the event in a way that mirrored the function of bystanders at outdoor baptisms across the South. The connections between southern religion and lynching were so compelling to Walter White, leader of the NAACP, that in 1929 he wrote, "It is exceedingly doubtful if lynching could possibly exist under any other religion than Christianity." White thought that southern evangelical Protestantism fostered "a particular fanaticism which finds an outlet in lynching."

Yet the same religion that White thought culpable in the lynching of black southerners also furnished the black community with the powerful counter-symbol of the lynched Christ. In the contrast between the rage of the white crowds and the innocence of its black victims, blacks saw a parallel to the sacrificial death of an innocent and ultimately victorious Christ. After all, wrote author Gwendolyn Brooks, "The loveliest lynchee was our Lord." A common evangelical faith also underlay alliances between white antilynching advocates like Jessie Daniel Ames and her black counterparts in the Committee on Interracial Cooperation, formed in 1919. Indeed the antilynching campaign carried out by the Association of Southern Women for the Prevention of Lynching, which Ames founded in 1930, drew on a century-long history of evangelical reform movements in America.

Religion was integral, as well, to the nonviolent way in which African Americans carried out their campaign for civil rights in the South in the mid-20th century. Rev. Martin Luther King Jr., a Baptist minister, saw the nonviolent approach to protest as not only an effective political strategy but also a religious imperative. In 1956, during the Montgomery Bus Boycott, King preached, "There is still a voice crying out in terms that echo across the generations, saying: 'Love your enemies, bless them that curse you, pray for them that despitefully use you, that you may be the children of your Father which is in heaven.'" In the face of violent and sometimes deadly attacks by white southern segregationists, black leaders like King sustained the civil rights movement's nonviolent approach to political protest in part by appeals to the common religious background shared by many of its members. King even looked past the immediate, necessary conflict of the push for civil rights to describe the ultimate ends of the movement in religious terms. "The end is reconciliation," King preached in Montgomery in 1956, "the end is redemption, the end is the creation of the beloved community." Thus, although W. J. Cash and others may sometimes have seen in southern religion the specter of southern violence, the historical relationship of the two in the American South has not always followed this pattern. For if southerners' violence has sometimes resembled their religion, their resistance to violence has drawn from their religion explicitly, making any simplistic explanation of the relationship between these two facets of southern life impossible.

ROBERT ELDER
Emory University

W. J. Cash, *The Mind of the South* (1941); Jacquelyn Dowd Hall, *Revolt against Chivalry: Jessie Daniel Ames and the Women's Campaign against Lynching* (1979); Charles

Marsh, *The Beloved Community: How Faith Shapes Social Justice from the Civil Rights Movement to Today* (2005); Donald Mathews, *Journal of Southern Religion* (August 2000); Randolph Roth, *American Homicide* (2009); Amy Louise Wood, *Lynching and Spectacle: Witnessing Racial Violence in America, 1890–1940* (2009); Bertram Wyatt-Brown, *Southern Honor: Ethics and Behavior in the Old South* (1982).

Slave Culture, Violence within

Masters physically punished slaves, and slaves lashed out at their owners in individual acts of confrontation or, very rarely, in organized rebellion. Slaves and nonslaveholding whites came to blows in their working or social lives. But not all violence in the Old South crossed racial lines. Slaves also sometimes fought with one another as well.

Violent conflicts within southern slave culture began as early as childhood. Especially in Texas and other westerly slaveholding states, some masters fed enslaved children like pigs, at long troughs, forcing them to jostle and throw elbows as they competed for morsels of food. Teenage male slaves and young enslaved men also wrestled, sometimes for fun and recreation but other times at the instigation of the master. Occasionally slaveholders orchestrated wrestling matches or other competitions of physical prowess among their own slaves or against those living on neighboring plantations.

Slaves' working lives invited violent encounters. Bondmen sometimes clashed over the proper means of completing their labors, arguing over such matters as how best to build a fence or plow a field. Slave owners, especially in the South Carolina Lowcountry, might employ an enslaved man as a slave driver. They expected him to wield the whip as necessary against his fellow slaves to ensure that he achieved the master's production goals. At cornshuckings, masters often supplied slaves alcohol as an incentive to work more quickly during extended, nighttime hours. It was no coincidence that violence frequently erupted among inebriated slaves who had imbibed too much whiskey at these events.

Leisure time activities sparked violence in the slave quarters. On Saturday nights and Sundays, slaves customarily took time off from work and enjoyed a brief respite from their exhausting physical labors. Much more frequently than their female counterparts, enslaved men gained the ability to travel off the plantation in pursuit of leisurely pastimes. Whether they took the opportunity to gamble at cards or dice, play marbles, or participate in sporting contests, erstwhile friendly competitions sometimes ended in violence among rivals. At dances and other social gatherings, the alcohol slaves consumed often contributed to violent outbreaks.

Property disputes among slaves frequently culminated in violence. Many slaves in the South Carolina Lowcountry participated in a thriving internal economy and amassed impressive quantities of property of their own. Elsewhere in the South, particularly on the cotton frontier of the Old Southwest, slaves found it difficult to reconstruct an informal economy like that farther east and therefore accumulated comparatively meager amounts of property. Across the South, however, slaves treasured their material possessions. They often responded violently when other slaves pilfered from them. Slaves stole cash and a range of commodities from one another. In their cramped cabins, most slaves lacked a secret, safe repository for their possessions. Theft typically cost enslaved women clothing, enslaved men such goods as tobacco. Slaves also purloined foodstuffs from nearby plantations. Slaves sometimes physically attacked those who stole from them, protecting their personal property as well as that belonging to the master. Safeguarding slaveholder property prevented slaves from taking the blame and punishment for goods missing from the plantation. In other cases, slaves charged with theft assaulted their enslaved accuser, resentful of the allegation. Those caught in the act might pummel—and, in rare cases, murder—the slave who spied their covert activities in an effort to silence the enslaved informant and prevent the exposing of wrongdoing to the master.

Slaves throughout the South engaged in violent confrontations over the repayment of debts they contracted with one another. They frequently made informal economic arrangements among themselves, exchanging goods or purchasing a commodity for cash. Many of these agreements entailed some obligation—either a future payment or transfer of goods—to complete the bargain. When one party failed to fulfill a verbal contract, the aggrieved slave sometimes engaged in violent retribution. Assiduous custodians of their limited financial resources, slaves fully expected to be reimbursed when fellow slaves owed them money. The very slave economy that fostered a sense of independence and autonomy among slaves also engendered conflict within the quarters.

Although a source of love and support, relationships in the slave cabin also sometimes turned violent. Masters maintained ultimate authority over the slave family, and when they paired enslaved couples with gross disregard for their own preferences, they created a breeding ground for domestic abuse. Some enslaved men took it as their marital prerogative to exercise control over their spouses and families through violence, which offered them a limited sense of power in a society that routinely denied their manhood. Even if male slaves could not protect their wives from the physical or sexual abuse of the master, prevent the sale of family members, serve as the exclusive provider of the slave household, or conceal their own whippings from kin, physical aggression offered some enslaved men a path to authority within the slave cabin.

The process of courtship invited violent encounters between slaves. Gender conventions held that male slaves lead the courtship process. Contests for female affection sometimes thrust rival slave suitors into violent engagements. Competition over enslaved women was particularly acute in the South Carolina Upcountry and other regions where holdings were small. Unlike on sprawling plantations with ample eligible partners, smallholdings offered few if any potential spouses from which to choose. As a result, cross-plantation unions were necessarily common in these areas. Abroad marriages appealed to enslaved men, who gained the privilege to travel to visit a sweetheart nearby. Bondmen on neighboring plantations occasionally resented the arrival of enslaved men intent on wooing eligible female slaves or enslaved women already married. The domestic slave trade only exacerbated competition for spouses in the older slaveholding states of the Atlantic seaboard as the lingering half of an enslaved couple torn asunder searched for a new spouse.

Whether during courtship or marriage, enslaved men jealously defended the women they claimed from the sexual overtures of other bondmen. Though recognized as a cultural institution across the Old South, slave marriage lacked legal sanction. Many slaves valued their marital unions, but some did not. Infidelity and adulterous liaisons ignited violence in the quarters. Cuckolded slave men sometimes physically punished an unfaithful wife but more commonly sought violent retribution upon the enslaved interloper for his sexual conquest. In the context of the slave family, enslaved men used violence to exercise dominance in the slave cabin, defend enslaved women from competing bondmen's sexual incursions, and take vengeance upon male slaves who successfully violated their sexual claims.

For enslaved men, violence served as one available pathway to the construction of a masculine identity. Although southern whites denied slaves' pretensions to honor, slaves believed otherwise. The culture of honor that they shared with whites could be expressed only among other slaves within the quarters, however. As they vied for rank, status, and reputation among themselves, enslaved men boasted of their manhood in the presence of other slaves and verbally challenged and insulted other bondmen. When enslaved men defended themselves, families, or friends with violence, they prevented a loss of honor and proclaimed their masculinity. The fights that erupted frequently involved fists, sticks, rocks, knives, and fence rails. On rare occasion bondmen brandished guns or utilized the rough-and-tumble fighting techniques such as ear biting and eye gouging more common among lower-class white brawlers. The ethic of honor in southern white society had its counterpart in masculine slave culture as well.

Examining slave life through the lens of violence is useful in prying into the culture of not only enslaved men but also enslaved women. Female slaves generally expressed themselves verbally rather than physically, but they sometimes resorted to violence as well, most commonly in defense of family. Women were more likely than men to poison their adult victims, although female slaves were more likely to murder enslaved infants and children than other adults.

Masters preferred to maintain peace in the slave quarters. Violent scrapes inflicted harm on valuable property. Injured slaves might be less productive in their labors or unable to work as they recovered. Serious wounds impaired their monetary value. Slaveholders established rules to govern conflicts between bondmen on the plantation and handled most violent episodes privately, without recourse to the legal system. If, however, slaves belonging to different masters inflicted harm upon one another, owners of injured, maimed, or murdered slaves were more likely to pursue redress in courts of law. Court records offer the best evidence of violent conflict among slaves but privilege the more sensational cases in which a slave was killed. Slaves convicted of murdering other slaves faced punishments that varied by state. In Virginia, death was the standard sentence until changes to the slave code authorized as an alternative the punishment of sale and transportation out of the United States. Virginia governors frequently commuted slated executions to sale and transportation or, beginning in the 1860s, hard labor on the public works. Georgia employed a combination of lashes and branding for slaves convicted of murdering other bondmen. A few in Louisiana were sentenced to life at hard labor in the state penitentiary.

JEFF FORRET
Lamar University

Edward E. Baptist, in *Southern Manhood: Perspectives on Masculinity in the Old South*, ed. Craig Thompson Friend and Lorri Glover (2004); Eugene D. Genovese, *Roll, Jordan, Roll: The World the Slaves Made* (1974); Jeff Forret, *Journal of Southern History* (August 2008); Lawrence T. McDonnell, in *Developing Dixie: Modernization in a Traditional Society*, ed. Winfred B. Moore Jr., Joseph F. Tripp, and Lyon G. Tyler Jr. (1988); Christopher Morris, in *Over the Threshold: Intimate Violence in Early America*, ed. Christine Daniels and Michael V. Kennedy (1999); Dylan C. Penningroth, in *New Studies in the History of American Slavery*, ed. Edward E. Baptist and

Stephanie M. H. Camp (2006); Brenda Stevenson, in *In Joy and in Sorrow: Women, Family, and Marriage in the Victorian South, 1830–1900*, ed. Carol Bleser (1991); Bertram Wyatt-Brown, *American Historical Review* (December 1988).

Slave Patrols

The first slave patrols appeared in southern colonies during the early or mid-18th century: South Carolina passed its first patrol law in 1702, Virginia followed in 1726, North Carolina enacted laws for patrols in 1753, and Georgia instituted its patrols in 1757. These colonial assemblies drew upon their knowledge of slave control methods used in Caribbean slave societies when they established patrols. Other southern colonies, and states, would pass laws authorizing patrols until every state had them by the early 19th century. Patrollers (also called paddyrollers, pattyrollers) used white-on-black violence to carry out their duties, and in many ways their actions mimicked the routine, nonpaternalistic side of master-slave relations.

Patrols were designed to supplement the sometimes ineffective mastery of white slave owners. To maintain control (theoretically) over slaves at all times, owners relied upon patrollers to police the roads and woods surrounding plantations. Like masters, patrols could and did use violence to enforce curfews and catch runaways. Working mostly at night, patrols had the legal authority to enter farms and slave quarters without warrants, and they also worked in southern cities, which often established their own urban patrol groups. Urban patrols preceded and in some cases supplanted town police forces. As appointed local officials, patrols functioned like other civil officers—for relatively low compensation and little thanks. Fines for nonperformance kept some men on the job, and with enough money, one could hire a substitute to serve the typical three-month appointment to a patrol group. In the 18th century, patrols reflected a cross section of southern white society, but by the 1830s in many southern states, patrollers were increasingly drawn from the lower social and economic tier of white communities. Slave owners and nonowners both served as patrols, although women and free blacks apparently did not.

In Virginia and South Carolina, and in many parts of the Deep South that copied South Carolina patrol laws, patrollers were closely tied to local militia, often drawn directly from militia membership rolls. In North Carolina and Kentucky, however, the county courts had authority over the appointment and supervision of patrol groups. In North Carolina, parts of Virginia, and in most cities, patrollers were also paid for their efforts on an hourly or nightly basis.

Slave patrols were charged with breaking up unauthorized slave meetings at night, catching local runaway slaves, and stopping slave insurrections before they happened by taking preventative measures. As they moved through slave cabins, patrollers looked for missing persons but also for prohibited guns, papers, and means of communication. Slaves found with stolen property or weapons would be punished summarily, and the goods confiscated (and frequently given to the observant patroller as a reward). Patrollers' activities brought them into conflict with slaves seeking fewer restrictions, and not surprisingly, slaves fought back against patrols. Folktales and Works Progress Administration (WPA) narratives abound with stories of slave-patroller confrontations, and in rare cases, slaves committed acts of arson or murder to deter overly conscientious patrols from their duties. During rumored insurrections or wartime, patrols became more active, but in more common periods of peace, patrols might work only one night a week.

When slavery ended in the 1860s, slave patrols no longer had the legal authority to enter the homes and churches of African Americans, nor would former slaves permit them the same liberties. Nonetheless, behaviors common to prewar slave patrols (night riding, white-on-black violence) continued under the guise of the Ku Klux Klan. Former bondmen and slave owners alike commented on the striking similarity of the Klan's outrages to actions previously taken by slave patrols.

SALLY E. HADDEN
Florida State University

J. Michael Crane, *Journal of Mississippi History* (1999); W. Marvin Dulaney, *Black Police in America* (1996); Sally E. Hadden, *Slave Patrols: Law and Violence in Virginia and the Carolinas* (2001); E. Russ Williams, *Louisiana History* 13, no. 4 (1972).

Slave Revolts

Few slaves in the antebellum South readily accepted their fate, yet large-scale slave revolts were fairly uncommon. Since the inception of slavery in colonial America, small-scale slave revolts had been frequently attempted, some even carried through to bloodshed. But perhaps because of fear and the lack of any substantial prior success, slaves primarily, and more effectively, used other day-to-day methods to anonymously protest their bondage. They participated in work slowdowns, broke tools, stole from their masters, set fire to barns and haystacks, and implemented other methods of impeding or sabotaging the efficiency of the farm or plantation upon which they worked. Nevertheless, the occasional large-scale revolt did occur—with dire and violent consequences.

One of the first effective mass slave revolts in colonial America was recorded in South Carolina on 9 September 1739. With the English and Spanish at war, the Spanish looked to disrupt English colonies by granting freedom to any slave who successfully deserted to St. Augustine. On that morning approximately 20 slaves gathered near the Stono River in St. Paul's Parish, which lay less than 20 miles from Charlestown (Charleston). The slaves fell upon a shop that sold firearms and ammunition, killed the two proprietors, armed themselves, and headed south toward St. Augustine. By 11 o'clock that morning the band of slaves was about 50 strong. Within a few hours between 20 and 25 whites had been murdered. That evening a growing army of whites found the slaves resting in a field, killed half them, capturing and executing all but one—who eluded capture for three years—within the next three months. A Negro Act that was quickly finalized thereafter severely limited the autonomy of black slaves by re-stricting their freedom to learn to read, grow their own crops, and assemble in groups.

An aftereffect of Stono was an increasingly heightened southern awareness of the unrest of slaves and the instability of the institution. Escapes and run-aways became common, and unexplained burning barns and haystacks were often blamed on malcontented slaves. As a result, southern whites meted out brutal and vicious penalties for acting out to keep any form of revolt to a minimum. After the 1790s, when the French island of Santo Domingo (also known as Saint-Domingue) was rocked by a savage slave insurrection that cost some 60,000 lives and established an independent Haiti, both slave-owning and non-slave-owning whites lived in constant fear of slave uprisings. Until then, the vast majority of rebellion in colonial and postcolonial America had taken the form of escape and vandalism (notwithstanding isolated inci-dents such as Stono), but once word of the Santo Domingo revolt reached the American South, fear of rebellion spread like wildfire.

Three large-scale insurrections epitomize the virulent anger present within slaves in postcolonial America. Each of the three revolts was inspired in part by religion, the former two in particular by the Old Testament accounts of Moses's delivery of the children of Israel from bondage in Egypt and the Israelite in-vasion of the land of Canaan. Of primary influence for the latter was the New Testament's story of Christ in Jerusalem and the apocalyptic promise of a New Jerusalem. There is none more infamous than any one of the three, and none did more to show the country what a potential powder keg slavery was.

The first recorded large-scale postcolonial conspiracy was conceived in 1800 in Richmond, Va., by a 24-year-old slave named Gabriel Prosser. At the time slavery was under attack by abolitionists across Virginia. Thomas Jefferson's antislave tract *Notes on the State of Virginia* had been through seven editions by then, and Judge St. George Tucker, a law professor at William and Mary College, had recently published his *A Dissertation on Slavery, with a Proposal for the Gradual Abolition of It in the State of Virginia.* Antislavery pamphlets circulated freely. Much talk focused on liberty and equality as a result of the recent American and ongoing French revolutions. But there was no liberty or equality for those who wore black skin, and the antislavery chatter added up to little more than political rhetoric. Prosser, an articulate blacksmith, and his revolutionary conspirators were enraged at the hypocrisy. If they were not to be freed of their bonds by enlightened politicians, they would take their freedom by force, arguing that "we have as much right to fight for our liberty as any men."

Prosser and his conspirators plotted to march their more than 1,000 recruits into Richmond—then a town of 8,000 inhabitants—and set it ablaze, taking hostages such as Gov. James Monroe. Afterward slaves were to rise up together and fight for their freedom, as did those on Santo Domingo. But the conspiracy was doomed by infighting, confusion, floods, and, ultimately, slave informants. Whites alerted to Prosser's plan mobilized the Richmond militia, and Prosser was arrested before the first shot was fired. He and 34 of his collaborators went to the gallows.

The next large-scale insurrection came in 1822 in Charleston, S.C., when Denmark Vesey was inspired by the congressional debates on slavery that resulted in the 1820 Missouri Compromise. A literate free slave, Vesey still had wives and children in bondage and was outraged by their condition and the institution of slavery itself. Soon Vesey had plotted a revolt that would include city and country slaves alike. The plot was simple. At midnight six battle units would fall upon Charleston, capture the guardhouse and arsenal, seize major roads, and kill any who attempted resistance. From there Vesey intended to sail his now-free army to Haiti, while one lieutenant wanted the army to remain and hold Charleston indefinitely. Again infighting, communication breakdowns, and informants thwarted the plan. Five of the six battle units did invade Charleston, throwing the city into sheer terror, but the unorganized units were quickly suppressed by authorities. Vesey and 34 of his conspirators were hanged. Between Prosser's and Vesey's revolts not a single white person lost his life, but 70 insurgents were hanged.

Nine years later, rebels finally proved that they could pull off revolt, albeit just shy of success. In 1831 an intellectually gifted and religiously inspired field hand by the name of Nat Turner formed an insurrectionist plot in Southampton County, Va. "Nat the Prophet," as he was known, believed he had been called by God to lead a slave insurrection and had seen visions instructing him on his mission. Practically none was to be spared. Every man, woman, and child between Turner's master's plantation and Jerusalem, Va., some 12 miles away, was to be destroyed. Keeping the plan to himself until he had received the final sign, Turner recruited seven other slaves to march across the countryside killing every white person they came across en route to destroying Jerusalem.

Just after midnight Monday morning, 22 August, Turner and four of his seven soldiers marched on the home of Turner's master, Joseph Travis. Soon all five white inhabitants, including two teenagers and an infant, were savagely executed. Turner and his band marched farm to farm massacring with bloodthirsty vengeance nearly every white person they came across, enlisting as many slaves and gathering as many weapons as they could along the way. By Monday, unorganized and now drunk on apple brandy, the army was repelled at Jerusalem, and Turner fled into the swamp. The majority of the insurrectionists, along with other innocent blacks, were captured and killed or jailed during a white counter frenzy.

Turner remained at large for two months while all of Virginia and neighboring North Carolina waited, paralyzed with fear. Eventually he was caught and hanged, but not before approximately 60 whites and nearly 200 blacks had lost their lives. From that point on, no white slaveholder lived comfortably with slavery. He now fully understood the fury and rage that lay beneath its burden.

JAMES G. THOMAS JR.
University of Mississippi

John B. Duff and Peter M. Mitchell, *The Nat Turner Rebellion: The Historical Event and the Modern Controversy* (1971); John Hope Franklin and Loren Schweninger, *Runaway Slaves: Rebels on the Plantation* (1999); Thomas Wentworth Higginson, *Black Rebellion: Five Slave Revolts* (1998); Winthrop Jordan, *Tumult and Silence at Second Creek: An Inquiry into a Civil War Slave Conspiracy* (1993); Stephen B. Oates, *The Fires of Jubilee: Nat Turner's Fierce Rebellion* (1975); Henry L. Tragle, *The Southampton Slave Revolt of 1831: A Compilation of Source Material* (1971).

Slaves, Violence toward

Slave owners in the American South convinced themselves that theirs was a just social order, one in which both masters and slaves benefited from institutionalized human bondage. In their view, slaves accepted, and even enjoyed, their fates; indeed, enslavement was the only condition in which they could be happy. Behind this internalized rationalization was the reality: violence and the threat of violence were the forces that established slavery and made it work. Most of this violence took the form of corporal punishment designed to keep slaves subordinate, but some was the product of spontaneous clashes between masters, mistresses, overseers, and other whites. Perhaps the most heinous type of violence—short of murder—was the rape and sexual exploitation of slave women. As with most other aspects of slavery, the law sanctioned the great majority of this violence.

When colonists first established slavery in the 17th century, slave owners did not feel the need to cloak their use of violence in religion or ideology; however, use of these methods of coercion became increasingly problematic in the Western world as time went on. The Enlightenment brought with it the conviction that relationships between individuals should be based on reason and mutual consent, not violence. The Enlightenment also gave rise to abolitionist movements, which cited violence against slaves as damning evidence of the inhumanity and immorality of slavery. Finally, over the course of the 18th and 19th centuries Americans became more religious. Masters had to reconcile slavery and its associated violence with these new sensibilities.

Slave owners adopted an ethos of paternalism to hide the brutality of slavery from themselves and the world. In this worldview, masters considered themselves the benevolent Christian stewards of their black slave "families." Ideally, the relationship between master and slave would be one of mutual, familial, obligation: the master would provide food, shelter, clothing, health care, and protection, and in return the slave would provide labor, loyalty, and love. To the extent that corporal discipline would be necessary, one could liken it to a loving father disciplining his disobedient children, with the severity of punishment being no more than necessary to bring the wayward slave son or daughter back in line. Paternalism might have been sufficient to assuage the consciences of slave masters, but it was not enough to ensure the subservience of the slave population, nor did it render invisible the truly violent nature of slavery.

Slave owners resorted to violence when slaves failed to live up to their myriad expectations. The whip was the most commonly used instrument of punishment. From the colonial period through the Civil War, whipping was an accepted form of discipline in many contexts, from prisons to naval vessels. Masters beat slaves for a variety of reasons. They could be whipped for disobeying a command, failing to pick their required quota of cotton or tobacco, assaulting a fellow slave, running away, or breaking any other farm or plantation rule. The brutality of these whippings varied based on the offense and the conscience—or lack thereof—of the person administering the beating. A minor infraction might result in only a couple of lashes in one instance but could end in death if an especially sadistic owner or overseer wielded the whip. There are no definitive statistics on the frequency of whippings, but if the testimonies of slaves and

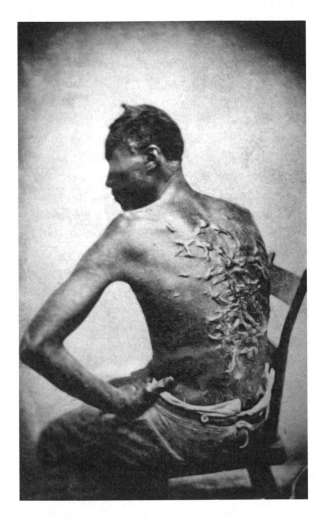

Photograph of a slave named Gordon who was brutally whipped by his overseer in Mississippi on Christmas Day and who escaped some time later to Union troops in Baton Rouge. This image was widely circulated as cartes de visite by abolitionists during the Civil War. Gordon later joined the Union forces as a soldier. (Photograph by McPherson & Oliver of New Orleans, National Archives/War Department)

other contemporary observers are to be believed, they were a regular feature of farm and plantation life.

Whipping represented the lenient end of the continuum of corporal violence; other, more draconian, forms of violence were also visited on the bodies of slaves. Some masters applied thumbscrews to secure the obedience of their slaves; others hanged their slaves upside down from overhead beams and whipped them. On one Georgia plantation, an overseer employed "the buck": slaves were forced to squat with their hands tied behind their backs; a large stick was placed through their arms and behind their knees. The slaves would be kept in this position for hours or whipped in it. On another southern plantation a master devised his own version of the medieval "Iron Maiden." He drove nails into a barrel, placed a slave inside it, and rolled it down a hill. Masters and overseers regularly branded slaves or cut off portions of their ears. The varieties of torture that slaves could be forced to endure seemed to be limited only by the imaginations of those who devised them and a few legal prohibitions.

Not all violence directed against slaves was a product of white attempts at discipline; some came out of interpersonal conflicts between slaves, free blacks, and nonslaveholding whites. Whites assaulted or killed slaves during the course of arguments, while gambling with each other, while committing crimes together, and even during disputes over lovers. Perhaps the most egregious form of this interpersonal violence was the rape and sexual exploitation of slave women. As with whippings, there are no reliable statistics on the incidences of rape, but it occurred with sufficient frequency to merit discussion in slave narratives and the memoirs of slaveholders themselves.

Slave women found themselves at the mercy of several different groups of white men: masters, masters' sons and other male relatives, overseers, and even visitors. Some masters saw sexual access to their female slaves as a right of ownership, and overseers used their power to secure sexual favors from unwilling slave women. Violence could be used directly in the course of a rape or merely implied. Slaves responded to these assaults in several ways. Some women met violence with violence to stop the attacks; others believed that fending off their assailants would only result in retribution against themselves or their families. The male relatives of rape victims confronted the perpetrators, but this, too, had its risks. These men might be sold away—or worse—for attempting to defend the honor of their female kin.

Compounding the physical, emotional, and psychological injuries caused by the rapes themselves was the fact that rape of a slave woman was not a crime. The rape statutes of the slave states only covered white women. This lack of legal protection for the bodies of slave women was representative of the enabling role the law played in violence against slaves. Because violence was essential to maintaining slave discipline, the law was crafted in such a way as to allow masters and communities the widest possible latitude. The only violent crimes against slaves with which whites could be charged were murder and serious assaults that maimed slaves in some way; lesser physical assaults went unpunished. While murder of a slave was a criminal offense, few masters or overseers were successfully prosecuted as a result of deaths that occurred during the disciplining of slaves.

The law in most states did allow slaves to defend themselves against violent attacks—but only against those likely to result in death or serious bodily injury. (This defense also protected owners' investments in their slave property.)

Courts could reduce a murder charge to the lesser charge of manslaughter if the victim had in some fashion provoked the attacker; whites could avail themselves of this leniency, but slaves could not. Southern legal systems did not want there to be any circumstance that permitted a slave to lawfully attack a white person out of anger or honor.

When the South entered the Civil War in 1861 white southerners claimed they were defending a just social system, one based on benevolence, mutual obligation, and hierarchical but democratic order. Each race, class, and sex had its place in society, and each group willingly played its assigned role and was rewarded in return. This idealistic view of the southern socioeconomic order accepted the reality that the entire structure was based on slavery but ignored the fact that slavery itself rested on a foundation of violence. Slaves were routinely whipped, beaten, raped, tortured, and killed to preserve slavery and white racial supremacy. The law was corrupted to make this violence legitimate. Only the greater violence of the Civil War could bring this violent regime to an end.

GLENN MCNAIR
Kenyon College

Ira Berlin, *Generations of Captivity: A History of African American Slaves* (2003); John Hope Franklin and Loren Schweninger, *Runaway Slaves: Rebels on the Plantation* (1999); Elizabeth Fox-Genovese, *Within the Plantation Household: Black and White Women of the Old South* (1988); Eugene D. Genovese, *Roll, Jordan, Roll: The World the Slaves Made* (1974); Glenn McNair, *Criminal Injustice: Slaves and Free Blacks in Georgia's Criminal Justice System* (2009)

Song, Black, Violence in

Black songs in the South, from spirituals and ballads to blues, southern soul, and hip-hop, have oftentimes prominently featured acts of violence. This is not surprising, given the history of slavery and white supremacist violence that has persisted through Jim Crow segregation, the civil rights era, and even the post–civil rights period. Violence is a complex issue in music of African Americans from the South as it encompasses the glorification of brutality and misogyny in blues, murder ballads, and southern rap, as well as the resistance against white supremacist and black male violence in these very same styles of music. Sometimes both even occur in the same song, creating an ambiguity that reflects the way many southerners feel about their history.

Spirituals were not the only songs slaves sang, but they were the ones that were remembered and preserved the most, partly because they helped to support the abolitionist cause and later the Harlem Renaissance's sanitized idea of a black past. In most spirituals, violence was downplayed, and salvation in the afterworld served as a less threatening topic. However, detailed accounts of Christ's Crucifixion worked as coded descriptions of the day-to-day violence of slavery: "Dey pierced Him in the side, dey nail Him to de cross, dey rivet His feet, dey hanged Him high, dey stretch Him wide." Sacred music was not the only music of slaves, of course, and secular music, such as work songs, occasionally depicted white supremacist violence more openly, as in a song that mocked the double standard of white patrols: "Run, nigger, run, patteroler'll ketch yer, hit yer thirty-nine and sware 'e didn' tech yer." One can assume that there were many such songs that depicted violence more openly and mocked slave masters, but most of them presumably never reached the ears of those who could have written them down.

White supremacist violence was rampant during and after Reconstruction in the segregated South and found its most gruesome expression in lynchings. Rarely commemorated in songs by African American southerners, lynchings were possibly most effectively criticized in the haunting jazz song "Strange Fruit," written in 1936 by Lewis Allan and most famously performed by Billie Holiday, neither of whom were from the South. The song depicts lynch victims as "strange fruit hanging from the poplar trees," appeals to senses of sight, sound, and smell, and juxtaposes images of a pastoral South with the "bulging eyes," the "twisted mouth," and the "burning flesh" of the tortured men. Although not typical for Billie Holiday's repertoire, "Strange Fruit" became one of her best-known songs and is remembered as a significant example of black protest against white oppression.

The representation of violence in murder ballads from the turn of the century and in blues music, which originated around the same time, is much less clearly focused on white supremacy, although domestic and black-on-black violence was oftentimes unquestionably a result of white-on-black racism. Black ballads that celebrated violent masculinity were numerous and included "Railroad Bill," "Casey Jones," "Jody the Grinder," and "John Henry." These ballads walked a fine line between asserting black agency and reverting to white stereotypes of the black brute that were used as the justification for many lynchings. The two best-known black murder ballads, both of which exist in hundreds of different versions and have been recorded by artists as diverse as Mississippi John Hurt, Sam Cooke, Tina Turner, and Taj Mahal, are most likely "Frankie and Johnny" (or "Frankie and Albert") about a black woman killing her man out of jealousy and "Stagger Lee" (or "Stack O'Lee") about a black "badman," Stagger Lee, who kills another black man, Billy, in a gambling dispute and/or a fight over a Stetson hat that takes place in Memphis, New Orleans, or St. Louis.

In 1958 Lloyd Price had a surprise No. 1 pop hit with his version of the song, a rare depiction of violence in rhythm and blues (he also recorded a sanitized version in which no murder takes place). Black Panther Party founder Bobby Seale described what he saw as the relevance of the mythical black "badman" by calling Stagger Lee "Malcolm X before he became politically conscious" and naming his son Malik Nkrumah Staggerlee Seale.

The celebration of black masculinity, often at the expense of black women, was not just a feature of "badman" ballads, but also of Delta blues. Furry Lewis sang, "I'm gon' get my pistol, 40 rounds of ball, I'm gon' shoot my baby just to see her fall," and Robert Johnson proclaimed in the rape fantasy of his "32-20 Blues," "if she gets unruly and thinks she don't want do, take my 32-20 and cut her half in two." One should note that Johnson also recorded the tender "Come on in My Kitchen" and that his frequent images of evil could refer to misogyny (as when he sang "me and the devil was walkin' side by side, I'm goin' to beat my woman until I get satisfied"), but also to white supremacist violence ("and the days keeps on worryin' me, there's a hellhound on my trail"). Some blues songs presented the male singer as victim, not perpetrator, of violence, for instance Eddie Boyd's "Third Degree" (written by Willie Dixon), in which he sang, "got me accused of murder, I ain't harmed a man." And while many blues songs could be interpreted as misogynist, the female blues singers talked back. Classic blues singers from the 1920s and 1930s like Bessie Smith and Gertrude "Ma" Rainey challenged traditional notions of femininity by presenting themselves as aggressive, sexually assertive, and complex. One could speculate whether Smith's "Send Me to the 'Lectric Chair" was a revenge fantasy or the depiction of actual violence, since, in typical blues fashion, it involved a good amount of braggadocio: "I cut him with my Barlow, I kicked him in the side, I stood there laughing over him while he wallowed 'round and died." While Smith's song was a clear vindication of a black woman, Ma Rainey's "Sweet Rough Man" involved a masochistic enjoyment of domestic violence: "He keeps my lips split, my eyes black as jet, but the way he love me makes me soon forget." Taken together, the two songs show the complexity of violence as it was depicted by female blues singers from the South.

The civil rights era brought some clear indictments of white supremacist violence by black artists. The bombing of the 16th Street Baptist Church in Birmingham, Ala., and the murder of civil rights activist Medgar Evers in Mississippi inspired songs of two black musicians that had been raised in North Carolina, John Coltrane's free jazz elegy "Alabama" (1963) and Nina Simone's "Mississippi Goddamn" (1964). Simone's song was consequently boycotted in several southern states, allegedly because of the word "Goddamn" in the title.

In 1968, one day after Martin Luther King's assassination, Simone quipped in a live performance of her song, "I ain't 'bout to be 'non-violent,' honey," echoing the black-power stance of another black southerner, James Brown, who had released his funk anthem "Say It Loud (I'm Black and I'm Proud)" a few months earlier. Although rarely depicting violence, soul and funk involved many southern "badman" performers like James Brown and Isaac Hayes, the latter of whom wrote the theme to the Blaxploitation movie *Shaft* (1971).

Violence, more akin to that expressed in blues music, became part and parcel of another musical genre that evolved from funk and soul: hip-hop. Originating in the South Bronx, the genre spread to the West Coast and eventually to the South. Inspired by West Coast gangsta rap, Houston's Geto Boys released "Mind of a Lunatic" in 1989, a disturbingly antisocial first-person account of murder, rape, torture, and necrophilia. Partly blues-style braggadocio, partly a reflection of urban poverty and violence, the song includes lines such as, "the sight of blood excites me, shoot you in the head, sit down and watch you bleed to death." In the more complex "Mind Playin' Tricks on Me," a No. 1 rap hit in 1991, the Geto Boys moved from sadism to a more introspective depiction of violence in which white supremacy is a strikingly similar undercurrent as in Robert Johnson's "Hellhound on My Trail." Southern rap was as varied in its depiction of violence as earlier genres and also included Arrested Development's "Tennessee" (1992) with its reference to "Strange Fruit": "Climbed the trees my forefathers hung from, ask those trees for all their wisdom." Southern rap, dominating hip-hop since the mid-1990s, has involved many rappers like Lil' Wayne who have been connected to violence in their lyrics and in their private lives.

ULRICH ADELT
University of Wyoming

Angela Y. Davis, *Blues Legacies and Black Feminism* (1998); Adam Gussow, *Seems Like Murder Here: Southern Violence and the Blues Tradition* (2002); Lawrence W. Levine, *Black Culture and Black Consciousness: Afro-American Folk Thought from Slavery to Freedom* (1977); Greil Marcus, *Mystery Train: Images of America in Rock 'n' Roll Music* (1997); Roni Sarig, *Third Coast: OutKast, Timbaland, and How Hip-Hop Became a Southern Thing* (2007); Brian Ward, *Just My Soul Responding: Rhythm and Blues, Black Consciousness, and Race Relations* (1998).

Song, White, Violence in

The songs of white southerners have tended to be rather gory things. We may trace some of this to the bloody imagery of southern religion, and perhaps more of it to an attempt to represent and comment upon a reality that was frequently violent and dangerous. The simple truth is that the environment, both natural and man-made, in Mississippi was much more likely to kill you than in New Hampshire, and it would be surprising if the musical culture did not reflect that fact. The mixture of honor, independence, and violence that characterized southern society is captured perfectly by the speaker in the song "Darling Corey" when he claims, "I ain't no man for trouble, but I'll die before I'll run." The musical traditions of white southerners encompassed a significant body of religious song but also built upon the ballad and lyric forms of the British Isles, songs violent enough in themselves and perfect vehicles to adapt to the violent context of the American South. When those musical traditions combined with vaudeville and Tin Pan Alley music in the early 20th century to produce the varieties of country music that came to define the region, the violent themes remained prominent.

W. J. Cash described southern religion as full of "primitive frenzy and blood sacrifice," and if his account is a bit theologically simplistic, there is no denying the violent imagery of southern religion, imagery conveyed not just in pulpit-thumping sermons but in dozens of songs as well. Much southern Protestantism follows Paul in preaching "Jesus Christ, and him crucified," and its hymns echo this sanguinary theme: "Remember the Cross," sings Ricky Skaggs, for example, and Johnny Cash asked, "Were You There When They Crucified My Lord?" In addition to songs about the cross, many sacred songs focus specifically on the blood of Jesus and its redemptive power. "Are You Washed in the Blood?" one song asked because, as another asserts, "There Is Power in the Blood." Those who are saved can rejoice that "Blood Done Sign My Name." The violent imagery of these religious songs likely comes out of the camp meeting tradition, where a heightened emotional state was part of the conversion process, as was an emphasis on Christ's sacrifice for the sinner.

The music white southerners inherited from Britain was full of death and killing. In the Child ballads, a collection of British and American ballads collected in the 19th century by Francis James Child, sisters killed sisters, mothers killed children, sons killed fathers, and sweethearts stabbed feckless lovers with wee penknives. Particularly relevant among the oldest traditional ballads were the border ballads, depicting the endemic raiding between England and Scotland. Appalachian scholar Rodger Cunningham argues that the instability of life on the frontier between "civilized" England and "barbaric" Highland Scotland shaped Scottish Lowlanders, who then moved to Ulster and eventually to the mountains and piedmont of the American South. The ballads about border raids such as Johnnie Armstrong and Dick o' the Cow do not seem to have come across the ocean, but the world of arbitrary and even petty violence they depict remained familiar. Beginning in the mid-16th century, broadside ballads were printed in Britain, especially about people hanged for murder; several of these did become traditional in the United States, including the South.

When we consider the violent environment of the South, it is important to remember that it was not just humans who were to blame. We see this reflected in topical ballads recounting events from the region. In one song a little girl cries, "Hurry Daddy, there's an awful, dreadful snake," but the father "reached our darling girl too late." Storms and floods could carry people away. A. P. Carter wrote "The Cyclone of Rye Cove" in 1929 about a tornado that wrecked a school and killed 13 people, and "The Mississippi Flood" recounted the events of 1927. As life in the South began to involve more machinery, people were mangled by it, and inevitably someone wrote a song. While there do not appear to be any songs about arms caught in cotton gins, "The Wreck of the Old 97" is but the most famous of a long line of songs about railroad disasters. By the 1930s, automobiles inspired songs like Dorsey Dixon's "Wreck on the Highway."

The South saw plenty of interpersonal violence, and it provided an inherently dramatic subject for song. The classic form is the "murder ballad," such as "Pretty Polly" or "The Banks of the Ohio" or little-known local ones such as "Patsy Beasley" from Anson County, N.C., or "The Story of Freeda Bolt" from Floyd County, Va. While there might be many occasions for murder, these murder ballads tend to involve the murder of a young woman by her lover, often followed by the disposal of her body and the eventual discovery of the crime and culprit. The murder ballads that originate in Britain contain an important detail that the American versions leave out: the murdered woman is killed because she is pregnant. To a great extent, we may understand this as the response of a man trying to avoid the social shame of having an illegitimate child. But in a society where pregnant brides were quite common, it is probably more accurate to read these songs as the response of a man who feels manipulated by a powerful woman. They are, in a very real sense, the extreme manifestation, in song, of the domestic violence that was, and sadly still is, all too prevalent in the South. While British ballads before the early 18th century often gave accounts of women who killed their men (a later American example is "Frankie Silver"), American murder ballads recounted frustrated men who had crossed the line between controlling women, which men had to do to be considered men, and killing them.

This sense of a man being controlled by a powerful woman is also expressed in a disturbing body of songs about wife beating. The conflicts of marital life are an age-old topic for song, and the Irish song "Who Wears the Britches" introduces the theme. In the 1930s, Cliff Carlisle presented the theme of domestic violence in a humorous light in "A Wild Cat Woman and a Tom Cat Man" and "Pay Day Fight." The fight in the first song begins when the woman accuses her man of infidelity, but there is little to laugh about in a story where "he grabbed her by the hair of the head and bumped her head against the wall." "Pay Day Fight" depicts physical violence as an acceptable method to decide how to allocate household resources.

Much of the violence in the South grew out of social conflicts that went beyond the simple binary relationship of attacker and victim. Of course, the largest episode of social violence in the South's history was the Civil War, and it spawned wagonloads of songs. "Shiloh's Hill" is one of the finest, with its depiction of "streams of blood" and its patricidal climax. Simpler and perhaps more bloodthirsty is "I Am a Good Old Rebel," written by Innes Randolph after the war: "Three hundred thousand Yankees lie stiff in Southern dust / We got three hundred thousand before they conquered us / They died of Southern fever, Southern steel and shot / And I wish it was three million instead of what we got."

In a society that bore down on its members to stay in line, through the fierce strictures of Jim Crow and the harsh requirements of evangelical religion, some men broke free from conventional expectations, lashing out violently at anyone who stood in their way. "Badman" songs often captured the career, and usually the eventual downfall, of such characters with a mixture of fear and admiration. Hanged for murder in 1894, West Virginia's John Hardy became the subject of a widely known song. Hardy "was a desperate little man / Carried two guns every day." Otto Wood was a persistent robber and escape artist in North Carolina memorialized in a song written by Walter "Kid" Smith in 1931. "He was a man they could not run," Smith's song went, "And he always carried a .44 gun / He loved the women and he hated the law / And he just wouldn't take anybody's jaw." Perhaps the most terrible form of social control in the South was lynching, and lynching was described in a number of ballads. Most of the time, these lynching ballads reflected the triumphant attitude of the mob. After a North Carolina mob lynched Alec Whitely for (allegedly) murder, robbery, incest, and a few other things, some people in his neighborhood sang, "They hung Alec Whitley to a red oak limb / Just to show the world what they'd do for him." Yet, just a few years later and a few miles away, another North Carolinian wrote about his neighbor, J. V. Johnson, who was lynched. In that song, Johnson admits, "I know my crime was awful black / I wish that I could call it back / It is so dark, I cannot see / My soul what will become of thee?" but the mob's answer is "Come out, come out, your time has come / When you'll repay the deed you've done."

The South has been a land both musical and violent. In a place where people routinely use music as a way to think through their lives, it is inevitable that there would be a body of music reflecting on the experience of living, and simply surviving, in a place suffused with violence and the potential for violence.

BRUCE E. BAKER
Royal Holloway, University of London

Bruce E. Baker, in *Under Sentence of Death: Lynching in the South*, ed. W. Fitzhugh Brundage (1997); Edward E. Baptist, in *Over the Threshold: Intimate Violence in Early America*, ed. Christine Daniels and Michael V. Kennedy (1999); George Pullen Jackson, *White Spirituals in the Southern Uplands: The Story of the Fasola Folk, Their Songs, Singings, and "Buckwheat Note"* (1933); G. Malcolm Laws, *Native American Balladry: A Descriptive Study and a Bibliographical Syllabus* (1950); Guthrie T. Meade, *Country Music Sources: A Biblio-Discography of Commercially Recorded Traditional Music* (2002).

Southwestern Violence

The roots of the apparently casual mayhem in the Wild West can be found in the violence-prone ethic of Texas and the South, specifically in the history of the Scots-Irish who immigrated to America in the 18th century. Conditioned to border war by generations of fighting first the English across the Tweed and then, as colonists in the province of Ulster, the turbulent Irish, by 1730 they were leaving for America by the thousands. Avoiding existing settlements, these Scots-Irish headed immediately for the western, Indian frontier.

Independence of thought and action, which was a primary benefit of frontier life, was not without its costs. The threat of Indian hostilities existed for all whites living on the fringe of Anglo-American civilization. The settlers valued the virtues of strength, physical courage, and self-reliance; Augustus Baldwin Longstreet observed in 1833 that to be "the very best men in the county . . . in the Georgia vocabulary, means that they could flog any other two men in the county." Life on the Indian frontier was savage, and the frontiersman was familiar with violence.

With the crossing of the Sabine River, new circumstances combined to make frontier conditions even more violent for the Anglo-American pioneer. Texas was the place where western and southern violence overlapped. The brief but bloody revolt against Mexican sovereignty spawned border warfare that lasted for generations and mutual antagonism and mistrust that linger to the present day. In Texas, also, the frontiersman encountered for the first time Indians who were superbly skilled horsemen—Comanche and Kiowa warriors—who fought westward expansion to a standstill until the development of repeating firearms. Finally, the unsettled conditions of a newly won independence and a virtually nonexistent legal system drew like a magnet the derelicts and outlaws of the more developed states in the East. One longtime Texan observed that before 1836 fighting was no more common among the Anglo-American colonists in Texas than in the United States. With the inauguration of the "powder-stained Republic," however, turbulence prevailed in many places. Hundreds of American—mostly southern—soldiers of fortune flocked to the Texas army in 1836, and with its disbanding after San Jacinto, its footloose men stayed on. During the 10 years before annexation to the United States, war spirit in Texas continued to run high: legal authority was minimal, bars to immigration were nonexistent, and all sorts of people left the United States for Texas. The western frontier developed too swiftly for its courts of justice.

Texans, like other frontiersmen, commonly settled differences with personal violence, whether by fighting, shooting, stabbing, or dueling. More than two-thirds of the indictments in the district courts of the Republic were for the crimes of assault and battery, affray, assault with intent to kill, or murder. About 60 percent of the assault and battery cases resulted in convictions, but sentences were light—ordinarily $5 or $10 and costs. Prosecutors in trials for more serious offenses encountered great difficulty in obtaining convictions because juries tended to give serious consideration to pleas of self-defense or "unbearable provocation." Only two men, in fact, were executed for murder in the republic. A Texas doctor wrote that "the killing of a fellow was looked upon with greater leniency than theft," a crime of rare occurrence and harsh punishment on the frontier. Homicide, moreover, was most often a crime without malice. Hot-tempered, armed men, on a sudden and often trivial irritation, killed their fellow men. Personal honor was a thing of great value, and in a raw new land no recourse to the courts existed. The very presence of armed, reckless men, imbued with such an ethic, made any quarrel a potential homicide.

While the middle and lower classes did away with each other in street brawls, barroom shootings, and knife fights, the gentry followed the prescribed form of manslaughter for their class, the formal duel. During the period of the republic alone, Texas witnessed "affairs of honor" between many officers of the army, including one in which the principals were its general-in-chief, Albert Sidney Johnston, and its acting commander, Felix Huston. Soldiers were not alone in resorting to the "code duello." Numerous Texas senators and representatives exchanged shots on the field of honor, and a fight between President Mirabeau B. Lamar and a member of his cabinet was barely averted.

This heritage of organized and personal violence naturally produced a corps of proficient, if ill-disciplined, soldiers. Ten years of brutal raiding and counter-raiding from San Antonio to the Rio Grande followed the Texas Revolution's apparent end at San Jacinto, and as scouts, escorts, and mounted infantry, the Texas Rangers serving under Zachary Taylor and Winfield Scott in Mexico took a full measure of revenge for the Texan dead at the Alamo and Goliad. So ruthlessly efficient was Col. John Coffee Hays's ranger regiment that General Taylor reportedly said of them, they "are the damndest troops in the world; we can't do without them in a fight, and we can't do anything with them out of a fight." As atrocities attributed to the Texas troops multiplied, the exasperated Taylor sent home all companies but one, Ben McCulloch's spy company, whose daring and precise reconnaissance activities discovered and reported Santa Anna's secret movement toward Taylor's army in February 1847, just in time to allow the American general to assume a strong defensive position at Buena Vista and thus salvage the United States war effort in northern Mexico.

Not surprisingly, Texas soldiers carried the same ardent martial spirit into the Civil War. Upon the arrival of the leading elements of the Texas brigade at Richmond in 1861, Jefferson Davis observed that "the soldiers of the other states have their military reputations to gain, but the sons of the defenders of the Alamo have theirs to uphold." The Texas Brigade of the Army of Northern Virginia, for example, amassed one of the most glorious combat records of any Civil War unit, North or South. Its men were equally notorious as foragers. Recruited primarily from counties on or near the Indian frontier, this brigade displayed almost superhuman courage and élan at Gaines Mill, Sharpsburg, Gettysburg, and Chickamauga, as well as at the Wilderness, where its decimated regiments are credited with checking the assault of a full Union corps. Despite terrible losses—one of its regiments sustained the highest percentage of casualties of any Civil War unit in a single day at Sharpsburg—the Texas Brigade maintained its formation to Appomattox, with Lee vowing to call upon it "so long as a man remains to wave its flag."

Undoubtedly much of the violence experienced on the frontier was the result of the restlessness engendered by successive wars. The Texas Revolution, the Mexican War, and the Civil War all produced men who had tasted action and could not return to the discipline of the settled world. Jesse James looms largest among this group, but he is only one of scores who continued the war well beyond the passing of the armies.

Many cowboys were also southerners dispossessed by the late war. Among the classic protagonists of western literature is Shane, whose "folks came out of Mississippi and settled in Arkansas," and the model for all cowboys of American fiction, the Virginian of Shiloh Ranch. Like his predecessors on the American frontier, the cowboy values independence, self-reliance, hard work, austerity in manners and possessions, honesty, bravery, and a rugged stoicism born of life in nature. Like the long rifle and bowie knife of earlier frontiersmen, however, his six-gun is his most enduring icon, and in both legend and fact he was too often quick to react to a real or supposed affront with violence.

Along with the heroic Shane and the Virginian, western fiction also presents the evil Major Tetley of *The Oxbow Incident*, who leads a murderous lynch mob dressed in a Confederate uniform and cowboy boots. He represents an undesirable side effect of the frontier imperative of self-reliance and the quest for order—vigilantism and lynch law. Although in the older states of the Deep South both practices flourished well into the 1930s and beyond, long after the development of formal courts of law, it was on the frontier that mob violence, in the name of law and order, took root in America. Nowhere was lynch justice more swift or certain than on the frontier.

Perhaps the most notorious example of vigilante usurpation occurred in east Texas between 1839 and 1844. The so-called Regulator-Moderator War had its background in the influx of lawless characters into the Neutral Ground between the Mexican province of Texas and the state of Louisiana in the first three decades of the 19th century. After 1806 Mexican law forbade the settlement of any lands within 20 leagues of the border of the United States, yet by 1836 the east Texas borderlands had a greater combined population than all other areas of the new Republic combined. These uninvited citizens, largely refugees from justice in the "old states," had become so accustomed to administering their own affairs and giving summary punishment to criminals that they were unwilling to accept the courts of the Texas Republic.

When a killing resulted from a quarrel over fraudulent land certificates, Texas courts acquitted the accused killer. The former defendant quickly organized a posse of 30 "Regulators" to deal with continuing violence. Although their stated purpose was the suppression of crime, this band burned homes and intimidated personal enemies until a rival faction of "Moderators" arose to oppose them. The first act of the Moderators, the murder of the leader of the Regulators, was met with bloody reprisal, and Regulator guns and ropes soon further reduced their already inferior numbers. So powerful did these vigilantes become that they openly defied the courts of Shelby County and contemplated overturning the government of the Texas Republic and declaring their new leader dictator.

Regulator excesses, however, strengthened the Moderators' position, and open warfare broke out once again. East Texas experienced a reign of terror while fields went uncultivated, men were shot from ambush, and prisoners were hung without trial. Only when President Sam Houston ordered 600 Texas militiamen into the region to arrest the leaders of the two factions were peace and order restored.

Statehood strengthened civil government in Texas, but it could not erase the effect of generations of summary frontier justice. Too often mixed with vigilantism was an equally malevolent racism, a curious phenomenon on the American frontier. In some ways the frontier was the freest of places, in which a man was judged on the quality of his work and such virtues as honesty, bravery, and shrewdness. The southern frontier was, however, also heir to the Old South's legacy of black slavery. Anglo-Texans never forgot the Alamo and Goliad or forgave the nation that martyred Crockett, Travis, Bowie, and Fannin. Germans, a numerous, prosperous, aloof, and Unionist minority in central Texas, were viewed with great suspicion by their Anglo-Texan neighbors, a prejudice that culminated in the slaughter of German prisoners of war by Confederate irregulars following the battle of the Nueces in 1862. Indians most of all, especially the fiercely imperialistic Comanches, were regarded as a race of savages whose very existence was a bar to the progress of civilization, and raid and counterraid between these mutually antagonistic cultures escalated into a war of attrition, which the Native American could not hope to win. Finally, when an Anglo-Texan was brought before the bar of justice in Langtry, charged with the murder of a Chinese laborer on the Southern Pacific Railroad, Judge Roy Bean freed him, asserting that "nowhere in his lawbook could he find a rule against killing Chinese."

The courage and honor, the militarism and violence of the 19th-century frontiersman, soldier, and cowboy remain part of present-day Texas culture. Texas A&M University provided more general grade officers to the Allied cause in World War II than any other officer-training academy, and Texans received a higher per capita share of Congressional Medals of Honor in Vietnam than servicemen of any other state. Cowboys and would-be cowboys still carry rifles in the gun racks of their pickup trucks, and for recreation the good old boys still enjoy a good free-for-all at the local honky-tonk on a Saturday night. Here, culturally and geographically, the South and the West meet and are one. The only difference, a Texas Ranger once observed, is that to the east of a certain imaginary line running down the middle of the state, roadhouse brawls take place in the parking lot; to the west they are conducted indoors: a vestige, one may suppose, of the southern heritage of order and decorum juxtaposed to the western tradition of experiencing life "with the bark on."

THOMAS W. CUTRER
Arizona State University

Dickson D. Bruce Jr., *Violence and Culture in the Antebellum South* (1979); Marcus Cunliffe, *Soldiers and Civilians: The Martial Spirit in America, 1775–1865* (1968); Thomas W. Cutrer, *Ben McCulloch and the Frontier Military Tradition* (1993); John Hope Franklin, *The Militant South, 1800–1861* (1956); Joe B. Frantz, in *Violence in America: Historical and Comparative Perspectives*, ed. Hugh Davis Graham and Ted Robert Gurr (1969); Eliot Gorn, *American Historical Review* (February 1985); William Ransom Hogan, *The Texas Republic: A Social and Economic History* (1946, 1969); Robert Marshall Utley, *Lone Star Justice: The First Century of the Texas Rangers* (2002); Jack K. Williams, *Dueling in the Old South: Vignettes of Social History* (1980).

Suicide

Like the other forms of violence explored in this volume, suicide, the intentional and voluntary act of ending one's own life, provides a useful window into the changing social and cultural fissures in southern society. Building on the work of sociologist Emile Durkheim and philosopher Albert Camus, historians of suicide have recognized that while suicide may be an individual act, it provides insight into the relationship between the individual and his or her community. Although gender and class undoubtedly had a significant impact in the social and cultural construction of suicide, race provides the most important prism through which suicide was understood.

British colonization of the American South brought together three disparate traditions about the meaning and significance of suicide. While white colonial southerners inherited centuries of Christian tradition that condemned suicide, African and American Indian southerners demonstrated a considerable diversity in the meaning of suicide. Until the Civil War, white southerners thought of suicide as among the most deplorable acts an individual could commit. In their public and private discourse, they affirmed a deeply held belief that suicide violated divine, social, and natural order. Despite this stigma, British colonists in the American South did not transplant the practice of denying Christian burial to suicide victims or having suicide victims forfeit their property to the state, as had been the case in Great Britain since the Middle Ages. The rise of a cult of honor, however, pushed white southerners to repudiate suicide in no uncertain terms. For instance, the Philanthropic Society, one of the University of North Carolina's two debating societies, unanimously concluded in 1798 that suicide was never justifiable, even in the case of the legendary Roman matron Lucretia, suggesting that the shame of rape was preferable to that of suicide. Not surprisingly, given this deep social stigma, colonial and antebellum white southerners rarely committed suicide, or at least suicide was so shameful that friends and family members obscured suicides, making them invisible in the historical record.

By contrast, suicide is a common theme in many accounts of slave life, appearing regularly in fugitive slave narratives, Works Progress Administration (WPA) oral histories, and other sources. Despite suicide's ubiquitous presence in the historical records, however, there is no present-day consensus about the frequency or meaning of slave suicide. Some historians have interpreted slave suicide as a form of resistance; others see it as evidence that bondage so psychologically crippled slaves that it drove them to kill themselves. Some slaves threatened to commit suicide as a form of negotiation with an owner, using the threat of suicide as a tool, for instance, to prevent the sale of a family member. They recognized that suicide, like running away or other forms of active resistance, deprived their owners of their labor. Many more slaves, however, appeared to have taken their own lives when confronted with desperate circumstances from which they saw no escape or possibility of improvement. These suicides appear to have been more of an act of futility rather than one of defiance or resistance. "Surely if any thing can justify a man in taking his life into his own hands, and terminating his existence, no one can attach blame to the slaves on many of the cotton plantations of the South, when they cut short their breath, and the agonies of the present being, by a single stroke," argued Virginia slave Charles Ball. "What is life worth, amidst hunger, nakedness, and excessive toil, under the continually uplifted lash?" Faced with these alternative explanations, some scholars have concluded that many slave suicides might be best understood as both an act of desperation and a form of resistance.

Slave owners actively attempted to prevent their human property from committing suicide. "Suicide amongst the slaves is regarded as a matter of dangerous example," wrote Charles Ball, "and one which it is the business and the interest of all proprietors to discountenance and prevent." Some slave owners denied suicides proper burial; others, particularly on Caribbean sugar plantations, publicly mutilated the bodies of slaves who had taken their own lives in an effort to dissuade others from following their example.

Slave attitudes toward suicide derive from African beliefs that survived the Middle Passage. The West African cultures displayed an array of attitudes towards suicide, ranging from absolute condemnation to widespread acceptance. Among slave traders, some West African cultures developed reputations for being particularly prone to suicide. For example, Igbo slaves from the Calabar region of the Niger delta were stereotyped as suicidal, while the Fantee were believed to rarely commit suicide. Some slaves evidently believed that after death, they would return to an earthly paradise in Africa and that suicide provided the quickest route to this paradise. According to Charles Ball, "They are universally of opinion, and this opinion is founded in their religion, that after death they shall return to their own country, and rejoin their former companions and friends, in some happy region, in which they will be provided with plenty of food, and beautiful women, from the lovely daughters of their own native land."

Certain locations and situations tended to trigger slaves to take their own lives. Suicide appears to have been more common in the Caribbean than in North America and among newly imported rather than seasoned slaves. Suicide appears to have been particularly frequent during the Middle Passage. Olaudah Equiano recalled in his 1791 memoir that he repeatedly thought of taking his own life during his transatlantic voyage, and other accounts of the Middle Passage suggest that suicide was endemic. Certain events appeared particularly prone to drive slaves to commit suicide. Forced separations from family members, imminent punishment, and fear of capture after escaping often prompted slaves to commit suicide.

Like imported African slaves, American Indians in the South demonstrated a considerable diversity of opinion about suicide, although most American Indians appeared to have condoned suicide, particularly group suicide, under certain circumstances. For instance, according to Bartolomé de las Casas in 1527, "The exploited Indians, seeing themselves die daily, . . . sometimes as entire households together, fathers and sons, the old and the young, adults and children, and some villagers urged others to hang themselves as a way out of the endless torment and calamity that had befallen them." Similarly, according to James Adair in 1783, during a smallpox epidemic, many Cherokee men "shot themselves, others cut their throats, some stabbed themselves with knives and others with sharp-pointed canes; many threw themselves with sullen madness into the fire and there slowly expired, as if they had been utterly divested of the native power of feeling pain."

The Civil War fundamentally reoriented how southerners understood suicide in its social and cultural contexts. Many white southerners believed that suicides had increased dramatically in the years after the Civil War, in what was variously described as "suicide mania," "the suicide epidemic," or the "self-slaying epidemic." Further, the Civil War brought about a revolution in cultural attitudes toward suicide. Widely condemned by the white community in social, moral, and religious terms before the Civil War, suicides became a tolerable, albeit regrettable, choice by the end of the 19th century. Although suicide never lost its stigma as a deviant behavior, white southerners came to sympathize with the plight of suicide victims in ways unthinkable to their antebellum forbearers. Suicidal Confederate veterans, many of whom suffered from what would now be diagnosed as post-traumatic stress disorder (PTSD), played a critical role in this postbellum reorientation. As revered social figures, their deaths helped to moderate how white southerners understood suicide.

Virginian Edmund Ruffin's 1865 suicide marked a symbolic shift in the meaning of suicide among white southerners. A committed Confederate nationalist and outspoken fire-eater, Ruffin had epitomized many of the features of southern manhood and honor in the decades preceding the Civil War. In the conflict's final months, however, Ruffin began contemplating suicide. Turning to his Bible and his journal, Ruffin began to reevaluate the morality of suicide. "One of the many subjects," he wrote in his final diary entry, "in regard to which a close examination of the words of the Bible would serve to correct mistaken popular opinion of the supposed contents, is suicide. It is the almost universal & unquestioned vulgar belief that this act is pronounced a crime by the acknowledged laws of God, as set forth in both the Old & New Testament. So far as I have learned, & believe, there is no ground for this opinion as to either." After reiterating his hatred of Yankee occupation, Ruffin placed a silver plated musket in his mouth, depressed the trigger with a short stick, and ended his life.

While white southerners became more tolerant of suicide after the Civil War, the region's African American population demonstrated the opposite propensity. After emancipation, the tolerant attitude that black southerners displayed toward suicide while enslaved disappeared. In its place, black southerners constructed a new ethos that abhorred suicide regardless of the circumstances. Indeed, many black leaders from throughout the South argued that that suicide was an almost entirely white phenomenon, from which black southerners virtuously abstained.

This racialized conception of suicide was affirmed by the white medical community, who assumed an increased role in treating suicidal patients in the decades after the Civil War. Insane asylum superintendants from across the South repeatedly asserted that suicide only afflicted whites. The medicalization of suicide at the end of the 19th and beginning of the 20th century caused many southerners to increasingly view suicide not as a sign of moral weakness, but as a symptom of mental illness. The medicalization of suicide also produced a proliferation in statistical data related to suicide. While many scholars remain skeptical about the value and accuracy of these figures, almost all of early national studies of suicide conducted between 1880 and 1930 indicate that the South had a significantly lower suicide rate that the rest of the nation.

The distinctive regional qualities of southern suicide seem to have moderated in the 20th century, especially after World War II. The suicide rate in the South, as reported by the Centers for Disease Control, has increased gradually over the past 50 years, while the national incidence of suicide has declined. The South no longer has the lowest regional rate of suicide in the nation (a position now occupied by New England). The marked gulf between white and black suicide rates in the South that was so pronounced in 1900 had moderated significantly by the dawn of the 21st century. While white southerners continue to commit suicide at a higher rate than black southerners, this difference is almost entirely a result of very high rates of suicide among elderly white men. Although it has lost many of its regional particularities, suicide has become a significant theme in southern literature during the 20th century. Starting with Kate Chopin's *The Awakening* (1899), suicide has featured prominently in the works of such diverse southern writers as Walker Percy, Toni Morrison, William Styron, and William Faulkner.

DAVID SILKENAT
North Dakota State University

Richard J. Bell, "Do Not Despair: The Cultural Significance of Suicide in America, 1780–1840" (Ph.D. dissertation, Harvard University, 2006); Sheldon Hackney, *American Historical Review* (February 1969); David Silkenat, *Moments of Despair: Suicide, Divorce, and Debt in Civil War Era North Carolina* (2010); Terri Snyder, *History Compass* (February 2007).

Vigilantism

Much of the collective violence that occurred in the historical South was conservative, meaning that its purpose was to maintain the status quo against individuals or groups perceived as threats. The consummate expression of conservative violence is vigilantism. Simply understood as taking the law into one's own hands, vigilantism involves some degree of organization by a group of people. There is no agreement on the minimum number required, but the concept excludes individuals acting alone. Moreover, vigilantes take the law into their own hands to reinforce existing power relationships, not to subvert them. Indeed, vigilantism has been aptly defined as "establishment violence," because it was traditionally used to defend the established distribution of power, even if the vigilantes themselves were not members of the elite. Vigilantes clearly broke the law by resorting to violence, but they defended their methods as "lawless lawfulness" that was intended to protect society, not undermine it.

The first American vigilante movement appeared on the South Carolina frontier in 1767. People living in the backcountry faced a wave of crime and violence by outlaws who engaged in robbery, arson, and kidnapping. In the absence of effective law enforcement, men in the backcountry formally organized the South Carolina Regulators. According to the *South Carolina Gazette*, the purpose of "the peaceable inhabitants" was "to expel the villains from wherever they can get at them, and to do justice themselves in a summary way." Numbering several thousand, the South Carolina Regulators were led by members of the frontier elite, including large planters and public officials. They held mock trials and used whippings, forced labor, and banishment as punishments. Largely successful in restoring order during their two-year campaign, the South Carolina Regulators became a model for other frontier communities, beginning with the North Carolina Regulators in 1768. The term "regulator" was commonly used for "vigilante" until the late 19th century when "regulator" faded from use.

The South contributed another term to America's vigilante tradition. In 1780 Col. Charles Lynch led a group of settlers who dispensed private justice in western Virginia. Their resort to "Lynch law" took the form of mock trials of Tory outlaws who were punished with floggings. Drawing on the practices of regulators and similar 18th-century movements, vigilantism spread west with the frontier. Texas experienced more outbreaks of vigilantism than any other state. Before the Civil War, vigilantes primarily targeted common criminals and relied largely on corporal punishment and banishment. Occasionally, lynching resulted in death. In 1835 a mob hanged five gamblers in Vicksburg, Miss.

Vigilantism proved so popular and effective in eliminating threats that it persisted even after government institutions became well established in the South. As new challenges to the status quo arose, the targets of vigilantes expanded beyond common criminals to encompass anyone whose activities threatened dominant ideas and institutions. Indeed, one problem with many unpopular causes was their activities were perfectly legal and hence outside the domain of law enforcement, so vigilantes sought to fill the void. The practice of vigilantism peaked during the decades after the Civil War when it was widely used by groups like the Ku Klux Klan to suppress African Americans who attempted to exercise new rights, such as voting.

With the close of the frontier in the late 19th century, vigilantism in the form of lynching became increasingly a southern phenomenon that was used most often to enforce white supremacy. Between 1880 and 1940 lynch mobs in the South murdered more than 3,200 African Americans. In addition, white mobs initiated race riots that took the lives of dozens of African Americans, notably in the southern cities of New Orleans, Atlanta, Wilmington, N.C., and Knoxville, Tenn., between 1866 and 1919. Whatever the specific cause, these race riots resembled other forms of vigilantism in that rioters used violence to enforce white dominance over African Americans.

On a much smaller scale, southern vigilantes also targeted immigrants, ethnic and religious minorities, union organizers, and other so-called radicals who appeared to threaten dominant values. In 1891 a mob lynched 11 Italians accused of killing the police chief of New Orleans, La. In 1910 vigilantes in Tampa, Fla., hanged two Italian immigrants accused of committing a murder during a strike by cigar workers. In 1915 anti-Semitism figured in the lynching of Leo Frank in Atlanta. In 1935 a socialist was flogged to death by Tampa vigilantes. Even more frequently, vigilantes used nonlethal violence, such as beatings and expulsion, to discourage or eliminate real or imagined threats.

Whatever the alleged motive, vigilante attacks in the 20th century usually occurred in areas with well-established systems of law enforcement. The problem was that police and the courts could not easily repress the perfectly legal activities of union organizers, radicals, and others who peacefully challenged the status quo. Therefore, vigilantes resorted to private violence to eliminate perceived threats. During the 1930s members of the Southern Tenant Farmers Union experienced a reign of terror in Arkansas, where vigilantes kidnapped, beat, and flogged supporters of the interracial, socialist-led union. In 1936 a former University of Alabama professor was kidnapped and flogged after he went to the defense of communist organizers in Birmingham. Although he identified one of the vigilantes as a local lawyer, no indictments were forthcoming. One grand juror declared: "I still don't think outsiders should take the law into their own hands, but what are you going to do when there's no law to deal with radicals and Communists?"

This widely held view meant that vigilantes rarely faced legal consequences for their actions even though they violated the law. Because they claimed to defend dominant groups and ideas, they usually gained acceptance, even approval, from the local press and public authorities who were responsible for prosecuting crimes. Vigilantes often tried to hide their identities, but members of the elite sometimes participated. In 1901, during a strike by immigrant cigar workers in Tampa, the owner-editor of the city's afternoon newspaper joined a citizens' committee that kidnapped 13 strike leaders and forced them onto a chartered boat that dumped them in Honduras. One defense of vigilantism invoked the concept of popular sovereignty to justify people taking the law into their own hands to dispense "justice," especially when law enforcement officials seemed impotent in eliminating supposed threats. Reflecting this view, the governor of Florida declared in 1937 that "a man ought to be hung on a tree if he advocates overthrow of government."

Despite a sharp decline in the number of lynching deaths after World War II, outbursts of vigilante violence erupted across the South during the 1950s and 1960s. Defenders of white supremacy attacked black and white civil rights activists in outbursts of violence that ranged from kidnappings and beatings to murder, notably in the 1964 case of three young men who were killed while working on voter registration in Mississippi. Often operating through chapters of the Ku Klux Klan and with the consent, even participation, of local police, antiblack vigilantes went largely unpunished at the time. When Mississippi authorities failed to prosecute anyone for the 1964 slayings, the federal government charged 18 persons for their involvement, and a Mississippi jury convicted seven, including a deputy sheriff.

Gradually, national publicity and federal investigations helped curb vigilante activities. In addition, changing attitudes in the South meant that by the 1960s Klansmen and other vigilantes increasingly risked prosecution if they took the law into their own hands. A shift in dominant southern values eventually placed vigilante violence outside the bounds of acceptable behavior, making it more likely to be successfully prosecuted by local, state, and federal officials. In 1979 members of the Ku Klux Klan and the American Nazi Party shot and killed five protesters in a communist-led march in Greensboro, N.C. Two criminal trials led to the acquittal of the accused shooters, but injured survivors of the attack later won a civil suit for damages from the city, the Klan, and the Nazi Party. In 2005 the state of Mississippi finally took action against one of the surviving perpetrators of the 1964 killing of three civil rights workers, and a local jury found the former Klansman Edgar Ray Killen guilty of manslaughter.

Vigilante violence now occurs infrequently in the South, and its perpetrators are more likely to face punishment. In 1998 James Byrd Jr., an African American, died in Jasper, Tex., after being kidnapped and dragged behind a truck by three white men, all of whom were convicted of murder. In 2006 three white college students were arrested in Alabama for burning nine black churches, and the trio pleaded guilty to both federal and state charges. Such cases reflect a growing respect for the due process of law, and this undoubtedly helps deter those inclined to take the law into their hands.

ROBERT P. INGALLS
University of South Florida

Richard Maxwell Brown, *Strain of Violence: Historical Studies of American Violence and Vigilantism* (1975); Robert P. Ingalls, *Urban Vigilantes in the New South: Tampa, 1882–1936* (1993); H. Jon Rosenbaum and Peter C. Sederberg, eds., *Vigilante Politics* (1976).

Alamo

The Alamo is the site of the most remembered battle in the Texas Revolution, fought 23 February to 6 March 1836. Founded by the Spanish in 1718 as Mission San Antonio de Valero, it became a military post called the Alamo because of a cavalry company from Alamo de Parras stationed there in the early 1800s.

When some Anglo Texans and Tejanos organized to oppose the centralized government in Mexico under Antonio Lopez de Santa Anna, they captured the town of San Antonio and the Alamo from Mexican soldiers in December 1835. Some Texans then went home while others left to attack Matamoros, leaving a small force to hold San Antonio. Santa Anna gathered an army of 6,000 men to recapture the town in February 1836. His advanced units on 23 February surprised the Texans, under James Bowie, William B. Travis, and newly arrived David Crockett, who occupied the Alamo as the most defensible position. They gathered supplies, rejected a surrender demand, and held off light attacks while calling for reinforcements from other Texans. James W. Fannin at Goliad with about 400 men started to respond until some of his wagons broke down. Only 33 men from Gonzales joined the Alamo garrison.

After a 12-day siege Santa Anna rejected his officers' preference of waiting for heavy artillery to batter down the Alamo walls. He ordered a predawn assault on 6 March by about 1,800 troops. In the dark they advanced close to the Alamo walls, faltered under Texan rifle fire, then broke through the outer wall defenses at two points. Most Texans died fighting, including about 100 who broke out of the Alamo only to be killed by Mexican cavalry. Santa Anna ordered the execution of a few who were captured, probably including Crockett. Between 180 and 250 Texans died at the Alamo, their bodies burned by command of Santa Anna. Mexican casualties totaled between 350 and 600 killed and wounded. The Mexican commander allowed women and an African American slave to depart the Alamo and tell of the battle. The Alamo defenders hoped for aid until the end, but delayed the Mexican advance enough to allow the Texas government to declare independence. Organization of another Texas army to oppose Santa Anna came only after the Alamo fell.

Memories of the battle ranged from strong emotions to neglect of the Alamo or debates over its meaning. Texas troops defeated Santa Anna at San Jacinto in April 1836 shouting "Remember the Alamo." One Texan leader compared the Alamo battle to the famous struggle at Thermopylae in 480 B.C.E. where Greek defenders died holding back a Persian army. During the Texas Republic the Alamo lay in ruins; then the United States Army and later merchants used the remaining buildings for storing supplies. In the early 20th century the Daughters of the Republic of Texas, led by Adena de Zavala and Clara Driscoll, convinced the state government to acquire and preserve the buildings as a historic site and shrine. Preservation led to celebrations of the Alamo as the birthplace of Texas independence, a creation myth with strong Anglo overtones. Portrayals in paintings and early movies reinforced that theme. Then the Disney television series about Davy Crockett made the Alamo a national icon in 1955. In the 1960s President Lyndon Johnson compared the Alamo and the Vietnam War.

In the late 20th century new research appeared that questioned some aspects of the heroic battle narrative. Accounts by Mexican soldiers noted that some defenders including Crockett had been captured and executed. That stirred efforts at refutation by those reluctant to give up a more heroic version. Debate developed over the source for Travis drawing a line to challenge the Texans to stay and fight. Reactions to Alamo mythology by some Mexican Americans pointed to Tejanos among the defenders. Others sought to eliminate negative stereotypes of Latinos that had arisen from Santa Anna's refusal to take prisoners. Still others argued for recognition of the Alamo's history as a Spanish mission. From these debates came a more realistic history of the battle. Yet the Alamo in more muted and diverse terms retains a popular image as a Texan and American icon.

ALWYN BARR
Texas Tech University

James E. Crisp, *Sleuthing the Alamo: Davy Crockett's Last Stand and Other Mysteries of the Texas Revolution* (2005); Stephen L. Hardin, *Texian Iliad: A Military History of the Texas Revolution* (1994); Timothy M. Matovina, *The Alamo Remembered: Tejano Accounts and Perspectives* (1995); Randy Roberts and James S. Olson, *A Line in the Sand: The Alamo in Blood and Memory*

(2001); Phillip Thomas Tucker, *Exodus from the Alamo: The Anatomy of the Last Stand Myth* (2010).

American Indian Blood Revenge

In the mid-1700s, James Adair resided in Indian country traveling the Southeast as a merchant trader. During his journeys he learned of the demise of a fellow trader, killed by a group of Creek (Muskogee) Indians. This unnamed Englishman, presumably working in western South Carolina, had apparently had a heated exchange with a local Indian who attempted to steal his wares. The two men engaged in physical combat, resulting in the Indian leaving empty-handed and the trader retaining his merchandise to offer paying customers. Presumably, the two never met again. Sometime after their encounter, the Indian died of respiratory complications. The deceased's heads of family convened and held the trader responsible for his death. Unknowledgeable of the issued execution, the trader was easily found and shot. The man's employer even aided the Indian party in getting to the trader. His employer both withheld news of the impending death sentence and insured that he would be absent at the time of the Indian party's arrival. A simple warning to the trader would have afforded him the opportunity to find refuge in an English settlement. Nevertheless, none tried to prevent the killing, and no one sought to apprehend those involved. When the colonial governor of South Carolina learned of the killing, he was, according to Adair, "passive, and allowed [the Indians] with impunity to shed this innocent blood." The governor, the employer, and the Indians all knew that the law of blood revenge was a fundamental part of southeastern Indian culture that should not be disrupted.

While from our modern vantage point it seems unlikely that the trader was responsible for the Indian's illness and resulting death, once the Creek man's family found the Englishman at fault, it was the obligation of the deceased's kin to exact revenge. Intent and motive were irrelevant in fulfilling the unwritten law of blood revenge. One was responsible for any loss of life. Retaliatory action ensured cosmological balance, and once the debt was paid, the matter was concluded. The victim of the revenge killing was to accept his fate stoically and without fear. As in this example, everyone understood the law of blood revenge, even across ethnic borders.

Among southern Indians, blood revenge does not have any identifiable historical origin. Taking a life necessitated balance, thus demanding a life in return. The regulation of blood revenge fell to large kinship groupings called clans. While the majority of southern Indians identified an allegiance to their town, clan relationships united members of different Indian towns across an Indian nation. An individual was typically born into a clan, taking the mother's affiliation. Clan identification was the single most important definition of an Indian's social affiliations. As a clan member, an individual received lifelong advocates who promised to protect him in life and seek redress in the event of death caused by an outsider.

Clan relationships formed the basis for seeking balance through blood revenge. When an outsider was held responsible for the death of a clan member, the *Cherokee Phoenix* stated in 1829 that retaliation "belonged to the clan." Among southern Indians, a killing or other offense, accidental or intentional, was not an act between individuals but a clan matter. In retaliation, the debt of a life did not explicitly have to be taken by the offending slayer. There were other ways to reinstate balance when an offense, injury, or death occurred. In some cases, it was possible for the offender's clan to sacrifice another member to satisfy the debt. In other instances, the clan would accept compensation of some sort, perhaps in goods or labor.

Within southern Indian society, blood revenge did not necessarily perpetuate murder. In *A Law of Blood Revenge*, John Phillip Reid characterizes blood revenge as a law of peace in which slayers unequivocally knew the repercussion. It is unclear if there was any uniform method for a retaliatory killing, but the closest male clan relative was frequently the individual to satisfy the debt. Although the law did not always provide individually ascribed justice, it provided a clear dictum of order. However, this American Indian sense of order increasingly came in conflict with European expectations of justice. Beginning in the late 18th century, southern Indians initiated attempts to curb retaliatory killings. The Creek Indian National Council agreed to outlaw revenge killings and punish murders by implementing a more American sense of justice. In 1810 the Cherokees abolished blood revenge outright. While the practice of blood revenge faded over the 19th century, vestiges of the cultural law remained as late as 1895 in such forms as the Choctaw law that allowed the brother of a murder victim to act as the executioner in place of the local sheriff.

F. EVAN NOOE
University of Mississippi

James Adair, *The History of the American Indians* (1775); Robbie Ethridge, *Creek Country: The Creek Indians and Their World* (2003); John Phillip Reid, *A Law of Blood Revenge: The Primitive Law of the Cherokee Nation* (2006).

American Indian Slave Trade

Amerindians enslaved one another before European contact. Though not similar in scale or purpose to European slavery, Indian slavery was a complex cultural arrangement where war captives were ritualistically sacrificed, adopted, traded in peaceful gift exchanges among Indian nations, or used for menial labor. European arrival dramatically changed these traditional patterns of life by purchasing captives to labor on colonial plantations in the South and West Indies. Death rates among laborers in the West Indian sugar plantations created a voracious appetite for labor and prompted an active growth in the exportation of captured Indians. A growing trade network, groundbreaking commercial and trade policies, religious toleration, colonial self-sufficiency, a booming New England shipping industry, and the consolidated economic web tying the West

Indies to North America all helped produce a bustling Atlantic economic world. Indian slavery acted as one of the many fibers that sustained this growing global system.

The transformation of the Native American world chronicled by members of Hernando de Soto's expedition of the 1540s to the one recognized by colonial travelers of the mid-18th century was violent and decidedly chaotic. From the 1620s to the 1720s, what would become the southeastern United States was aflame with violence and dislocation on a scale not to be rivaled until the American Civil War. Indians of the South preyed on other Indians in a lucrative trade system that would help fuel the creation of a viable plantation economy in Virginia and the Carolinas. As a practice it was brutal and destructive to native peoples with estimates ranging between 30,000 and 50,000 Amerindians being enslaved from 1670 to 1715. While clearly damaging and demographically scarring, the Indian slave trade did not entirely destroy southeastern Native American societies. The caustic effects instead illustrate the adaptability of Indian social institutions such as matrilineal kin relations, clan structure, tribal government, hunting and gathering, corn cultivation, and revenge killings to the changing economic and social climates of the 18th and early 19th centuries.

According to Robbie Ethridge, in the introduction to *Mapping the Mississippi Shatter Zone*, as Europeans vied for position in North America, warfare among native groups "became entwined with market interests and international commerce." Capturing members from neighboring Indian towns necessitated the use of force on a grand scale—far beyond what was necessary to maintain the fur and skin trade. As the dependency on European goods increased, native societies became more militaristic. Debt and the need for more European goods pushed many Indians to pursue captives from weaker, less organized groups as a means to enhance the regular traffic in pelts and feed a growing demand for labor in the West Indies. Specific Indian groups specialized in slave raiding.

During the 1660s many southern Indians allied with the Spanish were susceptible to attack from the north. With limited access to European weaponry, the scattered mission Indians lying on the northern boundaries of Spanish-controlled Florida were constantly marauded by slaving parties of Westo Indians (Eries that migrated from the northeast to the Virginia and Carolina settlements respectively). The Spanish were unable to offer anything more than token assistance, forcing natives along their territorial periphery to seek shelter closer to mission garrisons. Indian polities nearest the English settlements (especially after Charles Town's establishment in 1670) sought similar protection.

The range of these slaving expeditions was considerable, and attacks by groups such as the Westos forced disparate southeastern Indians, who did not seek the protection of European fortifications, to amalgamate for sur-vival. In addition to the dangers brought from slaving expeditions, the threat of disease was also constant for Indians. Epidemics like small pox seem to have traveled along the same routes as the slavers, inflicting comparable damage to native societies. The Yamasees, Creeks, Catawbas, and Choctaws are perhaps the best examples of these confederations, owing much of their existence to Westo aggressions. Accepting refugees seems to have been nothing new for some of these chiefdoms. Archaeological evidence indicates some of these societies in the distant past dealt with chaotic circumstances in similar ways, especially the forbearers of the Creeks. The Westo terror ended in 1680 when a group of Shawnee refugees assisted the Carolinians in destroying and enslaving the group.

The English continued to entice groups like the Creeks to target Indians allied with the Spanish and French, both for slaves and to advance their own imperial agenda in the region. Debt also fueled raiding and violence. Extending credit to Indians was a common practice for traders, much to the chagrin of South Carolina's Lords Proprietors. War with neighboring communities for captives and hunting for deerskins were the quickest way out of debt. This created a dangerous spiral, especially as options for indebted Indians diminished. Vulnerable Indian towns migrated beyond the reach of slaving expeditions, disease and years of slaving depopulated large areas of the southeast, old hunting grounds were cultivated for plantation agriculture, and devious trading practices continued to stress Indian relations. In many cases, traders enslaved a debtor's family to settle an account.

The combination of abuses by traders, white encroachment, and the fear of becoming enslaved pushed the Tuscaroras in North Carolina to act in the fall of 1711. The element of surprise brought initial successes for the Indians, but these victories were overshadowed by coordinated assaults from an English and Indian coalition (Yamasees, Cherokees, Catawbas, and Apalachees). Victory for the English in 1713 was followed by enslavement and displacement of Tuscarora lands and property.

Fear of losing their lands and their families to enslavement because of mounting debts eventually sparked retaliation when Yamasee warriors preemptively massacred a peace delegation sent to their town of Pocotaligo in April 1715. The Yamasees, along with their Lower Creek allies, launched a series of attacks on South Carolinian settlements, forcing the panicked abandonment of plantations and eventual retreat of the colonists behind Charles Town's gates where starvation and disease hindered colonial resolve.

The Yamasee War called into question the practices of Indian slaving on an economic level. The slave trade did not end with the defeat of the Yamasees, but it did slow considerably, changing it in purpose and meaning. Enslaving natives continued in the Southeast beyond the removal period of the early 19th century, albeit on a much more limited scale. The Yamasee War proved that old slaving practices were too costly and dangerous. As the Atlantic slave trade grew, the influx of Africans into places like South Carolina became more profitable and, in many ways, safer.

KEVIN HARRELL
University of Mississippi

Robbie Ethridge, *From Chicaza to Chickasaw: The European Invasion and the Transformation of the Mississippian World, 1540–1715* (2010); Robbie Ethridge and Sheri Shuck Hall, eds., *Mapping the Mississippi Shatter Zone: The Colonial Indian Slave Trade and Regional Instability in the American South* (2009); Alan Gallay, *The Indian Slave Trade: The Rise of the English Empire in the American South, 1670–1717* (2002); William Ramsey, *The Yamasee War: A Study of Culture, Economy, and Conflict in the Colonial South* (2008); Christina Snyder, *Slaving in Indian Country: The Changing Face of Captivity in Early America* (2010).

Ames, Jessie Daniel

(1883–1972) SOCIAL REFORMER.
Jessie Daniel Ames, born 2 November 1883, had moved three times in Texas by the time she was a teenager. Her father, a stern Victorian eccentric, migrated from Indiana to Palestine, Tex., where he worked as railroad stationmaster, and in 1893 the Daniels moved to Georgetown, Tex., the site of Southwestern University, from which Ames later graduated.

The brutal Indian Wars and vigilantism of the period created a violent atmosphere, which strongly affected the sensitive young Jessie. A strong-willed child, she had resisted the perfect table manners expected of her and often was sent to the kitchen. In the Daniel kitchen, young Jessie heard about a lynching nearby in Tyler, an event she remembered for years and that influenced her lifelong efforts to abolish lynching.

In June 1905 Jessie Daniel married a handsome army surgeon, Roger Post Ames, who later died in Guatemala. In 1914 she rose to prominence in Texas as an advocate of southern progressivism and women's suffrage. Unlike most suffragists in the early 1920s, she understood the grave injustice against blacks in this country. She served as a vital link between feminism and the 20th-century struggle for black civil rights.

In 1924 she became field secretary of Will Alexander's Atlanta-based Commission on Interracial Cooperation. She immediately began organizing against lynching in Texas, Arkansas, and Oklahoma. Alexander brought her to Atlanta in 1929 as director of Women's Work for the commission, and in 1930 she began Southern Women for the Prevention of Lynching, which in nine years had 40,000 members. Alerted by friendly law officers and her contacts in the press when a lynching threatened, Ames contacted women in that county who had pledged to work against violence. Her work was not always appreciated. Opposition came from women as well as men. The Women's National Association for the Preservation of the White Race claimed that Ames's women "were defending criminal Negro men at the expense of innocent white girls."

Ames did not support the federal antilynching law in 1940 as being practical. She said the bill would pass the House and southern senators would then defeat it. She was soon at odds with her boss, Dr. Alexander, as well as her old allies in the NAACP.

From May 1939 to May 1940 in the South, for the first time since records had been kept, not a single lynching occurred. World War II, however, dealt a deathblow to Southern Women for the Prevention of Lynching, just as it did to the attempt to abolish the hated poll tax in the South. The alliance between women and victimized blacks, which Ames hoped for, was postponed.

In 1943 Southern Women for the Prevention of Lynching was absorbed by the newly formed Southern Regional Council, as was the Interracial Commission. Ames wanted to work for the new agency but found her services were not needed.

In the foothills of the Blue Ridge Mountains, Ames set about to rebuild her life. Elected superintendent of Christian Social Relations for the Western North Carolina Conference of the Methodist Church, she welcomed the opportunity "to get back into public life and be remembered." She later returned to Texas and was honored in the 1970s as a pioneer who combined feminism with civil rights activism. Jessie Daniel Ames died on 21 February 1972 at the age of 88.

MARIE S. JEMISON
Birmingham, Alabama

Jessie Daniel Ames Papers, Texas Historical Society, Dallas, Texas State Library, Austin, and Southern Historical Collection, University of North Carolina, Chapel Hill; Jacquelyn Dowd Hall, *Revolt against Chiv-*

alry: *Jessie Daniel Ames and the Women's Campaign against Lynching* (1979); Association of Southern Women for the Prevention of Lynching and the Commission on Interracial Cooperation Papers, Trevor Arnett Library, Atlanta University; Jon D. Swartz and Joanna Fountain-Schroeder, eds., *Jessie Daniel Ames: An Exhibition at Southwestern University* (1986).

Andersonville Prison

Andersonville Prison, also known as Camp Sumter, served as a Confederate prison during the U.S. Civil War from February 1864 to May 1865. Originally situated on 16 acres of land in Macon County, Ga., the prison was colloquially referred to as Andersonville after the railroad station beside it. During the short time it was open, Andersonville had the highest mortality rate of all Civil War prisons, with more than a quarter of its inmates dying while incarcerated.

Though Andersonville was initially built to hold 10,000, its population grew to about 33,000. An expansion in the summer of 1864, where prisoners and slaves constructed a hospital, bakery, more barracks, and extended the stockades to include an additional 10 acres of lands to the site, was insufficient to adequately house all of Andersonville's prisoners.

Andersonville's guards were a collection of troops from various units, but as they were sent into combat, they were replaced by reserves and militia from Georgia and Florida. This rotation of ill-armed and outnumbered guards used guard towers, packs of dogs, cannons, and a "deadline" to control inmates. The deadline was drawn three feet into the stockade wall. Any prisoner who stepped beyond it would be shot to death by guards.

In March 1864 Captain Hartmann Heinrich "Henry" Wirz became commander of Andersonville. Though he tried to improve conditions in the prison, overcrowding and his lack of authority over his staff made it impossible.

The remote location of Andersonville, chosen for its isolation from land and coastal attacks, made access to supplies difficult. Even when there was an adequate food supply, rations were limited and the food was of poor quality. Malnutrition was the foremost cause of inmate death at the camp. Disease spread through a contaminated water supply. After some of the 80 escape tunnels dug by inmates were found to be concealed in on-site wells, the wells were covered and a nearby stream was used as the primary water source for drinking and bathing. Sewage and garbage were dumped into nearby swamps that fed the stream, and inmates suffered from bouts of scurvy and dysentery as a result of the unsanitary conditions.

A gang of inmates, who called themselves the Andersonville Raiders, robbed inmates of food and personal belongings. Illegal gambling and inmate-run "stores" stripped them of any remaining valuables. In response, a second group of inmates called the "Regulators" sprang up to police the inmates, enforcing sanitation rules and reducing the number of robberies. The Regulators rounded up the remaining Raiders and tried them before an all-

Andersonville Prison, Ga., August 17, 1864. Southwest view of stockade showing the deadline.
(Photographer unknown, Library of Congress [LC-USZ62-122695], Washington, D.C.)

inmate jury. Their sentences ranged from running the gauntlet, wearing a ball and chain, and being sent to the stocks. The six leaders of the Raiders were hung in the summer of 1864.

By August 1864, 33,000 prisoners were being housed at Andersonville, its highest population. Prisoners were transferred to other camps in Georgia and South Carolina in anticipation of attack, as Gen. William Tecumseh Sherman and his troops marched deeper into Georgia.

In May 1865 Henry Wirz was tried on counts of war crimes by federal military courts. He was sentenced to death by hanging and was executed on 10 November 1865 in Washington, D.C. He was the only man who was executed in connection with war crimes during the Civil War. In the town of Andersonville, Wirz was seen as a martyr. The United Daughters of the Confederacy erected a monument and holds an annual ceremony in Wirz's honor on the anniversary of his execution.

The site of Andersonville Prison is now home to the National Prisoner of War Museum, which chronicles the capture, living conditions, and hardships of American POWs throughout history. Also on-site is Andersonville National Cemetery, which was the burial place of prisoners who died while incarcerated there. Clara Barton, founder of the American Red Cross, led the effort to identify and mark each grave. Of the 13,714 graves, only 921 of them are marked "unknown." The Andersonville National Cemetery remains an active burial site where soldiers can still be buried.

In 1956 MacKinlay Kantor's historical novel *Andersonville* won the Pulitzer Prize for fiction. Famed landscape painter Winslow Homer's *Near Andersonville*, which depicts a slave woman watching from her cabin door as captured Union soldiers are led past by Confederate captors, touched on the irony of Union liberators taken captive.

NOVELETTE BROWN
University of Mississippi

Robert Diel Dean, *Echoes of Andersonville* (1999); Ovid L. Futch, *History of Andersonville Prison* (1968); James M. Gillispie, *Andersonvilles of the North: The Myths and Realities of Northern Treatment of Civil War Confederate Prisoners* (2008); William Marvel, *Andersonville: The Last Depot* (2006); John McElroy, *Andersonville: A Story of Rebel Military Prisons* (2008).

Angola Prison (Louisiana State Penitentiary)

Angola Prison is the oldest prison farm and the largest maximum-security penitentiary in the nation, with 5,260 prisoners residing on 18,000 acres of land. More than 90 percent of Angola's inmates will never be released, serving terms averaging 88 years. Once dubbed the bloodiest prison in America, Angola's history is steeped in inmate abuse and exploitation.

Through convict leasing, former Confederate general Samuel James purchased the lease of the Louisiana State Penitentiary and all inmates in 1880 and moved them to the 8,000-acre Angola Plantation, named for the region in Africa from which slaves were brought. Its isolated location, surrounded on three sides by the Mississippi River, kept it far from state supervision. Inmates were housed in Angola's old slave quarters, packed into barracks without blankets or linens. Meals were scarce and barely edible. Inmates worked between 60 and 90 hours per week on the farm

planting and harvesting cotton, corn, and sugarcane, as well as building the prison levee system. Those accused of not working hard enough were often beaten with straps, shaved pipes, and spare pieces of lumber. During the 1890s, the death rate of convicts in the Louisiana Penal System, which consisted primarily of Angola, was four times greater than that of any other state in the country. Though Louisiana repealed convict leasing in 1898, the state did not regain full control of its inmates until 1901.

After the Great Depression, Angola's staff was reduced from 150 to 50, and the trusty system was set in place, allowing inmates to fill the vacant positions. Prisoners were given authority over others, holding jobs as farm line guards and gun-tower guards. Trustees were paid minimal salaries and given perks such as conjugal visits, additional meals, and roaming privileges. Inmate and institutionalized violence at Angola skyrocketed, and by 1952 working conditions and abuse had grown to such a level that 31 inmates slashed their Achilles tendons in protest. By the 1970s the prison, which was still the primary corrections facility in Louisiana, was both overcrowded and understaffed. Gang violence, drug trafficking, sexual slavery, and theft were common occurrences. Inmates had taken to sleeping with phone books on their chests in case they were stabbed during the night. During this period, Angola was given the title of Bloodiest Prison in America, averaging one to two inmate stabbings each night.

Even though current warden Burl

Cain is credited with decreasing inmate assaults by 72 percent, there are still reports of brutality. Herman Wallace and Albert Woodfox, known Black Panthers, spent 36 years in solitary confinement for the murder of a prison guard in 1973. They were finally released into maximum security in 2008. In 2008 25 inmates reported that following an inmate revolt in the 1990s guards beat them with batons and fists until they lost control of their bodily functions, left them naked inside freezing cells, and threatened to sexually assault them with batons. Even though the inmates claim that they were not involved in the uprising, they were beaten and threatened until they signed confessions. Though the prison is still a working farm, inmates now have the opportunity to work for KLSP, the prison radio station, and the *Angolite*, the uncensored, award-winning magazine. The prison also hosts a twice-yearly rodeo.

Because of its reputation, Angola has been widely represented in popular culture, particularly in film. The 1995 film, *Dead Man Walking*, is based on nun Sister Helen Prejean and her relationship with Angola inmates Elmo Patrick Sonnier and Robert Lee Willie while they were on death row. Death row conditions at Angola during the 1930s were the inspiration for the 1999 film adaptation of Stephen King's *The Green Mile*, and scenes for the 2001 film *Monster's Ball* were filmed at Angola. In 1934 legendary folk singer Huddie "Lead Belly" Ledbetter was "discovered" by musicologist John Lomax while incarcerated at Angola for attempted murder. Bluesman Robert Pete Williams was pardoned from the prison after serving 12 years of his life sentence for murder, and musicians in nearly all genres of music have referenced the infamous prison, including spoken-word artist Gil Scott-Heron, New Orleans soul band the Neville Brothers, pianist James Booker, and rapper Juvenile.

NOVELETTE BROWN
University of Mississippi

Daniel Bergner, *God of the Rodeo: The Quest for Redemption in Louisiana's Angola Prison* (1999); Anne Hamilton and C. Murray Henderson, *Dying to Tell: Angola, Crime, Consequence, Conclusion at Louisiana State Penitentiary* (1992); Dennis Shere, *Cain's Redemption: A Story of Hope and Transformation in America's Bloodiest Prison* (2005); Liz Garbus, Willbert Rideau, and Jonathan Stack, *The Farm: Life inside Angola Prison* [DVD] (1998); Alan Lomax, *Prison Blues of the South: Live at the Mississippi and Louisiana State Penitentiaries* [CD] (1994).

Antiabortion Violence

The South has figured prominently in the larger conflict over abortion rights in the United States since 1973. *Roe v. Wade* (1973), the controversial U.S. Supreme Court case that decriminalized abortion, originated in Dallas as a challenge to abortion statutes in Texas. Within months the first freestanding abortion clinic in the nation opened in San Antonio and, by the 1990s more than 400,000 women obtained abortions in the South each year, second only to the Northeast. Although Catholic organizations outside the South were the most visible early opponents of abortion rights, the first legal injunction against antiabortion protesters in the United States occurred in Virginia in 1974, and the first arrest of protesters occurred in Maryland the following year. By the early 1980s the opposition of President Ronald Reagan and the Republican Party to abortion allowed increasing Republican inroads into southern politics, fueled in part by the growing political power of fundamentalist Christianity often identified with the Moral Majority and cultural conservatism. Reflecting the traditional concern of southern fundamentalists for public morality, the Southern Baptist Convention adopted a strong opposition to legalized abortion in 1984. As a result, the emergence of numerous antiabortion organizations in the South, such as the American Life League, Pro-Life Nonviolent Action League, Life Dynamics, and Rescue America, reflected how much of the more dramatic social activism concerning abortion had shifted to the South. Four years later, Atlanta became the central battleground over abortion as supporters of Operation Rescue, an organization that claimed that its direct-action protests at abortion clinics were the latest chapter in the southern civil rights movement, protested at the 1988 Democratic National Convention. Authorities arrested more than 1,200 activists during the convention.

As the movement grew after 1980, in part owing to frustration with the Reagan administration's inability to overturn *Roe*, abortion clinics in the South faced increasing violence ranging from blockades, vandalism, and intimidation to chemical attacks, arson, bombings, and murder. In 1982 three

men from Texas calling themselves the "Army of God" destroyed three abortion clinics in Florida and Virginia and kidnapped an abortion doctor. From 1982 to 1998 arsonists damaged 56 abortion clinics in the South and bombed 15 clinics in Virginia, Florida, Washington, D.C., Maryland, North Carolina, Alabama, and Georgia. In an attempt to disrupt services and cause expensive repairs, abortion opponents attacked clinics in the South with butyric acid more than 30 times during the period. In 1992 Pensacola, Fla., became the epicenter of the more radical antiabortion movement as leaders from throughout the nation organized a training program for Christian antiabortion activists called IMPACT. The following year David Gunn, a doctor in Pensacola, became the first casualty of the war over abortion in the United States when he was shot outside his clinic by an abortion opponent named Michael Griffin. Five months later George Patterson, a doctor who performed abortions in Mobile, Ala., was shot and killed. Although the case remains unsolved, antiabortion activists circulated a "WANTED" poster with Patterson's face in the months preceding his murder. As a result of such violence and more common efforts to harass and intimidate clinic workers and patients, Congress passed the Freedom of Access to Clinic Entrances (or FACE) Act in 1993, which prohibited the use of force to interfere with abortion services. The legislation curbed many of the blockades, but in 1994 a former minister from South Carolina named Paul Hill shot and killed a doctor and a clinic escort in Pensacola. Although condemned by more moderate anti-abortion activists, Hill enjoyed support from others such as Michael Bray, a minister from Maryland who published a book in 1994 entitled *A Time to Kill* that argued such murders were "justifiable homicide." Before receiving the death sentence, the defiant Hill evoked the words of radical abolitionist John Brown in 1859 in claiming that "You may mix my blood with the blood of the unborn and those who have fought to defend the oppressed." As a result of years of escalating clinic violence, the number of abortion providers in the South declined by the mid-1990s with 91 percent of southern counties lacking abortion services by 2000.

RICHARD L. HUGHES
Illinois State University

Patricia Baird-Windle and Eleanor J. Bader, *Targets of Hatred: Anti-abortion Terrorism* (2001); Dallas A. Blanchard, *Anti-abortion Movement and the Rise of the Religious Right: From Polite to Fiery Protest* (1994); Lawrence B. Finer and Stanley K. Henshaw, *Perspectives on Sexual and Reproductive Health* (Jan.–Feb. 2003); National Abortion Federation, www.prochoice.org; James Risen and Judy L. Thomas, *Wrath of Angels: The American Abortion War* (1998).

Antilynching Activism

In 1901, Mark Twain, the prolific writer and observer of American culture, sarcastically noted that America had become the "United States of Lyncherdom." For Twain, lynchings were becoming so commonplace that he predicted that the number of lynchings per year would exceed the 500-mark by 1903 and that a spectacle lynching would occur in downtown New York City. Although Twain's prediction did not come to fruition, lynching did gain widespread approval, which inspired a number of activists to organize antilynching campaigns during the first half of the 20th century.

Lynchings were extralegal public executions meant to punish alleged criminals and deviants. What distinguished lynchings from simple murders was that they were typically carried out by a group with the intent that the execution would be viewed by a collective either during the execution or afterward. Therefore, a lynch mob's desire for the public consumption of extralegal violence was one of lynching's distinguishing features.

The antilynching movement emerged in response to the dramatic rise of lynching in the 1890s and the American public's seeming acceptance (even glorification) of lynch mob violence. From the beginning, women played crucial roles in antilynching crusades. Ida B. Wells emerged as a national and international celebrity for her outspoken denunciations of white-on-black lynchings and the rape of black women by white men. Wells's antilynching activism sprang from witnessing the lynching of Thomas Moss, a successful black grocer, and several other black men in Memphis in 1892. Wells penned three significant antilynching pamphlets that provocatively challenged white southerners' justifications of lynching. In particular, Wells's pamphlets challenged the idea that black men were increasingly raping white women and that lynching was needed to deter black criminality and restore white womanhood. Instead, Wells argued that lynchings were an attempt to deprive blacks of economic opportunity and citizenship rights. Through her tireless campaigns to alter public opinion, Wells laid the foundation for future female antilynching activism.

Most notably, in 1930, Jessie Daniel Ames founded the Association for Southern Women for the Prevention of Lynching (ASWPL). Ames's primary message was that lynchings denigrated white womanhood rather than upheld it. Ames believed that if white women openly rejected lynching as a chivalrous practice, they would delegitimize lynching and over time lynchings would cease. By the end of the 1930s, dozens of ASWPL chapters had been organized throughout the South. The ASWPL's success in organizing white southern women against lynching lent creditability to antilynching rhetoric among southern whites—creditability that black antilynching activists such as Ida B. Wells had never been able to achieve.

While Ida B. Wells and the ASWPL did much to alter how lynchings were perceived, the National Association for the Advancement of Colored People (NAACP) led the most sustained assault against lynch mob violence. Between 1920 and 1950 the NAACP tirelessly campaigned for federal antilynching laws. The NAACP contended that southern localities routinely failed to punish lynch mob participants and the police officers who allowed lynchings to occur. The organization reasoned that if federal antilynching statues were adopted,

it would make punishing lynching more likely, and as a result fewer whites would participate in lynch mob violence. The NAACP's lobbying efforts paid dividends. On three separate occasions (1922, 1937, and 1940), the House of Representatives passed antilynching legislation; however, each time southern lawmakers defeated antilynching legislation in the Senate. Although federal antilynching laws were never adopted, the NAACP's activism placed greater pressure on southern states to pass antilynching laws and southern localities to punish whites who aided and abetted lynch mob violence.

KARLOS K. HILL
Texas Tech University

Crystal Feimster, *Southern Horrors: Women and the Politics of Rape and Lynching* (2009); Amy Louise Wood, *Lynching and Spectacle: Witnessing Racial Violence in America, 1890–1940* (2009); Robert Zangrando, *The NAACP Crusade against Lynching, 1909–1950* (1980).

Atlanta (Georgia) Race Riots (1906)

At the turn of the 20th century, racial tensions in Atlanta were heightening rapidly, largely a result of the population boom brought on by Reconstruction. Despite disenfranchisement efforts, African Americans were voting and were becoming more involved in the city's political sphere while also forming black businesses and communities. Pushing racial tension in Atlanta over the edge, in the summer of 1906 the *Atlanta Journal*'s former publisher, Hoke Smith, ran for governor on a platform that played on white southerners' prejudices, equating black political power with black male sexual dominance and encouraging the disenfranchisement of blacks.

On Saturday, 22 September 1906, various newspapers in Atlanta reported four alleged, sensationalized assaults upon local white women by black men. At least 5,000 white men and boys gathered in the Five Points area of downtown Atlanta, quickly forming a violent mob. City leaders failed to contain the mob, and the men rushed through the city's central business district, beating and shooting hundreds of blacks and destroying black-owned businesses along the way. The state militia took control of the city around midnight, yet sporadic fighting continued in the next few days. The riots finally ceased on Tuesday, 25 September, after prominent businessmen, city leaders, and members of the press and clergy gathered and demanded an end to the violence, as it was harming Atlanta's reputation as a progressive New South city.

The effects the riots had on Atlanta were immediate. The official death count was 12 blacks and 2 whites killed in the riots. More than 1,000 African Americans left the city, and the number of black businesses decreased. While the riot negatively affected the city in many ways, by the end of the year elite white and black leaders had met and formed the Atlanta Civic Lead and the Colored Cooperative Civic Lead in order to ensure future interracial cooperation in the city.

MEGHAN LEONARD
University of Mississippi

Mark Bauerlein, *Negrophobia: A Race Riot in Atlanta, 1906* (2001); Rebecca Burns, *Rage in the Gate City: The Story of the 1906 Atlanta Race Riot* (2006); Gregory Mixon, *The Atlanta Race Riot: Race, Class, and Violence in a New South City* (2005).

Bacon's Rebellion

Bacon's Rebellion was a colonial uprising in Virginia that united poor blacks and whites to seek relief from American Indian raids and unfair treatment by Gov. William Berkeley. Berkeley, a successful attorney in England, had been appointed governor of the Virginia colony by Charles I in 1642. During his first decade in office, he called for explorations of Virginia's frontier and successfully handled relations with hostile Indians tribes. In fact, he encouraged settlers to increase trading with them, and in return traders gave him a portion of their profits.

Berkeley was temporarily removed from office during the English Civil War but resumed the governorship of Virginia in 1660. During his second term, Berkeley appointed wealthy friends to high political positions, deeded them large plots of land, and used tax revenue for personal purposes. By the 1670s, high taxes, drought, low tobacco prices, and American Indian raids weighed on Virginia's working class. These problems and a lack of representation from the colonial government united laborers, indentured servants, and slaves in their discontent.

In September 1675 a band of Doeg Indians confiscated hogs from settler Thomas Matthews as compensation for unpaid trade debts. Colonists retaliated by murdering two of the Doegs, after which the Doegs killed shepherd Robert Hen. During an attack on the Doegs, two militia captains killed 14 Susquehanna Indians, who were British allies. The Susquehanna killings resulted in several retaliatory raids between the Indians and the frontiersmen.

Berkeley's solution to the escalating situation between the American Indians and the frontiersmen was to disarm the Indians and tell the settlers that they were not hostile. In addition, Berkeley called the Long Assembly and set up a number of defensive forts around Virginia. The assembly declared war on all hostile tribes, which was financed by taxes levied on the colonists.

Discontented farmers gathered at the home of wealthy planter Nathaniel Bacon to form a new raiding party. Bacon and Berkeley were distantly related, and because of this connection, Berkeley had appointed him to the Virginia Counsel. However, Bacon's views aligned more with the frontiersmen than with Virginia's ruling class, and Bacon became leader of the burgeoning rebellion. The band traveled south until it reached a tribe of Ochannechee Indians. After coercing them into killing the Susquehannas, Bacon and his followers brutally murdered the majority of the Ochannechee settlement. Upon returning home, they learned that Berkeley had held an election to find a more effective solution to the American Indian hostility.

The House of Burgesses imposed reforms that limited Gov. Berkeley's power and granted landless freedmen suffrage rights. Bacon brought 500 men to Jamestown to petition for a commission to lead troops against the Indians. Berkeley was steadfast in his refusal, even when Bacon's men aimed their weapons at the Burgesses. When Bacon ordered them to aim at Berkeley, he relented.

On 13 July 1676 Bacon issued the Declaration of the People of Virginia, which criticized Berkeley's nepotism toward his friends in politics, unfair taxes, and failure to defend farmers against Indian attacks. The document also called for all American Indians in Virginia to be removed or killed. Following the declaration, Bacon and his men began attacking Indians on the frontier. Among those they terrorized were the Pawmunkey Indians, who had been allies with the English and uninvolved in attacks on the settlers.

On 19 September 1676, Bacon returned to Jamestown and burned down the capital. Berkeley fled to the safety of England, where a naval squadron embarked to quell the rebellion. Before it could arrive, Bacon died from dysentery on 26 October 1676. John Ingram became the rebellion's new leader, but a number of followers left the movement. The rebellion finally came to an end after Berkeley launched a series of successful amphibious attacks. Berkeley returned to Jamestown and briefly resumed his post as governor in 1677, during which he punished some of Bacon's rebels by seizing their property and hanging 23 of them. Upon receiving the results of an investigative committee, King Charles II stripped

Berkeley of his governorship and recalled him to England.

NOVELETTE BROWN
University of Mississippi

Warren M. Billings, *Sir William Berkeley and the Forging of Colonial Virginia* (2010); Michael Leroy Oberg, *Samuel Wiseman's Book of Record: The Official Account of Bacon's Rebellion in Virginia, 1676–1677* (2009); Stephen Saunders Webb, *1676: The End of American Independence* (1995); Howard Zinn, *A People's History of the United States: 1492 to Present* (2005).

Birmingham Church Bombing

After a summer of nearly 200 riots, protests, and marches throughout the country, Birmingham, Ala., recaptured the nation's attention as the violent epicenter of the civil rights movement when a dynamite bomb exploded through the 16th Street Baptist Church near downtown on Sunday, 15 September 1963. Although there were nearly 50 unsolved bombings on African American homes and churches in Birmingham since 1949, this explosion was the first to kill. Addie Mae Collins, Carole Robertson, and Cynthia Wesley, all aged 14, and Denise McNair, aged 11, died in the bombing planned by Ku Klux Klan (KKK) members Thomas Edwin Blanton, Herman Frank Cash, Robert Chambliss, and Bobby Frank Cherry. Within hours of the explosion, two more black teenagers fell victim to white supremacists who used violence to terrorize the city that day: 16-year-old Johnnie Robinson, shot in the back by a white police officer for throwing rocks at cars near the church, and 13-year-old

Virgil Ware, shot by two white teenagers after they attended a National States Rights Party (NSRP) rally protesting recent school desegregation in the western part of the city.

The 16th Street Baptist Church bombing was part of a larger political struggle between white supremacists, white moderates, and black activists over race and power in postwar Birmingham. On 1 April 1963 voters elected Albert B. Boutwell over T. Eugene "Bull" Connor for mayor as part of a yearlong movement to reform municipal government. On the next day Rev. Martin Luther King Jr. and Rev. Fred L. Shuttlesworth led a six-week campaign to desegregate the city. These two events challenged the power of white supremacists to maintain segregation. Connor, who refused to leave office, reacted by ordering city workers to use dogs and fire hoses against protesting African Americans. In response to a settlement between King, Shuttlesworth, and white business elite announced on 12 May, KKK members bombed the home of Rev. A. D. King and the black-owned A. G. Gaston Motel, prompting outraged African Americans to protest through mass rioting in downtown. Lawyer David J. Vann, who coordinated the reform movement, remarked Birmingham was in a "civil war."

Throughout the summer, white segregationists attempted to enforce segregation, from boycotting downtown department stores to bombing the homes of prominent black leaders. Their activities reached a fever pitch after a federal court approved the city's

In Washington, D.C., the Congress of Racial Equality conducts a march in memory of the four young girls killed in the Birmingham bombing of 16th Street Baptist Church. (Thomas J. O'Halloran, photographer, Library of Congress [LC-U9-10515-6A], Washington, D.C.)

school desegregation plan, in which five black children would attend three all-white schools. In early September members of the KKK and the NSRP provoked enough violence to prompt municipal officials to close all public schools. Sensing political gain, Alabama governor George C. Wallace sent state troopers to protect the rights of white protestors. It was against this backdrop of state-sanctioned violence to uphold white supremacy that four KKK members bombed the church.

Since that Sunday morning, the bombing has been remembered as an isolated yet nationally significant event. The death of four young women gave the movement new martyrs and a national sense of urgency, but by the late 1960s national opposition to civil rights strengthened in the face of the move-

ment's shifting dynamics, urban riots, and white flight. Wallace would capitalize on this "backlash" conservatism in his 1968 and 1972 presidential bids, but he also sought forgiveness for his defense of white supremacy in his later gubernatorial career. By the late 1970s his plea for racial reconciliation converged with the rise of black politicians, forcing a reckoning of unresolved civil rights issues. The Birmingham church bombing was one of them. From 1977 to 2002 Alabama state prosecutors won convictions against Chambliss (1977), Blanton (2001), and Cherry (2002). In each trial, prosecutors effectively silenced a discussion of the political culture that sanctioned white supremacist violence. In doing so, they placed the onus of the South's racism, symbolized by the death of four young women, on the surviving bombers rather than its people or leaders such as Wallace. Instead of achieving full justice, the trials revised the southern past, leaving it without a historical context of racial violence, to conform to a "racially innocent" present.

CATHERINE A. CONNER
University of North Carolina at Chapel Hill

Spike Lee, director, *4 Little Girls* (film, 1997); S. Willoughby Anderson, *California Law Review* (April 2008); Diane McWhorter, *Carry Me Home: Birmingham, Alabama; The Climatic Battle of the Civil Rights Revolution* (2001); Renee C. Romano, in *The Civil Rights Movement in American Memory*, ed. Renee C. Romano and Leigh Raiford (2006).

The Birth of a Nation

The Birth of a Nation (1915) is perhaps the most controversial film in the history of American cinema. A pioneering tour de force by the first great U.S. director, David Wark Griffith (1875–1948), the film both overwhelmed viewers with its visual and narrative power and inspired heated protests because of its content.

The story upon which the film is based originated in the fevered imagination of Thomas Dixon (1864–1946), a racist ideologue and author from North Carolina. In a trilogy of novels — most notoriously *The Leopard's Spots* (1902) and *The Clansman* (1905) — and in his incendiary stage production *The Clansman* (1905), Dixon used the post–Civil War South as the historical stage on which to draw out his obsessive themes of miscegenation, imperiled feminine virtue, and Aryan honor.

A scenario based upon the play came to D. W. Griffith's attention in 1914. The story and themes resonated powerfully with Griffith, a native Kentuckian and the son of a Confederate officer. A middling stage actor who turned to motion pictures in 1908, Griffith by 1914 was an experienced director committed to the artistic possibilities of film. Production of what was originally known as *The Clansman* began in California on 4 July 1914, and the picture premiered in Los Angeles on 8 February 1915.

The Birth of a Nation, as the film was ultimately titled, traces the relationship of two families — the Camerons of South Carolina and the Stonemans (whose patriarch, Austin Stoneman, is modeled on Radical Republican representative Thaddeus Stevens) of Pennsylvania. The families establish a close friendship during the antebellum years. Then the Civil War shatters the idyllic plantation existence of the Camerons and pits the sons of the two families against one another in battle.

The film's second half portrays Reconstruction as a vicious assault upon southern womanhood and white civilization. In one of the film's most infamous scenes, the Cameron family's youngest daughter, the innocent Flora, leaps to her death off a cliff rather than submit to the seductions of Gus, a freed slave, who, emboldened by the liberties Reconstruction bestowed upon him, had chased her through the woods. The film's hero, Ben Cameron, forms the Ku Klux Klan to avenge his sister's death and his family's honor. Cameron and his men, in full Klan regalia, lynch Gus in an elaborate ritual. Later, they rescue

Reconstruction violence against blacks portrayed in the film The Birth of a Nation, 1915
(Film Stills Archives, Museum of Modern Art, New York, N.Y.)

Ben's lover, Elsie Stoneman, when her father's "mulatto" protégé, Silas Lynch, attempts to force himself upon her. In the famed climax of the film, the riders of the KKK rush to the rescue of a small band of whites who are about to fall victim to riotous black troops. In this regard, *The Birth of a Nation* not only offered a grossly white supremacist interpretation of Reconstruction but, in the context of 1915, also dramatized white supremacist rhetoric that defended lynching as a necessary and righteous response to black aggression.

Nothing like *The Birth of a Nation* had been seen before—Griffith had revolutionized filmmaking. At more than two-and-one-half hours in length, costing more than $100,000 to produce, accompanied by an orchestra in larger venues, and timed perfectly to commemorate the fiftieth anniversary of the war's end, the film was a revelation to the moviegoers of the day. Audiences all over the country found themselves carried away by its almost irresistible power. As one awestruck Atlanta reviewer exulted, "It makes you laugh and moves you to hot tears unashamed. It makes you love and hate. It makes you forget decorum and forces a cry into your throat." Proving enormously popular in spite of its unprecedented two-dollar ticket price, the film played for a full 48 weeks at the Liberty Theater in New York City and earned some $60 million nationwide in its first run. Thomas Dixon even persuaded his old friend Woodrow Wilson to make *Birth* the first movie screened at the White House, where, after his viewing, the president reportedly stated, "It is like writing history with lightning. And my only regret is that it is all so terribly true."

Anticipating the film's premiere in Atlanta, William Simmons reestablished the Ku Klux Klan as a nativist, Protestant organization in a ceremony atop Stone Mountain, just outside the city. The night before the premiere, Klan members paraded through the streets of Atlanta, firing their rifles in front of the theater where the film would play. Through the 1920s, the Klan used *Birth* as a recruitment tool, appearing at screenings around the country in full regalia to distribute organizational material. Simmons credited the film for giving "the new order a tremendous popular boost."

Praise for *The Birth of a Nation*, however, was far from universal. The movie appeared at a dismal period in the history of American race relations, and though less vicious than the novels and play on which it is based, it is nonetheless filled with odious racial stereotypes, most ominously that of the lustful black male intent upon molesting white women. In response, the fledgling National Association for the Advancement of Colored People (NAACP) protested the film in city after city, calling for either an outright ban or the removal of offensive scenes. Despite making little headway against the movie itself, the protests proved a landmark in the development of African American protest in general and of the NAACP in particular.

To the end of his life, Griffith refused to concede that there was any justification for such criticism of his masterpiece. So while *The Birth of a Nation* is undoubtedly a historic milestone that stunningly transformed motion pictures, it remains a work deeply and sadly tainted by the social pathologies of its day.

STEVE GOODSON
University of West Georgia

Thomas Cripps, *Slow Fade to Black: The Negro in American Film, 1900–1942* (1977); Steve Goodson, *Highbrows, Hillbillies, and Hellfire: Public Entertainment in Atlanta, 1880–1930* (2002); Richard Schickel, *D. W. Griffith: An American Life* (1984); Amy Louise Wood, *Lynching and Spectacle: Witnessing Racial Violence, in America, 1890–1940* (2009)

Black Militias

Black militias and paramilitary organizations in Reconstruction trace their roots to the black military experience during the Civil War and, before that, to kin-based networks of resistance during slavery. Taking many forms across the post–Civil War South, black militias served as a vital tool of community solidarity in the face of the Ku Klux Klan and other forms of white paramilitary violence. They were often—but not always—defensive in nature. In some situations, however, black militias served to extend and consolidate black political power and cultural hegemony rather than simply respond to white violence.

The first black militias emerged in Louisiana during the Civil War itself, as free black elites formed paramilitary companies in support of the developing radical constitution in 1864 and especially after the New Orleans Riot of 1866. Black militias would appear in other southern cities in the immediate postwar years as well, including in Mobile, Savannah, Charleston, Richmond, and Memphis—many of them geared toward neighborhood self-defense against the likes of the 1866 Memphis rioters. But it was not until March 1867 that black militias expanded into the rural African American heartland on a sizable scale.

The most famous black militias in Reconstruction organized themselves through the auspices of the Union League. Though white Republicans organized many of these leagues, African Americans formed the backbone of the leagues throughout much of the South. And in many cases blacks took leadership positions in local and statewide Union Leagues. Importantly, many black militias, including the Union Leagues, combined paramilitary activity with more peaceable means of community-building and political consolidation. Union Leagues played a central role in the construction of local Republican Party organizations, formation of independent African American churches, construction of schools, and development of benevolent organizations for former slaves.

The Union League as a national organization was created in the North during the early years of the Civil War. Its first expansion into the postwar South was restricted to white Unionist areas in the hill country of east Tennessee, north Georgia, north Alabama, and western North Carolina. But, as the Congressional Reconstruction Act took effect in March 1867, the league served as the vanguard of political mobilization among ex-slaves throughout the South. And while it employed many of the rituals and vows of secrecy present in the Northern Union League, the black Southern Union League expended a greater portion of its energy on the armed defense of the right of ex-slaves to vote, hold office, and exercise basic civil rights.

Union Leagues were hardly the only form of black militia to emerge in the Reconstruction South. Local black elected officials, including especially sheriffs and justices of the peace, organized state-backed black paramilitary organizations in South Carolina, Louisiana, Mississippi, and Texas. These took on various names including State Guards, Loyal Leagues, and the Heroes of America. As former defenders of the federal government in the Union army, they typically adopted monikers stressing loyalty to the formal and triumphant post–Civil War Union.

Not all black militias were formally organized. In the border states of Kentucky and Missouri incipient black militia organizations armed either in defense of the right to vote or to protect black prisoners facing potential lynching at the hands of white Regulators. In Delaware and Maryland black neighborhood groups marched to the polls with arms to prevent attacks from various Democratic paramilitary organizations. These would manifest themselves even in cities with relatively small black populations.

Black militant organizations were not restricted to men. Many black women publicly encouraged men to bind themselves together, threatening humiliating violence against men unwilling to protect black homes and rights. This was true in urban as well as rural centers and lent a sort of gendered politics of militancy that reflected the uniformly working-class position black women found themselves in during and after slavery.

Black militias typically disappeared as a formal entity with the demise of Radical Reconstruction. They were dismantled by force, economic threats, or dispersal. But the militancy inherent in the militias merely transferred to new forms of activism, including the encouragement of emigration, the armed struggle for sharecroppers' rights, and less organized modes of armed resistance to the wave of lynchings and riots in the 1890s. Early 20th-century black militant organizations, including the Garveyite United Negro Improvement Association and the various Communist Party factions in the Deep South, drew upon the experience and organization of the Reconstruction and post-Reconstruction black militias.

AARON ASTOR
Maryville College

Elsa Barkley Brown, *Public Culture* (Fall 1994); W. E. B. DuBois, *Black Reconstruction in America* (1935); Michael Fitzgerald, *The Union League Movement in the Deep South* (2000); Eric Foner, *Reconstruction: America's Unfinished Revolution* (1988); Steven Hahn, *A Nation under Our Feet: Black Political Struggles in the Rural South from Slavery to the Great Migration* (2003).

"Bonnie and Clyde"

(BONNIE PARKER, 1910–1934, AND CLYDE BARROW, 1909–1934) OUTLAWS.

On the morning of 23 May 1934 six law officers fired more than 160 shots at a car driving down a road near Arcadia, La. Fifty shots hit the car's passenger and driver—Bonnie Parker and Clyde Barrow, better known as "Bonnie and Clyde." The fatal ambush was the culmination of months in pursuit of the notorious outlaws, who had killed at least 12 people since April 1932.

Bonnie Parker was high-spirited and intelligent. Her family moved from Rowena, Tex., to Dallas when her father died in 1914. There, she met Clyde Barrow, the quick-tempered, uneducated son of desperately poor parents. By the time they met, Barrow had already been involved in petty crimes. Bonnie's criminal association with him began when she smuggled a gun into a Texas prison where he was being held, thus allowing him to escape.

Often with various other gang members, Bonnie and Clyde drove for miles along the back roads of Texas, Oklahoma, Missouri, Arkansas, and Louisiana. They lived mostly in stolen cars, and they survived on the spoils of their victims. Panic and criminal incompetence characterized Barrow's escapades and often resulted in purposeless killings.

When news spread that Texas Ranger Frank Hamer and his men had killed Bonnie and Clyde, crowds gathered at the scene, tearing off parts of the car, hacking away locks

Bonnie Parker and Clyde Barrow, better known as simply "Bonnie and Clyde," were considered outlaws by some but considered outlaw-heroes by others. (Texas/Dallas History & Archives Division)

of Bonnie's hair, taking whatever they could that had belonged to the infamous pair. One determined souvenir seeker even tried to amputate Clyde's trigger finger. The desire to possess anything with which Bonnie and Clyde had been associated was compulsive, and it has continued. The death car itself sold at auction in 1973 for $175,000.

For two years, Barrow's gang terrorized residents in and around Texas and, in doing so, sparked the phenomenal growth of a legend. The image of a tiny, cigar-smoking woman and a daring gangster together, living dangerously and outrunning poorly organized pursuers, evoked great excitement. Bonnie's devotion to Clyde and Clyde's successful rise from the anonymity of dire poverty further incited the romanticization of their exploits; and books and movies, such as *Bonnie and Clyde* (1967), have sustained their memory. Many of their contemporaries cheered the outlaws' deaths, but, in a decade when Americans needed heroes, countless others sympathized with and celebrated the careers of Bonnie and Clyde.

JESSICA FOY
Cooperstown Graduate Programs
Cooperstown, New York

Blanche Caldwell Barrow, John Neal Phillips, and Esther L. Weiser, *My Life with Bonnie and Clyde* (2004); Jeff Guinn, *Go Down Together: The True, Untold Story of Bonnie and Clyde* (2010); James R. Knight and Jonathan Davis, *Bonnie and Clyde: A Twenty-first Century Update* (2003); Paul Schneider, *Bonnie and Clyde: The Lives behind the Legend* (2009); John Treherne, *The Strange History of Bonnie and Clyde* (1985).

Bowie Knife

The romance of the Bowie knife is one of the great American legends. James "Jim" Bowie (1796–1836) was born in Kentucky but grew up in the wilds of Louisiana with his brother Rezin as part of a large extended Bowie family of American pioneer planters. A natural adventurer and land speculator, he came to national attention as a result of a deadly brawl following a duel on a Mississippi River sandbar above Natchez in September 1827, where in self-defense he killed a man with a large single-edge hunting knife that had been made and given to him by his brother Rezin. Even though he nearly died from his wounds, newspaper reports made Bowie famous as a courageous knife fighter, and thereafter stories about him and his knife began to work into American folklore.

By 1835 the public demand for "Bowie knives" was such that eastern industry cutlers had begun selling massive fighting knives under that name. When Bowie then died leading the volunteer forces at the Alamo in 1836, he was instantly immortalized as an iconic American hero. The demand skyrocketed for "Bowie knives," a concept that quickly evolved into a deadly and intimidating weapon with a very heavy straight single-edge blade having a cross guard and a concave clipped point with false edge. American industry could not keep up, and the cutlery industry of Sheffield, England, became leading manufacturers and exporters of Bowies for much of the remainder of the 19th century.

The knife became popular early on as a southern weapon and was carried in large numbers into the western frontier. Although knife fights of the time were common, stories of its use in formal duels became greatly exaggerated in popular lore. However, in 1860 U.S. congressman John F. Potter from Wisconsin actually did accept a duel challenge from Roger Pryer, representative from Virginia, with the stipulation that it be fought with Bowie knives. The duel was never fought, but the nickname "Bowie Knife" Potter stuck. During the Civil War soldiers on both sides carried these knives, and many were sold with patriotic slogans etched on their blades, such as "Death to Traitors," or "Death to Abolition." Most versions today are smaller and lighter than those of the 1800s.

NATHAN E. BENDER
University of Idaho Library

William C. Davis, *Three Roads to the Alamo: The Lives and Fortunes of David Crockett, James Bowie, and William Barret Travis* (1998); Norm Flayderman, *The Bowie Knife: Unsheathing an American Legend* (2004); Harold L. Peterson, *American Knives: The First History and Collector's Guide* (1958); Geoffrey Tweedale, *The Sheffield Knife Book: A History and Collectors' Guide* (1996).

Byrd, James, Murder of

On 7 June 1998 a modern-day lynching tragedy in the small East Texas town of Jasper shocked the world and sparked a controversial push for stronger hate-crime legislation in the next decade. In the wee hours of the June morning, James Byrd Jr., a 49-year-old African American man, accepted a ride from three young, inebriated white men. Byrd, who had also been drinking, was walking home after a friend's wedding anniversary celebration. After the white men drove their pickup truck onto a dirt logging road, they stopped, pulled Byrd from the back of the truck, and kicked him and beat him with a baseball bat. Then they chained Byrd by his ankles to the truck and dragged him for almost three miles before dumping the remains of his torso near a black cemetery. About a mile before the cemetery, Byrd was decapitated by a culvert pipe, which also severed his right arm from his body. Byrd's blood and remains were later found scattered along the three-mile stretch of road.

The next day, authorities arrested John William King, 23, and Shawn Berry, 23, both of Jasper, and Lawrence Brewer, 31, of Sulphur Springs, for Byrd's murder. Items found at the crime scene belonged to King and Berry. Berry was the first man arrested, and he claimed involvement only as a bystander, giving an affidavit that led to the arrests of King and Brewer. The trial proceedings revealed that King and Brewer had been interested in starting a white supremacist group and that the incident may have been a hoped-for publicity garner for the group. King, the first of the three to be tried, was convicted in February 1999 and given the death penalty—the first time since 1854 that a white man in Texas received such a sentence for killing a black man. Brewer was also given the death penalty, but Berry received a life sentence.

The following decade saw growing state and national calls for stronger hate crime legislation, much of which would bear Byrd's name. In March 1999, as a result of the Byrd family's activism, the Texas legislature proposed tougher sentencing for perpetrators of hate crimes. George W. Bush, governor of Texas at the time, refused to support the bill, citing that all three men involved in the horrific Jasper case were convicted of capital murder, the highest felony level in Texas, so no sentencing would be any more severe than what the three men had been given. After Bush's election to the presidency, though, new Texas governor Rick Perry signed the James Byrd Hate Crimes Act into state law. In 2007 the U.S. Congress proposed a similar bill, the Matthew Shepard and James Byrd Jr. Act. Matthew Shepard was a homosexual University of Wyoming student who was also brutally murdered in 1998. Though President Bush and several conservative groups opposed the bill because they thought it came too close to "thought crime" legislation, the bill was signed in October 2009 by Democratic president Barack Obama and officially named the Matthew Shepard and James Byrd Jr. Hate Crimes Prevention Act. The addition to the original 1968 Hate Crimes Act contained the controversial extension for investigation and prosecution of violence motivated by bias against a victim's "actual or perceived race, color, religion, or sexual orientation."

The murder of James Byrd was an unsettling event, especially at a time when many thought the era of lynchings had long been over. While the incident's most tangible national result was the passing of hate crime legislation, international news, a globally reaching documentary film, *Two Towns of Jasper*, aired in 2002 on BBC and the Discovery Channel and increased international awareness about the dangers of prejudice between any different groups of people. The community of Jasper, confronted with its own attitudes about race, began to effect small changes that moved toward hope for more harmonious race relations. The Byrd family established the James Byrd Jr. Foundation for Racial Healing, which continues to grant scholarships to minority students, host diversity workshops, and conduct oral-history projects to promote racial understanding. In 1999 the town of Jasper built the James Byrd Jr. Memorial Park and removed a fence that had separated black and white graves in the town cemetery since 1836.

MARY AMELIA TAYLOR
University of Mississippi

Joyce King, *Hate Crime: The Story of a Dragging in Jasper, Texas* (2002); Dina Temple Raston, *A Death in Texas: A Story of Race, Murder, and a Small Town's Struggle for Redemption* (2002).

Chain Gang

The profit motive and a desire to eliminate tax burdens dominated post–Civil War southern discussions of criminal punishment. The region was impoverished by the war and yet had now to deal judicially with free blacks as well as white offenders. Convict lease to private contractors and corporations became a standard alternative to government maintenance throughout the southern states. Because convict labor was most profitable when used for large-scale work projects such as levee repair, railroad building, and road construction,

Convicts working on a road, Oglethorpe County, Ga., 1941 (Photographer unknown, Library of Congress [LC-USF-344-7541-2B], Washington, D.C.)

the chain gang was closely associated with the lease system. By 1886 it was the chief form of convict labor in eight southern states, and it persisted in these states long after its abolition in the North and West.

Unlike antebellum chattels, chain gang crews cost lessees little if anything—an 1867 Georgia railroad lease stipulated a $25 annual fee per inmate—and convicts were infinitely expendable because those who died were quickly replaced. Men, women, and often children sentenced for crimes ranging from the theft of a keg of nails and vagrancy to premeditated murder worked on gangs under armed guard, joined together by a long squad chain attached to ankle irons. Escape was further impeded by stride or hobble chains that allowed a span of about eight inches between leg irons. Throughout its history, a dispro-portionate number of those sentenced to this form of labor were black, for example, 846 out of 952 in an 1878 survey, and 2,113 out of 2,221 in Georgia in 1902.

Whether moving the sand and earth required to shore up levees in the Delta mud or "chipping" turpentine in Florida swamps, crews of convicts worked from 10 to 14 hours per day. They were transported to work camps in mule-drawn boxcars or windowless cages with tiers of plank beds on either side. Once at a campsite, these portable cages served as permanent housing when tents or rough-hewn cell houses were not set up. Food, typically fatback, corn bread, and cowpeas, was rationed, often spoiled, and, in summer, swarmed with flies. Sanitation in the work camps was not even rudimentary. Convicts lacked washbasins, towels, and soap; they slept, secured by a logging chain, in their work clothes, on bare vermin-infested mattresses. No attempt was made to isolate tubercular or syphilitic prisoners.

Medical care was unknown, and entire gangs fell prey to diseases such as meningitis. Shackle poison (an infection caused by the constant friction of ankle irons), malnutrition, overwork, beatings, or self-inflicted mutilations, such as hamstringing, claimed others. Those who tried to escape or who failed to work hard or fast enough were often punished by confinement to a coffin-like sweatbox, flogging, or the riveting of 20- to 50-pound iron weights to leg shackles. At the height of the lease system, the death rate was so appalling (45 percent of the prisoners working the Greenwood-to-Augusta railroad died annually in the period 1877–79) that leading critics such as the editor of the *New Orleans Daily Picayune* argued that imposing the death sentence on any convict with a term in excess of six years was more humane and expedient.

The hostility of free labor, especially when convict crews were brought in as strikebreakers, led to the abolition of the private lease system in most southern states by the turn of the century. The chain gang, however, did not disappear. Used by state or county officials primarily as road crews, gangs actually became more important, and more visible, with the advent of the automobile. Reformist activity increased in the 1920s, and exposés of abuses culminated in the 1932 Warner Bros. release of Robert Burns's *I Am a Fugitive from a Chain Gang*—"A gruesome experience," according to *Variety*, "and dynamite for the state of Georgia." Sub-

sequently the use of chain gangs was greatly reduced, although even in the early 1960s small details were still in evidence. Georgia was the last southern state to completely abolish the practice.

Although images of the chain gang in literature (Richard Wright's *Black Boy*) and film (Stuart Rosenberg's film *Cool Hand Luke*) are vivid reminders of the institution, its most enduring legacy is musical. Tunes range from the mournful "holler," a "strange wailing chant" unintelligible to white "walking bosses," to blues lyrics directly inspired by the experience of gang work—such as "Chain Gang Blues" by Ma Rainey and Kokomo Arnold, "Levee Camp Blues" by Robert Pete Williams, and George "Bullet" Williams's "Escaped Convict Blues," with its evocation of tracking hounds. Particularly important is the work song. Supplying a meter for manual labor that required coordination of axes, hoes, and hammers, work songs also provided a partial outlet for frustration and anger. Along with the harsh nonmechanized work that sustained them, the songs have now largely disappeared.

ELIZABETH M. MAKOWSKI
University of Mississippi

Edward L. Ayers, *Vengeance and Justice: Crime and Punishment in the Nineteenth-Century American South* (1984); Mark Colvin, *Penitentiaries, Reformatories, and Chain Gangs: Social Theory and the History of Punishment in Nineteenth-Century America* (2000); Bruce Jackson, *Wake Up Dead Man: Afro-American Worksongs from Texas Prisons* (1972); Daniel A. Novak, *The Wheel of Servitude: Black Forced Labor after Slavery* (1978); Paul Oliver, *Blues Fell This*

Morning (1960); J. C. Powell, *The American Siberia* (1891); Carl Sifakis, ed., *Encyclopedia of American Crime* (1982); Jesse F. Steiner and Roy M. Brown, *The North Carolina Chain Gang* (1927); Walter Wilson, *Forced Labor in the United States* (1933).

Convict Leasing

Convict leasing provided southern employers with cheap, manageable, and readily available workers for two generations before the last remnants of the system disappeared in the 1930s. Although the practice of hiring out or leasing convicts originated in the pre–Civil War penal systems of Alabama, Kentucky, and Louisiana, the system was not adopted by all southern states until the 1870s.

Before emancipation, most southern black offenders were slaves and were punished by their masters as permitted or required by the state slave codes. Thus, penal facilities in the prewar South were largely for "whites only." Some of these offenders were turned over to private contractors, typically textile manufacturers. But, as free persons after 1865, black offenders constituted a sudden and sizable addition to southern prison populations, which the economically depressed states found difficult to handle. The solution was convict leasing on a vast, biracial scale.

The zenith of the brutal and exploitative system lasted from about 1880 to 1910. During those years convict leasing was in reality a legal postwar form of slavery for white and black prisoners alike, although blacks far outnumbered whites (especially in the Deep South) and received much harsher treatment.

Depending on where they had been convicted, postwar southern convicts were leased to cotton, rice, sugarcane, and tobacco planters; levee builders; coalmines; timber companies; and railroad construction firms. Prisoners of both races and sexes, sometimes no more than eight or nine years of age, suffered from overwork, physical abuse, meager diets, and little or no medical care. Death and injury rates were appalling. As the most despised element in the population, convicts had few spokesmen or defenders. Several states had established "penitentiary rings" supported by politicians who favored leasing because the practice relieved their states of responsibility for maintaining convicts and because the system brought "easy" revenues to public treasuries at no sacrifice to voting taxpayers. Beginning in the 1890s, however, coalitions of political opponents, labor interests, and humanitarian reformers were able to abolish leasing gradually state by state.

Convict leasing should not be considered identical to state or county "chain gangs," which continued to exist in the post–World War II South. "Chain gang" prisoners were also badly treated, but they were under the custody of public authorities rather than the more insensitive, inhumane, and publicly unsupervised private contractors of the lease system.

MARK T. CARLETON
Louisiana State University

Mark T. Carleton, *Politics and Punishment: The History of the Louisiana State Penal System* (1971); Dan T. Carter, "Convict Lease" (M.A. thesis, University of Wisconsin, 1964); Hilda Jane Zimmerman, "Penal Systems and Penal Reform in the South since the Civil War" (Ph.D. dissertation, University of North Carolina at Chapel Hill, 1947).

Copeland, James

(1823–1857) OUTLAW.

The name of no other outlaw in southern Mississippi and Alabama is more shrouded in mystique and controversy than that of James Copeland, who was hanged 30 October 1857 on the banks of the Leaf River near Augusta in Perry County, Miss. Indeed, Copeland was a household word from Mobile Bay to Lake Pontchartrain not only because his clan had terrorized folks in that region during the flush times of the 1830s and 1840s, but also because he dictated his memoirs to a highly literate young sheriff, J. R. S. Pitts. Published first in 1858 with later editions in 1874 and 1909, *The Confession of James Copeland* created a furor that still persists amid the piney woods and coastal counties.

Tales about Copeland, born in Jackson County on the Mississippi Gulf Coast, are still spun. His brutal life of larceny, arson, and murder captivated the imagination of generations who either admired him as a latter-day Robin Hood or scorned him as a contemptible desperado. His errant ways began as a lad of 12 with the theft of a pocket knife, followed shortly thereafter by grand larceny, and the burning of the local courthouse, assisted by an older accomplice, Gale H. Wages, whose clan he soon joined—a clan eventually bearing the name Copeland.

Though the clan operated mainly in south Mississippi and Alabama, Copeland's criminal path took him as far east as the Chattahoochee River, as far west as the Rio Grande, and as far north as the Wabash. In his confession he related crimes committed in the company of his mentor Wages and one Charles McGrath, a quintessential fraudulent frontier preacher. Copeland, who credits himself with only two murders, stole anything readily converted to cash, but he specialized in the theft of horses and slaves. Before the trio split up to avoid capture, Wages supposedly buried their savings of $30,000 in gold in the Catahoula Swamp in southwestern Mississippi. The gold coins are still sought by treasure hunters.

Hoping to escape the grasp of Mississippi officials who had indicted him for murder, Copeland surrendered to Alabama authorities to serve a term for larceny. However, deputies of Sheriff Pitts awaited his release, and after four more years in custody, James Copeland—in the words of Pitts—"expiated his blood stained career on the scaffold" before a massive October crowd in 1857.

JOHN D. W. GUICE
University of Southern Mississippi

J. R. S. Pitts, *Life and Confession of the Noted Outlaw James Copeland* (1980).

Cortez, Gregorio

(1875–1916) FOLK HERO.

Gregorio Cortez was a legendary figure from the Texas-Mexico border. In 1901 Cortez became a fugitive from the law after he killed a sheriff who attempted to arrest him for allegedly having stolen a horse. Details pertaining to the actual shooting are clouded, but significant misunderstanding clearly occurred because of language problems.

For 10 days Cortez managed to elude hundreds of men who chased him throughout the rough country of the Rio Grande region. Finally he was captured and tried in court. He was acquitted of murdering the sheriff but was convicted of killing a member of the posse that sought to capture him. Cortez was pardoned in 1913 and died in 1916 under mysterious circumstances.

The importance of Gregorio Cortez lies in what his story reveals about Mexican American–Anglo-American relations along the United States–Mexican border in the early 1900s. This was a time of marked racial friction influenced by border tensions between Mexico and the United States. The dominant society saw Cortez as a killer and fugitive, but people of Mexican background viewed him as a folk hero who had defied oppressive Anglo lawmen.

Popularized by border balladeers at the time, Cortez's story became the subject of Américo Paredes's *With His Pistol in His Hand: A Border Ballad and Its Hero* (1958). In the early 1980s Jack Young directed the film *The Ballad of Gregorio Cortez*, which played before a national television audience and in theaters across the United States.

OSCAR J. MARTINEZ
University of Texas at El Paso

Deliverance

Deliverance (1972), based on James Dickey's first novel of the same name (1970), which was adapted into a screenplay by Dickey and director John Boorman, focuses upon four Atlanta businessmen who attempt to escape the constraints of suburbia by taking a weekend trip to mountainous north Georgia. Persuaded by athletic outdoorsman Lewis Medlock (played by Burt Reynolds) to immerse themselves in a rapidly vanishing wilderness, the men agree to canoe down a wild river that will soon be dammed—and tamed—to make way for a hydroelectric plant. Shot on location on the Chattooga River in Rabun County, Ga., the film was a critical and commercial success. It launched the career of Reynolds, and featured performances by Jon Voight as adman Ed Gentry, Ned Beatty as victimized salesman Bobby Trippe, and Ronny Cox as sensitive musician Drew Ballinger.

On the second day of the foursome's journey, two "hillbillies" emerge from the woods. Bobby is raped at gunpoint, and Ed escapes the same fate only when the macho Lewis kills the rapist. The second hillbilly flees, but the suburbanites soon come to fear that he is hunting them from a vantage point above the gorge. The men's canoes capsize after Drew is mysteriously thrown from the lead canoe—perhaps shot to death—and Lewis is seriously injured. The mild-mannered Ed must rise to the occasion and save his remaining companions. Like Marlow in Joseph Conrad's *Heart of Darkness*, Ed must confront the terrifying possibility that savagery lurks beneath the facade of civilization—and, further, decide upon a course of action in the face of this knowledge. When he scales an impossibly dangerous cliff and kills the remaining mountain man after a violent struggle, he sets about crafting a story to escape the dubious justice system of a county in which all jurors might be kin to the dead mountaineers.

Deliverance was nominated for three Academy Awards—for best picture, best director, and best film editing. North Georgians were far less impressed with the film. Already suspicious during Boorman's location shooting, many locals, according to one Dickey correspondent, traveled great distances to see the movie (because local theaters refused to show it) and were repelled by the villains' portrayal as overalls-wearing, toothless, inbred sodomites. The film's $2 million in production expenditures helped fuel the national trend toward on-location filming as state governments, including Georgia, increasingly offered incentives to filmmakers.

During the film's Atlanta premiere, then-governor Jimmy Carter told Dickey, "It's pretty rough. But it's good for Georgia . . . I hope." The "rough" dimensions of *Deliverance*, however, were inextricably connected to its "good" effects. The film's immediately iconic moments—the haunting image of local actor Billy Redden stonily playing his half of "Dueling Banjos" as a warning of the nightmare to follow, and a sodomizing hillbilly commanding a trembling insurance salesman to "squeal like a pig"—left indelible impressions of Georgia's "local color." Before 1970 the Chattooga River averaged about 100 visitors each year, but within four years of the film's release the number skyrocketed to 50,000, only to double by 2005. To be sure, however, a signifi-

cant portion of these visitors included drunken college-age males "squealing like a pig" through the whitewater. At least 24 deaths occurred on the Chattooga as a result of the popularity of rafting among such novices, a phenomenon that came to be called the "Deliverance Syndrome."

The film's influence continues to be felt in the 21st century, thanks in part to regular television broadcasts through at least 2007. In 2004 the *New York Times* listed *Deliverance* in "The Best 1,000 Movies Ever Made," and in 2005 *Maxim* magazine named the *Deliverance* hillbillies the all-time top movie villains. From ubiquitous imitations of the "Dueling Banjos" theme to "Paddle faster, I hear banjos" bumper stickers to allusions in popular films like *Pulp Fiction* (1994), *Deliverance* has powerfully shaped national perceptions of Appalachia, the South, and indeed all people and places perceived as "backwoods."

EMILY SATTERWHITE
Virginia Tech

Chris Dickey, *Summer of Deliverance: A Memoir of Father and Son* (1998); Henry Hart, *James Dickey: The World as a Lie* (2000); J. W. Williamson, *Hillbillyland: What the Movies Did to the Mountains and What the Mountains Did to the Movies* (1995); James Dickey Papers, Manuscript, Archives, and Rare Book Library, Emory University.

Donald, Michael, Lynching of

On 21 March 1981 Henry Francis Hays and James "Tiger" Knowles, two members of the Mobile chapter of the United Klans of America, kidnapped 19-year-old Michael Anthony Donald from a street in downtown Mobile. They took Donald to a wooded area where they beat and strangled him to death with a hangman's noose. The Klansmen hung Donald's body from a tree on a downtown Mobile street, near the home of Klan leader Bennie Jack Hays, Henry's father. The act was in response to the acquittal of Josephus Anderson, a black man accused of murdering a white police officer. The Donald lynching shocked the local community, and national and international media outlets covered Donald's funeral. Coming 26 years after the murder of Emmett Till and 16 years after the bloody confrontations in Selma, Ala., the Donald lynching focused attention on Mobile's racial climate as never before. The lynching came at the end of a 15-year period of violence in Mobile and occurred two months before arguments resumed in *Bolden v. City of Mobile*, a lawsuit alleging that Mobile's at-large election of commissioners was inherently discriminatory to minorities.

Local police were quick to characterize the lynching as a drug-related crime despite Donald's clean record. The NAACP and Michigan Congressman John Conyers called for an immediate federal investigation. A month after the murder, Jesse Jackson and Joseph Lowery led a march through Mobile in protest of the city's lack of action. The march ended on Herndon Avenue, the residential street where Donald's body was found.

Alabama state senator Michael Figures and his brother, Thomas, the U.S. attorney for Mobile, urged the FBI to open its own investigation into the Donald lynching. In June 1983, after a two-year investigation, Hays and Knowles were charged with Donald's murder. Knowles struck a plea bargain with prosecutors and testified against Hays. Knowles stated that Bennie Jack Hays, the leader of the local United Klans of American (UKA), instructed them to kill a black person in retaliation for Josephus Anderson's acquittal. The jury found Henry Hays guilty, and he was executed in June 1996. He was only the second white man in the state's history to be executed for the murder of an African American. Knowles was sentenced to 25 years in prison. Bennie Jack Hays died while awaiting trial for his role in the lynching.

Shortly after the criminal trial, Morris Dees, cofounder of the Southern Poverty Law Center in Montgomery, Ala., filed a civil suit against the UKA on behalf of the Donald family. Dees's strategy was to charge the UKA using a statute from corporate law that held corporations responsible for the actions of its members. The lawyers used Klan documents and tax records in their argument. Michael Figures, a state politician and Mobile civil rights leader, served as co-counsel. On 12 February 1987 the all-white jury awarded the Donald family an unprecedented $7 million in damages. The case, *Beulah Mae Donald v. United Klans of America*, was a landmark decision. The victory propelled the Southern Poverty Law Center to the forefront of civil rights litigation, which has since tried several similar cases using the same statute. The judgment bankrupted the United Klans of America and its long-time leader,

Robert Shelton. Beulah Mae Donald, Michael's mother, was hailed as "the woman who beat the Klan," and she traveled throughout the country with Morris Dees after the case. Using the money from the judgment, she bought her first home. She died of a stroke in Mobile in September 1988.

In 2006 the City of Mobile voted to rename Herndon Avenue in Michael Donald's honor. That same year, Ravi Howard published *Like Trees, Walking*, an award-winning fictional account of the murder and its effect on Mobile's African American community. In 2008 veteran journalist Ted Koppel placed the Donald Lynching at the center of his documentary *The Last Lynching*, analyzing the long-term effects of racial violence on America. In January 2009 the tree from which Donald's body was hung was added to Mobile's African American Heritage Trail.

SCOTTY E. KIRKLAND
University of South Alabama

Morris Dees and Steve Fiffer, *A Lawyer's Journey: The Morris Dees Story* (2001); Ravi Howard, *Like Trees, Walking* (2007); Scotty E. Kirkland, "Pink Sheets and Black Ballots: Politics and Civil Rights in Mobile, Alabama, 1945–1985" (M.A. thesis, University of South Alabama, 2009); Bill Stanton, *Klanwatch: Bringing the Ku Klux Klan to Justice* (1991).

Elaine (Arkansas) Massacre (1919)

The aftermath of World War I contributed to the atmosphere and circumstances surrounding the 1919 massacre of perhaps hundreds of African Americans in and around Elaine, Ark., in Phillips County. The Delta region of eastern Arkansas experienced rapid economic growth preceding and during the war, becoming an important center for hardwood and cotton. The region's white elite, heavily outnumbered by black workers, anticipated continued high profits by means of cheap and exploitable black labor, including sharecroppers and tenant farmers.

For their part, many blacks returned from war service to Phillips County with heightened economic expectations. Farm laborers, and a few black landowners, expected to continue to reap the benefits of high cotton prices. Black sharecroppers and tenants sought to sell their own crops on the market, or secure a fair price from their white landlords. This tension between planters, who wanted to roll back the wartime gains of black laborers and enhance their control over labor, and workers, who believed they were fighting for their just economic rewards, underlie the violence of the Elaine massacre.

The nationwide wave of strikes and labor-capital clashes also contributed to tension in eastern Arkansas. News of organizing by the radical Industrial Workers of the World (IWW), for example, was front-page news in Phillips County. So when many black laborers around Elaine joined the Progressive Farmers and Household Union of America (PFHUA), founded by Robert L. Hill, some white planters viewed their organizing efforts as preparation for a significant challenge, possibly violent, to their economic and social hegemony. In fact, the PFHUA was preparing to sue some members' landlords in the fall of 1919 for their share of that year's crop.

In early October, gunshots were exchanged at a PFHUA meeting at a church in Hoop Spur, Phillips County. It is not clear who fired the first shot, but black union guards killed one white gunman. What followed was a swift escalation of violence perpetrated by white posses numbered at 600 to 1,000 individuals and consisting of land-owners, war veterans, law enforce-ment personnel, and even strangers to Phillips County. Arkansas governor Charles Hillman Brough personally es-corted 583 federal troops to the area. These troops were directed to shoot on sight any blacks who refused to sur-render. There were charges of torture and barbarism over several days of vio-lence. The highest estimate of African American men, women, and children killed stands at 856.

By the end of October, 122 African American men and women had been indicted, the charges ranging from murder to night riding. A Committee of Seven composed of local law enforce-ment officials and landowners released their version of the events. The com-mittee suggested Robert L. Hill had misled the PFHUA members and staged an insurrection intending a general massacre of whites. The NAACP and Ida Wells-Barnett investigated the violence and emphasized the inequalities in the sharecropping system, the violent re-sponse by landowners to black union-ization, and the torture of several black detainees. The "Elaine Twelve," a dozen blacks who received the death sentence for their alleged role in killing several whites, were eventually released after Arkansas courts and the U.S. Supreme Court, in the landmark case of *Moore v. Dempsey*, found the rushed proceedings against them unsustainable.

University of Arkansas

Kieran Taylor and Jeannie M. Whayne, *Arkansas Historical Quarterly* (Autumn 1999); Grif Stockley, *Blood in Their Eyes: The Elaine Race Massacres of 1919* (2001); Nan Elizabeth Woodruff, *American Congo: The African American Freedom Struggle in the Delta* (2003).

Evers, Medgar, Assassination of

Political assassinations and extreme violence have been an unfortunate but all-to-real part of America's historical landscape. During the 1950s and 1960s white Mississippians had a well-earned reputation for using unbridled violence and murder to uphold white supremacy. In May and August of 1955 alone, whites murdered Rev. George Lee and Lamar Smith for advocating voting rights and 14-year-old Emmett Louis Till for failing to truly understand Mississippi's racial rules of order. In all three murders, those involved escaped punishment. Born on 2 July 1925 in Decatur, Medgar Evers rose to civil rights prominence within this sociopolitical milieu of vio-lent repression.

In December 1954 Evers joined the National Association for the Advance-ment of Colored People (NAACP) as its first full-time Mississippi field secretary; he and his wife, Myrlie, moved from Mound Bayou to Jackson the following year. As field secretary, Evers led and organized voter registration drives and economic boycotts and assisted individuals fighting against discrimination. His activities commanded attention from covert organizations such as the White Citizens' Council and the Mississippi State Sovereignty Commission. Both groups relied on intimidation and violence to stifle black activism. Racial tensions in Jackson, however, heightened during the early 1960s as African Americans intensified attacks against segregation. The dangers associated with civil rights activism, for Evers, rose considerably after 20 May 1963.

On 20 May, Evers delivered a televised response to an earlier speech Jackson mayor Allen Thompson made, which, in part, disparaged the NAACP and touted race relations in the city. During the 17-minute address, Evers declared that "racial segregation" benefited neither blacks, whites, nor the state, and thus all should work for its destruction. More whites, he argued, would have to join the civil rights struggle if meaningful social progress were to happen. Despite death threats made in response to the speech, Evers continued organizing in Mississippi, with conservative groups and local police officers providing their own brand of daily harassment. On 11 June, President John F. Kennedy delivered a televised civil rights address. Evers watched the speech, attended a meeting afterward, and finally headed home to his wife and three children.

At a little past midnight 12 June 1963, Evers pulled his car into the family's driveway. Moments after he exited the vehicle, a bullet from a high-powered rifle fatally struck the 37-year-old in the back. He died at the University Hospital moments later. The city of Jackson mourned his death where some 6,000 individuals, including Martin Luther King Jr., attended the funeral. President Kennedy also expressed his condolences by sending a letter of sentiment to Myrlie Evers acknowledging that the ideals her husband promoted "will enable his children and the generations to follow to share fully and equally in the benefits and advantages our nation has to offer." On 19 June, Evers was buried at Arlington National Cemetery with full military honors. His murder would inspire those across the country to continue fighting for social and political justice but his murderer would escape punishment for decades.

In 1964 white supremacist Byron De La Beckwith twice escaped conviction for Evers's murder. Beginning in 1989, however, a series of articles by reporter Jerry Mitchell placed Beckwith back in the public spotlight. After a third trial, on 5 February 1994 the state pronounced Beckwith guilty of murder and sentenced him to life imprisonment; he died in 2001. Beckwith remained adamant about and unapologetic for his beliefs and actions regarding racial issues. Upon his demise, he took to the grave an unyielding commitment to white supremacy. The dedication to equality and fair play that Evers exhibited, however, continued to inspire positive social change. Although a profound tragedy, Evers's death helped strengthen the civil rights struggle in Mississippi by bridging social gaps between individual groups. His death also impacted civil rights legislation at the federal level.

When the Evers family visited the White House, President Kennedy signed a draft copy of his civil rights bill and assured Myrlie Evers that her husband's death would "make this possible." Although neither Evers nor Kennedy witnessed the final outcome, the 1964 Civil Rights Act resulted from the violent deaths of both men and the progressive ideals their lives represented.

MICHAEL VINSON WILLIAMS
Mississippi State University

Myrlie Evers and William Peters, *For Us, the Living* (1967); Charles Evers and Andrew Szanton, *Have No Fear: The Charles Evers Story* (1997); Bobby Delaughter, *Never Too Late: A Prosecutor's Story of Justice in the Medgar Evers Case* (2001); Myrlie Evers-Williams and Manning Marable, *The Autobiography of Medgar Evers: A Hero's Life and Legacy Revealed through His Writings, Letters, and Speeches* (2005).

Filibusters

"Filibusters," in the 19th-century meaning of the word, were individuals who led, enlisted in, or helped outfit private military expeditions designed to invade foreign lands. The term came into vogue during the years between the Mexican and Civil wars, when thousands of Americans defied proscriptive clauses in the American Neutrality Act of April 1818 and participated in expeditions to such regions as the Mexican Yucatan, Spanish Cuba, Central America, and Ecuador. This form of filibustering has continued to the present. In 1981 a group of American adventurers drew considerable public notice when they were charged by the FBI with plotting an armed invasion of

the island of Dominica, for the purpose of overthrowing its government. Two more times within five years after that, federal agents foiled plots conceived in Louisiana and Mississippi to overthrow a foreign government, the last a 1986 attempt to seize Surinam in Central America.

The United States was by no means the only country to spawn such expeditions in the 19th century, nor was there anything uniquely southern about filibustering. The famous plot of Aaron Burr (1805–7), for instance, occurred during the Jefferson administration, before the rise of sectional consciousness in the South. It would be misleading, moreover, to simplify even the pre–Civil War expeditions as purely southern endeavors. Men of all regions enlisted in filibuster ranks, for a variety of personal and ideological reasons, including mere adventurism and an ethnocentric belief—sometimes called Manifest Destiny—that Americans had a God-given mission to impose their republican institutions upon peoples presumed to be less fortunate. New York City and California were two of the country's flagrant centers of filibuster activity. On the other hand, many people could be found throughout the United States who opposed filibustering. Several scholars have suggested that filibustering was an expression of antebellum American romanticism.

Nevertheless, when James Stirling, an English visitor to the United States, informed his countrymen in 1857 that filibustering was "essentially a thing of the South" (*Letters from the Slave States*), he was hardly the victim of a far-fetched delusion. Filibustering found its strongest popular support in the Deep South; in several instances federal authorities found it virtually impossible to prosecute blatant violations of the Neutrality Act in the Gulf states because of the force of public opinion. More significantly, several expeditions either began with, or developed, a southern, sectional orientation. Certainly this was the case with former governor John A. Quitman's Cuba conspiracy in 1853 to 1855. Southern governors, congressmen, newspapermen, and even judges and preachers helped Quitman assemble ships, arms, and men to invade Cuba, because they wanted to prevent Spain from "Africanizing" (abolishing slavery in) Cuba, and they shared Quitman's belief that new slave states would provide security from the American antislavery movement. In the most successful filibuster of the age, a native Tennessean named William Walker, who invaded Nicaragua and became its president in 1856, won widespread southern support when he reestablished slavery in his conquest.

Several commentators, therefore, have presented filibustering as a southern cultural trait. The noted historian John Hope Franklin, for instance, interpreted filibuster expeditions as an element within the general category of southern militarism and violence. However, given northern participation in the filibuster movement, the idea of filibustering as peculiarly southern is a fusion of myth and reality.

ROBERT E. MAY
Purdue University

Charles H. Brown, *Agents of Manifest Destiny: The Lives and Times of the Filibusters* (1980); Robert E. May, *The Southern Dream of a Caribbean Empire, 1854–1861* (1973); Edward S. Wallace, *Destiny and Glory* (1957).

Forrest, Nathan Bedford

(1821–1877) CONFEDERATE GENERAL.
In 1877, in its published obituary for Nathan Bedford Forrest, the *New York Times* summarized the Confederate general as "a man of obscure origin and low associations, a shrewd speculator, negro trader, and duelist, but a man of great energy and brute courage." This viewpoint was shared by many northerners at the time of Forrest's death as they confronted the legacy of a former slave trader, brutal warrior, and the first leader of the Ku Klux Klan. Violence defined Forrest's life and his image for contemporaries—as witnessed by the national press coverage of his exploits—but also animated and sustained his public memory throughout the 20th century. Many of Forrest's enthusiasts came to embrace this violent image as a central part of the general's appeal and often described him in terms very similar to those used by his 19th-century detractors. Because of this legacy, Forrest has served as a symbol of the culture of violence in the South and his image provides an important window into southern society and Civil War memory.

Two particular events bolstered Forrest's persona as the aggressive and violent southern warrior: the general's involvement in the Fort Pillow Massacre and his leadership in the founding of the first incarnation of the Ku Klux

Klan. On 12 April 1864, Confederate soldiers under the command of Forrest launched an attack on Fort Pillow, a Union redoubt with a garrison comprised of black artillerymen and white cavalry troops. The disproportionate number of black soldiers killed during and after the battle (many of these deaths rumored to be after their surrender) led to charges of a massacre and this battle soon came to epitomize the racialized horrors experienced during the Civil War. Forrest's actual involvement in the battle has been regularly debated, but the violence at Fort Pillow would serve as the most identifiable aspect of Forrest's military career during his life. Although Forrest was repeatedly connected to Fort Pillow in the 19th century—and cartoonist Thomas Nast could simply identify his caricature of the general with the shorthand "FP"—his involvement with the first Ku Klux Klan would have a larger impact on the way he was viewed in the 20th century. Several months after the end of the Civil War, a group of Confederate veterans founded the first Ku Klux Klan in Pulaski, Tenn., in an extralegal and violent attempt to reimpose white supremacy. By 1867 Forrest allegedly emerged as the first Grand Wizard of the Klan, a position routinely disputed by many proponents of the general.

Despite—and oftentimes because of—the ambiguities surrounding the general's actions at Fort Pillow and with the Klan, these two stories helped define Forrest's legacy in the 20th century as he came to symbolize the virility of the Confederacy and the South. By the 1930s many admirers of the general

Nathan Bedford Forrest, Confederate general and the first Grand Wizard of the Ku Klux Klan (Photographer unknown, Library of Congress, Washington, D.C.)

came to claim this bloodthirsty image, too, and Forrest's violent life came to signify his virtues rather than his flaws. In 1931 Andrew Nelson Lytle, the Southern Agrarian writer, crafted Forrest as the patriarchal defender against the horrors of northern industrialism as well as the last protector of the Old South. His biography of the general, *Bedford Forrest and His Critter Company*, energized the violence within the Forrest narrative and, in so doing, animated his legacy with a distinctively brutal form of masculinity. Significantly, Lytle's opening chapter features a young Forrest killing and mutilating a panther, an act that presages the author's reading of most elements of the general's life. In addition, unlike other writers who attempted in various ways to disassociate Forrest from the Klan, Lytle clearly argues for Forrest as an unambiguous representative of the violent aspects of southern culture. Overall, Lytle's book would profoundly shape later interpretations of the general's life, including those made by Shelby Foote as well as organizations such as the Sons of Confederate Veterans.

In 1998 sculptor Jack Kershaw unveiled his giant fiberglass rendering of Forrest outside of Nashville surrounded by Confederate flags and barbed wire. Clutching both a pistol and sword, Kershaw's glowering Forrest signaled the increased prominence of the general's image in popular culture during the 1990s. Forrest materialized as the anti–Robert E. Lee: the belligerent, unrepentant Confederate capable of absolute terror. Just as the *New York Times* labeled Forrest at the time of his death as "notoriously bloodthirsty and revengeful," the general's image in the late 20th century resonated around this blood-soaked representation of aggression. From Thomas Nast's Reconstruction cartoons and many of Forrest's obituaries, to Andrew Lytle's biography in 1931 and the culture wars of the 1990s, Nathan Bedford Forrest has consistently served as a stark reminder of the culture of southern violence seen not only in the Civil War but also in remembrances of the Lost Cause.

COURT CARNEY
Stephen F. Austin State University

Court Carney, *Journal of Southern History* (August 2001), in *White Masculinity in the Recent South*, ed. Trent Watts (2008); John Cimprich, *Fort Pillow, a Civil War Massacre, and Public Memory* (2005); Richard Fuchs, *An Unerring Fire: The Massacre at Fort Pillow* (1997); Tony Horwitz, *Confederates in the Attic: Dispatches from the Unfinished Civil War* (1999); Jack Hurst, *Nathan Bedford Forrest: A Biography* (1993); Andrew Nelson Lytle, *Bedford Forrest and His Critter Company* (1931); Brian Steel Wills, *A Battle from the Start: The Life of Nathan Bedford Forrest* (1992).

Frank, Leo

(1884–1915) LYNCHING VICTIM. Described by Leonard Dinnerstein as "one of the most infamous outbursts of anti-Semitic feeling in the [history of] the United States," the Leo Frank case inspired formation of both the second Ku Klux Klan and the Anti-Defamation League of B'nai B'rith. The case began on Confederate Memorial Day in 1913 with the murder and mutilation of Mary Phagan, a 13-year-old employee of an Atlanta pencil factory. The mayor and an anxious populace, aroused by yellow journalism, demanded that the police find her killer quickly. They responded by arresting the victim's boss, Leo Frank. A Jew from New York, Frank rapidly became a focal point for the resentment toward factories and outsiders that rapid industrialization had ignited in southern traditionalists.

Frank's Atlanta trial took place in an atmosphere of hysteria, amid threats of mob violence. The prosecution, led by Solicitor Hugh Dorsey (who rode the publicity he gained from this case into the governorship), portrayed Frank as a lecherous employer who preyed on young factory girls. The state relied heavily on the testimony of Jim Conley, a black janitor with a criminal

Postcard of a crowd milling about after the lynching of Leo Frank, Marietta, Cobb County, Ga., August 1915 (Courtesy of Georgia Archives, Vanishing Georgia Collection)

record, who claimed Frank asked him to help hide a body and write two notes found next to Phagan's remains. Evidence available to police and prosecutors strongly suggested he, not Frank, was the killer; but the jury convicted the Jewish factory manager. Although he believed Frank was innocent, Judge Leonard Roane denied his motion for a new trial and sentenced him to death.

A good deal of new evidence soon surfaced, which raised further doubt about Frank's guilt. Efforts to secure a new trial failed, however, despite an appeal carried to the United States Supreme Court. The Court also spurned a petition seeking Frank's release on a writ of habeas corpus. He gained a temporary reprieve when Governor John Slaton sacrificed a promising political career by commuting his sentence to life in prison. Then, on 16 August 1915, a group of respectable citizens from Mary Phagan's hometown, Marietta, Ga., abducted Frank from the state prison farm at Milledgeville and hanged him.

Frank's death and the events preceding it aroused intense interest throughout the country. Governors, state legislators, and members of Congress joined more than 100,000 other Americans in efforts to save Frank's life. This outpouring of public sentiment and the nationwide press coverage of the case owed much to the efforts of Jewish leaders, who viewed this incident as a threatening manifestation of anti-Semitism, comparable to France's infamous Dreyfus affair.

Concerned Jewish groups persisted in trying to clear Frank's name, and evidence continued to surface. In 1982

a former office boy at Frank's factory, Alonzo Mann, came forward and said that he had seen another man carrying Mary Phagan's slain body. As of 1983 Governor Joe Frank Harris publicly supported a posthumous pardon of Leo Frank, but the Georgia Board of Pardons and Paroles refused to take such action. The Anti-Defamation League, the American Jewish Committee, and the Atlanta Jewish Federation submitted another petition focusing on the denial of justice to Frank, and the Board of Pardons and Paroles reversed itself and granted the pardon in March 1986, 71 years after the lynching of Leo Frank.

MICHAEL R. BELKNAP
University of Georgia

W. Fitzhugh Brundage, *Lynching in the New South: Georgia and Virginia, 1880–1930* (1993); Leonard Dinnerstein, *The Leo Frank Case* (repr., 1999); Steve Oney, *And the Dead Shall Rise: The Murder of Mary Phagan and the Lynching of Leo Frank* (2003); Mary Phagan, *The Murder of Little Mary Phagan* (1987).

Greensboro (North Carolina) Massacre (1979)

Greensboro, N.C., was the site where on 3 November 1979 members of the Ku Klux Klan and the American Nazi Party fired on a crowd of labor activists at a Death to the Klan March, leaving five marchers dead. The violence came out of tensions in the area between the Maoist Workers Viewpoint Organization, which attempted to organize textile workers, and white terrorist groups. Activists who survived the attack insisted it was the result of a conspiracy between violent reactionary groups and the civil authorities of the area wanting to prevent unionization of the work force. The incident illustrates continuing violence in the post–Jim Crow South, violence related to long-standing cultural forces.

In July 1979 the Klan showed the film *The Birth of a Nation* in the textile town of China Grove, N.C., hoping to use its white supremacist story to recruit new members. Communist activists disrupted the event, which was the beginning of months of increasingly harsh verbal conflict. Communist organizers scheduled the anti-Klan march for November in Greensboro, challenging Klansmen to come and observe the will of the people against fascism. Beginning at Morningside Homes, a predominantly African American housing project, the march proceeded until cars drove up containing the attackers wielding pistols, rifles, and shotguns. Local television film crews documented the attack. The police knew of the planned march, but few police officers were present, enabling the attackers to escape. The absence of the police suggested collusion with the attackers.

Authorities later arrested 16 of the assailants and brought six to trial. An all-white jury in a state trial failed to convict those with criminal charges. A later federal trial took place around charges of conspiracy to violate the marchers' civil rights, a case that resulted from the Federal Bureau of Investigation's (FBI) most extensive criminal civil rights investigation to that point, but another all-white jury acquitted the defendants. In 1985 a jury in a civil lawsuit awarded survivors of the attack $350,000 from the city of Greensboro, the Klan, and the American Nazi Party.

Despite the official opposition of the Greensboro city government, Greensboro citizens launched a Truth and Reconciliation Commission modeled on the South African example after apartheid ended, taking testimony and assessing the causes and results of the massacre. The commission found blame on many sides — the failure of demonstrators to get the full support of the black housing project residents, the deliberate effort by the assailants to provoke violence, the violent rhetoric on both sides, and the failure of both the FBI and local law enforcement to prevent an attack they knew was coming.

CHARLES REAGAN WILSON
University of Mississippi

Sally Avery Bermanzohn, *Through Survivors' Eyes: From the Sixties to the Greensboro Massacre* (2003); Signe Waller, *Love and Revolution: A Political Memoir; People's History of the Greensboro Massacre, Its Setting and Aftermath* (2002); Elizabeth Wheaton, *Codename GREENKILL: The 1979 Greensboro Killings* (1987).

Guerrilla Bands

Few parts of the Civil War South escaped the violence of guerrilla fighting and its associated evils. Indeed, in some places, guerrillas posed the gravest threats of death, theft, and destruction. Their numbers are unknown, but a minimal estimate would be 25,000, although that figure should most likely be doubled. Guerrillas acted from very mixed motives and played a number of roles, but their dramatic impact on the course and outcome of the war has been severely underestimated by scholars.

The geographical scope of the guerrilla conflict was unlimited. It erupted spontaneously within days of the firing on Fort Sumter all along the North-South border, from Maryland and Virginia westward to Kansas and Missouri. Thereafter, it kept pace with the advance of Union armies into the South. By war's end, the guerrilla war had infected every Confederate state and had spread, as well, to the southern counties of the Midwest, from Iowa to Ohio.

This irregular war grew so rapidly and became so pervasive because both sides had their guerrilla bands. While Confederate guerrillas were the most numerous, southern Unionists also resorted to irregular warfare. Each side waged war against two enemies. There was, of course, the opposing army, Union or Confederate, to be harassed and bothered. Steering clear of large bodies of troops, Confederate guerrillas specialized in destroying or endangering enemy lines of supply and communication. They also "bushwhacked" Union pickets, stragglers, and isolated contingents of soldiers. Union guerrilla bands, being smaller in number and generally operating in hostile territory, had to be more cautious, but they, too, could prove a misery to enemy troops.

More often, though, and especially in politically divided communities, Confederate and Union guerrillas fought each other. Local defense, including the protection of homes and economic and political control of neighborhoods, was the essential purpose of both sides. This meant that, in addition to fighting each other, guerrillas also targeted the families and property of neighbors who disagreed with their views on secession and the war. Kinship ties could also define the enemy, as did personal grudges and old feuds about politics or property. In addition, rebel guerrillas helped to police the slave population and break up illegal trade, especially in cotton. In this sense, the Civil War was not as much a contest between two nations, or even two sections of the country, as a showdown to determine who would control and maintain law and order in hundreds of communities across the South. It was this intense brand of local fighting that accounted for most of the wickedness associated with the guerrilla war.

Further complicating matters, there were three types of guerrilla bands. Most numerous were the traditional, homegrown variety, which organized spontaneously for both local defense and to harass enemy troops. Second, beginning in the spring of 1862, were Partisan Rangers. Not so much bands as formally organized military companies and battalions, they were sanctioned by the Confederate government to serve as adjuncts to the conventional army. Third, and quite apart from these two legitimate groups, were bands of deserters, draft dodgers, and ne'er-do-wells. These armed malcontents sometimes claimed to serve either the Union or Confederate cause, but their larger purpose was to loot and pillage while staying clear of the armies and local authorities.

Contrary to their popular image, most guerrillas do not appear to have been restless, reckless young thugs. More research is needed on this issue, but what we know about the composition of guerrilla bands suggests that their members did not differ markedly from conventional soldiers. While some bands included men either too old or too young for the armies, most members were either men of property and position or from respectable families. They chose to serve as irregulars, rather than in the armies, because of family circumstances, the nature of their occupations and professions, or the vulnerability of their communities.

DANIEL E. SUTHERLAND
University of Arkansas

Michael Fellman, *Inside War: The Guerrilla Conflict in Missouri during the American Civil War* (1989); John C. Inscoe and Gordon B. McKinney, *The Heart of Confederate Appalachia: Western North Carolina in the Civil War* (2000); Robert R. Mackey, *The Uncivil War: Irregular Warfare in the Upper South, 1861–1865* (2004); Clay Mountcastle, *Punitive War: Confederate Guerrillas and Union Reprisals* (2009); Kenneth W. Noe, *Civil War History* (March 2003); Daniel E. Sutherland, *A Savage Conflict: The Decisive Role of Guerrillas in the American Civil War* (2009).

Harlan County, Kentucky

The 1930s were a time of labor upheaval in the United States. There were strikes, picket lines, lockouts, riots, sit-down strikes, marches, protests, musterings of national guardsmen, and many charges

of police brutality. Amid this labor unrest that was truly national in scope, one place caught the attention of the nation and much of the Western world. Previously almost unknown, it accumulated a huge literature in newspapers and magazines and generated a voluminous body of folk music. The place has since been known as "bloody Harlan."

The 1930 census revealed a population of 64,577, nearly all of which was dependent in one way or another on coal mining. John W. Hevener has published a careful study of the county's labor strife in the troubled decade, concluding that the struggle caused 11 deaths and 20 woundings. When viewed against the background of the region's grim history these casualties appear startlingly low—but bloody enough to justify the county's reputation. Harlan County earned its niche in the folklore of American labor violence. However, in considering Harlan's reputation for lawlessness and bloodshed, the labor struggles mark only a brief and relatively minor facet of its turbulent history.

Harlan County lies between two great barrier walls—the long steep parallel ridges known as the Cumberland and Pine mountains. The area was settled sparsely and late. After the first settlers had built their cabins, forbidding hills kept out new waves of settlers and preserved intact the mores and culture, the ignorance and cunning, the crankiness and suspicion, the narrowness and prejudices, the loyalties and clannishness that marked the pioneer families. Sam Howard, a Revolutionary War veteran, was the county's first permanent settler. His family and the 30 or 40 other backwoods families who followed around 1800 had been hardened by decades of warfare. As a people they had been seasoned by two centuries of scrabbling in the backwoods, clearing endless new ground, fighting with the French, struggling over wilderness lands with the British, and countering almost incessant raids from both southern and northern Indians. It was inescapable that the people who stopped off at such places as the Poor Fork and Wallins Creek were a hard-bitten, self-reliant lot who would be quick with knife and gun whenever it appeared to them that they were being "picked on."

The county was established by the legislature in 1819, and the county seat was "established" at Sam Howard's old place, which he called Mount Pleasant. By any standard meaningful to contemporary Americans, this backwoods bailiwick was desperately poor. The people there fished, hunted until most of the game was exterminated, and gained such money as came into their hands by bartering ginseng, feathers, whiskey, brandy, hides, and saw logs to stock drovers and backwoods merchants. These settlers became remarkably interrelated, an important circumstance in a society that valued "blood kin."

The county was of the most rudimentary character, with a budget of $6,025.60 in 1857. Data on this period are hard to come by, but there is no reason to believe that the population was unusually violent in those years. During the Civil War Harlan County residents were Unionists (except for a

prosouthern enclave on Clover Fork) and formed strong home guard units to keep the peace. Unlike neighboring Letcher County, which split on the issue and fostered a little war within a big one, Harlan Countians did little fighting among themselves. Instead, they relentlessly bushwacked Confederate forces that ventured into their midst between 1862 and 1864.

The struggle left many mountain counties impoverished, divided, and hate filled so that numerous little "wars" followed Appomattox. In the half century after Lee surrendered, scarcely a county was without one of these vendettas that spread from valley to valley until practically the entire population was at peril. Breathitt County was wracked by one struggle after another, as were Clay, Letcher, Pike, Knott, and Bell. The dead were beyond count and included a circuit judge, a United States commissioner, a county attorney, a city marshal, a trustee of the State College of Kentucky, a physician, and a witness guarded by a company of state militiamen armed with a Gatling gun.

This bloody record reflected a lingering statewide frontier mentality that endorsed murder as a form of private justice. In that bloody period only Arkansas and Mississippi ranked with Kentucky in violent crime. It was the considered judgment of the *New York Times* (26 December 1878) that Kentucky was "the Corsica of North America," its people considerably less civilized than the Italian Mafia.

Harlan County did not escape these troubles. In April 1882 Wilse Howard won a few dollars from Bob Turner in a card game. Turner drew a gun and compelled Howard to return the money. Three days later Howard killed Turner from ambush. There is no credible tally of the deaths in the ensuing Howard-Turner War. It ended when the Turner faction caught the Howards in "Harlan Town," killed four of them, and wounded seven others.

The whirlwind industrialization of Harlan radically changed its society and economy. In the years from 1900 to 1920 the population increased from 9,838 to 31,546. Subsistence farmers left their hollows and river valleys to mine coal in "company towns." Their dependence on family or "clan" was abandoned for day wages and an erratic coal market. People who had lived all their lives amid "blood kin" and friends found themselves in small houses in communities that were totally dominated by the omnipresent power of coal and iron policemen. When the market for coal evaporated in recurrent depressions, famine and rebellion followed. The rebellions were repressed by a political system that grew directly out of the coal economy: the circuit judge, sheriff, and county chairmen of both political parties were in the coal business. That the men revolted in such uprisings as the "battle of the Evarts" and the "battle of Fork Ridge" is understandable. The only surprise lies in the small number of casualties.

Harlan was never as violent as its sister counties 70 miles away in West Virginia — "Bloody Mingo" and "Bloody Logan." In 1922 the Logan County War saw veritable armies of miners pitted against formations of deputy sheriffs and national guardsmen. Nonetheless it must be conceded that "Bloody Harlan" was not a gratuitous nickname. In 1916 a homicide rate of 0.8 per 100,000 persons was recorded in New Hampshire (a different kind of Appalachian state), and rural America as a whole reported 5.2. Harlan's rate was a horrendous 63.5. Perry reported 30.4. Harlan's neighbor to the south, Wise County, Va., came up with 39.3, and its eastern neighbor, Letcher, led the nation with 77.9 — nearly 80 times that of New Hampshire.

HARRY M. CAUDILL
Whitesburg, Kentucky

John W. Campbell, *The Southern Highlander and His Homeland* (1922); Joe Daniel Carr, *Filson Club History Quarterly* (April 1973); Mabel Green Condon, *A History of Harlan County* (1962); David A. Corbin, *Life, Work, and Rebellion in the Coal Fields: Southern West Virginia Coal Miners, 1880–1922* (1981); Paul Frederick Cressy, *American Sociological Review* (June 1934); John W. Hevener, *Which Side Are You On? The Harlan County Coal Miners, 1931–39* (1978); G. C. Jones, *Growing Up Hard in Harlan County* (1985); Winthrop Lane, *Civil War in West Virginia* (1922); Howard W. Lee, *Blood-Letting in Appalachia* (1969); Elmon Middleton, *Harlan County, Kentucky* (1934); John Ed Pearce, *Days of Darkness: The Feuds of Eastern Kentucky* (1994); George W. Titler, *Hell in Harlan* (1972).

Hatfields and McCoys

The Hatfield-McCoy feud, the most famous southern Appalachian vendetta, was one manifestation of general late 19th-century American violence — bloody labor troubles, western lawlessness, and political assassination. It was also part of the cultural milieu of

*"Devil Anse" Hatfield, Kentucky fighter, 1880s
(West Virginia Department of Archives and
History, Charleston)*

the isolated Tug River valley along the
West Virginia–Kentucky border, an area
known for widespread illiteracy, fundamentalist churches, and disrespect for
law. Exaggerated family and clan loyalties and acute sensitivity to affronts
often mixed with the consumption of
moonshine whiskey to produce explosive situations.

Numerous incidents, such as a dispute over ownership of a razorback
hog, a romance between "Devil Anse"
Hatfield's son Johnse and Randolph
McCoy's daughter Rose Anna, and a
deadly election altercation, were behind
the Hatfield-McCoy feud. Home guard
and bushwhacking activities by the two
families during the Civil War had also
set the stage for conflict. Some historians see the feud as a conflict between
an emerging industrial order (repre-

senting miner, railroad, and timber
companies) and traditional, precapi-
talist local culture.

Several bloody events in the 1880s
drew national attention to the feud: the
killing of Ellison Hatfield, a brother of
"Devil Anse," at an election in 1882 and
the retaliatory murder of three sons of
Randolph McCoy by enraged Hatfields;
the battle of Grapevine Creek, a pitched
battle on the Jug Fork River; and a mer-
ciless raid on New Year's night 1888 in
which Hatfields burned McCoy's house
and killed two more of his children.
The feud was elevated to an interstate
battle when West Virginia governor
Willis Wilson refused to extradite Hatfield partisans indicted in Pike County,
Ky., for the 1882 murders and when he
instituted habeas corpus proceedings
for return of nine who were seized later
by Kentucky authorities in raids into
West Virginia. Sensational journalists
on large city newspapers provided the
nation with gory and sometimes fabri-
cated accounts that did much to encrust
the feud with myth and legend.

The hanging of one Hatfield partisan and the sentencing of others to
prison terms following an April 1897
trial in Pike County signaled an end to
the feud. By then many of the participants, including "Devil Anse," who had
become a symbol of the bloodthirsty
mountaineer, were weary of the killing.
The entry of industry and improved
transportation broke the bonds of isolation and fostered a new society that
had far less patience with violent feuds.
The Hatfields and the McCoys turned
to peaceful pursuits, and both families
produced important business, indus-

trial, and political leaders for the New South.

OTIS K. RICE
West Virginia Institute of Technology

Virgil C. Jones, *The Hatfields and the McCoys* (1948); Otis K. Rice, *The Hatfields and the McCoys* (1978); Altina Waller, *Feud: Hatfields, McCoys, and Social Change in Appalachia, 1860–1900* (1988).

James Brothers

(FRANK, 1843–1915; JESSE, 1847–1882) OUTLAWS.

Noted outlaws Alexander Franklin James and Jesse Woodson James were born and raised on a western Missouri farm, sons of a prosperous, slave-owning family that had moved from Kentucky in 1842. Like many Missourians, they were southern in origin and outlook. Before and during the Civil War, violence over slavery and secession divided Missouri and consumed the James family. In the absence of regular Confederate troops in Missouri during the war, organizations of pro-southern guerrillas formed to respond to the harsh treatment of southern sympathizers by Union troops and Kansas guerrilla raiders. In 1862 Confederate private Frank James joined guerrilla leader William Clarke Quantrill. Seventeen-year-old Jesse rode with William "Bloody Bill" Anderson's guerrilla band in 1864 after Union militia reportedly attempted to hang Jesse's stepfather, harassed his pregnant mother, and gave him a severe whipping. Both brothers were deeply involved in violent irregular warfare. In this crucible of blood and fire America's best-known outlaws were created.

PROCLAMATION
$5,000⁰⁰
REWARD
FOR EACH of SEVEN ROBBERS of THE TRAIN at WINSTON, MO., JULY 15, 1881, and THE MURDER of CONDUCTER WESTFALL
$ 5,000.00
ADDITIONAL for ARREST or CAPTURE
DEAD OR ALIVE
OF JESSE OR FRANK JAMES
THIS NOTICE TAKES the PLACE of ALL PREVIOUS REWARD NOTICES.
CONTACT SHERIFF, DAVIESS COUNTY, MISSOURI IMMEDIATELY
T. T. CRITTENDEN, GOVERNOR
STATE OF MISSOURI
JULY 26, 1881

Wanted poster for the arrest or capture of the outlaws Frank and Jesse James (Broadsides, 1860–1886 [C3252], Western Historical Manuscript Collection–Columbia, Mo.)

After the war many guerrillas resumed normal lives though they were denied amnesty and the right to vote. The James brothers, however, did not settle down. Their family had been banished from Missouri, and according to legend, when Jesse attempted to surrender in 1865, he was shot by federal troops. By 1866 Frank and Jesse James had begun their long careers as bank and train robbers. Supporters argued that their treatment during and after the war forced them outside the law and justified their actions. This notion was reinforced when Pinkerton detectives hired by the railroads threw an explosive device into their parents' home, killing their nine-year-old half brother and blowing their mother's arm off.

When the James brothers were involved in an 1869 bank robbery and murder, newspaperman John N. Edwards began an influential 20-year crusade to idealize their lives as guerrillas and outlaws. He portrayed them as dashing southern gentlemen who protected women and children from northern persecution during the war and defended helpless victims of northern banks and railroads afterward. Many people of southern background agreed that the James brothers were knights of the South's Lost Cause and frontier Robin Hoods.

As people in all regions felt the pinch of big business in the post–Civil War decades, the James brothers were praised nationally in folklore and popular culture as bold western outlaw heroes who robbed the rich and gave to the poor. This widespread romantic portrayal of the James brothers played a significant role in bringing qualities of the southern gentleman to the western hero. Like later fictional western heroes such as the Virginian and Shane, the James brothers of legend lived on the wild frontier but upheld the chivalrous code of their southern background: they protected the weak and righted wrongs with a fierce sense of honor, pride, and style.

Despite the romantic image of the James brothers, Governor Thomas Crittenden felt they had given Missouri a bad name. In 1881 he offered a $10,000 reward of railroad money for their capture. On 3 April 1882 gang member Robert Ford betrayed Jesse James with a deadly shot from behind while visiting Jesse and his family in their home. Ford was sentenced to hang for murder, but the governor gave him a full pardon.

The manner of Jesse's death was the final step in his ascent to the rank of hero. Frank James surrendered his pistol six months later and was tried but acquitted of several crimes.

The James brothers were outlaws for a remarkable 16 years. Thanks to local and public support for their role in the Civil War and their attacks on banks and railroads, they were never apprehended and never convicted of any crimes. A century after the end of their outlaw careers, Frank and Jesse are still celebrated in movies, songs, and novels as heroes of the Lost Cause and Robin Hoods of the West.

GEORGE B. WARD
Texas State Historical Association

David Brion Davis, *American Quarterly* (Summer 1954); John Newman Edwards, *Noted Guerrillas; or, The Warfare of the Border* (1877); William A. Settle Jr., *Jesse James Was His Name* (1966); T. J. Stiles, *Jesse James: Last Rebel of the Civil War* (2002).

King, Martin Luther, Jr., Assassination of

At 6:01 P.M. on 4 April 1968, James Earl Ray fatally shot Martin Luther King Jr. at the Lorraine Motel in Memphis, Tenn. This violent act bound together two vastly different individuals—one a lifetime criminal, the other a lifetime advocate for equality and justice. Though these men could hardly be more different, they each represented tensions and conflicts within the American experience. In their violent encounter, they dramatized these conflicts even as they transformed American society forever.

Ray was born only 10 months before King on 10 March 1928 in Alton, Ill. He faced a troubled childhood, experiencing grinding poverty that made him the ridicule of his teachers and peers. His father's side of the family had a century-long tradition of crime, and early on, James learned criminal ways from his father and uncle. At age 14 he committed his first crime, initiating a lifelong career of criminal behavior, especially theft. Growing up in poverty amid uprooted southerners, James was exposed to intense racism towards blacks. He reflected his deep, though hardly unique, racism in his flirtation with Nazism both during and after World War II. As he grew older and spent time in and out of notorious prisons like Leavenworth, Ray revealed the potent mixture that would ultimately prompt him to assassinate King: a desire for criminal fame, a deep racism, and a longing for quick money. Though many believed that James's fatal act was part of a larger governmental conspiracy, no clear evidence suggests the assassination was more than an individual or familial act.

Even though the murder was not part of a wider plot, it did reveal deep fault lines in American society. King's undisputed leadership of the civil rights movement made him the target of death threats and vitriol. He became the symbol of black power that threatened many Americans, especially white southerners, bent on keeping blacks marginalized. His visibility and his importance to the movement made him a prime target to whites frustrated with the prospect of black empowerment, some of whom offered bounties on King's head—bounties that finally motivated criminals like Ray to act.

White hostility to civil rights was only one conflict in a society ensconced in violence. For one, the U.S. was waging a global Cold War that was "hot" in the Third World. The height of the Vietnam War came in 1968, and only three weeks before King's assassination, the My Lai Massacre demonstrated the terrible atrocities that could stem from racism and militarism. Second, violence permeated national politics like never before, as the 1960s witnessed the assassination of several high-profile figures, including John F. Kennedy, Malcolm X, and Robert F. Kennedy. Third, the turmoil of the 1960s exposed the pervasiveness of violence in American society. The South's social system, in particular, relied upon the threat of violence to disenfranchise and impoverish blacks. This became readily clear during the civil rights movement, which, though its activists practiced nonviolent resistance, fomented violence among segregationists. The movement was actually rife with violence, as whites engaged in massive resistance resorted to acts of terror, police brutality, and murder to punish and control black protestors. In this way, the civil rights movement only made manifest the latent violence endemic to American society.

Just as King's assassination reflected this wider American context of violence, it also transformed the American scene. Upon hearing of King's assassination, riots broke out across the nation for a week, marking the most extensive coterminous rioting in the nation's history. In the end, 39 peopled were killed, 2,600 were injured, 21,000 were arrested, $65 million of damage was done, and scores of inner-city neighborhoods were destroyed. More importantly, this rioting coincided with national trends of black frustration, white backlash, and the breakdown of the liberal state to turn most Americans against fighting for civil rights and social justice. Yet, even as the assassination signaled crisis for the movement King led, his charisma, his dedication, and, most of all, his message would continue to inspire for generations to come.

DAVID A. VAREL
University of Colorado at Boulder

Taylor Branch, *At Canaan's Edge: America in the King Years, 1965–68* (2006); David J. Garrow, *Bearing the Cross: Martin Luther King Jr. and the Southern Christian Leadership Conference* (1986); Gerald Posner, *Killing the Dream: James Earl Ray and the Assassination of Martin Luther King Jr.* (1998); Clay Risen, *A Nation on Fire: America in the Wake of the King Assassination* (2009).

Knights of the Golden Circle

The Knights of the Golden Circle (KGC) was a secret antebellum organization promoted by George W. L. Bickley, a Virginia-born editor, adventurer, and doctor of eclectic medicine. He hoped to create a great slave empire encompassing the West Indies, the southern United States, Mexico, Central America, and part of South America—hence the name Golden Circle. But his main goal was annexation of Mexico, whose relations with the United States were strained in the late 1850s.

Hounded by creditors, "General" Bickley, self-styled "President and Commander-in-Chief of the KGC American Legion," left his Cincinnati base in 1860, toured the East and the South, and promoted a filibustering expedition into Mexico. He received his chief support in Texas, where at least 32 "castles" (lodges) were established under local leadership. Bickley had limited newspaper support elsewhere in the South, and there were rumors that linked prominent southern politicos to the KGC (Jefferson Davis, William L. Yancey, John B. Floyd, John C. Breckinridge), but these were probably fabrications.

Bickley's attempted invasion of Mexico was ineptly handled; he failed to secure the support of Gov. Sam Houston, who had seemed interested; and he failed to show up at the appointed time with a large force he claimed he was collecting in New Orleans. In April a number of his disgusted supporters met in New Orleans and expelled Bickley. He retaliated by calling for a convention in Raleigh in May, at which time he was reinstated.

Once more Bickley turned his attention to Mexico. This time he was sidetracked by the 1860 campaign. With Lincoln's election Bickley became an ardent advocate of southern secession and supported it in Tennessee and Kentucky.

The "General" served a stint as a Confederate surgeon, deserted, and for a short time lived with a backwoods woman at Shelbyville, Tenn. In July 1863 Bickley was arrested in Indiana for spying and consequently was imprisoned until October 1865, although nothing was proved. He died a broken man in August 1867.

The KGC was a prime antebellum example of the South's aggressiveness and expansionism. Nevertheless, it was a militancy that failed to achieve its goals. The Republicans in the 1864 campaign tried to link antiwar Democrats to the treasonable plots of the KGC, but, in fact, no "castles" were established in the North. The KGC gained a widespread but unfounded reputation for popularity, and it embittered relations between the North and South.

ERNEST M. LANDER JR.
Clemson University

Ollinger Crenshaw, *American Historical Review* (October 1941); Roy S. Dunn, *Southwestern Historical Quarterly* (April 1967); Robert E. May, *The Southern Dream of a Caribbean Empire, 1854–1861* (1973).

Ku Klux Klan, Civil Rights Era to the Present

The Ku Klux Klan (KKK) is the United States of America's oldest documented white supremacist group. Historically, the KKK precipitated, engaged in, and supported numerous acts of intimidation and violence in the South. Bombings, murders, assaults, and other violent acts were sanctioned by the social norms of southern culture during a time in which KKK members were also employed in positions of power (i.e., sheriffs, judges). Their place in society contributed to the disproportionate enforcement, prosecution, and sentencing of whites who antagonized and victimized blacks and others in the South. Although the first two waves of KKK

members benefited from a cohesive unit of organization, members of the third wave arose from dozens of independent groups that utilized the KKK moniker during the 1960s in resistance to the civil rights movement.

The rise of black freedom struggles in the 1950s provoked a massive resistance on the part of southern whites. The KKK reemerged as the most violent expression of this resistance. KKK members were implicated in a series of incidents, including the 1963 church bombing that killed four young girls, the 1963 assassination of National Association for the Advancement of Colored People (NAACP) organizer Medgar Evers, and the 1964 murder of three civil rights workers in Neshoba County, Miss. The nationwide media coverage of the aftermath of these violent incidents contributed to the KKK's increasingly unfavorable image outside the South.

During the 1970s and 1980s racially motivated acts of violence perpetrated by KKK members did not cease entirely. For instance, in 1979, in what came to be known as the Greensboro Massacre, KKK members (in collaboration with Nazi members) murdered five protesters at an anti-Klan rally in Greensboro, North Carolina. In 1980 four older black women were shot after a KKK initiation rally in Chattanooga, Tennessee. In 1981 the murder of Michael Donald became the last documented lynching in Alabama. Unlike earlier incidences where cases were dismissed or offenders acquitted by all-white juries, the perpetrators of these acts were criminally prosecuted for their crimes. In some instances, KKK organizations faced civil

United Klans of America Rally, Mobile, Ala., 1977 (Photograph by
Dave Hamby, courtesy of the Mobile Press-Register)

opposition, resulting in their financial collapse (i.e., United Klans of America, Imperial Klans of America). The Southern Poverty Law Center's founder, Morris Dees, led civil cases against these groups, and the U.S. government increased its oversight. These factors made it increasingly unacceptable for the KKK to resort to violence as a means to further its political agenda.

Today the Southern Poverty Law Center estimates that thousands of KKK members are split among at least 186 KKK chapters. These fragmented factions have been weakened by "internal conflicts, court cases, and government infiltration." However, they still disseminate hate against blacks, Jews, Latinos, immigrants, homosexuals, and Catholics. Instead of violence, some of today's KKK organizations focus on collective political action by participating in and restructuring the government. Others focus on marketing strategies in order to appeal to mainstream America with the intention of increasing recruitment and disseminating their ideology to a wider audience. Although violent acts, like the 2008 murder of a woman in Louisiana after a failed KKK initiation, do still randomly occur, violence is no longer considered a socially accepted means to achieving white hegemony in the South.

STACIA GILLIARD-MATTHEWS
West Virginia University

Josh Adams and Vincent Roscigno, *Social Forces* (December 2005); Chip Berlet and Stanislav Vysotsky, *Journal of Political and Military Sociology* (Summer 2006); David Chalmers, *Hooded Americanism: The History of the Ku Klux Klan* (1987), *Backfire: How the Ku Klux Klan Helped the Civil Rights Movement* (2005); David Holthouse,

The Year in Hate (2009); Diane McWhorter, *Carry Me Home: Birmingham, Alabama; The Climactic Battle of the Civil Rights Revolution* (2001); Pete Simi and Robert Futrell, *American Swastika: Inside the White Power Movement's Hidden Spaces of Hate* (2010).

Ku Klux Klan, Reconstruction-Era

The Ku Klux Klan was the name popularly given to hundreds of loosely connected vigilante groups that emerged in the early Reconstruction era in locations throughout the South. These groups used violence and threats, primarily against freed people, local white Republicans, immigrants from the North, and agents of the federal government, to gain political, social, cultural, and economic benefits in the wake of the war. Although some prominent figures attempted to organize the Klan and use it as political tool, the Klan was never effectively centralized. Klan groups proliferated rapidly in 1868 and saw a second peak in 1870–71. The Klan movement was in decline by late 1871 and had almost disappeared by the end of 1872.

The first group to call itself the Ku Klux Klan began in Pulaski, Tenn., probably in the summer of 1866. The six original members were young, small-town professionals and Confederate veterans. This group was at first fundamentally a social club. Members performed music and organized entertainments. Significantly, they also introduced a particularly elaborate version of the rituals and costumes common to fraternal associations.

As the Pulaski Klan spread, local elites became interested in its poten-

An original Klansman from Pulaski, Tenn. He was part of the original Ku Klux Klan and is pictured here wearing an original robe. (Courtesy of the Tennessee State Library and Archives)

tial as a political organization in opposition to the government of William Gannaway Brownlow. In an April 1867 meeting in nearby Nashville, they produced a governing document called the "Prescript." The Prescript described the Klan as a political organization opposed to black enfranchisement and in favor of southern autonomy and the strengthening of white political power. It also detailed a complex and rigidly hierarchical organization. At this time, Nathan Bedford Forrest was probably chosen as the Klan's first Grand Wizard. Other prominent men like Albert Pike, Matthew Galloway, and John B. Gordon joined around this time and used their influence to spread the organization.

The tightly organized, politically focused regional Klan envisioned by the Prescript never materialized. Each state faced substantially different political situations, making coordination difficult; Klan groups had few effective ways to organize or communicate; and the federal government soon became aware of the Klan and worked to suppress it. The Tennessee leaders disbanded the group in 1869. Klan activity persisted, and even increased, after this disbandment, but the disbandment spelled the end of attempts to centralize the Klan.

The Klan, instead, became an amorphous movement including a range of clandestine groups in many parts of the South who exploited postwar political, social, and economic disorganization for various ends. Each group had its own composition, goals, and tactics. Some had political goals, such as intimidating Republican voters, politicians, and local government officials. Others hoped to prevent the establishment of schools for freed people. Some styled themselves after western lynch mobs and portrayed themselves as protecting the weak and punishing crime and immorality. Some were conventional criminal gangs using a Klan identity to escape detection or punishment for theft, illegal distilling, rape, or various violent and sadistic acts. Others had apparently economic goals, such as driving away freed people competing with them as laborers or tenants, terrifying workers into compliance, or forcing tenants to abandon their crops, animals, or improvements. Still others engaged in

Klan violence to settle personal disputes involving land use, social status, feuds, or sexual competition.

Perpetrators of Klan violence varied from place to place. Some Klan groups consisted largely of privileged, though temporarily dispossessed, southern elites, who rode horses and wore extravagant costumes. Other, probably most, Klan groups consisted of poor whites. Many Klan groups, for instance, too poor to own horses, committed their attacks while riding mules or on foot, and either did not disguise themselves or simply covered their faces with cheap materials like painted burlap sacks or squirrel skins.

Klan tactics differed as much as did membership and apparent motives. Some Klan groups were largely performative, parading through the streets and leaving cryptic messages about town. Most, however, exercised intimidation and/or violence against specific targets. Even when they were pursuing goals that were not primarily political, their victims were almost always Republicans, and usually freed people. By targeting these groups, Klansmen frequently gained broad support among local Democratic whites. The most common form that intimidation and violence took was the nighttime visit, in which Klansmen would descend upon the home of their victim and either force their way in or demand that their victim come outside. Klan visits frequently involved property theft from victims, whether the Klansmen were "confiscating" firearms or simply stealing money, food, or household goods. Some Klansmen threatened their targets, requiring that they renounce a political party, leave town, or otherwise change their behavior. Other Klan groups whipped their victims. A number of Klan attacks were sexual in nature: Klansmen raped victims, whipped them while naked, forced them to perform humiliating sexual acts, or castrated them.

Klansmen sometimes killed their victims. Because of the weak and disorganized nature of local government at the time, and because of the difficulty in defining which attacks should count as Klan attacks, it is impossible to get reliable numbers on how many people the Klan killed, but the number is in the several hundreds. In most cases, Klansmen killed victims execution style, either by shooting or hanging them. Klansmen shot others while they were attempting to escape. Klan groups killed some victims, particularly those who were politically connected, through ambush. Additionally, Klan groups committed some larger collective murders, such as the abduction and killing of ten freedmen in Union County, S.C., in the spring of 1871.

Freed people and white Republicans often attempted, sometimes with success, to prevent or resist Klan threats and violence. Those anticipating attack fled to nearby cities for safety or "laid out," spending the night out of doors in their fields. Others gathered friends and family, or, in South Carolina, black militiamen, to stand guard for them. At the same time, Republican leaders and local agents of the federal government gathered information about Klan activity and plans and sent it urgently to state and federal officials, in hopes of gaining protection. Klan survivors and witnesses often agreed to testify to state or federal committees, even at grave personal risk. In the face of threatened violence at election time, Republicans tried various strategies, such as approaching the polls in groups. Faced with an attack, some, who had managed to arm themselves, met approaching Klansmen with gunfire. Unarmed victims sometimes used household implements as weapons. Others attempted to reason or plea with their captors; frequently, they recognized some of their attackers and directly called upon their protection.

The federal government, convinced that local and state efforts were ineffective, took several steps to suppress the Klan, but could intervene only when Klan violence had a political nature. Congress passed a series of bills popularly referred to as the Enforcement Acts, intended to enforce the voting rights granted to freedmen under the Fifteenth Amendment. The first, passed on 31 May 1870, then strengthened and supplemented by another act passed 28 February 1871, made it a federal crime for individuals to conspire or wear disguise to deprive citizens of their constitutional rights and set up a federal mechanisms for the arrest, prosecution, and trials of accused offenders. The most controversial, popularly called the Ku Klux Force Act, passed on 20 April 1871, gave the president the authority to suspend the writ of habeas corpus and to send federal troops to areas incapable of controlling Klan violence even without the invitation of a governor.

It also made punishable by federal law several common forms of political Klan behavior and forbad Klansmen from serving on juries. President Ulysses S. Grant took limited advantage of this legislation, sending small numbers of troops to some of the hardest-hit areas. South Carolina became the focus of federal Klan enforcement: Grant suspended habeas corpus briefly in nine counties, federal marshals and troops made hundreds of arrests, and the federal district court began a high-profile series of trials of accused Klan leaders in the fall of 1871.

The Ku Klux Klan was significant in federal politics, particularly during the Johnson impeachment and in the federal elections of 1868 and 1872. The Klan first emerged to national notice during the impeachment trials, as Johnson's opponents attempted to associate him with the Klan. In the election of 1868 supporters of Ulysses S. Grant, the Republican candidate, labeled supporters of Democrat Horatio Seymour as the "Ku-Klux Democracy." Though the election of 1872 occurred after the Klan's decline, the Klan was even more central to it than to the election of 1868. Grant's supporters attempted to tie Horace Greeley, the Liberal Republican and Democratic candidate, to the Klan, claiming that a vote for Greeley was a vote for Klan resurgence. Greeley's supporters claimed that Grant was using the Klan as a "bugbear" and that Klan suppression was a pretext for unconstitutionally increasing the reach of federal power.

In the months after winning reelection, Grant stopped federal Klan arrests and trials and quietly released those dozens of men who had been committed to federal prison as Klansmen. Besides some interest surrounding the publication of Albion Tourgée's 1879 Klan-themed novel, A Fool's Errand, the Ku Klux Klan would not be significant in American social and political life, or even in cultural representation, until its 20th-century revival.

ELAINE FRANTZ PARSONS
Duquesne University

Steven Hahn, *A Nation under Our Feet: Black Political Struggles in the Rural South from Slavery to the Great Migration* (2003); Kwando Mbiassi Kinshasa, *Black Resistance to the Ku Klux Klan in the Wake of the Civil War* (2006); Scott Reynolds Nelson, *Iron Confederacies: Southern Railways, Klan Violence, and Reconstruction* (1999); Mitchell Snay, *Fenians, Freedmen, and Southern Whites: Race and Nationality in the Era of Reconstruction* (2007); Allen Trelease, *White Terror: The Ku Klux Klan Conspiracy and Southern Reconstruction* (1971); Xi Wang, *The Trial of Democracy: Black Suffrage and Northern Republicans, 1860–1910* (1997); Lou Faulkner Williams, *The Great South Carolina Ku Klux Klan Trials, 1871–1872* (1996).

Ku Klux Klan, Second (1915–1944)

The Ku Klux Klan was never more powerful than it was in the 1920s. At that time, it thrived as a nativist and racist organization, championing the rights and superiority of white Protestant Americans. Unlike the first Klan of the Reconstruction era, the second Klan was a nationwide movement. At its height, it boasted 5 million members in 4,000 local chapters across the country, although some historians contend that it never had more than one and a half million active members at any one time. The Klan's main appeal was its promise to restore what it deemed traditional values in the face of the transformations of modern society, and it was most popular in communities where it acted in support of moral reform. Klansmen opposed the social and political advancement of blacks, Jews, and Catholics, but they also virulently attacked bootleggers, drinkers, gamblers, adulterers, fornicators, and others who they believed had flouted Protestant moral codes.

Although the Klan was strongest in the Midwest, in states like Indiana and Illinois, where it peddled its slogan of "100% Americanism" to great effect, it was still in many ways a distinctly southern organization. William Simmons, a former Methodist preacher from Alabama, reestablished the Klan in an elaborate ceremony atop Stone Mountain, just outside of Atlanta, Georgia, on Thanksgiving Day in 1915. Even as the organization spread across the country, its leadership and base of operations remained in Atlanta. Moreover, Klansmen regularly engaged in rituals and rhetoric that drew on southern traditions from the Reconstruction Klan and Lost Cause mythology to enact their nationalistic agenda.

Klans throughout the country held public rallies, staged parades, and engaged in various political activities, mostly attempting to influence political leaders to adopt Klan positions. Klansmen tended to be solid, churchgoing middle and working-class men, who were concerned about the loss of traditional white, patriarchal power in the face of urbanization, immigration, black migration, feminism, and the cracking of Victorian morality. As much as they expressed contempt toward those at the bottom of the social ladder, they railed against the excesses of Wall Street and Hollywood, leading one historian to characterize their politics as a kind of "reactionary populism."

In wanting to present itself as a mainstream movement that stood for law and order, the Klan, as an organization, prohibited and disavowed acts of violence. That did not stop individual Klansmen, in full Klan regalia, from committing numerous acts of terror and violence, especially in southern states. Klansmen whipped and tortured blacks who transgressed Jim Crow racial codes, but they also targeted whites who had violated moral codes. They engaged in threats, beatings, and tarring and featherings to humiliate their victims. During the 1920s, probably more than 1,000 violent assaults took place in Texas and Oklahoma alone, and more than 100 assaults each in Florida, Georgia, and Alabama. In 1921 the *New York World* published a three-week serial exposé on the Klan, highlighting its money-making scams, its radical propaganda, and its violence. The articles led to a congressional hearing on the organization, which ended abruptly with no conclusion.

Although the Klan supported traditional gender roles, white women received their own recognition in the formation of the Women's Ku Klux Klan in 1915. Implemented as a separate organization, the Women's Ku Klux Klan bound itself to the Klan's ideals but remained independent of the men's organization. As Klanswomen, members marched in parades, organized community events, and recruited new Klan members—primarily children. As it grew in numbers and visibility, the Klan expanded to include youths. In 1923 the Klan voted to create two auxiliaries: the Junior Ku Klux Klan for adolescent boys and the Tri-K-Klub for teenage girls. The Junior Klan sought to promote the principals of the Ku Klux Klan in preparation for adult male membership. The Tri-K-Klub, under the umbrella of the Women's Ku Klux Klan, taught girls the ideals the Klan desired in wives and mothers, such as racial purity, cheerfulness, and determination.

In the late 1920s, the Klan's power began to wane and its membership declined. After the 1921 hearings, both mainstream newspapers and the black press increased their reportage of Klan violence, and the National Association for the Advancement of Colored People began its own documentation of Klan terror. In addition, a number of prominent Klan leaders were caught in embarrassing scandals, exposing the hypocrisy of the organization. Finally, the Klan's insistence that its movement was democratic and patriotic began to appear contradictory. For some, the Klan in America began to resemble the rising fascism in Europe, a perception only furthered by the increasing radicalism of Klan leaders. By 1930 the national Klan movement had gradually retreated into the South, where the economic crises of the Great Depression further weakened the organization. In

that year, it claimed barely 50,000 members. In 1944, the Internal Revenue Service presented the Second Ku Klux Klan with a bill for $685,000 in unpaid taxes. Unable to pay, the Imperial Wizard on 23 April 1944 revoked the charters and disbanded all Klaverns of the Klan.

KRIS DUROCHER
Morehead State University

AMY LOUISE WOOD
Illinois State University

Charles C. Alexander, *The Ku Klux Klan in the Southwest* (1965); Kathleen M. Blee, *Women of the Klan: Racism and Gender in the 1920s* (1991); David Chalmers, *Backfire: How the Ku Klux Klan Helped the Civil Rights Movement* (2003); Kenneth T. Jackson, *The Ku Klux Klan in the City, 1915–1930* (1967); Nancy K. MacLean, *Behind the Mask of Chivalry: The Making of the Second Ku Klux Klan* (1995); Wyn Craig Wade, *The Fiery Cross: The Ku Klux Klan in America* (1997).

Long, Huey, Assassination of

The events surrounding the assassination of former Louisiana governor and senator Huey P. Long remain controversial. Two dominant theories cloud the murder. The traditional narrative contends that a lone gunman, Carl Weiss, assassinated Long. Alternative theories hold that Weiss may not have pulled the trigger, but perhaps the bodyguards who were hired to protect the Kingfish shot him accidentally.

The traditional narrative asserts that on Sunday morning of 8 September 1935 Long's team of bodyguards drove him from his house in New Orleans to a special legislative session in Baton Rouge. That same evening Long went to the capitol building and attended the legislative session. The session ran until 9:30 P.M.; then Long walked to the corridor leading into the governor's suite, well ahead of his team of bodyguards. At that moment, Carl Weiss stepped out from a large marble pillar and fired a .38 caliber pistol toward Long's chest. Just then (before or simultaneously) several of Long's bodyguards gunned down Weiss, firing 30 shots and killing him. Long died 31 hours later, after a failed operation.

Carl Weiss was a young physician, family man, and a lover of music and art who hardly fit the typical profile of an assassin. However, he had several possible motives for murdering the Kingfish. First, Long was trying to gerrymander a political district to remove longtime political rival Judge Benjamin Pavy—the father-in-law of Weiss, who was married to his daughter, Yvonne. Also, before to the assassination, Long had arranged for the firing of Paul and Marie Pavy, Yvonne's uncle and sister. Most significant, though, is the specter of Long's reintroducing a rumor that the Pavy family had African American "blood."

In the years following Long's assassination, skeptics challenged the official reports of his assassination. There was no autopsy performed on Long, the alleged murder weapon disappeared (only to be found and analyzed in a later investigation), and records surrounding the Louisiana State Police and other institutions disappeared, as did hospital records regarding Long's brief stay before his death. Also troubling were the conflicting testimonies from witnesses, mostly among Long's bodyguards. There were so many questions and peculiarities surrounding the assignation that observers suspected either a conspiracy or a cover-up.

The controversy peaked in late 1991 and 1992. In October 1991 Professor James E. Starrs, a criminal forensic expert from George Washington University, led a team of investigators to exhume the body of Carl Weiss. Starrs gained national notoriety for work in similar, high-profile, historical killings. He also attempted to gain permission to exhume Long's body, but the family denied the request. However, Starrs's investigation netted key pieces of evidence, including the alleged murder weapon. Starrs found that Mabel Guerre Binnings, the sole survivor of Louis P. Guerre, the head of the original state team that investigated the murder, still had the weapon. Legal wrangling ensued and impelled the State of Louisiana to reopen the case. The courts finally awarded the weapon to investigators. The renewed interest in the controversy elicited a barrage of local and national media coverage.

The Starrs team released its conclusion at the 44th Annual Meeting of Forensic Sciences at the Hyatt-Regency Hotel in New Orleans on 21 February 1992. Starrs stated that "it is submitted there is significant scientific and other evidence establishing grave and pervasive doubts that Carl Austin Weiss was the person who killed Huey Long." Starrs violated a state-mandated gag order that prohibited revealing evidence surrounding the reopened case, although no contempt of court was pursued.

Four months later, Lt. Don Moreau released the conclusions of the state investigation. The probe relied on the same two pieces of evidence that the Starrs team examined: pictures of Long's blood-stained clothing and the spent round found with the weapon in Mabel Guerre Binnings's safety deposit box, believed to be the round (or one of the rounds) involved in Long's murder. Moreau's findings differed from Starrs's. Moreau stated that, "nothing we found was in conflict with the original historical theory. He further argued that if Weiss survived, he would have been arrested and convicted of the crime."

Despite new forensic evidence, neither the Starrs team nor the reopened state investigation resolved the controversy. Both groups claimed that the significant time lag in the renewed efforts to uncover the real truth of Long's assassination impeded investigators from reaching definitive conclusions. Further, both of the new investigations placed Weiss at the scene of the crime with possible motivations, but who exactly pulled the trigger remains a mystery.

CHRISTOPHER L. STACEY
Louisiana State University at Alexandria

Richard Briley III, *Death of the Kingfish! Who Did Kill Huey Long?* (1960); Alan Brinkley, *Voices of Protest: Huey Long, Father Coughlin, and the Great Depression* (1983); Hermann B. Deutsch, *The Huey Long Murder Case* (1963); Glen Jeansonne, *Huey*

at 100: Centennial Essays on Huey P. Long (1995), *Messiah of the Masses: Huey P. Long and the Great Depression* (1993); William Ivey Hair, *The Kingfish and His Realm: The Life and Times of Huey P. Long* (1991); Donald Pavey, *Accident and Deception: The Huey Long Shooting* (1999); Ed Reed, *Requiem for a Kingfish: The Strange and Unexplained Death of Huey Long* (1986); Richard White Jr., *The Reign of Huey P. Long* (2006); T. Harry Williams, *Huey Long: A Biography* (1969); David H. Zinman, *The Day Huey Long Was Shot: September 8, 1935* (1993).

Lynching Photography

Today, hundreds of lynching photographs sit in archives or have been exhibited on Web sites and in books. Mostly taken between the 1890s and 1930s, they depict hanged and, sometimes, mutilated corpses, mobs standing proudly next to their victims, or crowds of spectators surrounding the gruesome scene. Although these images represent only a fraction of the lynchings that were committed, news accounts and other pieces of evidence suggest that it was not an uncommon practice for lynchings to be documented on camera, either by local professional photographers called to the scene or members of the crowd brandishing their Kodaks. The resulting photographs were then sold from storefronts, sent as postcards to family and friends, or stored away as souvenirs. They have attracted considerable scholarly and public attention in recent years because of what they reveal about the practice of lynching. Most significantly, they stand as chilling reminders that lynching was a community-sanctioned, even celebrated, act of violence, one to be commemorated in a photograph. Indeed, although photographs of war and atrocities are not unusual, lynching photographs are striking because they were taken from the perspective of the perpetrators, not journalists or unsympathetic witnesses.

Like the practice of lynching itself, photographing a lynching was not confined to the South. A number of sensationalistic lynchings occurred in western and midwestern states and were photographed. But since the overwhelming majority of lynchings in the Jim Crow era took place in the South, most existing photographs also come from there. The more crowds and attention that a lynching drew, the more likely it was to be photographed. In some of these cases, local photographers were given prime spots to capture the mob's work on camera. But even mobs that lynched their victims out of the public eye at times documented their violence.

Lynching photographs tended to follow particular conventions, as certain poses and perspectives appear over and over again. These conventions mirrored common photographic practices that mobs and spectators would have been familiar with, such as hunting photographs. By visually associating the lynching with socially acceptable practices, the photographs would have served to sanction and normalize both the violence and the act of photographing the violence for the public. Images of lynching also tended to reflect and thus reinforce narrative justifications for lynching, which posited that the violence was a necessary defense against black criminality. Like prolynching narratives, photographs tended to depict the white mob not in the midst of its fury, but as orderly and restrained, in sharp contrast to the "black beast" it hunted and subdued. In this sense, they provided visual force to white supremacist ideology.

Although lynching photographs were meant to be seen and circulated, only rarely did local or national media outlets publish them. When they did appear in the press, they elicited strong public reaction. White readers found them to be unseemly and potentially incendiary. In 1908 the U.S. Post Office banned the distribution of material that depicted lynchings for this same reason. Civil rights activists and the black-run press, however, found lynching photographs to be powerful tools in their efforts to expose the violence to a disbelieving public and advocate for antilynching legislation. Ida B. Wells published a postcard from an 1891 lynching in Clanton, Ala., in her 1894 antilynching pamphlet, *A Red Record*. And soon after its founding in 1909, the National Association for the Advancement of Colored People began collecting lynching photographs to publish in its magazine, the *Crisis*, and on political flyers, ads, and pamphlets.

Through the 1920s and 1930s, as print technologies developed and as efforts to pass federal antilynching legislation heated up, the black press reprinted photographs with increasing frequency. At this point, the national media, such as *Time* and *Life* magazines, selectively published some photographs, in conjunction with stories about anti-lynching legislation. In these contexts, lynching photographs stood as visual evidence no longer of white superiority but of white barbarism. Activists, in this respect, were able to shift the message of these images quite effectively. Lynching came to be seen as a shameful practice, out of step with American ideals and modern notions of justice. Racial violence persisted in the South but not with the same kind of public display or bravado.

Lynching photographs continue to serve as potent symbols of Jim Crow oppression and its damaging effects. They garnered renewed national attention in 2001 with the publication of *Without Sanctuary*, which drew from Atlanta antique collector James Allen's extensive collection of lynching photographs. Subsequent exhibits of this collection in various cities around the country drew large crowds and sparked some debate over the most appropriate ways to exhibit this sensitive material.

AMY LOUISE WOOD
Illinois State University

Dora Apel, *American Quarterly* (September 2003), *Imagery of Lynching: Black Men, White Women, and the Mob* (2004); Dora Apel and Shawn Michelle Smith, *Lynching Photographs* (2007); Grace Elizabeth Hale, *Making Whiteness: The Culture of Segregation in the South, 1890–1940* (1998); Amy Louise Wood, *Lynching and Spectacle: Witnessing Racial Violence in America, 1890–1940* (2009).

Night Riders

If Reconstruction brought a twinkle of progressive thought to the South, it also bred fiery resentment and rabid emotions. Slavery had been demolished, and, overnight, former plantation owners were without labor. A depressed, war-weary southern economy now had an even larger labor force in which poor whites competed for jobs with newly freed blacks. Out of this climate hatred sprouted, and in southern communities throughout the region night riders and Klansmen rose up in efforts to psychologically and physically intimidate blacks.

In *Night Riders in Black Folk History*, Gladys-Marie Fry discusses the function of the night rider or "Ku Klux" in controlling blacks before and after the Civil War. This form of intimidation was used before the Civil War to discourage unauthorized movement, to guard against slave insurrections, and, after the war, to repeatedly let blacks know their behavioral boundaries. Black oral history is rich with stories of evil white men joining together to incite the fears of black families and entire towns. Night rider incidents are stored in the minds of elderly blacks, and although many do not recall the chronological specifics of the events, they well remember acts of intimidation, often having heard tales from older family or community members.

Night riders were not unique to Reconstruction. Although the practice flourished then, black folk history shows that night-riding existed throughout slavery. The Reconstruction Ku Klux Klan was probably a modern version of the antebellum patrol system. The patrols or "paterollers" set out to check the passes of the slaves, to maintain curfew, and to physically abuse rule breakers. Folklorist William Lynwood Montell writes that slave owners in the Kettle Creek area of Tennessee relied on the patrol system because they had trouble keeping slaves on the plantation.

Though the stereotype of a masked, robed Klansman was in many cases a true image, many night riders often traveled without the disguise of a white garment. In the Cumberland plateau community of Free Hill, Tenn., not one resident remembers a Ku Klux disguise or mask; rather, as one resident explained, "these were people that they knew, they knew from down in town." The absence of a mask or hood, however, did not mean that there was no attempt to disguise. Groups of men always came at night and assumed the community would flee out of fear. For them, night itself was some disguise, and there was little risk of recognition.

TOM RANKIN
Duke University

Gladys-Marie Fry, *Night Riders in Black Folk History* (1975); William Lynwood Montell, *The Saga of Coe Ridge: A Study in Oral History* (1970); Elizabeth Peterson and Tom Rankin, *Free Hill: A Sound Portrait of a Rural Afro-American Community* (Tennessee Folklore Society recording, 1985).

Orangeburg (South Carolina) Massacre (1968)

Violence against blacks in the South erupted on 8 February 1968 when a fusillade of gunfire by state highway patrolmen killed three students and wounded 27 others on the campus of South Carolina State College at Orangeburg. The killings, known in civil rights

circles as the "Orangeburg massacre," attracted little national attention at the time—despite the fact that the Orangeburg massacre was the first time students on an American college campus had been slain by law enforcement officers. Some historians have suggested that the subsequent lack of media attention was a result of the victims being black and the case of segregation being a localized event. Others suggest that the violence of the Vietnam War had desensitized the American public to violence. In 1970 historian Dave Nolan put forth another explanation, writing that had the shooting happened "earlier, there might have been a public outcry. But this was 1968, not 1964, and in the intervening years civil rights demonstrations had come to be seen as 'riots'—and most whites seemed to feel that it was justified to put them down as brutally as possible."

The shooting occurred on the third night of confrontations that had begun when students at the predominantly black college protested the segregation policy of the town's only bowling alley, five blocks from the campus. Although South Carolina governor Robert E. McNair called the event "one of the saddest days in the history of South Carolina," he blamed the circumstances that led to shooting on "black power advocates" and inaccurately claimed that the officers had responded to gunfire in self-defense. Over a year later, nine South Carolina state troopers involved in the shooting were tried in federal court for use of excessive force but were acquitted.

The episode preceded by more than

two years an event that became a cause célèbre—the slaying of four white Kent State University students by National Guardsmen in May 1970. A few days later in that same month, Jackson, Miss., city police and state highway patrolmen opened fire on protesting black students at Jackson State University (then Jackson State College), killing two students. A President's Commission on Campus Unrest investigated the Kent State and Jackson State shootings, but its historical section failed to mention the killings two years earlier at Orangeburg.

In 1999 a state historical marker about the Orangeburg Massacre was erected on the South Carolina State campus. In 2003, Gov. Mark Sanford issued a statement saying, "I think it's appropriate to tell the African American community in South Carolina that we don't just regret what happened in Orangeburg 35 years ago—we apologize for it."

JACK BASS
University of South Carolina

Jack Bass, *Nieman Reports* (Fall 2003); Jack Nelson and Jack Bass, *The Orangeburg Massacre* (1970); Bestor Cram, director, *Scarred Justice: The Orangeburg Massacre, 1968* (film, 2009).

Parchman (Mississippi State Penitentiary)

The intervention of the convict lease system stalemated the penitentiary movement in the postbellum South. Because convicts, most of whom were black, were leased, southern states stopped maintaining existing prisons, and penitentiaries became "mere shells of buildings, depositories for the old,

the sick and the most dangerous." The state of Mississippi outlawed convict lease (though not the equally infamous chain gang) by constitutional amendment in 1890 and sought institutional alternatives for using convict labor that would not jeopardize the interests of free labor. Legislators authorized the purchase of several tracts of land on which penal farms were erected to provide convicts with "healthful agricultural labor" and the state with significant profit.

The largest of these farms was established at the turn of the 20th century on some 13,000 acres purchased from a Sunflower County planter, James Parchman. When folksong collector John Lomax visited Parchman in the 1930s, more than 2,000 inmates tilled 17,000 acres of rich Delta land, channeling large sums into the state treasury. Lomax found his blues and ballad recording hindered by the length of convict workdays and noted that part of the farm's profit came from the "economies" practiced: labor from 4:00 A.M. until dark and a total lack of mechanization. Former inmate Bukka White's "Parchman Farm Blues" describes the long workdays: "We go to work in the morning, just at the dawn of day. / Just at the setting of the sun—that's when the work is done."

John Lomax's son Alan also visited Parchman several times to make recordings, and in 1959 he recorded woodchopping prisoners led by James Carter in a work song called "Po' Lazarus." The recording became the opening track in the film *O Brother, Where Art Thou?* (2000), whose main characters

Camp B, Mississippi State Penitentiary, more commonly known as Parchman or
Parchman Farm, 1975 (William R. Ferris Collection, Southern Folklife Collection,
Wilson Library, University of North Carolina at Chapel Hill)

escape from Parchman. In 1996 a film adaptation of John Grisham's novel *The Chamber* was set and filmed at Parchman, and in 1999 Eddie Murphy and Martin Lawrence starred as two Parchman inmates wrongfully convicted and given life sentences in *Life*.

William Faulkner's character Mink Snopes is imprisoned at Parchman in *The Mansion*, which once names the prison "destination doom." A 1968 regional prison report confirmed the gloomy conditions at Parchman. After outlining conditions at Parchman and penitentiaries in Arkansas and Louisiana, the report concluded that "the three states put together could not out of presently available funds and facilities provide the components of one prison which would meet minimum national standards." Parchman's brutality and corruption were not unique. Angola in Louisiana was also

infamous, but by the 1960s Parchman had become legendary. Mose Allison's "Parchman Farm" suggests the harsh conditions working inmates faced: "I'm putting that cotton in an eleven-foot sack . . . with a twelve-gauge shotgun at my back." Beatings were routinely administered for infractions ranging from failure to address an officer properly to attempted escape. Inmates employed as armed guards — 170 out of a total force of 210 guards as late as 1968 — abused and often killed fellow prisoners.

In 1971 documented instances of brutality against several hundred incarcerated civil rights workers led to sweeping changes. Within three years, the trusty system was abolished; inadequate, segregated facilities were abandoned; and vocational training was implemented. Conditions improved only temporarily, however. In 2002 the American Civil Liberties Union filed charges against Parchman for inhumane treatment, especially in its Unit 32 (Death Row). Calls for reform culminated in June 2010 with a deal to close Unit 32 and eventually transfer its inmates to other facilities.

As of September 2010, 3,454 inmates were held at Parchman Penitentiary. It is still Mississippi's only maximum-security prison, and it still implements inmate work programs. Its Agricultural Enterprises program grows fruits, grains, and vegetables and raises poultry for the prison's food services, and the Mississippi Prison Industry manufactures textile, metal, and wood products while teaching inmates nonagricultural vocational skills. Adult education independent study programs are offered, as well as a religious education program, in which inmates can earn a bachelor's degree in Christian ministry from New Orleans Baptist Theological Seminary. Parchman's religious education program began in 2004, and in 2009, 28 inmates graduated with B.A. degrees. Since 1949, inmates have published a magazine called *Inside World*, which contains penitentiary news, inmate questions to wardens and commissioners, intercamp sports reports, artwork and cartoons, poetry, and editorial sections about both penal and "outside world" issues. Apartments for family and conjugal visiting are still maintained at Parchman; the practice of allowing conjugal visiting in prisons was first implemented in Mississippi at Parchman in 1918.

Notable Parchman inmates have included bluesmen Bukka White, Son House, and Vernon Presley, Elvis Presley's father. After a young B. B. King

visited his uncle, Bukka White, at Parchman, he conveyed a sense of fear that is, despite Parchman's reforms, still associated with the prison: "After that . . . I knew I wanted to stay far away from the place."

ELIZABETH M. MAKOWSKI
MARY AMELIA TAYLOR
University of Mississippi

Donald Cabana, *Death at Midnight: The Confession of an Executioner* (1996); L. C. Dorsey, *Cold Steel* (1982); William Ferris, *New Journal* (25 January 1973), *Give My Poor Heart Ease: Voices of the Mississippi Blues* (2009); Christopher Hensley, Sandra Rutland, and Phyllis Gray-Ray, *American Journal of Criminal Justice* (2000); Columbus Hopper, *Sex in Prison: The Mississippi Experiment with Conjugal Visiting* (1969); Marvin Hutson, "Mississippi's State Penal System" (M.A. thesis, University of Mississippi, 1939); Alan Lomax, *The Land Where the Blues Began* (1993); John A. Lomax, *Adventures of a Ballad Hunter* (1947); Roy Reed, *New York Times* (27 January 1973); David M. Oshinsky, *Worse than Slavery: Parchman Farm and the Ordeal of Jim Crow Justice* (1997); Dunbar Rowland, *Mississippi* (1907); Southern Regional Council, *The Delta Prisons: Punishment for Profit* (1968); W. B. Taylor, *Down on Parchman Farm: The Great Prison in the Mississippi Delta* (1999); Margaret F. Winter and Stephen Hanlon, *Litigation* (Fall 2008); www.mdoc.state.ms.us.

Redfield, H. V.

(1845–1881) JOURNALIST.

H. V. Redfield's *Homicide, North and South* was the most careful and extensive study of the differences in regional homicide rates produced in the 19th century. Although the work of a little-known amateur, it is an outstanding example of the American social science of the period.

Horace Victor Eugene Redfield was born about 1845 in Erie County, N.Y., into a family with Vermont origins. However, after his father's early death, he accompanied his mother to the South and in 1860 was residing in Jasper, Marion County, Tenn. A journalist in adult life, he wrote no other known book. Redfield died in 1881 in Washington, D.C., where he had been based for several years as correspondent for the *Cincinnati Commercial*. In the preface to *Homicide*, he emphasized his southern upbringing and claimed to have spent most of his life in the South. The author went out of his way to praise southern life and the treatment he had received there. He realized that many would view his work as an attack on the South, but he wished that it could be viewed as friendly criticism that might lead to reform.

Redfield began his book by noting that the rural rates for homicide in England, New England, and the Upper Midwest were very similar, but that rates for the South were much higher than for any civilized country in at least the previous two centuries. He tried to document this remarkable fact and inquire into its causes. He traveled widely throughout the country, collecting data from official sources where it was available (primarily in the North) and developing complete newspaper files where this was possible. He compared rates in the late 1860s and 1870s for "old states" North and South and for frontier states, finding that South Carolina's were as many times greater than New England's as Texas's rates were greater than Minnesota's. In both cases he estimated well over 10 times as many murders per 100,000 population in the South as in the North. He pointed out that Texas was populated largely from the Old South and Minnesota from the North. By comparing homicide rates and population origins in Ohio, Indiana, and Illinois, he demonstrated that the line between North and South ran through these states, whereas Iowa more clearly belonged to the North.

Redfield saw several patterns in southern homicide. Drunken brawls might not be too different from those in the North, yet they more often led to murders, both because of the attitudes of those involved and the general practice of carrying weapons. Murder often occurred to redress insult to personal honor or because of a tough's desire to show off. Groups, whether gangs or clans, often attacked rival groups out of animosity or for political ends. Feuds as such played less of a part in his analysis than one might expect, given his familiarity with Kentucky.

Although very close to the Civil War, he could not see the war as a major cause of southern patterns that greatly antedated it. He saw the most general cause of southern violence as a lack of regard for human life. He thought an exaggerated sense of honor contributed to the high rates of homicide, as did the unnecessary carrying of weapons, particularly concealed weapons. In many rural areas he pointed out that a lone law officer was often powerless or afraid to intervene. Even if caught, the murderer would seldom be convicted or would be given a light sentence. Redfield cited many cases illustrating the difficulty of getting convictions in the South. Convictions were seldom achieved for several reasons: the jurors did not take killing as seriously as in the North, they would be more likely to accept the reasons justifying the killing than would northern jurors, the jurors knew they might themselves later be involved in murder and would not want to meet a juror related to a person they had helped convict, and they feared imminent retaliation by relatives of the murderer should they convict.

A great deal has changed since Redfield's study. In his time, for instance, he found whites more involved in murder than blacks. (This may have been because of the availability of weapons, or simply because he did not have sufficient information on black homicide.) Redfield may well have contributed to the amelioration of the situation as he found it, but lethal violence still casts a shadow over southern culture and thus the nation as a whole.

RAYMOND D. GASTIL
Freedom House

H. V. Redfield, *Homicide, North and South: Being a Comparative View of Crime against the Person in Several Parts of the United States* (1880); J. H. Redfield, *Genealogical History of the Redfield Family* (1860); *New York Times* (18 November 1881).

Regulator Movement

The Regulator movement (1766–71) was a farmer's reform movement in the North Carolina Piedmont. It aimed to hold corrupt government officials accountable and to create greater economic and political democracy in the area. At the movement's height, some 5,000 to 6,000 men, the great majority of free Piedmont males, took part in it. Regulators engaged in a variety of activities, some of them legal and some of them extralegal. Early in 1771, North Carolina's Gov. William Tryon defeated Piedmont farmers in a military battle, ending the Regulation.

The movement began in 1766 when a group of farmers started the Sandy Creek Association, named after the creek where most of the leaders lived. Leader and spokesman was Herman Husband, a Quaker who had moved from Cecil County, Md., and whose religiously inspired ideas about social justice became tremendously influential among Piedmont farmers. Early in 1768 members of the Sandy Creek Association joined with other reform-minded farmers. They called themselves "Regulators" — a name that indicated that they intended to "regulate" and reform government abuse.

Regulator grievances included difficulties in obtaining clear deeds to land, high legal costs and high taxes, the embezzlement of tax moneys, fee grabbing on the part of court officers, and the collusion between creditors and public officials. Initially farmers tried peaceful means of redress — they petitioned the governor and the Assembly, took local officials to court, and entered local elections.

While the governor and Assembly were unsympathetic and did not succeed in getting corrupt officials convicted, the Regulators were surprisingly successful in the elections. They were outnumbered in the legislature, however, so their calls for a land bank, anti-speculation laws, fair debt collection laws, court reform, more equitable taxation, secret ballots in elections, the right to instruct their representatives, and the disestablishment of the Anglican Church went unheeded.

When Regulators repeatedly tried such legal measures without results, they grew exasperated and began to resort to extralegal measures. They refused to pay taxes until they could be assured their money would not be embezzled, they repossessed property seized for public sale to satisfy debts and taxes, and they closed courts to prevent miscarriages of justice. They urged people to boycott the courts and resort to mediation.

Moreover, in September 1770 Regulators disrupted the Superior Court in Hillsborough, beat up a few lawyers and merchants, and destroyed the house of the most hated official in the Piedmont. The provincial authorities retaliated forcefully. The Assembly passed a sweeping Riot Act that gave Gov. William Tryon the authority and funds he needed to raise the militia and to march against the Regulators.

On 16 May 1771 about 1,100 militiamen confronted some 2,000 to 3,000 farmers on a field near Alamance Creek. The army was top-heavy with officers, many of them leading eastern citizens who would in just a few short years lead the colony into independence. Two hours after the first shot was fired, 17 to 20 farmers were dead, along with 9 militiamen. More than 150 men on both

sides were wounded. The next day, the governor ordered one Regulator hanged on the spot without benefit of trial. He then undertook a punitive march through the backcountry, burning fields, requisitioning produce and supplies, and forcing more than 6,400 men to take an oath of loyalty to the king. After a hasty trial, six more Regulators were hanged in Hillsborough in June. Some of the best-known Regulator leaders were outlawed and fled the province.

As a result of the violence and repression, the Regulation as an organized movement was crushed by the summer of 1771, though individually many people remained defiant and continued to support their leaders. Hundreds of families left the Piedmont in bitterness. Despite formidable odds, however, the Regulator dream of farmer independence and economic democracy persisted in pockets of the South, throughout the 19th century and beyond.

MARJOLEINE KARS
University of Maryland,
Baltimore County

A. Roger Ekirch, *"Poor Carolina": Politics and Society in Colonial North Carolina, 1729–1776* (1981); Marjoleine Kars, *Breaking Loose Together: The Regulator Rebellion in Pre-revolutionary North Carolina* (2002); William S. Powell, James K. Huhta, and Thomas J. Farnham, eds., *The Regulators in North Carolina: A Documentary History, 1759–1776* (1971).

Rosewood (Florida) Incident (1923)

Florida did not escape the racial violence of the 1920s. Blacks who lived in the small, mostly African American community of Rosewood, located in north-central Florida near Cedar Key, endured a week of violence in January 1923, which resulted in the loss of property and lives. Two very different versions of what led to the week of death and destruction exist.

On Monday morning, 1 January 1923, a white woman, Fannie Taylor, who lived in Sumner, accused an unidentified black man of attacking her. Although the wife and mother did not claim that she had been sexually assaulted, her husband and other white men assumed that she had been and began a search for the attacker. Sarah Carrier, of Rosewood, was at the Taylor home that morning to do laundry, though, and the account that emerges from the black community differs. That version claims that Fannie Taylor's white lover had beaten her, and she concocted the story of being assaulted by a black man to explain her bruises to her husband.

The search for the reputed black attacker led the mob to Rosewood, approximately three miles east of Sumner. By Monday afternoon, one black man, Aaron Carrier, was rushed out of the area by the sheriff to prevent angry whites from harming him, but another black man, Sam Carter, was killed. Carter had supposedly befriended Taylor's attacker, and for this he was tortured and murdered. Carter's body was found on Tuesday, 2 January.

Armed whites began congregating in Sumner and on Thursday night, 4 January, attacked the Carrier home, where family members had gathered for safety. When the shooting ended,

Sarah Carrier and her 32-year-old son, Sylvester, were dead, as were two white men, Henry Andrews and C. P. Wilkerson. The cold, wet swamps soon provided protection for the black residents of Rosewood, who could hear the gunshots and see the flames as angry whites torched several buildings, including a church, that night. Lexie Gordon, a 50-year-old black woman, too ill to join her friends and neighbors in the swamps, was shot and killed when she ran out of her burning house.

Sheriff Bob Walkers informed Gov. Cary Hardee on Friday, 5 January, that everything was under control, although a group of white men on their way to Rosewood murdered Mingo Williams, a black man with no connection to Rosewood or the alleged attack on Fannie Taylor. Also on Friday, 5 January, James Carrier, the son and brother of the Carriers who were killed the night before, was forced to dig his own grave, before being killed by whites. On Saturday, 6 January, a train arrived to evacuate the women and children still hiding in the swamps. They were taken to Gainesville, where the black community provided refuge. Whites, on Sunday, 7 January, returned to Rosewood to finish the burning they had begun on Thursday night.

A grand jury appointed to investigate the incident at Rosewood found "insufficient evidence" to prosecute; thus no one was ever charged with the murders of the six black men and women, the killing of the two white men, the attack on Fannie Taylor, or the theft and arson that occurred at Rosewood. The lack of action by the state of Florida, coupled with fear and silence buried what happened the first week of 1923 in Levy County, Fla.

Though the incident attracted little national attention when it took place in 1923, it garnered national and international press in 1993 and 1994 when survivors and their descendants filed a claims bill in the Florida legislature. The law firm of Holland and Knight represented the claimants who sought $7.2 million in damages. The Florida legislature passed the Rosewood Compensation bill in April 1994, which provided $150,000 to each of the nine survivors, compensation for those who could demonstrate property loss, and a state university scholarship fund for the families and the descendants of Rosewood residents. Gov. Lawton Chiles signed the approximately $2.1 million compensation measure on 4 May 1994. Gov. Jeb Bush dedicated a Historical Marker at Rosewood in June 2004. Florida became the first state to acknowledge that its officials failed to protect its black citizens and to award compensation.

MAXINE D. JONES
Florida State University

Maxine D. Jones, *Florida Historical Quarterly* (Fall 1997); Maxine D. Jones, with David Colburn, Tom Dye, Larry E. Rivers, and William W. Rogers, "A Documented History of the Incident Which Occurred at Rosewood, Florida, January 1923," commissioned by the Florida Legislature (December 1993); Michael D'Orso, *Like Judgement Day: The Ruin and Redemption of a Town Called Rosewood* (1996).

Scottsboro Case

The "Scottsboro case" was the cause célèbre of American race relations in the 1930s. Touching on both the North's outrage at southern racism and the South's defensiveness about northern claims of moral superiority, this trial of nine black youths for rape in Scottsboro, Ala., reminded the nation of its failure to reconcile its image as the world's leading democracy with the squalid reality of bigotry and repression daily faced by its black citizens.

On 25 March 1931 the deputy sheriff of Jackson County, Ala., reacting to reports of a fight among "hobos" on a Southern Railway freight bound for Memphis, stopped the train at Paint Rock, Ala., and arrested nine black youths, jailing them at the county seat of Scottsboro. The deputy also removed several white hobos from the train, including two white women. Minutes later, the women accused the blacks of rape, and only courageous action by the Jackson County sheriff saved the blacks from a lynching. The first rape trial took place in Scottsboro just three weeks later, and despite the trumped-up nature of the charges, the jury convicted eight of the nine and sentenced them to death.

The severity of the youths' sentences galvanized public opinion throughout America. When an appellate court overturned the verdicts, the state of Alabama immediately launched a second prosecution of the "Scottsboro boys" in 1933. During the second trial the International Labor Defense, an organization closely aligned with the Communist Party, defended the youths, and the case became front-page news. Five years of legal maneuvering followed in both the state and federal courts. In 1937 defense attorneys and the prosecution finally reached a compromise, which freed four of the defendants while sentencing the others to long prison terms. Not until 1950 did the last of the Scottsboro boys emerge from the Alabama prisons. For many southerners, the Scottsboro case marked a low point in 20th-century race relations because it starkly revealed white southerners' oppression of blacks.

CARROLL VAN WEST
Center for Historic Preservation
Middle Tennessee State University

Dan T. Carter, *Scottsboro: A Tragedy of the American South* (1969); James E. Goodman, *Stories of Scottsboro* (1994); Kwando Mbiassi Kinshasa, *The Man from Scottsboro: Clarence Norris and the Infamous 1931 Alabama Rape Trial, in His Own Words* (2002).

Sumner-Brooks Affair

On 22 May 1856 one of the most egregious acts in the history of the United States Senate ensued when South Carolina representative Preston Brooks assaulted Massachusetts senator Charles Sumner. Sumner, a Republican and abolitionist, had given an impassioned speech on the floor of Congress three days before the beating. The speech, "Crimes against Kansas," was a vehement objection to and condemnation of the Kansas-Nebraska Act and its authors. The act, passed in 1854, allowed states to vote on the issue of slavery regardless of whether they were above the 36 degrees 30 minutes latitude — a boundary previously established by the Missouri Compromise of 1820.

Northern Republicans, who wished to prohibit slave labor in new territories, scrambled to create a more fiery objection to the issue. It was with a new sense of urgency that Sumner was chosen to write and orate this highly controversial speech. Sumner had delivered the speech previously at private venues; many of the proslavery southern Democrats had read the speech and objected to it being read in Congress.

On the floor of Congress, Sumner singled out Illinois senator Stephen A. Douglas of Illinois and Andrew Butler of South Carolina as the conspirators of the Kansas-Nebraska Act. Sexualizing the proslavery position, Sumner declared that Butler had "chosen a mistress to whom he has made his vows, and who, though ugly to others, is always lovely to him — though polluted in the sight of the world, is chaste in his sight. I mean the harlot slavery." This innuendo enraged Preston Brooks, a representative of South Carolina and relative to Butler, who saw Sumner's claim as a challenge to Butler's, and by extension, his family's honor. Brooks entered the Senate chamber two days after the speech holding a short cane with a hard metal handle. Before Sumner could acknowledge his presence, Brooks struck him in the head with the cane. As Sumner feebly tried to protect himself, Brooks continued the bombardment upon his skull until the cane finally shattered against it.

In this incident, politics collide with southern values of masculine honor. In issuing a caning Brooks trampled both Sumner's body and his honor. But the caning also signaled that Brooks did not consider Sumner a gentleman. Had he viewed him as an equal, Brooks would have challenged Sumner to a duel. Canings, however, were issued to those of lower social classes and therefore served as the greatest of indignities.

The event would serve as a rallying cry for both sides of the slavery issue heading into the Civil War. Brooks, after resigning under censure, would be re-elected immediately and become celebrated as a defender of southern honor. Sumner, after taking more than a year to recover, saw his political career revitalized after his near martyrdom.

CASEY D. GAWTHROP
Illinois State University

David Donald, *Charles Sumner and the Rights of Man* (1970); Michael D Pierson, *New England Quarterly* (December 1995); Manisha Sinha, *Journal of the Early Republic* (Summer 2003); Charles Sumner, *The Works of Charles Sumner* (1870); William Welch, *New England Quarterly* (June 1992).

Texas Rangers

When the first English-speaking colonists moved into Mexican Texas, they brought their own customs, social values, laws, and officials. Among these were the Rangers.

Since the beginnings of the Anglos' westward drive—in the case of Texas settlers, generally through the South—armed, mounted men ranged the line of advancing homesteads to protect them from Indians and outlaws. These men were usually civilians locally paid, armed with their own guns, and not in uniform.

Rangers may have had their origin hundreds of years ago in English estates in the role of protectors of their employers' lands, patrolling or ranging at will. Once across an ocean and on the southern frontier, they came to deal with whatever trouble could not be appropriately solved by local police, sheriffs, or the army. Rangers were never intended as a substitute for either the police or the army. They were volunteer, but, unlike local lawmen, they were willing to pursue their foe as far as was necessary and were much more mobile than regular army detachments. They would fight on their opponents' terms and settle trouble as they saw it without the delays of formal legal process.

When Stephen F. Austin's Texas colony was threatened by Indian attacks in 1823, he called out a company of rangers for protection. They were not the first such men in the field, but they were probably the first officially called Rangers.

For more than 40 years, Ranger units in Texas were temporary, raised when necessary, dismissed when not needed. They were called "Rangers," "spies," "volunteer companies," "Corps of Rangers," and "Ranging Companies." Later the term Texas Rangers was commonly used, as in 1866 legislative finance bills.

The duties of the Rangers varied with the times. First, they opposed small groups of hostile Indians. When the Republic of Texas was established in 1836, sporadic conflict between Mexico and Texas continued. The Rangers then faced two enemies, Indians and Mexicans. For a dozen years Rangers were irregular fighting units, riding as scouts, guerrillas, and cavalry support for regular troops. Some groups became virtual border guards on the Rio Grande between Texas and Mexico. Others ranged the northwest frontier of Texas in pursuit of Indians. In time, the Indians were driven from Texas, and the Rio Grande—with exceptions—became a stable, recognized international border.

The next Ranger opponent was the outlaw. Rangers turned to the role of peace officers, serving somewhat as a state police force, though never that in name. They regulated cattle rustling, fence cutting, mob violence—any breach of the law that was too widespread or too violent for local officers.

Of debatable efficiency against Indians, Rangers were demonstrably effective against outlaws. They established a lasting reputation for quick striking power over a vast area. To the Anglo businessman and settler, the Ranger meant courage, peacekeeping, and frontier resourcefulness. To his opponents, he represented unhesitating violence, unrelenting pursuit, and a willingness to use any means, including firepower, to enforce the law.

Over the years, Rangers established a standard of personal bravery. The claim that only one Ranger was necessary to quell any riot was certainly myth, but individual acts of courage supported the belief that it just might be true. The Rangers have also attracted considerable criticism. They have been accused of brutality, racism, and illegal arrest. In recent years, Mexican Americans have been especially critical of the Rangers, seeing them as an authoritarian force used against minorities. Rangers have been called strikebreakers and paid assassins. But they have more supporters than critics, as their continued service indicates. The most common feeling is that "as long as there is a state of Texas, there will be Rangers."

Established as a permanent service in 1874, the Rangers were authorized by the Texas legislature to enlist 450 men. Temporary enlistments in earlier years had risen as high as a thousand. The number of Rangers has since varied from a low of about 20 in 1900 to 94 in 1982.

For many years the Texas Rangers served the state directly under the governor and an adjutant general. In 1935 the service became a division of the Texas Department of Public Safety. Today they are charged with suppressing riots and insurrections, apprehending fugitives, assisting peace officers anywhere in the state, and dealing with major crime on their own initiative.

JOHN L. DAVIS
Institute of Texas Cultures

John L. Davis, *The Texas Rangers, Their First 150 Years* (1975); James B. Gillett, *Six Years with the Texas Rangers* (1921); Ben H. Procter, *Just One Riot: Episodes of Texas Rangers in the 20th Century* (1991); Walter Prescott Webb, ed., *The Handbook of Texas* (1952), *The Texas Rangers* (1935).

Till, Emmett

(1941–1955) LYNCHING VICTIM.
On the evening of 24 August 1955, 14-year-old Emmett Louis Till walked into a grocery store in the hamlet of Money, Miss. Young Till, Chicago born and bred, had been in the Deep

South for three days. Before letting her son board the train for Mississippi, his mother, Mamie Till Bradley, had warned him to take care around southern whites, and her words would prove prophetic. Exactly what happened that evening in the grocery store is hard to determine. According to Till's cousins and other eyewitnesses, the young boy from Chicago entered the store intent on making a simple purchase. Other accounts, hotly contested but highly influential, suggest that Till had been boasting of his friendships with white people up North and was dared to go into the grocery to talk to Carolyn Bryant, the 21-year-old white woman working the cash register. Whatever the reason, something occurred between the young black boy and the older white woman, who was clearly flustered by the exchange, and after leaving the store, Till let out a wolf whistle in her direction. Till's cousins immediately perceived the danger, and they rushed him into their car and sped away.

For several days, nothing happened. Then, around 2:30 A.M. on Sunday, 28 August, Roy Bryant (Carolyn's husband) and his half brother J. W. Milam arrived at the home where Till was staying. Demanding to see the boy from Chicago, the two armed men barged into the home and rousted Till from bed. What happened over the next few hours is difficult to discern. In their post-trial confession to journalist William Bradford Huie, Bryant and Milam claim to have acted alone that evening. The two men insisted that they wanted only to scare Till. However, as the night wore on, Till would not stop

bragging about his white girlfriends back in Chicago, so the two men had no choice but to kill him. Against this self-serving and highly unreliable account, other witnesses provide evidence to suggest that multiple men were involved in the murder. The trial testimony of one such witness locates several men, including Milam, at a nearby plantation the morning after the kidnapping. According to this account, Till was taken to a shed on this plantation, where he was beaten, tortured, and shot in the head. His body was then tossed into the back of Milam's pickup truck, weighted with a gin fan, and thrown into the Tallahatchie River.

When Till's corpse surfaced three days later, the arrest, trial, and eventual acquittal of his murderers became one of the most sensational news stories of the century. Many factors made this so, but perhaps none was more influential than Mamie Till Bradley's decision to host a four-day, open-casket viewing of her son's corpse. Warned that the state of Mississippi was planning to bury her son down South, she demanded that his body be returned to Chicago, and wanting the whole world to see what had been done to her son, she unsealed his casket. The viewing was attended by thousands of Chicagoans, and black newspapers around the country published gruesome pictures of her son's decomposed and disfigured face (which had been beaten so badly that it had to be stitched back together).

Not surprisingly, when the trial opened in late September nearly 100 journalists and photographers, some from as far away as Europe, descended upon Mississippi. In addition, all three national news networks assigned correspondents to the case, and each evening those networks rushed footage back to their studios for immediate broadcast. All of this media attention, however, could not ensure justice. After a swift five-day trial, and an even swifter 67 minutes of deliberation, the all-white jury, against all reasonable evidence, acquitted the two defendants. The national and international outrage in response to this verdict was heightened three months later when *Look* magazine published the murderers' confession. Protected from double jeopardy and confident that they had done nothing wrong, Bryant and Milam sold their story for approximately $4,000 and were never brought to justice.

The lynching of Emmett Till and the brazen acquittal of his murderers energized a generation of civil rights activists and helped to ignite the black freedom struggle of the 1950s and 1960s. Although he found no justice in his day, his story resonates in our cultural memory and shapes the way we talk about race and violence in America.

CHRISTOPHER METRESS
Samford University

Keith Beauchamp, director, *The Untold Story of Emmett Louis Till* (2004, documentary film); Christopher Metress, ed., *The Lynching of Emmett Till: A Documentary Narrative* (2002); Mamie Till-Mobley, *Death of Innocence: The Story of the Hate Crime That Changed America* (2003); Stanley Nelson, director, *The Murder of Emmett Till* (2003, documentary film); Harriet Pollack and Christopher Metress, ed., *Emmett Till in Literary Memory and Imagination*; Stephen J. Whitfield, *A Death in the Delta* (1981); Simeon Wright and Herb Boyd, *Simeon's Story: An Eyewitness Account of the Kidnapping of Emmett Till* (2010).

Trail of Tears

In 1838 the U.S. government uprooted some 13,000 Cherokee Indians from their land east of the Mississippi River and forced them westward into the Oklahoma territory. The 1,000-mile route they took to Oklahoma is called the Trail of Tears because of the hardships of weather, disease, and starvation that accompanied the Native Americans.

The forced migration along the Trail of Tears was a dismal journey, much of which took place in the middle of a harsh winter. Eyewitness accounts by missionaries, soldiers, government officials, and the uprooted Indians themselves describe how natives marched and suffered for hundreds of miles before reaching Oklahoma. Thousands of Native Americans died on the trip, which took them from north Georgia through middle Tennessee, southern Kentucky, and Missouri, and into present-day Oklahoma. The trip itself was only part of the harrowing experience the Indians endured in this stage of the removal. Federal troops held as many as 15,000 Cherokees in detention camps before the trip. Many of the detainees died of starvation or disease while in the camps.

The Trail of Tears has become a symbol for the historic oppression of Native Americans by whites, of which the forced removal of Indians to the west between 1820 and 1840 is only a part. Many southern Indians were tricked with unfamiliar legal practices or intimidated into giving up their land. The federal government demoralized the Native Americans by reducing the supply of game and negotiating separate treaties with certain tribesmen who were willing to accept white civilization. The Removal Acts of 1830 proposed the "final solution"—the exile of the southeastern Indians to the territories west of the Mississippi. At the time of the Indian removal, some Cherokees, like John Ross, advocated the move as the natives' only hope of survival; others, like John Ridge, argued for remaining in the Southeast and preserving traditional ways.

Today, the Trail of Tears has become a historic route developed by the Tennessee Department of Conservation in conjunction with the Department of Tourist Development. Along the route the tourist can see the final capitol of the Cherokee nation near Cleveland, Tenn., the only remaining stockade where the Indians were imprisoned before removal, and Andrew Jackson's home outside Nashville. The inclusion of Jackson's home, the Hermitage, is ironic because, as president, Jackson was a staunch advocate of many of the brutal policies against the Indians, and he was instrumental in implementing the forced migration policy. Sixty thousand Indians were relocated west of the Mississippi under Jackson's direction.

KAREN M. MCDEARMAN
University of Mississippi

John Ehle, *Trail of Tears: The Rise and Fall of the Cherokee Nation* (1988); Gloria Jahoda, *The Trail of Tears: The Story of the Indian Removal, 1813–1850* (1975); Vicki Rozema,

ed., *Voices from the Trail of Tears* (2003); *Southern Exposure* (November–December 1985).

Tulsa (Oklahoma) Race Riot (1921)

On the evening of 31 May 1921, the rising aspirations of African Americans in the wake of World War I clashed with the expectations of others in Tulsa who wanted a return to the patterns of white supremacy prevalent before the war. That clash began the Tulsa Riot (31 May–1 June), the last of the major riots that rocked the United States around the time of the war. Dozens, perhaps hundreds, of people died in it, and more than 35 blocks of Greenwood, the African American section of Tulsa, burned to the ground.

The riot was set in motion when the *Tulsa Tribune* printed a front-page story on 31 May announcing the arrest of a young African American man, provocatively identified as "Diamond Dick" Rowland, for the alleged assault of a young white woman, Sarah Page, in an elevator in downtown Tulsa the day before. That evening, African American World War I veterans met in Greenwood to talk about their fears that there would be a lynching. That story appeared in the context of rising expectations for justice and the rule of law in the African American community in the wake of the United States' campaign to save democracy in Europe. For instance, W. E. B. Du Bois told readers of the *Crisis* in May 1919 to "Make way for Democracy! We saved it in France, and by the Great Jehovah, we will save it in the United States of America, or know the reason why."

A postcard of a victim of the Tulsa Race Riot, 1 June 1921 (Tulsa Race Riot of 1921 Archive, 1921–2000, Department of Special Collections and University Archives, McFarin Library, University of Tulsa, Tulsa, Okla.)

Some sense of the immediate ideas of Greenwood residents appeared in an editorial in the *Tulsa Star*, Greenwood's weekly paper, in September 1920. The editorial, written in response to a lynching in Oklahoma City, urged that "while there was a danger of violence, any set of citizens had a legal right—it was their duty—to arm themselves and march in a body to the jail and apprize the sheriff . . . of the purpose of their visit and to take life if need be to uphold the law and protect the prisoner." The Greenwood community acted on such sentiments. At several times on the evening of 31 May, armed veterans crossed the railroad tracks separating black and white Tulsa, went to the courthouse, and told the sheriff they were there to protect the prisoner. The sheriff waived them away, but at their final trip that evening, sometime around 10:00 P.M., there was a struggle and a gun went off, which set off the riot.

Throughout the evening, the Tulsa police department worked in conjunction with local units of the National Guard and with hastily deputized men to put a plan in place to deal with what some at the time called a "negro uprising." Deputies were issued weapons taken from a sporting goods store or told to go home and get a gun, and around dawn on 1 June, the deputies, local Guardsmen, and police officers began to sweep through Greenwood, disarming and arresting the residents. Those who resisted were shot, as were some who surrendered peacefully. As a result, mobs looted and burned Greenwood. The Oklahoma Supreme Court acknowledged in a lawsuit after the riot that some of the mob were wearing deputy badges and others police uniforms.

In the aftermath of the riot, thousands were left homeless; many fled to Chicago, Kansas City, and even farther, to Boston and Los Angeles. The city's response included an attempt to relocate Greenwood farther away from white Tulsa and a grand jury investigation that arrived at what seemed a preordained conclusion. One newspaper headlined the report, "Grand Jury Blames Negros for Inciting Race Rioting; Whites Clearly Exonerated." But the *Oklahoma City Black Dispatch*'s interpretation of the grand jury report is closer to correct: there was "a white wash brush and a big one in operation in Tulsa."

Following on the heels of a 2001 report by a state commission to investigate the riot, many in Tulsa and elsewhere began to campaign for reparations to riot survivors. A lawsuit, *Alexander v. Oklahoma*, was filed in federal court on behalf of riot victims and their families in 2003 but was dismissed in 2004, though the campaign to remember the riot and to pay victims continues in Congress and in Oklahoma.

ALFRED BROPHY
University of North Carolina at Chapel Hill

Alfred L. Brophy, *Reconstructing the Dreamland: The Tulsa Race Riot of 1921; Race, Reparations, Reconciliation* (2002).

Turner, Nat

(1800–1831) SLAVE.
Born in Southampton County, Va., Turner was a black American slave who led the Southampton insurrection, which has often been seen as the most effective slave rebellion in the South. In recent years, Turner has been a focus of cultural and historical debate.

Turner is the dominant figure among a trio of insurrectionists who led major uprisings, beginning in 1800 with Gabriel Prosser, continuing with Denmark Vesey in 1822, and ending with Turner in 1831. Famous in the folklore and oral history of black Americans, these rebels expressed the powerful urges of blacks to be free. Called "Ol' Prophet Nat" and leader of the most violent of the rebellions, Turner became an especially vivid figure in the underground history of American slavery.

Turner was born to a black woman owned by a plantation aristocrat also named Turner. Transported from Africa in her youth, Nat Turner's mother imbued in him a passion for freedom. Always dreamy and visionary, he learned to read, probably taught by his master's son, and early displayed strong religious feelings. As an adult he became a preacher among the slaves. Sold by the Turner family to a less prosperous farmer and sold again to a Southampton craftsman named Joseph Travis, Turner bitterly withdrew into religious fantasies marked by omens, signs, and visions. Turner burned for his freedom, but he also saw himself as a savior of his people. Following an eclipse of the sun, taken as a sign from the Lord, Turner and four trusted lieutenants embarked upon the bloody insurrection on the night of 21 August 1831, beginning with the slaughter of the Travis family. By 23 August, when the rebellion was thwarted by militia, Turner's rebels had killed almost 60 white men, women, and children. Turner escaped capture for six weeks, but eventually was caught, tried, and executed, as were some 16 others involved with him.

The cultural debate over Turner was sparked in 1967 by the publication of William Styron's novel *The Confessions of Nat Turner*. Though Daniel Panger published *Ol' Prophet Nat* (1967), it was Styron's best seller that challenged black Americans, historians, and social critics, for it raised questions on Turner, black history, and the "true" character ("Sambo" or "rebel") of the slave in the South. The co-opting of Turner by a white author prompted, for example, a polemical outcry called *William Styron's Nat Turner: Ten Black Writers Respond* (1968). Coming in the midst of the social revolution of the 1960s, Panger's, Styron's, and many others' works devoted to the Southampton Revolt soon made Turner a symbol of "Black Power and social liberation."

JAMES M. MELLARD
Northern Illinois University

John B. Duff and Peter M. Mitchell, *The Nat Turner Rebellion: The Historical Event and the Modern Controversy* (1971); Kenneth S. Greenberg, ed., *Nat Turner: A Slave Rebellion in History and Memory* (2003); Thomas Wentworth Higginson, *Black Rebellion: Five Slave Revolts* (repr., 1998); Stephen B. Oates, *The Fires of Jubilee: Nat Turner's Fierce Rebellion* (1975); Henry L. Tragle, *The Southampton Slave Revolt of 1831: A Compilation of Source Material* (1971).

Waco Siege (Branch Davidians)

On the morning of 28 February 1993, the Bureau of Alcohol Tobacco and Firearms (BATF) attempted the execution of a search warrant for the compound of a religious organization consisting of 124 residents, known as the Branch Davidians, for illegally stockpiling weapons, and an arrest warrant for the organization's leader, David Koresh, who was suspected of physically and sexually abusing the children in the compound. In the BATF's raid-style attempt, gunfire erupted, killing four BATF agents and five Davidians, wounding 16 BATF agents and four Davidians (including Koresh who was shot in the hand and the hip, grazing the bone). Who shot first remains a contested issue.

Negotiations began with the local police to cease fire. They continued with BATF agent John Cavanaugh, who negotiated several children out of the compound. However, Koresh took most of the time preaching biblical messages from the book of Revelation. On the second day of negotiations, he agreed to surrender himself after the FBI allowed one of his Bible lectures to be aired on the radio. But after the airing, he told negotiators he was not coming out because God spoke to him, telling him to "wait." At that point the FBI took over as the lead agency, and negotiations continued, though Koresh dominated them with biblical reasoning for why he could not surrender. The FBI also used its Hostage Rescue Team (HRT) to secure a perimeter around the compound with several combat vehicles.

The Davidians had lived in a secluded area near Waco, Tex., that they called Mt. Carmel, for more than 50 years. They were a sect of Seventh-day Adventism, whose primary covenant with God was the spirit of prophecy with particular focus on Judgment Day and the end of time. Koresh became leader of the Davidians in 1988 and in 1989 claimed to have a vision in which God told him he was the chosen one predicted by the book of Revelation to open the Seven Seals and usher in the apocalypse. The Davidians' daily life included the selling and collecting of guns as revenue. While this was (and perhaps still is) a popular enterprise in Texas where gun shows were abundant, accounts suggest that another intent for the 300 firearms (including fully automatic assault rifles) and millions of rounds of ammunition they stored was to help God in His apocalyptic wrath on the earthly world around them.

The negotiations were intractable as the Davidians refused to come out on religious grounds. To them, surrendering meant disobeying God's direct command and giving their souls to the devil. The HRT strengthened the Davidians' position by taunting them with threatening tank maneuvers, floodlights at night, and loud annoying sounds to cause sleep deprivation. On the 45th day of negotiating, U.S. attorney general Janet Reno approved a plan to force the Davidians out with tear gas. During the tear gas raid on the morning of 19 April, the compound caught fire. Nine survived the fire by running out, and 75 died.

The Waco siege remains one of the longest and largest police actions in United States law enforcement history, involving nearly 700 federal, state, and local law enforcement personnel from the U.S. Attorney's office, the FBI, the BATF, the Texas Rangers and Department of Public Safety, the county sheriff's office, and the Waco Police Department. Approximately 25 different FBI negotiators recorded nearly 200 hours of negotiations over 51 days. By all accounts, the BATF and the FBI failed. But after numerous FBI reports and congressional hearings, the standoff prompted improvements in the FBI's handling of hostage and barricade situations, particularly in negotiation strategy and communication between negotiators and tactical teams.

The siege might better be called a "standoff" because neither side backed down—the unstoppable force of the law against the immovable object of religious conviction. It is this idea, combined with the vast scale and deadly consequences, that makes the confrontation significant in Texas-American history.

ROBERT R. AGNE
Auburn University

Jayne S. Docherty, *Learning Lessons from Waco: When the Parties Bring Their Gods to the Table* (2001); James R. Lewis, ed., *From the Ashes: Making Sense of Waco* (1994); Kenneth G. C. Newport, *The Branch Davidians of Waco: The History and Beliefs of an Apocalyptic Sect* (2006); James D. Tabor and Eugene V. Gallagher, eds., *Why Waco? Cults and the Battle for Religious Freedom in America* (1995); U.S. Department of Justice, *Report to the Deputy Attorney General on the Events at Waco, Texas* (1993); Stuart Wright, ed., *Armageddon in Waco: Critical Perspectives on the Branch Davidian Conflict* (1995).

Wells-Barnett, Ida B.

(1862–1931) JOURNALIST AND SOCIAL ACTIVIST.

For Ida B. Wells-Barnett, "southern culture" was an embattled site of identification. She was a native of Holly Springs, Miss., born a slave in 1862. There she attended Rust College, run by the American Missionary Association, and was strongly influenced by its "Yankee" teachers. Wells-Barnett was baptized in the Methodist Episcopal Church. After her parents' death in the yellow fever epidemic of 1878, she moved to Memphis, Tenn., around 1880 and lived there until 1892. That year, she published her most important writing, a pamphlet entitled *Southern Horrors: Lynch Law in All Its Phases*. This essay placed southern codes of honor in the horror of the lynching-for-rape scenario, part of a violent, morally hypocritical, crassly economic system of white supremacy. White men justified the murder of "bestial" black men by claiming the role of protectors of "weak" white women; Wells-Barnett proved that statistically the rape charge was rarely in play during actual, documented lynchings. Instead, the cry rape was often a cover to punish black men who in any way challenged the social, political, or economic status quo of the South. She also pointed out that white women sometimes participated in both mob activity and in consensual sex with black men. When a death threat appeared in print in 1893 because of Wells-Barnett's newspaper criticism of lynching and southern honor, the region became off limits and she left for the North. She returned only once, in 1917, to investigate the plight of 16 Arkansas farmers imprisoned for labor organizing activity and sentenced to die in Helena, and then she went in disguise.

Ida B. Wells-Barnett became famous—to opponents, infamous—for her critique of the South, but she accomplished the work largely outside of it. In 1895 she settled in Chicago, Ill., married lawyer Ferdinand L. Barnett, and raised four children. She died there in 1931. She arguably achieved greatest prominence outside the United States during 1893 and 1894, when she traveled to England and Scotland to mobilize opposition to lynching in the United States. At strategic points, however, she referred to herself as a "southern girl, born and bred" or by the pen name "Exiled." Such identifications established her credibility as a native witness to history, especially since a black woman's moral authority was by definition suspect in U.S. society. After a difficult period of political retrenchment in Chicago and the brutal race riot of July 1919, Wells-Barnett again accented her southern roots and reached out to the progressive elements of the white South in renewed efforts toward interracial understanding in the region, but this offer likely did not even reach ears that had long since tuned her out.

Ironically, some of the best evidence of Ida B. Wells-Barnett's sparsely documented personal life dates from the 1880s, when she lived in Memphis and participated in a wide array of activities that mark her as a product of the post-Reconstruction New South. She left a diary dating from December 1885 to September 1887, and it provides vivid details of her life during this dynamic period. Entries describe a context not, perhaps, stereotypically "southern" or dominated by folkways. She studied Shakespeare and elocution, attended lectures by national figures like Dwight Moody, and was present at gender- and racially inclusive meetings of the Knights of Labor. The diary further documents her anger at injustice and violence directed at African Americans,

some of which touched Wells-Barnett directly, as in her forced removal from a railroad "ladies" car. She was also the godmother of a child whose father was murdered, along with two business associates, during a conflict in the spring of 1892. This triple lynching in Memphis was a life-changing event that directed her attention to full-time antimob violence protest.

Ida B. Wells-Barnett organized against southern violence outside of the region, resulting in scores of local antilynching committees and the founding the National Association of Colored Women (1896) and the National Association for the Advancement of Colored People (1909). Her efforts successfully positioned antilynching as a legitimate focus of national reform, but based in the urban North. In that context, individuals and groups more securely positioned than she by academic credentials, social status, or political connections in publishing, philanthropy, and government assumed leadership of the issue in the World War I era. Although Ida B. Wells-Barnett's southernness enabled her powerful voice to emerge in the 1890s, she became eclipsed by the competitive, money-driven, and consolidating trends that came to characterize social reform in the United States over her lifetime.

PATRICIA A. SCHECHTER
Portland State University

Miriam DeCosta-Willis, ed., *The Memphis Diary of Ida B. Wells: An Intimate Portrait of the Activist as a Young Woman* (1995); Paula J. Giddings, *Ida B. Wells and the Campaign against Lynching* (2008); Trudier Harris, ed., *Selected Works of Ida B.*

Wells-Barnett (1991); Patricia A. Schechter, *Ida B. Wells-Barnett and American Reform, 1880–1930* (2001); Ida B. Wells-Barnett, *Crusade for Justice: The Autobiography of Ida B. Wells*, ed. Alfreda M. Duster (1970).

Whitecappers

Whitecapping, also known as night-riding, was a communal form of vigilantism that occurred throughout North America during the late 19th and early 20th centuries but perhaps with greatest intensity and political salience in the South. Participants almost always disguised their identities, sometimes by wearing sheets over their heads, thus giving rise to the generic term applied to them. The term also suggests the inspiration such groups may have derived from the Ku Klux Klan and similar organizations of the Reconstruction era.

Enforcement of moral standards and defense of local economic interests were the most common goals of night riders. The latter rationale produced the most dramatic episodes of vigilantism. Small bands of night riders could punish adulterers, wife beaters, or prostitutes and then quickly disband, having put other potential offenders on notice. Resisting the new political and economic relationships promoted under industrial capitalism, however, required more concerted efforts. During the 1890s, moonshiners in northern Georgia, who had resisted the efforts of federal revenue agents to regulate and tax whiskey since immediately after the Civil War, organized secret societies that targeted informers for the revenue agents through campaigns of barn burning and terror. Similarly, communities of squatters

in northwestern Tennessee during the first decade of the 20th century banded together to intimidate land agents who had obtained title and fishing rights to an area surrounding Reelfoot Lake. Two of the most extensive whitecapping movements pursued goals not dissimilar to those of farmers' cooperative groups such as the Grange and Alliance. In southwestern Mississippi white farmers combined resistance against the merchant-credit system with attempts to control black labor by banding together to drive African American tenants off land seized by merchants in foreclosure. In the Black Patch region of western Kentucky and Tennessee, tobacco growers attempted to monopolize the storage of the area's crop so that they could better negotiate with the buyers sent by the tobacco trust. Night riders terrorized farmers willing to sell their tobacco on an independent basis, burned warehouses not affiliated with the farmers' organization, and were strong enough at one point to raid the area's largest town.

Whitecappers challenged legal institutions that they believed were either incapable of serving their local needs and interests or were abetting outside influences that threatened communal social and economic traditions. They usually consisted of a cross section of local societies and saw themselves as legitimate and orderly defenders of community standards. In almost all cases, however, what may have started as well-organized, often elite-led vigilantism degenerated into more random acts of night-riding or enactments of long-standing feuds, with African

Americans the most frequent targets. Such acts divided organizations and enabled local, state, and federal officials to reassert legal authority.

The violence of whitecappers has been a prominent undercurrent of black folk testimony and has been featured in the works of some southern writers. For many African Americans, whitecapping has appeared as yet another manifestation of white efforts to terrorize and control blacks, closely aligned to the slave patrols and to the Reconstruction-era Klan. Novelists, much like historians, have examined the ways that whitecapping simultaneously defended and destroyed community values. Robert Penn Warren's first novel, *Night Rider* (1939), narrated the Black Patch War of his native Kentucky largely from the point of view of a fictional tobacco planter who organizes the vigilantism but eventually loses control over the violence he has helped unleash. Tom Franklin's *Hell at the Breach* (2003), like Warren's novel based on a real incident, concerns a showdown in an isolated area of southwestern Alabama between rural whitecappers and town-based authorities. Both novels stress the tendency of violence to resist containment. As in historical cases of whitecapping, violence, once pursued as a means to an end, quickly becomes the end itself.

W. BLAND WHITLEY
Papers of Thomas Jefferson
Princeton University

Richard Maxwell Brown, *Strain of Violence: Historical Studies of American Violence and Vigilantism* (1975); Gladys-Marie Fry, *Night Riders in Black Folk History* (1975); William F. Holmes, *Journal of Southern*

History (May 1969), *Journal of American History* (December 1980); Paul J. Vanderwood, *Night Riders of Reelfoot Lake* (1969); Christopher Waldrep, *Night Riders: Defending Community in the Black Patch* (1993).

Wilmington (North Carolina) Race Riot (1898)

At the entrance of the Cape Fear River, about 30 miles from the east coast of North Carolina, rests the port city of Wilmington. On the morning of 10 November 1898—two days after a statewide election, in which terrorized blacks had largely refrained from voting—an armed and angry mob of about 500 white men gathered in front of the headquarters of the Wilmington Light Infantry. From there, in military order and led by Col. Alfred M. Waddell, they marched to the office of the black newspaper. They forced the door open, broke windows, destroyed furniture, and then burned the building down.

Thus began one of the worst massacres of the Progressive Era. In 1898 Wilmington was, ironically, perhaps the most racially tolerant post-Reconstruction southern city. Blacks figured prominently in the city's political and economic life, occupying high positions in government and holding jobs as restaurant owners, barbers, and artisans. The collector of customs at the port of Wilmington, one of the city auditors, the coroner, 30 percent of the aldermen, clerks, firemen, policemen, and justices of the peace were all black. Conspicuous also were black lawyers, a black voting majority, and Alex Manly's black-run newspaper, the *Wilmington Record*.

At the same time, masses of poor whites and blacks lived in abject poverty. Many Democrats were poor, lower-class whites, who scolded employers for giving blacks preference in hiring.

In the 1894 state election the Fusionist forces, a coalition of Populists and Republicans with their black allies, triumphed. Two years later they elected Wilmington's Daniel Russell as the first Republican governor since Reconstruction. In March 1897 they altered Wilmington's charter, which enabled the Republicans to usurp control of the city government from an office-holding Democratic clique. The old politicians (city bosses) unsuccessfully challenged the victorious allies in the courts.

For a period of months before the riot, the "Secret Nine"—a cabal of minor Democrats—clandestinely planned to overthrow the new government. The Wilmington race riot was preceded by a statewide supremacy crusade, which the resurgent Democrats launched to regain political ascendency in 1898. It was abetted by a propaganda campaign, and armed vigilantes terrorized the black population.

During mid-October the Democrats resurrected an Alex Manly editorial that had appeared in the *Wilmington Record* on 18 August. It refuted claims that black men were raping white women and committing other crimes and stated that black men "were sufficiently attractive for white girls of culture and refinement to fall in love with them." Printed out of context and headlined daily in the local papers, the article was a catalyst for the riot that exploded on 10 November.

Manly escaped days before a large mob, led by ex-congressman Alfred M. Waddell, burned his press. The wounding of William Mayo (white) roused the whites to a frenzy. A massacre ensued, but no whites were slain, and only three were injured. The number of blacks killed can never be known.

The Democrats subsequently overthrew the legally elected Republican government and unanimously elected Waddell mayor. The next day, amid jeering crowds, a militia with "fixed bayonets" banished prominent white Republican and black leaders. After two days the blacks who had hidden in the woods came out to find their property, businesses, artisan trades, municipal jobs, and even the traditionally black-occupied menial vocations taken over by the self-appointed new administration and its supportive clan.

H. LEON PRATHER
Tennessee State University

David S. Cecelski and Timothy B. Tyson, eds., *Democracy Betrayed: The Wilmington Race Riot of 1898 and Its Legacy* (1998); H. Leon Prather, *We Have Taken a City: Wilmington Racial Massacre and Coup of 1898* (1984).

INDEX OF CONTRIBUTORS

Page numbers in boldface refer to articles.

and peonage, 130; political violence in, 134; and Reconstruction, 150; and vigilantism, 187
Arnold, Kokomo, 219
Arrested Development, 172
Arson, **23–25**, 40
Ashby, Turner, 52
Ashley Gang, 21
Association of Southern Women for the Prevention of Lynching, 156, 197, 204
Atlanta, Ga.: and Civil War, 51; and Leo Frank case, 58, 64–65, 231; and Martin Luther King Jr., 118; riots in, 134, 143, 187, **204–5**; and Jessie Ames, 197; anti-abortion protests in, 202; and *Birth of a Nation*, 211; and Ku Klux Klan, 250
Atlanta Jewish Federation, 233
Atlanta Journal, 204
At the Cross Roads, 64
Austin, Stephen F., 266
Austin Southern Intelligencer, 108
Autobiography of an Ex-Coloured Man (Johnson), 94
Avenging a Crime; or, Burned at the Stake, 64
Awakening, The (Chopin), 185
Ayers, Edward, 8, 9, 10

Bacon, Nathaniel, 125, 206
Bacon's Rebellion, 132, **205–7**
Bailey, Alonzo, 129
Baker, Ella, 120
Ball, Charles, 93, 182, 183
Ballad of Gregorio Cortez, The, 222
Banty Tim, 64
Barbados, 55
Barbera, Joseph, Sr., 123
Bare-knuckle fighting, 30
"Barn Burning" (Faulkner), 24
Barrow, Clyde, 126, 128, **213–15**
Barton, Clara, 199
Batista, Fulgencio, 123
Baton Rouge, La., 251
Bean, Roy, 180
Beatty, Ned, 222

Beckwith, Byron De La, 227
Bedford Forrest and His Critter Company (Lytle), 230
Before They Die, 106
Bell, Madison Smartt, 96
Bell County, Ky., 89
Berkeley, William, 205, 206–7
Berry, Halle, 69
Berry, Shawn, 216
Beulah Mae Donald v. United Klans of America, 224
Bevel, James, 118, 120
Beverly, Robert, 91
Bickley, George W. L., 243
Bierce, Ambrose, 53
Binnings, Mabel Guerre, 252, 253
Birmingham, Ala.: and civil rights struggle, 28, 45, 46–47, 120; church bombing in, 39, 171, **207–9**; labor violence in, 88, 89; and vigilantism, 187
Birth of a Nation, The, 65, **209–11**, 234
Black armed resistance, **25–29**
Black Boy (Wright), 94, 219
Black codes, 57
Black Legion, 66
Black Liberation Army, 29
Black militias, **211–13**
Black Panther Party, 29, 48
Black Patch War, 105, 278
Black Power, 29, 47, 121, 132
Blake; or, The Huts of America (Delaney), 93
Blanton, Thomas Edwin, 207, 208
Blease, Cole, 101
Blood sports, 2, **30–34**
Bloomville, S.C., 41
Blues music, 170, 171
Blyew, John, 57–58
Boehm, Christopher, 62
Bogalusa, La., 29, 89
Bonnie and Clyde, 126, 128, **213–15**
Booker, James, 201
Boorman, John, 222
Boston, Mass., 141
Boston Tea Party, 115

sports in, 30, 33; labor violence in, 88; lynching in, 98; organized crime, 122–23; prisons, 137, 140; convicts, 138, 139, 220; race riots in, 141; and Reconstruction, 150, 151; slave culture in, 160; black militias in, 211, 212; filibusters, 228

Louisiana Sugar Planters Association, 88

Lowery, Joseph, 40, 224

Loyal Leagues, 212

Lumbee, 21, 22

Lynch, Charles, 97, 186

Lynching, 2, 6, 11, 12, 13, 15, 27, 77, **97–102,** 107, 148, 179, 187, 203, 275; and criminal justice, 58; films about, **63–66;** and labor disputes, 87; and memory, 104; police involvement in, 131; religious significance of, 155–56; in songs, 170, 175; photography, **253–55**

Lytle, Andrew Nelson, 230–31

Mabila, Ala., 19

Macon County, Ga., 198

Madden Branch, Ga., 52

Mafia, 122, 123

Malcolm X, 29, 242

Manifest Destiny, 228

Manly, Alex, 279

Mann, Alonzo, 233

Mann, Horace, 54

Mansfield High School, 45

Mansion, The (Faulkner), 258

Mao Tse Tung, 29

Mapping the Mississippi Shatter Zone (Ethridge), 194

Marcello, Carlos, 122–23, 124

March on Washington, 117

Marrow of Tradition, The (Chesnutt), 94

Martinsville Seven case, 149

Maryland: and fox hunting, 34; homicide in, 78; prisons, 137; antiabortion protests in, 202; black militias in, 212

Masculinity, 2–3, 8, 10, 12–13, 84, 159, 171

Mask of the Ku Klux Klan, The, 65

Massive resistance, 45

Matthews, Thomas, 205

Matthew Shepard and James Byrd Jr. Hate Crimes Prevention Act, 217

Maxim, 223

Mayo, William, 279

McCarthy, Cormac, 96

McComb, Miss., 47

McCoy, Randolph, 239

McCullers, Carson, 95, 96

McCulloch, Ben, 178

McCurry, Stephanie, 10

McGrath, Charles, 221

McIntosh County, Ga., 27

McNair, Denise, 207

McNair, Robert E., 256

Memory, **103–6**

Memphis, Tenn., 90, 134, 141, 150, 203, 212, 241, 276

Mencken, H. L., 14

Meredith, James, 46

Mexican Americans, 222, 267; violence toward, 3, 98, **107–11**

Mexico, 109, 178, 243, 266

Miami, Fla., 122, 144

Micheaux, Oscar, 65

Michigan, 35

Middle Passage, 183

Migration narrative, 94

Milam, J. W., 268–69

Militant South, 1800–1862, The (Franklin), 112

Militarism, 4, **111–15,** 180

Military education, 112, 113, 114

Mind of the South (Cash), 5

Mississippi: and American Indians, 22; black armed resistance in, 28; church burnings in, 40; and civil rights struggle, 43, 46, 47, 135; criminal justice, 56; and films about lynching, 65; and guns, 72; labor violence in, 88; lynching in, 100; and nonviolent protest, 120; convicts, 139; crime rate, 140; and Reconstruction, 151, 152; and vigilantism, 188; black militias in, 212; filibusters, 228; whitecappers in, 277

Mississippi, University of, 43, 46

Mississippi Plan, 151

Mississippi State Sovereignty Commission, 227

Missouri: and capital punishment, 37; and Civil War, 52, 104; and outlaw-heroes, 125, 128; convicts, 138, 139; black militias in, 212; and James Brothers, 240–41

Missouri Compromise, 164, 265

Mitcham Beat, Ala., 105

Mitchell, Jerry, 227

Mitchell, Margaret, 92, 95

Mobile, Ala., 56, 90, 202, 212, 223–25

Mob violence, 5, 6, 58, 97–101, 107–11, 113, 178. *See also* Lynching; Vigilantism

Money, Miss., 267

Monroe, James, 164

Monroe, N.C., 28

Monster, 69

Monster's Ball, 69, 201

Montell, William, 62, 256

Montgomery, Ala., 45, 118, 119, 120, 156

Moreau, Don, 253

Morgan, John Hunt, 127

Morrill Act, 113

Morris, Errol, 69

Morrison, Toni, 96, 185

Mosby, John Singleton, 52, 127

Moses, Robert "Bob," 47

Moss, Thomas, 203

Moviegoer, The (Percy), 96

Muni, Paul, 67

Murder. *See* Homicide

Murder ballads, 170, 174

Murietta, Joaquin, 110

Murphy, Audie, 112

Murphy, Eddie, 68, 258

Muste, A. J., 116

Myrdal, Gunnar, 14

Myths, American, 1

NAACP, 102, 197, 204, 211, 224, 226, 227, 251, 254, 276; Legal Defense Fund, 36

Narváez, Pánfilo de, 91

Nashville, Tenn., 51, 95, 139, 231

Nast, Thomas, 230, 231

Natchez Revolt, 19

National Assembly of Sportsmen's Caucuses, 85

National Association of Colored Women, 276

National Council of Churches, 41

National Recovery Act, 89

National Rifle Association, 73

National States' Rights Party, 46, 207, 208

National Turkey Federation, 82

National Wildlife Federation, 82

Native Americans. *See* American Indians

Native Son (Wright), 94

Navarette, Cesar and Geovanni, 130

Negro Act, 163

Nelli, Humbert, 122

Nelson, Willie, 127

Neshoba County, Miss., 244

Neville Brothers, 201

New Jersey, 39

Newman, Frances, 95

Newman, Paul, 68

New Mexico, 30, 39, 109, 140

Newnan, Ga., 101

New Orleans, Battle of, 104

New Orleans, La., 243, 251, 252; and Civil War, 51; criminal justice, 56; and dueling, 60, 61; homicide in, 77; lynching in, 100; organized crime, 122, 124; riots in, 134, 141, 150, 187, 211; and Reconstruction, 151

New Orleans Daily Picayune, 219

New South, 14

New York, N.Y., 25, 141, 203, 210, 228

New York Times, 223, 229, 231, 237

New York World, 250

Nicaragua, 229

Night Rider (Warren), 278

Night riders, 255–56, 277

Night Riders in Black Folk History (Fry), 255

Nisbett, Richard, 7

Nolan, Dave, 256

Nonviolent protest, 115–21, 156, 242

North Carolina: and American Indians,

Shawnee, 195
Shelton, Robert, 225
Shelton Laurel, N.C., 52
Shepard, Matthew, 217
Sheridan, Philip, 51
Sherman, William Tecumseh, 51, 199
Shiloh, Battle of, 50
Shridharani, Krishnalal, 116
Shuttlesworth, Fred, 28, 207
Silver, Frankie, 105
Simmons, William, 211, 250
Simone, Nina, 171
Singleton, John, 106
Skaggs, Ricky, 173
Slater, Morris, 125
Slaton, John, 233
Slave code, 55
Slave culture, violence within, **157–60**
Slave narratives, 93, 182
Slave patrols, 55–56, 75, 131, **161–62**, 255
Slave revolts, 25–26, **162–65**, 272
Slavery, 9–11, 51, 55, 130, 148, 220, 265; and
    capital punishment, 34; and homicide,
    74, 75, 76; and honor, 79; in literature,
    92–95; and rape, 146, 166, 168; court-
    ship in, 159; and violence toward slaves,
    165–69; and suicide, 182–83
Slotkin, Richard, 1
Smiley, Glenn E., 118
Smith, Bessie, 171
Smith, Hoke, 204
Smith, John, 91
Smith, Lamar, 226
Smith, Walter "Kid," 175
Social Forces, 71
Song: black, violence in, **169–72**; white,
    violence in, **172–76**
Sonnier, Elmo Patrick, 201
Sons of Confederate Veterans, 231
Sound and the Fury, The (Faulkner), 95
South Carolina: and American Indians,
    19, 20; and arson, 24; black armed re-
    sistance in, 27; and slave code, 55; and
    dueling, 61; labor violence in, 87; and
    outlaw-heroes, 125; and peonage, 130;

political violence in, 132–33; and Re-
    construction, 150, 151, 152; and slave cul-
    ture, 157, 158, 159; slave patrols, 161; slave
    revolts, 163; and vigilantism, 186; black
    militias in, 212; homicide in, 260
South Carolina Gazette, 185
South Carolina State University, 114, 256,
    257
Southampton County, Va., 26, 164, 272
Southern Baptist Convention, 202
Southern Christian Leadership Confer-
    ence, 47, 120
Southern Honor (Wyatt-Brown), 7
Southern Horrors (Wells-Barnett), 275
Southern Poverty Law Center, 40, 224, 245
Southern rap, 172
Southern Regional Council, 197
Southern Tenant Farmers Union, 187
Southern woods burning, 23–24
Southwestern violence, **176–81**
Spanish-American War, 112
Spirituals, 169–70
Springfield, Ill., 143
"Stagger Lee" ("Stack O'Lee"), 170
Starrs, James E., 252
State Guards, 212
Steamboat Round the Bend, 66
Stephens, Alexander H., 60
Stevens, Thaddeus, 209
Stirling, James, 228
Stockton Times, 109
Stono Rebellion, 25, 163
Stowe, Harriet Beecher, 92
"Strange Fruit," 170
Student Non-Violent Coordinating Com-
    mittee, 47, 120
Sturgis, Ky., 45
Styron, William, 96, 185, 273
Suicide, 2, **181–85**; medicalization of,
    184–85
Summer of Sam, 66
Sumner, Charles, 60, **265–66**
Sumner, Fla., 263
Sun Shines Bright, The, 66
Supreme Court, U.S., 36–37, 57–58, 59, 233;

MIX
Paper from
responsible sources
FSC® C013483

CLAYTON COUNTY LIBRARY
RIVERDALE BRANCH
420 VALLEY HILL ROAD
RIVERDALE, GA 30274